HOLMAN
Old Testament Commentary

HOLMAN
Old Testament Commentary

I & II *Kings*

GENERAL EDITOR
Max Anders
AUTHOR
Gary Inrig

HOLMAN
REFERENCE

Nashville, Tennessee

Holman Old Testament Commentary
© 2003 Broadman & Holman Publishers
Nashville, Tennessee
All rights reserved

ISBN 0-8054-9467-7
Dewey Decimal Classification: 223.8
Subject Heading: BIBLE. O.T. KINGS

1 & 2 Kings /Gary Inrig
p.   cm. — (Holman Old Testament commentary)
Includes bibliographical references. (p.).
ISBN
  1. Bible. O.T. 1 & 2 Kings—Commentaries.   I. Title.   II. Series.

—dc21

1 2 3 4 5 6 07 06 05 04 03
R

To Howard and
Jeanne Hendricks,
Alan and Shirley Hull,

models, mentors, friends,
whose value becomes more obvious
with the passing of time.

Gary Inrig
December 2002

Contents

Contents

Editorial Preface

Today's church hungers for Bible teaching, and Bible teachers hunger for resources to guide them in teaching God's Word. The Holman Old Testament Commentary provides the church with the food to feed the spiritually hungry in an easily digestible format. The result: new spiritual vitality that the church can readily use.

Bible teaching should result in new interest in the Scriptures, expanded Bible knowledge, discovery of specific scriptural principles, relevant applications, and exciting living. The unique format of the Holman Old Testament Commentary includes sections to achieve these results for every Old Testament book.

Opening quotations stimulate thinking and lead to an introductory illustration and discussion that draw individuals and study groups into the Word of God. "In a Nutshell" summarizes the content and teaching of the chapter. Verse-by-verse commentary answers the church's questions rather than raising issues scholars usually admit they cannot adequately solve. Bible principles and specific contemporary applications encourage students to move from Bible to contemporary times. A specific modern illustration then ties application vividly to present life. A brief prayer aids the student to commit his or her daily life to the principles and applications found in the Bible chapter being studied. For those still hungry for more, "Deeper Discoveries" take the student into a more personal, deeper study of the words, phrases, and themes of God's Word. Finally, a teaching outline provides transitional statements and conclusions along with an outline to assist the teacher in group Bible studies.

It is the editors' prayer that this new resource for local church Bible teaching will enrich the ministry of group, as well as individual, Bible study, and that it will lead God's people truly to be people of the Book, living out what God calls us to be.

Acknowledgments

I am privileged to serve a group of believers at Trinity Church who have been a constant source of encouragement and support. Their response to a series of messages based on 1 and 2 Kings reminded me again of the power of God's eternal Word to speak to every generation of believers.

Over the years I have served with many wonderful partners in ministry as fellow elders and pastoral team members. I owe a great debt to each one, and I especially thank the elders and pastoral team of Trinity Church for their permission, encouragement, and support. Their support made it possible for me to invest the time and energy it took to complete this project, which turned out to be far more demanding than I imagined. Special thanks to Tom Fort and Rick Langer.

My greatest human joy comes from my family, especially my marvelous wife Elizabeth. Nothing I do would be as meaningful or as much fun without her encouragement, love, and practical wisdom.

Above all, this book is written in honor of the One who is its source, with the prayer that it will help to explain rather than obscure the message he intended us to hear: "Now to him who is able to do immeasurably more than all we ask or imagine, according to his power that is at work within us, to him be glory in the church and in Christ Jesus throughout all generations, for ever and ever! Amen" (Eph. 3:20–21).

Holman Old Testament Commentary Contributors

Holman New Testament Commentary Contributors

Vol. 1, Matthew
ISBN 0-8054-0201-2
Stuart K. Weber

Vol. 2, Mark
ISBN 0-8054-0202-0
Rodney L. Cooper

Vol. 3, Luke
ISBN 0-8054-0203-9
Trent C. Butler

Vol. 4, John
ISBN 0-8054-0204-7
Kenneth O. Gangel

Vol. 5, Acts
ISBN 0-8054-0205-5
Kenneth O. Gangel

Vol. 6, Romans
ISBN 0-8054-0206-3
Kenneth Boa and William Kruidenier

Vol. 7, 1 & 2 Corinthians
ISBN 0-8054-0207-1
Richard L. Pratt Jr.

Vol. 8, Galatians, Ephesians,
Philippians, Colossians
ISBN 0-8054-0208-X
Max Anders

Vol. 9, 1 & 2 Thessalonians,
1 & 2 Timothy, Titus, Philemon
ISBN 0-8054-0209-8
Knute Larson

Vol. 10, Hebrews, James
ISBN 0-8054-0211-X
Thomas D. Lea

Vol. 11, 1 & 2 Peter, 1, 2, 3 John, Jude
ISBN 0-8054-0210-1
David Walls & Max Anders

Vol. 12, Revelation
ISBN 0-8054-0212-8
Kendell H. Easley

Holman Old Testament Commentary

Twenty volumes designed for Bible study and teaching to enrich the local church and God's people.

Series Editor	Max Anders
Managing Editor	Steve Bond
Project Editor	Dean Richardson
Product Development Manager	Ricky D. King
Marketing Manager	Stephanie Huffman
Executive Editor	David Shepherd
Page Composition	TF Designs, Greenbrier, Tennessee

Introduction to

1 and 2 Kings

I didn't get to see in person the damage at Ground Zero in New York City. Those who did struggle with words to describe both the site itself and their emotions. Television can convey accurately the nature of the damage, but it cannot convey the scale or the sights and sounds. When the massive towers of the World Trade Center collapsed, the wreckage covered an entire square mile. It is hard to grasp the enormity of such devastation, or, if you are familiar with what once stood there, the strange sense of empty space where once-great buildings had stood.

But hardest to describe are the emotions. How do you find words to convey the sense of anguish, the looks on the faces of workers as they resolutely carried on a search for the remains of friends and fellow workers? How do you communicate the agony and anger that this massive calamity was not due to a freak of nature—an earthquake or a hurricane? It was an atrocity planned and carried out by people who succeeded in wreaking havoc on unsuspecting people who were simply going about their daily business.

For the rest of our lives, visits to New York City will include trips to Ground Zero. There people will tell themselves the story of what used to be there, of how it came to disappear, and how we need to make sure that such a thing can never happen again. Ruins can cause us to look back in remembrance so we can move forward in wisdom.

The unknown author of 1 and 2 Kings had just that in mind when he picked up his pen to write an account of his nation's history for his fellow Jews who were in captivity in Babylon. Terrible as the September 11 atrocity was, this man was facing devastation on a far greater scale. It wasn't a sizable portion but the entire capital city of Jerusalem that had been destroyed by a powerful enemy. The population was destroyed, deported, or dispersed as refugees. The golden city was a heap of ruins, a monument to disaster. Even worse, the nation's identity as the people of God, with a special calling in the world, seemed to have come to an end. The writer stood, as it were, on the Ground Zero of Jerusalem and asked two questions: what happened, and where do we go from here? Where have we been, and where are we going? What did we do wrong, and how can we be sure not to make the same mistakes again?

Those are the questions that the books of 1 and 2 Kings were written to answer. On one level these books provide a history of the period of the monarchy in Israel, from the death of David to Judah's last king. But it is not a history written the way a modern historian would tell the story. It is not objective, dispassionate, and reportorial. It is "preached history," true to the facts but designed to bring a message. It is highly selective, covering almost four hundred years in very broad strokes. Large periods are passed over quickly, while much more attention is given to figures such as Solomon, Elijah, Elisha, Hezekiah, and Josiah. The books of 1 and 2 Kings are best described as theological narratives. As narratives, they tell a story; as theology, they contain a message about God and his dealings with his people.

The two books of Kings were written originally as one book. Even though they describe events long ago and far away, they bring a message that is surprisingly current and relevant. Some of the details will escape us, and certainly many of the customs will be strange and unfamiliar. But people are still people, and the dangers they faced and the failures they experienced are not very different from those of our time. With the advent of aggressive pluralism, the central issue of exclusive loyalty to the triune God has become the central issue of our time. Most of all God is still God. Although his people in the present age are the church rather than the political entity of the nation of Israel, his character and his essential requirements of faith and obedience remain the same.

Time spent in the books of 1 and 2 Kings has been a rich personal experience for me. As I have shared it with the congregation where I have served, they have felt its power as well. My prayer is that, through the help of this book, a portion of Scripture too often ignored will come alive with fresh power.

AUTHORSHIP

We do not know who wrote the books of 1 and 2 Kings. We do know that he wrote them as one book that was later divided into two for the sake of convenience. We also know, from the last verses of the book, that the book reached its final form after King Jehoiachin of Judah was released from prison in 561 B.C. The book was thus the work of an unknown writer, writing in Babylon in the time between Jehoiachin's release and the return of the first deportees to Jerusalem about 539/538 B.C. The book shows no indication that such a return was politically on the horizon. A probable date for its writing would be 555 B.C. The ancient rabbinic contention that Jeremiah was the author reflects the close connections between Jeremiah 52 and 2 Kings 24–25, but this theory has no convincing support.

As he wrote, the author of 1 and 2 Kings made use of existing materials. He mentions "the book of the annals of Solomon" (1 Kgs. 11:41); "the book of the annals of the kings of Israel" (eighteen times, see 1 Kgs. 14:19); and "the book of the annals of the kings of Judah" (fifteen times, see 1 Kgs. 14:29). Such annals were common in Babylon and Assyria. They contained an annual account of a king's reign, with the major political, religious, and military events noted. This appeared to be the pattern in Israel, although no trace of these annals remains. The author probably made use of other materials as well, although they are not noted. There is an obvious dependence on Isaiah 36–39 in 2 Kings 18–20, and 2 Kings 24–25 is closely linked to Jeremiah 52. It is possible that early forms of the history existed.

But the author was not just a compiler. Rather, he was a prophet, writing under divine direction. His knowledge was not limited to what he found in the annals. He knew the mind of God on certain events. He was thus writing on the basis of revelation, not just research. That is one reason the Jews catalogued the books of 1 and 2 Kings among the "former prophets" in their canon. The author was a prophet, not just a historian. It is also obvious that the author had been highly influenced by the Book of Deuteronomy. He evaluated much of what transpired in the light of the blessings and curses of that book. He shared that in common with the author of 1 and 2 Samuel.

There is a close connection between the two books of Samuel and the two books of Kings, with the books of 1 and 2 Kings obviously picking up the story where Samuel leaves off. It may be that the same author wrote both, or that there was a group of like-minded scholars who worked together on a "history of Israel" project, or that the writer simply followed what another author had done. Certainty on such matters is not possible.

Modern critical biblical scholarship has developed some highly complex and speculative theories about the authorship of 1 and 2 Kings. It is outside the scope of a book such as this to deal with them. Suffice it to say that their conclusions are driven by assumptions that tend to deny the unique nature of the Scriptures and that are intended to buttress other theories of the evolution of Israel's religion.

AN OVERVIEW OF 1 AND 2 KINGS

The books of 1 and 2 Kings are shaped around four significant dates. In 967 B.C. David's son Solomon, the king of a united Israel, began to build the temple in Jerusalem (1 Kgs. 6:1). Around 931, the nation split in two. Ten nations formed a new kingdom of Israel under the rebel Jeroboam, and Judah formed the basis of a new kingdom under the Davidic king, Rehoaboam (1 Kgs. 12:18–20). The next major date was 722, when the nation of Israel was attacked and destroyed by the Assyrians and vanished as a nation from the stage of history. The nation of Judah continued until about 587/586 B.C. until it was destroyed by Babylon.

It is possible to use these dates as the outline of the book—the united nation (1 Kgs. 1–11); the divided kingdom (1 Kgs. 12–2 Kgs. 17); and Judah alone (2 Kgs. 18–25). While that is certainly a valid division, it does not reflect the unique emphases of the writer. He spent much more time on some periods of the history than on others. What is especially significant is the emphasis placed on the ministries of Elijah and Elisha. More space is devoted to those two men than any single individual, with the exception of Solomon. The reason was the crisis represented by Ahab and Baal worship. The following outline conveys the major structure of the books of 1 and 2 Kings:

    I. The United Kingdom: Solomon's Reign and Temple
       (1 Kgs. 1:1–11:43)
   II. The Early Years of the Divided Kingdom: Israel and Judah
       (12:1–16:34)
  III. Elijah and the Battle with Ahab (1 Kgs. 17:1–2 Kgs. 1:18)
  IV. Elisha and the End of the House of Ahab (2 Kgs. 2:1–10:36)
   V. The Last Days of the Divided Kingdom (2 Kgs. 11:1–17:41)
  VI. Judah Alone: From Survival to Captivity (2 Kgs. 18:1–25:26)
 VII. A Sign of Hope in Babylon (2 Kgs. 25:27–30)

THEMES

Because the books of 1 and 2 Kings were intended to warn the people against perpetuating or repeating the sins that had brought the people to its bondage in Babylon, certain themes are woven through both books. These are noted here. The nature of each will become clear in the following exposition.

Yahweh, the God of Israel, alone is God. The gods of the nations are the inventions of men, and they are empty and powerless

The Lord insists on exclusive worship, free from any taint of idolatry. The first and second of the Ten Commandments are of crucial importance, if Israel is to be loyal to the covenant. God will not share his glory or his people with any rivals, so there is no place for pluralism or syncretism.

The hope of Israel is God's faithfulness to his covenants, especially his covenant with David, but also his covenant with Abraham, Isaac, and Jacob, and his promise to Solomon to place his "name" in the temple.

The Lord has revealed himself and his will through his law and also through his prophets.

God's people are responsible to obey what God has revealed.

Although the Lord is slow to punish, he is sure to punish the covenant disloyalty of his people.

THE CHRONOLOGY OF 1 AND 2 KINGS

If you travel in other countries, you will discover that little things can lead to significant confusion. For example, in Australia the street-level floor is called "ground level," and you go up to the first floor. In North America the ground floor is the first floor. So if you agree to meet an Australian on the tenth floor, both of you may end up frustrated. The same can happen with chronology. In some systems the first year of a king's reign begins the moment he assumes the throne; in others, the first year is the "accession year," and the count doesn't begin until the turn of the next calendar year. And not all calendar years begin on the same date. These are just some of the things that make it difficult to compare chronologies, especially in the absence of an agreed-upon general calendar.

The chronology of 1 and 2 Kings is one of the most challenging problems of Old Testament scholarship. The accession year computation and different calendars are part of the problem, compounded by using "round" rather than precise numbers ("two years" against "fifteen months"), and co-regency, where a father would share the throne with his son. For example, nineteen kings ruled in Israel from 931 to 722 B.C., a total of 209 years. But when the years the kings are said to reign are added, it comes to a total of 241 years. This is not an error but the result of the phenomenon of co-regencies.

This book is not the place to attempt to solve these problems. The work of Edwin Thiele is the classic in the field, and I have chosen to follow his calculations in the following chart. In some places numbers vary by one year. This reflects the fact that our calendar begins in January, but Israel and Judah used calendars beginning in the spring and the fall. The chart on the following page outlines the period covered by 1 and 2 Kings. The overlapping dates represent co-regencies.

Kings of 1 and 2 Kings	
Israel (North)	*Judah (South)*
Solomon (970–931/30)	
Jeroboam (930–909)	Rehoboam (930–913)
	Abijam (913–910)
	Asa (910–869)
Nadab (909–908)	
Baasha (908–886)	
Elah (886–885)	
Zimri (885)	
Omri (885–874)	
Ahab (874–853)	
	Jehoshaphat (872–848)
Ahaziah (853–852)	
Jehoram (852–841)	
	Jehoram (848–841)
	Ahaziah (841)
Jehu (841–814)	Athaliah (841–835)
	Joash (835–796)
Jehoahaz (814–798)	
Jehoash (798–782)	
	Amaziah (796–767)
Jereboam II (793–753)	
	Uzziah (792–740)
Zechariah (752)	
Shallum (752)	
Menahem (752–742)	
	Jotham (750–732)
Pekahiah (742–740)	
Pekah (753–732)	
	Ahaz (735–715)
Hoshea (732–722)	
	Hezekiah (729–686)
	Manasseh (696–642)
	Amon (642–640)
	Josiah (640–609)
	Jehoahaz (609)
	Jehoiakim (609–598)
	Jehoiachin (598)
	Zedekiah (597–587)

1 Kings 1:1–2:46

Transfer of Power

I. **INTRODUCTION**
Power Struggle

II. **COMMENTARY**
A verse-by-verse explanation of these chapters.

III. **CONCLUSION**
God's Will and My Responsibility

An overview of the principles and application from these chapters.

IV. **LIFE APPLICATION**
Lessons on Leadership

Melding these chapters to life.

V. **PRAYER**
Tying these chapters to life with God.

VI. **DEEPER DISCOVERIES**
Historical, geographical, and grammatical enrichment of the commentary.

VII. **TEACHING OUTLINE**
Suggested step-by-step group study of these chapters.

VIII. **ISSUES FOR DISCUSSION**
Zeroing these chapters in on daily life.

Q u o t e

"*L*eaders should lead as far as they can and then vanish.

Their ashes should not choke the fire they have lit."

H . G . W e l l s

BIOGRAPHICAL PROFILE: DAVID

- The Book of 1 Kings continues the story of King David from 2 Samuel
- David ruled as king for forty years (1011–971 B.C.). For the first years he was king over Judah alone, reigning from Hebron. Then, from 1004, he ruled over the united nation from Jerusalem
- David is the most dominant figure in 1 and 2 Kings. Although he was alive only in 1 Kings 1–2, his shadow lies over both books, where he is mentioned by name ninety-five times
- God's covenant with David, recorded in 2 Samuel 7, which promised David a lasting dynasty, was the enduring basis of the nation's hope (1 Kgs. 2:33,45; 5:5; 8:15,19,24–26; 9:5; 11:12–13, 32–38; 15:4; 2 Kgs. 8:19; 19:34; 20:6; 21:7)
- David and his obedience to the Lord is the standard by which the succeeding kings of Judah are measured
- David was the father of more than nineteen sons (see 1 Chr. 3:1–10). By the time we reach 1 Kings 1:1, the three oldest sons (Amnon, Chileab, and Absalom) have died, and Adonijah is the oldest surviving son. David's family relations have long been chaotic

1 Kings 1:1–2:46

I N   A   N U T S H E L L

As David grew increasingly frail in his old age, a crisis developed over succession to the throne. When David's oldest surviving son made a play for the throne, only decisive action by those closest to David ensured that David's intended successor, Solomon, would come to the throne. These chapters record the manner in which Solomon came to be David's successor, and they also reveal the basic principles upon which the Davidic dynasty will either flourish or founder.

Transfer of Power

I. INTRODUCTION

Power Struggle

$\mathcal{T}$he 2000 presidental election in the United States will go down as one of the closest, most confusing, and controversial in American history. Experts had predicted that the race between then Vice President Al Gore and Governor George Bush of Texas would be close. But no one imagined it would be so close! On election night it became evident that, although Gore had a higher tally in the national popular vote, the race would be settled in the state of Florida where Bush led by the narrowest of margins.

As the next weeks unfolded, the airwaves were full of charges of voting irregularities, judicial bias, shady tactics, and political corruption. Each day seemed to bring new accusations from one group or another, new legal maneuverings, and unexpected developments. It was a saga that took weeks to unfold, but finally, thirty-five days after the election, Gore conceded and George W. Bush became the forty-third president of the United States.

What is often overlooked is that the process, while complicated and convoluted, was peaceful. It reflected the deepest values of the American people. Demonstrators took to the streets to protest, emotions ran high, and heated words were exchanged. But there was no danger of armed rebellion and no serious threat of physical violence against the parties involved. The transfer of power may have been prolonged and painful, but it was democratic and peaceful. Confusion did not lead to chaos or catastrophe, and in the long annals of human history that is rare.

Israel may have been God's special people, but God's calling does not change the depravity factor that works in all of us. As the Book of 1 Kings begins, we are at a critical moment in the history of the united monarchy. David is the nation's second king, and there had never been a smooth transition of power from one generation to another. Israel's external enemies had been brought under control by the military genius of David. But two dangers remained. One was internal division over David's successor. Who would take his place? The other was more subtle but far more significant. What would happen in the heart of the king who followed David? That is why the central passage in the first two chapters of 1 Kings also is the key to the future of the nation.

The last recorded interaction between David and Solomon (2:1–4) shaped the movement of the entire history that followed. Surrounding that section is a historical account of the power struggle that resulted in Solomon's being firmly established on the throne. The entire section is about power, both political and spiritual.

II. COMMENTARY

Transfer of Power

MAIN IDEA: *God accomplishes his sovereign purposes, but his people are called to promote his purposes.*

A The Struggle for the Throne (1:1–53)

SUPPORTING IDEA: *God's people live in a fallen world, where they must act shrewdly and decisively to further the interests of God's kingdom.*

1:1–4. The dominating question of chapter 1, arising out of the account of the struggles within David's family recorded in 2 Samuel, is, Who will sit on David's throne? In one form or another, the phrase recurs eleven times. The reason it is important is given in these opening verses: David was not only growing old; he was becoming increasingly frail. The fact that **he could not keep warm** suggests poor circulation, perhaps linked to advanced arteriosclerosis. This was not just a personal problem; it also had significant political ramifications.

The leaders of the nation attempted to deal with the problem in a way that seems strange to us—providing David with a young woman who would provide nursing care and help him **keep warm**. The beautiful young woman they enlisted, **Abishag** (see "Deeper Discoveries"), became his concubine. In this context, the fact that David had no intimate relations with her is not a sign of David's purity but of his physical frailty. That weakness created a political vacuum.

1:5–10. David's oldest living son, **Adonijah**, determined to fill the political vacuum. He apparently knew that Solomon, and not he, was David's intended choice, or he would have been content to let events take their course. But David had not publicly named his successor, so the opportunistic Adonijah decided to make a play for the throne. The description of David's indulgence of Adonijah has an ominous tone, especially combined with the reference to Absalom. Like Absalom who rebelled against his father, Adonijah was spoiled, handsome, and willing to go behind his father's back in a bid for personal power. His determination was clear: **I will be king.**

In his play for the throne, Adonijah first surrounded himself with the trappings of power— **chariots and horses . . . with fifty men** as military attendants. This was a quasi-military force, using powerful cultural images. He also enlisted some of David's power brokers, especially two powerful figures,

Joab the military leader and **Abiathar** the religious leader. Third, he held a celebration just outside the city limits of Jerusalem as the final event before presenting himself to the nation as the new king. Those who attended were the people who would make his coup a reality. By their participation in this quasi-coronation meal, they were entering into a covenant with Adonijah.

1:11–27. Adonijah knew that his intentions were not universally acceptable. He had carefully excluded some of those closest to David: the prophet **Nathan . . . Zadok the priest, and Benaiah son of Jehoiada**. He had also been careful not to invite his brother **Solomon** to his celebration. At this point Nathan seized the initiative, fearing that David's frailty had made him unaware of the seriousness and urgency of events. Nathan was not just a godly and wise man, but the prophet through whom God had revealed his covenant to David. He was not willing to wait passively for the will of God to be done. Aware of the danger posed by men concerned only to further their own agenda, he acted shrewdly and decisively to protect and to promote the purposes of God.

Nathan approached the queen mother, **Bathsheba**, knowing that she would have unique access to David as well as concern for the best interests of her son. He informed her of Adonijah's actions and then charged her to remind David of his solemn promise to her: **Solomon your son shall be king after me.** We have no record of this promise in the biblical record, but there is no reason to doubt the truth of it. Nathan reminded Bathsheba that this was a life-and-death issue, both for Solomon and herself, since the normal pattern for a newly crowned king was to eliminate all potential rivals. Adonijah's failure to invite Solomon to his party showed that Adonijah viewed him as a dangerous rival.

Bathsheba followed Nathan's advice and gained an audience with the king. She came as a petitioner, reminding David that he had made a promise about Solomon, sworn **by the LORD your God.** Such an oath was inviolable, indicating that when David had made it he had been convinced that it was the will of God. Her reminder was accompanied by a warning (**you, my lord the king, do not know about it**) and an appeal (**the eyes of all Israel are on you, to learn from you**). She also reminded David that she and Solomon were in danger (**I and my son Solomon will be treated as criminals**).

At that point Nathan appeared, and he confirmed the report of Bathsheba. These two people had full knowledge of David's deepest secret—his sins against Uriah—and were trusted by the king. Nathan asked with great directness: **Who should sit on the throne of my lord the king after him?**

1:28–40. David may have been frail in the flesh, but he was sound of mind. He gathered his strength, summoned Bathsheba into his presence, and renewed his promise to her: **Solomon your son shall be king after me.** He then set out the course of action. A royal retinue was to be led by the leaders of the nation— **Zadok the priest, Nathan the prophet and Benaiah**. As leader of David's military guard, Benaiah was to take the lead. Solomon was to be placed on David's personal **mule** (a symbol of royalty) and taken to **Gihon**, the major gathering spot of the people.

In this public environment, surrounded by David's highest officials, Solomon was to be anointed by the prophet and the priest, while the ceremonial **trumpet** (shofar) was sounded, and the shout went up: **Long live King Solomon**. Solomon was then to be paraded back to the palace and seated on the throne. He would not be displacing David as king but would be ruling alongside him as co-regent.

David's officials immediately carried out his orders. Before the day was over, the succession crisis had been dealt with. David's designated successor had been publicly anointed by the nation's religious leaders and joyfully accepted by the people, who were **playing flutes and rejoicing greatly**.

1:41–53. Events had moved so rapidly that Adonijah and his party were caught unaware that their gathering had been rendered obsolete. En Rogel, where Adonijah's party was gathered (v. 9), was less than a mile down the valley from Gihon. The sound of the trumpet was the first clue, picked up by the old warrior Joab. Any doubt of what had occurred was quickly dispelled by the arrival of **Jonathan**, son of Abiathar the priest. For the third time the events of Solomon's anointing are recorded.

Adonijah's guests recognized the significance of these events and sought to distance themselves from Adonijah. They **rose in alarm and dispersed**. Adonijah also realized how the situation had changed. Fearing Solomon's reprisal, he fled to **the altar** of sacrifice, as a place of refuge (see "Deeper Discoveries"). Adonijah desperately clung to its horns, believing his life was in jeopardy. Since he had probably intended to kill Solomon, he expected to receive similar treatment at his brother's hands. Fearful, he sent a message to the king, pleading for mercy: **Let King Solomon swear to me today that he will not put his servant to death**. He was resigned to accept the legitimacy of Solomon's claim to the throne.

For the first time in the story, Solomon took action. Until now others had acted on his behalf. Now he showed his character, acting with royal authority without consulting his father. He offered Adonijah a release, conditioned on his being **a worthy man**. Adonijah was left no room to mount an insurrection against Solomon. The new king was in charge. Adonijah's power play had failed.

🅱 The Survival of the Throne (2:1–12)

SUPPORTING IDEA: *Even when a job or position is a gift from God, it is maintained only by spiritual obedience and practical wisdom.*

2:1–4. The final words of a father to a son are always significant, especially when royal power and the divine purposes are involved. It was common for God's great leaders to pass the torch to their successors (Jacob, Gen. 48–49; Moses, Deut. 32; Joshua, Josh. 23–24). Therefore, as death drew near, David gave Solomon a personal charge and some political advice.

David was a soldier, so he began his charge with words that have the ring of a battlefield charge (see 1 Sam. 4:9): **Be strong, show yourself a man.** What followed was of special importance: Solomon would be strong and manly only as he ordered his life by God's commands. The priority of his personal life and of his royal administration must be a commitment to God's will. The king of Israel was not like the pagan kings, a law to himself. He was a man under orders. Therefore, he must **walk in his ways, and keep his decrees and commands . . . as written in the Law of Moses.** These various terms reinforce one idea: The king's greatest responsibility was to honor the ways and word of God (see Deut. 17:18–20).

There would be consequences to such a lifestyle. First, Solomon would have personal success: **You may prosper in all you do.** "Prosper" contains the idea of acting with skill and insight, with the result of success. Royal and national prosperity would be the by-product of a life of obedience, a theme revealed in the chapters that follow. Second, such obedience would bring about dynastic continuity: **You will never fail to have a man on the throne of Israel.** This focuses on an important part of the Lord's promise made to David in the Davidic covenant (2 Sam. 7:11–16). The Lord's unconditional promise was of an everlasting dynasty for David, a promise that ultimately points to the Lord Jesus, God's Messiah from the line of David. This throne would be an eternal throne, based on God's sovereign promise, not David's descendants' appropriate performance.

But within the unconditional covenant was a condition: when any of David's descendants did wrong, "I will punish him with the rod of men, with floggings inflicted by men. But my love will never be taken away from him, as I took it away from Saul" (2 Sam. 7:14–15). The promise that there would always be someone eligible to sit on the throne did not mean that every generation would experience God's blessing. There was a condition for personal blessing of which David reminded Solomon: **If your descendants . . . walk faithfully before me with all their heart and soul.** Blessing was not automatic, and judgment was a possibility.

Faithfulness meant not only a life conformed to God's standards but also a heart committed to God. This condition is central to the theology of 1 Kings, and it is a theme to which the Lord himself directed Solomon over and over (see 1 Kgs. 3:14; 6:12; 9:4–9; 11:11). The throne of David was established on the unconditional covenant promise of God. The prosperity of each king and his kingdom was linked inseparably to that king's faithfulness to the Lord.

2:5–9. The throne would be maintained only by spiritual obedience. But David also was a realist who knew that Solomon's hold on the throne was fragile and needed to be protected by shrewd actions. Suddenly we are in the cold, hard world of politics in a culture that had its brutal side. David was dying and had unfinished business: Joab and Shimei. There had been compelling reasons why he himself could not act against these men; nevertheless, he knew they posed a danger to his son.

Joab was both a relative and a longtime military ally of David. But he was also a ruthless, self-serving man who could pose a great danger to the inexperienced Solomon. Twice he had taken the lives of fellow Israelites who were a threat to him (Abner, 2 Sam. 2–3; Amasa, 2 Sam. 20:9–10). He had also sided with Adonijah in the recent succession struggle. He was a man **stained** with blood before God, but David had not dealt properly with his sins. The dying king advised his son that this must be corrected and that he must see to it that Joab paid the price for his sins. Leaving this mess for his son surely doesn't represent David at his best!

In the same way, David warned his son about **Shimei**, a Benjamite and clansman of the former king, Saul. Resentful that David had displaced the old royal family, Shimei had publicly cursed and mocked David as the king fled before the rebellion of his son Absalom (2 Sam. 16:5–13). When events turned with the death of Absalom, Shimei had come to David with a thousand of his fellow Benjamites, begging for mercy, aware that his mockery had been a capital crime. In the euphoria of the moment, David had spared his life, but he knew that Shimei's bitterness had not vanished. As an influential and opportunistic adversary, he posed a continuing danger to the new king. So David advised his son to find an appropriate way to remove the danger and to execute justice by bringing **his gray head down to the grave in blood**.

But the third person mentioned in these verses was different. During Absalom's rebellion, when it looked as if David would be overthrown, **Barzillai** had shown loyalty by bringing him food (2 Sam. 17:27–29). Solomon was to repay Barzillai's kindness by allowing his family to be **among those who eat at your table**, the equivalent of a royal pension.

2:10–12. The passing of David was the passing of one of God's giants, but it is recorded with great simplicity. The writer's main concern was the fulfillment of God's promise as **Solomon sat on the throne of his father David, and his rule was firmly established**. This last phrase is the theme of the rest of the chapter, repeated in 2:24,45–46. But that throne would remain secure only as Solomon and his sons followed the Lord (see 2:2–4).

The Securing of the Throne (2:13–46)

SUPPORTING IDEA: *A leader is required to do some difficult things, but he must fight the temptation to indulge his dark side.*

2:13–25. The first person to represent a danger to Solomon had not been mentioned by David, but he soon showed his true colors. **Adonijah** had been given a good conduct reprieve by Solomon in 1:53. But his ambition to succeed to the throne had not abated. Perhaps he thought his true motives would not be detected. But his request for Abishag, David's concubine (1:2–4), was not the innocent appeal of a man for the hand of the woman he loved. Because he knew that Bathsheba, as the queen mother, had access to the king, he went to her with his request: **ask King Solomon . . . to give me Abishag . . . as my wife.** In the culture of the time, possession of the former king's harem was linked to a claim on the throne (see 2 Sam. 3:8; 16:20–22). Adonijah clung to the idea that he was the rightful king (**All Israel looked to me as their king**), and almost certainly this was the opening move for another attempt to displace Solomon.

It is likely that Bathsheba recognized his intent, but she agreed to present the request to her son. Solomon detected immediately what was involved. He was confident that he was on the throne by the will of God. So Adonijah's request represented defiance against God as well as a violation of his good-conduct reprieve. Solomon ordered Adonijah's execution, which Benaiah, as head of his military guard, carried out.

2:26–27. Determined to deal with the Adonijah threat, Solomon next moved against Abiathar, the priest who had been part of the conspiracy. But because of his sacred role and his longtime association with David, Solomon chose not to execute him but to sentence him to house arrest. Abiathar was removed from the office of high priest, a fulfillment of God's prophecy through his prophet in 1 Samuel 2:27–36. This introduces another important theme of 1 Kings: the fulfillment of prophecy.

2:28–35. **Joab**, astute as always, knew that the execution of Adonijah, with whom he had sided (1:7,41), meant that he was next. He fled to the altar for refuge, perhaps hoping to receive the same good-conduct reprieve as Adonijah had (1:49–53). But the altar was only a place of refuge for the innocent (Exod. 21:12–14). Joab bore the guilt of innocent blood. Therefore, Solomon ordered Benaiah to execute him, probably after he had dragged him away from the altar. David's advice to Solomon about Joab had been carried out, precipitated by Joab's own actions.

2:36–46. The last piece of unfinished business was **Shimei.** Solomon commanded him not to **cross the Kidron Valley** (the path to his home area) or to **go anywhere else.** He was confined to Jerusalem. The restrictions must have been onerous, but for three years Shimei complied. But then two of his slaves escaped and were captured in the Philistine city of Gath. Foolishly, Shimei went to recover his slaves without asking Solomon's permission. Hearing the news, Solomon reminded Shimei of their agreement and of **all the wrong you did to my father David**. He then ordered Benaiah to wield the executioner's sword for the third time (vv. 25,34).

All the unfinished business had been dealt with. **The kingdom was now firmly established in Solomon's hands**. It had not been without cost. But only three people had lost their lives, and there is no record of other bloodshed during Solomon's reign.

MAIN IDEA REVIEW: *God accomplishes his sovereign purposes, but his people are called to promote his purposes.*

III. CONCLUSION

God's Will and My Responsibility

The opening question of the Book of 1 Kings is, Who will sit on the throne of David? (see 1:20). The answer is given in these chapters. Solomon sat on the throne of his father David, and his rule was firmly established (2:12,24,46). This was not just the result of politics. It was the result of the will of God, as David (1:48), Solomon (2:24), and even Adonijah (2:15) recognized. But the succession of Solomon to the throne was not automatic. Significant parts of the kingdom had desired another king. But by the end of these two chapters, all of these enemies had been dealt with. Solomon sat securely upon his father's throne, the unrivaled king.

But Solomon's greatest enemy had not been removed. It was found in his own heart. The greatest threat to Solomon's reign was Solomon himself. The Lord had made clear, through the mouth of his son David, that Solomon's greatest need was to walk in obedience and faithfulness before the Lord. This principle of blessing or judgment will shape all that happens in the following story of the kings.

Pogo, an old comic strip, is famous for the words, "We have met the enemy, and he is us." Solomon's throne looks very secure as we come to the end of chapter 2. But as we shall see, it is only as secure as the condition of his heart.

PRINCIPLES

• The central battle of life is the battle of the heart. There is no substitute for maintaining a heart of faithfulness and a lifestyle of obedience

17

- Knowing that God has a sovereign purpose does not mean that we can wait passively for it to unfold. God's people are called to decisive actions to further his purposes.

- God's unconditional promises often have conditional requirements we must meet before we can experience his blessings.

- There are times when evil cannot be quietly contained; it must be surgically removed.

APPLICATIONS

- Don't sit passively while evil people pursue their selfish goals.

- Follow the advice of Solomon: "Above all else, guard your heart, for it is the wellspring of life" (Prov. 4:23).

- All that is necessary for evil to triumph is for good people to do nothing. Do something!

- Stay in touch with those whom you lead and the situation around you.

- Don't leave unfinished business for those who will follow you.

IV. LIFE APPLICATION

Lessons on Leadership

David's last words to his son contain some important insights into leadership, delivered by one of the great leaders in history. Solomon's strength would come not from military or administrative measures but from moral and spiritual vitality. A good leader is not above God's law but under it. Strength is rooted in a person's relation to God and his word.

These chapters are a manual on leadership. There is a danger of choosing leaders on the wrong basis—for their charm and their charisma—as seen in the person of Adonijah. There is also the danger of distracted or enfeebled leadership, of leaders getting out of touch with the situation around them and plunging their followers into conflict and uncertainty. There is also a need for the holy activism modeled by Nathan, who refused to wait passively for events to unfold. Knowing the will of God, he was bold, proactive, and shrewd. There is a need for leaders to seize their responsibility, as Solomon did when he came to the throne. And, in the actions of David and Solomon, there is a reminder of the dark side of leadership, of doing the right thing in the wrong way.

V. PRAYER

Father, thank you that you are the sovereign Lord of all things. You are work-ing all things according to your own purposes and glory. I am grateful that you have called me to be involved actively in carrying out your will in a sinful world. Give me the wisdom to know how to act in ways that further your purpose. Amen.

VI. DEEPER DISCOVERIES

A. Abishag

Abishag was a young, beautiful virgin who was recruited to "serve the king." She obviously acted as a servant and nurse. The fact that David did not have a sexual relationship with her is not a statement about his purity, but his frailty. Abishag's status is uncertain, but at most it was that of concubine, not queen. Some have suggested, on the basis that she was a Shunammite, that she was the Shulammite of the Song of Solomon (Song 6:13). But this is unlikely.

B. David's Oath: Fact or Fiction?

There is no explicit mention in 2 Samuel of a promise by David to Baths-heba that Solomon would be the successor to the throne. On the basis of this silence, some critics have suggested that the oath was a fiction, invented by Nathan to manipulate the senile David. But David is depicted as feeble, not senile. When he did act and speak, his mind was clear and his memory was strong. Adonijah clearly felt a need to act behind David's back and not to invite Solomon alone. Why, if he was considered the logical successor? The initial promise had apparently been private, not public. First Chronicles clearly indicates that David had designated Solomon as his successor (1 Chr. 22:5–19).

C. Seizing the Horns (1:50; 2:28)

The altar was the place where the priests offered the many sacrifices required by God. Since the blood of sacrifices was smeared on the horns of the altar (Lev. 4:7,25), they were considered especially sacred. The concept of the altar as a place of asylum is suggested by Exodus 21:12–14, where it is a provision for those who have committed involuntary manslaughter. It gave the accused opportunity for a hearing of his case. But Joab was a murderer. He had killed intentionally. The shedding of innocent blood polluted the land (Num. 35:33–34). Murderers like him were to be executed (Deut. 19:11–13).

VII. TEACHING OUTLINE

A. INTRODUCTION

1. Lead Story: Power Struggle

2. Context: First Kings tells the ongoing story of the reign of David, picking up the story in his old age. Because he is increasingly frail, the question of who will be his successor must be answered.

3. Transition: The writer of 1 Kings not only wants us to understand why it is Solomon, and not one of David's other sons, who came to the throne. He also wants to introduce us to some of the crucial themes that will play themselves out in the history of the nation, especially the critical idea that a king's relation to God through obedience to his commands will determine the fate of the nation.

B. COMMENTARY

1. The Struggle for the Throne (1:1–53)

2. The Survival of the Throne (2:1–12)

3. The Securing of the Throne (2:13–46)

C. CONCLUSION: GOD'S WILL AND MY RESPONSIBILITY

VIII. ISSUES FOR DISCUSSION

1. There are significant lessons about leadership, both negative and positive, in this section. Which ones do you find exemplified in David, Adonijah, Nathan, and Solomon?

2. The heart of this section is the advice given to Solomon by David in 2:1–4. How should his advice shape our understanding of our personal priorities?

3. A leader must do some difficult things, but there is always the possibility of doing them in a sinful way. Talk about the hard side of leadership, where a leader must deal with "enemies." How does a leader maintain godliness in such situations?

1 Kings 3:1–4:34

Defining Moments

| Q u o t e |

"$\mathcal{S}$eek wisdom. Wisdom starts in heaven, but works at street level, where we bump shoulders with others. It isn't satisfied with information retrieval: You can't access wisdom by the megabyte. Wisdom is concerned with how we relate to people, to the world and to God."

E d m u n d   P .   C l o w n e y

BIOGRAPHICAL PROFILE: SOLOMON

- Mentioned 294 times in the Old Testament, 12 times in the New
- Oldest surviving son of David and Bathsheba, he was also called Jedidiah ("beloved of the LORD") by the prophet Nathan (2 Sam. 12:25)
- Third king of the united kingdom of Israel, and the first dynastic king (as the son of David), he reigned from Jerusalem about 971–931 B.C.
- Not recorded as leading any major military campaigns, but was responsible for consolidating the territory acquired by his father, and he built a formidable army
- Responsible for the "Golden Age" of Israel. The Lord Jesus speaks of "the glory of Solomon" and "the wisdom of Solomon"
- Notorious for his seven hundred wives and three hundred concubines (1 Kgs. 11:3)
- Failed as a king because of his involvement in idolatry and violation of the divine covenant; his oppressive policies toward the northern tribes also led to the tribal rebellion at the beginning of the reign of his son Rehoboam

1 Kings 3:1–4:34

IN A NUTSHELL

At the beginning of his reign, Solomon showed his love for the Lord by leading his people in the worship of God. The Lord gave Solomon permission to ask whatever he wished. Solomon asked the Lord for a hearing heart, a heart of wisdom so he could govern his nation well. The Lord not only promised Solomon wisdom; he promised him wealth and fame as well. These chapters show the fulfillment of God's promise to Solomon of wisdom, wealth, and fame.

Defining Moments

I. INTRODUCTION

Make a Wish

*J*ulius Caesar had led the Roman army to victory in Britain and Gaul. But the Roman senate, fearing his ambition, had ordered him to relinquish command of his troops before he entered Italy. The decisive place was the Rubicon, the border between Gaul and Italy. To cross with his army would plunge the nation into civil war. In one of those moments on which history turns, Caesar rode his horse into the stream, shouting for his men to follow, with the words, "The die is cast."

There are times in life when we are faced with choices that are truly momentous. Sometimes we realize this at the time. More often we recognize their significance only as we look back. They are defining moments, times that expose our deepest values, test our commitment, and shape our character. We make our choices, and then they make us.

Defining moments don't come often, but when they do, they leave an indelible mark. Occasionally they come in dramatic form, in the shape of a great opportunity, a powerful temptation, or a personal tragedy. More often they come in quiet moments of reflection. Sometimes they are choices between good and bad; at others, between better and best. The most life-shaping defining moments involve encounters with the triune God, occasions that probe the depths of our being. Only rarely do we get to choose our defining moments, but we always get to choose our response to them.

One of our society's unique charities is the Make a Wish Foundation, an organization that seeks to grant the wishes of desperately ill children. When my five-year-old grandnephew was battling a life-threatening illness, kind and generous people made it possible for him to travel from Canada with his entire family to fulfill his desire to go to Disneyland.

Imagine that the sovereign God of the universe granted you the same opportunity. What would your wish be? For young King Solomon, this was not a theoretical scenario. The Lord actually did appear to him, and he gave him an opportunity to ask for whatever he wanted—a divine blank check!

Solomon is a puzzling man, as we shall discover. He accomplished great good and lived a life marked by massive achievements. But the outcome of his life was tragic. He was a wise man who did some foolish things. He was a godly man who did some ungodly things. But he began well. At the beginning of his reign, we see him at his best.

II. COMMENTARY

Defining Moments

> **MAIN IDEA:** *The wisdom that God delights to give his people is primarily a matter of the heart and not of the mind.*

Solomon was the great son of an even greater father, chosen by his father David to be the king of Israel. He would reign for forty years, becoming the "golden boy" who brought in Israel's golden age. But his golden age would not survive his death. Underneath the glittering surface, he had planted the seeds of its destruction. But that would be hidden for a time. The problem was found in Solomon's heart. His father David had been known as the man after God's own heart; Solomon would prove to have a divided heart.

A The Battle of Life Centers on the Heart (3:1–3)

> **SUPPORTING IDEA:** *Our exceptional achievements prove to be less decisive, in the long run, than the "except" of our hearts.*

3:1–3. Solomon's life was marked by great achievements. This opening description of his reign focuses on three of those. First, his marriage showed his international prominence: **Solomon made an alliance with Pharaoh king of Egypt and married his daughter.** Five times (3:1; 7:8; 9:16,24; 11:1) our attention is directed to this marriage, showing how significant the author of 1 Kings considered it. Marriage between ancient kings was not so much a romantic arrangement as a political arrangement—an alliance of royal families and nations, not just individuals.

The pharaoh in question was almost certainly Siamun (978–959 B.C.), one of the last kings of the relatively weak twenty-first dynasty. Such a marriage had special significance, because earlier Egyptian dynasties had refused to give their daughters in marriage to live outside the land. While pharaohs took foreign princesses, they did not give away their daughters. The marriage represents a profound reversal of fortunes for Israel and Solomon. The former slave people had become the ally of their old enemy, the traditional superpower of the region! Solomon was an international force to be reckoned with.

Marriage to an Egyptian princess did not technically violate the letter of biblical commands (see Deut. 7:1–4), but it was unwise, threatening the uniqueness of God's people. It will also become clear that Solomon married this woman without requiring her to become a worshiper of the only true God.

The second major achievement of Solomon was his building projects: **his palace and the temple of the LORD, and the wall around Jerusalem.** Solomon had inherited a huge territory from his father, the result of David's military campaigns. Solomon himself is never specifically said to go to war. His task was to turn acquired territory into a nation. This required a strong administrative, military, and religious capital. So Solomon focused his energy and fortune on Jerusalem, building the palace complex and the glorious temple and extending the city wall. Jerusalem became the centerpiece of his empire.

Solomon's third achievement involved the centralizing and regularizing of national worship. Over the centuries the Mosaic tabernacle had been neglected. Much of the people's worship took place at **high places**, local shrines and worship centers that were a constant temptation to idolatry (see "Deeper Discoveries"). These high places may have been tolerated by the Lord for a time, but they represented a danger. Solomon knew his father's passion to build a temple **for the Name of the LORD**. He caught his father's vision and made the project so central to his early reign that the author of 1 Kings devotes four and one-half chapters to describing it (5:1–9:9). The Solomonic temple centered the worship of God's people on the particular place the Lord had chosen and rendered the high places obsolete and sinful. So at the beginning of his reign, Solomon devoted his energies to making the worship of God central.

Having told us of Solomon's exceptional achievements, the author of 1 Kings tells us that **Solomon showed his love for the LORD by walking according to the statutes of his father David.** He is the only post-Davidic king said to love the Lord, which in the context of 1 Kings meant to give God exclusive loyalty, heartfelt devotion, and practical obedience. At this point Solomon was following David's example.

But all was not as it seemed. Solomon's love for the Lord was not unqualified. He loved the Lord, **except that he offered sacrifices and burned incense on the high places**. Throughout the Book of 1 Kings, kings are judged by their attitude toward the high places: good kings abolish them; mediocre kings tolerate them; and evil kings patronize them. This "except" which seems like such a small crack, will later became an open breach. Later we will read that Solomon "loved many foreign women" (11:1). This "except" became the central issue in Solomon's life: He had a divided heart. Eventually, the crack became a gaping hole.

B The Crucial Choices of Life Center on the Heart (3:4–15)

SUPPORTING IDEA: *God delights to respond to our prayers when they focus on the condition of our hearts, in light of his purpose for us.*

3:4–5. Solomon's defining moment came in the context of worship. Gibeon, a town about seven miles north of Jerusalem, was the most important high place, chiefly because, as 2 Chronicles 1:3 indicates, the ancient tabernacle constructed under the leadership of Moses was there. This was not a private ceremony but a national act of worship, as is indicated by 2 Chronicles 1:2–3 and by the massive number of sacrifices: **a thousand burnt offerings**. Solomon, as king, was making the Lord a priority.

In response to Solomon's worship and leadership, the Lord appeared to him in a dream with a stunning offer: **Ask for whatever you want me to give you**. This was the first of four occasions in his life that Solomon met his Lord in a very personal way (cp. 6:11–13; 9:1–9; 11:9–13). This was not an ordinary dream, since the Lord and Solomon carried on a conversation; it was a divine revelation. God's offer was a blank check, a remarkable act of divine generosity. But it was also a challenge for Solomon to decide his deepest values. What did he want his life and his reign to be about?

3:6–9. Solomon's response was a remarkable mixture of gratitude, humility, and boldness. He began by grounding himself in God's person and purpose. His praise centered on God's **great kindness**, his loyal love revealed in the covenant the Lord had made with his father David. His father had lived a faithful life before God, out of the integrity of his heart. But it was God's initiating grace and generosity that had been the prime mover of events. Solomon's presence on the throne was living evidence that God's great covenant love continued.

From praise Solomon turned to his problem. Succeeding a powerful figure like David was a daunting responsibility. Solomon was probably about twenty years old at this time. A comparison of other passages tells us that he was a married man with a son before he came to the throne (cp. 11:42; 14:21). But he felt like **a little child**, immature and inexperienced with respect to his new responsibility to lead a nation. He also felt incompetent: **I . . . do not know how to carry out my duties**. Solomon faced a responsibility that overwhelmed him. He had been thrown into the deep end of the pool. He found himself the king not of any nation, but of **the people you have chosen**.

There is a great deal to be learned about prayer from Solomon's model. He first filled his mind with a sense of God's greatness and grace. Then he humbled himself in dependence. Only then did he make his petition. Think of all the things he could have asked for. But because he focused on God and his own weakness, he made a request that brought pleasure to the heart of God: **Give your servant a discerning heart to govern your people**.

The expression "a discerning heart" is literally "a hearing heart." In the Hebrew language the same word conveys the idea of "hearing" and "obeying." Solomon felt a need to hear God, to have his guidance and direction as he sought to lead his people. He needed divine help to distinguish good from evil, right from wrong, and truth from falsehood as he led his people. He also needed to hear his people, to know their needs, their concerns, and their desires. Solomon was asking for divine help to carry out the responsibilities of the kingship.

3:10–14. When our prayers align with the purpose and program of God, it brings delight to him. God responded to Solomon by affirming his request. He had asked for what truly mattered and had prayed in God's will. He could have asked for the typical longings of kings—things such as longevity, prosperity, and peace. But Solomon asked for "a hearing heart."

God's promise to Solomon was that he would receive what he had asked for: **discernment in administering justice** and **a wise and discerning heart**. *Discernment* in Hebrew conveys the idea of being able to distinguish between options, seeing whether something is right or wrong, wise or foolish. *Wisdom* primarily describes "skill," in this context "skill in living." True wisdom is not about intellectual genius so much as it is about the ability to live in accordance with life as God has ordered it. It is a term that will be used to describe Solomon more than twenty times in the following chapters.

Three times in his response, the Lord told Solomon, **I will give you.** The first gift would be wisdom, to an extent that would set Solomon apart from all people. But the Lord's grace overflowed. He would also give Solomon what he had not asked for— **riches and honor**—so Solomon would be supreme in his generation. Finally, the Lord extended a conditional promise: **If you walk in my ways . . . I will give you a long life.** The earlier promises had been unconditional. But this promise was conditioned on obedience. The outcome of this part of the promise is indicated by the fact that Solomon died at about the age of sixty, while David lived for seventy years.

3:15. Solomon's promise came through a dream that contained a great promise. It was the sacred promise of the God of Israel. Solomon realized that, and he led the people back **to Jerusalem**. There, before another part of the ancient tabernacle, **the ark of the Lord's covenant**, which David had brought into the city, he completed his spiritual celebration. The **burnt offerings and fellowship offerings**, as well as the royal **feast**, served as public acknowledgment of God's generosity to him and his people.

C God Honors the Wise Choices of the Heart (3:16–4:34)

SUPPORTING IDEA: *When we live in wisdom by having a hearing heart before God, he fulfills his promises of blessing to us.*

The section that follows indicates how the Lord fulfilled his promise to Solomon. This is a central message of 1 Kings: God was faithful to his covenant and promises. In these chapters we see Solomon experiencing, in fulfillment of 3:12–13, God's gift of wisdom (3:16–28); God's gift of wealth (4:1–28); and God's gift of honor and fame (4:29–34).

3:16–28. The story of Solomon, the prostitutes, and the baby is one of the best known in the Bible. It was an event that solidified Solomon's reputation as one of the shrewdest men in history. It was customary in the Ancient Near East for any citizen to have access to the king as the court of final appeal. Prostitutes were one of the most disreputable and disrespected elements of Hebrew society, the kind of people who would be marginalized and overlooked in a quest for justice. But in the reign of wise King Solomon, even they could receive a fair hearing.

The facts of the case were not in dispute. Two prostitutes who shared a house gave birth to babies within three days of each other. During the night one of the babies died. The complainant claimed that the other woman had rolled over on her own baby, killing it. Awaking to this horror, she had switched the babies, placing the dead baby by the first woman's side. When she awakened, the first woman discovered the dead body, and she instinctively knew what had happened and that the living baby was hers. But her version of the story was hotly disputed by the other woman, who contended that the entire story was a fabrication. **And so they argued before the king**.

What was Solomon to do? There were no other witnesses who could be called and no medical tests that could determine maternity. Normal judicial procedures were of no value. Solomon's decision defied all judicial norms: **Cut the living child in two and give half to one and half to the other**.

The ruling stunned one of the women, who immediately cried out that the baby must be spared and given to the other woman. But her companion displayed a coldhearted concern for fairness; she was willing to sacrifice the baby. Solomon had exposed their hearts. His "hearing heart" heard the cry of the true mother, and he rendered his final verdict: **Give the living baby to the first woman . . . she is his mother**. The story of Solomon's ruling swept through the nation. His citizens delighted to retell the story with a kind of awe. What kind of ruler would come up with such an ingenious solution? And there was justice for the poor and disreputable, not just for the rich and the powerful. Surely this was proof that their king **had wisdom from God to administer justice**.

4:1–28. Solomon had inherited a large territory, acquired mainly by the military exploits of his father. But it is one thing to hold territory and another to build it into a kingdom. While David's administration had been minimal, Solomon's role was not to extend the kingdom militarily, but to solidify it administratively and economically. The major message of this section is that Solomon had administrative wisdom from God. This wisdom led to the God-given wealth described in verses 20–28.

Solomon built his administration around a carefully chosen group of senior leaders who are described in 4:1–6. A study of the list shows that some of the officials had first served under David. But under Solomon the government became more complex and centralized. We cannot be sure of the job descriptions of some of these individuals, but together they constituted the administrative, military, diplomatic, and religious branches of his government. One name that should be noticed is found in verse 6: **Adoniram . . . in charge of forced labor**. This appointment would have significant consequences for the future of God's people.

Verses 7–19 describe another innovation of Solomon. The nation had been organized around the twelve tribes. But not all of the tribes were of the same size. Neither did they live in regions that were equally productive. Solomon divided the nation into twelve regions, for the sake of taxation, to supply **provisions for the king and the royal household**. Each region was responsible to provision the royal household (the Jerusalem bureaucracy) for one month a year. The divisions sometimes followed the old tribal boundaries. At other times these tribal divisions were disregarded. This redistricting may have been intended to shift loyalties away from the tribes to the central government. It had the effect of making Jerusalem, not the tribes, the hub of the nation.

In verses 20–28, we see the results of Solomon's administrative skills. His nation was peaceful, productive, and prosperous. His kingdom reached **from the River** (the Euphrates) . . . **as far as the border of Egypt**. These were the boundaries of the land (repeated in v. 24) that God had promised Abraham (Gen. 15:18), a clear sign of divine blessing. Not only did Solomon have **peace** within these borders; **these countries brought tribute and were Solomon's subjects** throughout his life. Life for the average Israelite was very good as well.

This section also describes Solomon's lavish lifestyle and the luxury of the royal court. In a time when horses and chariots were signs of wealth and military power, Solomon developed a strong military machine. The most revealing phrase is **they saw to it that nothing was lacking**. Life in Solomon's kingdom was very good, because God fulfilled his promises to him. But we should note that this blessing brought a danger that Solomon would forget the warnings God had given to kings (Deut. 17).

4:29–34. The final part of God's unconditional promise to Solomon was that he would have honor. The key word in this section is **wisdom**. In one form or another, it occurs eight times in six verses. Here the variety of Solomon's wisdom is on display. It was not his achievement but God's gift of **wisdom and very great insight** (discernment) **and a breadth of understanding** (literally, heart).

Wisdom was a much-prized pursuit in the ancient world, and it often took the form of proverbs, songs, or nature observations. Solomon excelled in all of these, so much so that **his fame spread to all the surrounding nations**. The Lord had kept his promise to Solomon beyond all expectations.

MAIN IDEA REVIEW: *The wisdom that God delights to give his people is primarily a matter of the heart and not of the mind.*

III. CONCLUSION

Guarding the Heart

As Solomon went to sleep on the night of his worship in Gibeon, he did not expect to be confronted in his sleep with a question that would define his life and kingship. But when the Lord asked, 'What do you want me to do for you?" he found himself facing one of life's most searching questions: *If I could receive whatever I wanted from the Lord, what would I request? And how would the Lord respond to my request?*

Solomon's request for a hearing heart delighted the Lord. He was wise enough to recognize his need and selfless enough to ask for what furthered God's purposes and the nation's progress, not just his own. He also was wise enough to know that wisdom is not ultimately an issue of the head but a matter of the heart. The mind is clearly engaged in the matter of wisdom, but when the heart is detached from loyalty to God, even the most brilliant mind will begin to display foolishness. Solomon's wisdom was not only proverbial; it was practical. It enabled him to lead his people in ways that resulted in God's blessings.

A strong beginning is no guarantee of a good ending. Solomon had a heart defect. While his heart heard God, it also heard other voices—the high places and later his wives. In the long run his wisdom was rendered useless because he allowed his heart to drift from God.

PRINCIPLES

- The "except" of our lives, when it represents a holdout from full obedience, will eventually overwhelm our achievements.
- Without "a hearing heart" toward God, there can be no true wisdom ("the fear of the L ORD is the beginning of wisdom," Prov. 9:10).
- Wisdom is not primarily a matter of the head; it is a matter of the heart.
- God delights to answer the prayers of those whose supreme concern is the promotion of God's kingdom and purposes.
- A great beginning does not guarantee a good ending.

APPLICATIONS

- Guard your heart against the "excepts" that can devastate your love for the Lord.
- Value wisdom more than intellect and godliness more than education.

- Be less concerned about your kingdom than God's kingdom and more concerned about the welfare of others rather than your own.

- The higher you go in positions of leadership and responsibility, the deeper you need to go in your development of character and discipline.

IV. LIFE APPLICATION

The Way of Wisdom

One of the first lessons a novice pilot has drilled into him is that he must trust his instruments, not his instincts. In a cloud or at night, when visibility is restricted, a pilot can lose all sense of up and down. One's instincts may seem certain, but they may be profoundly wrong. The way of wisdom is not to obey one's feelings but to trust the instrument panel. If a pilot doesn't listen, if he adopts the principle of "live and learn," he will not live long. Experience is not always the best teacher. Wise people learn and live.

The way of wisdom is to learn and live. But it is important to understand what the Bible means when it talks about wisdom. One of the questions that inevitably comes from the life of Solomon is, How could such a wise man do so many foolish things?

Wisdom, as the Bible describes it, is not primarily an abstract or reflective concept but a practical element. The Hebrew word for wisdom, *hokmah,* has about it the idea of "skill." In Exodus 35:30–36:2, it is used six times to describe abilities of two master craftsmen, Bezalel and Oholiab, the mastery of skills and techniques. It is also used to describe skill that enables a person to be a gifted judge, leader, or administrator. It is in this sense that it describes Solomon in 1 Kings 3:28 and 5:12. However, in its most important sense, wisdom describes skill in living, a comprehensive term that describes skill in relationships, moral integrity, practical life issues, and, supremely, in spiritual matters. It is this most important sense that is primarily in view in the Book of Proverbs. The premise of such skill in living is that "the fear of the LORD is the beginning of wisdom" (Prov. 9:10).

The tragedy of Solomon is that he maintained the lesser kinds of wisdom, mastery of information and people, but he lost touch with the most important kind, skill in living, because he lost touch with God. Wisdom without a relationship with God is meaningless. Solomon became a very wise fool. His life is a powerful reminder that we not only need to be wise; we need to be wise in the right way. Only a vital, healthy relationship with the Lord Jesus makes this possible.

V. PRAYER

Lord, give me the wisdom to come before you, fully aware of your grace in my life, your purpose for my life, and your program for your people. Help me to learn not only how to ask wisely but also how to live wisely, by maintaining my heart diligently before you. Teach me to deal ruthlessly with the "except" in my heart. Amen.

VI. DEEPER DISCOVERIES

A. High Places

The high places were open-air sanctuaries used as places of worship. The translation "high places" is not quite precise, since they were also found in valleys (Jer. 32:35) and cities. They were a pagan Canaanite custom (Num. 33:52), but many of the high places were devoted to the worship of God. Worship in such places contradicted the command of Deuteronomy 12, which required worship only at the one place chosen by the Lord. There was great danger represented by these high places, because of their Canaanite associations, and they often became centers of idolatry and immorality.

B. Asking That Pleases God (3:4–14)

Important principles about prayer are taught in this section. Although Solomon had been invited by the Lord to ask for whatever he wanted, he did not rush into petition. First, he reviewed what God had done for him, in a way that quickly turned into praise for God's loyal love. He then recognized his own weakness and need, honestly confronting his limitations. At the same time, he reminded himself before God of the responsibility he had received from God himself. God had a purpose for his life that he was called to achieve. Only then did he make his request. Because he had focused on the mission of God for his life, his request was not self-centered and self-indulgent. Rather, it was focused on God's will and God's purpose for him.

C. The Twelve District Governors (4:7–19)

The primary task of these districts was to supply the central government, on a rotating basis, with food and other supplies and labor. The divisions may have crossed traditional tribal boundaries to make each district a more viable economic unit. But there is no mention of the tribe of Judah in the list. Solomon, who was from the tribe of Judah, may have exempted his own tribe from this taxation. If so, this was an act of favoritism that would breed deep resentment among the other tribes (a smoldering resentment that burst into flame in the civil disruption of 1 Kings 12). Solomon may have been wise, but he was still a sinner. And "wise" sinners do stupid things!

VII. TEACHING OUTLINE

A. INTRODUCTION
1. Lead Story: Make a Wish
2. Context: Solomon was now secure on the throne of Israel. He was the son of David, but what kind of king would he choose to be?
3. Transition: Before our author takes us to the specific event that becomes the defining moment for Solomon, he takes a few verses to give us an overview of Solomon's reign. He introduces an idea that will prove to be important to the reign of Solomon, because it gives us a glimpse into his heart.

B. COMMENTARY
1. The Battle of Life Centers on the Heart (3:1–3)
2. The Crucial Choices of Life Center on the Heart (3:4–15)
3. God Honors the Wise Choices of the Heart (3:16–4:34)

C. CONCLUSION: GUARDING THE HEART

VIII. ISSUES FOR DISCUSSION

1. "Solomon loved the Lord, except . . ." What are some of the "excepts" that we sometimes demonstrate in relation to our love of the Lord? Are these always bad things? What about the "excepts" in your own life?
2. Put yourself in Solomon's place. What would you have asked for if the Lord had promised to give you whatever you requested?

1 Kings 5:1–7:51

A House for God's Name

I. **INTRODUCTION**
Calling or Career?

II. **COMMENTARY**
A verse-by-verse explanation of these chapters.

III. **CONCLUSION**
Building the House of God

An overview of the principles and application from these chapters.

IV. **LIFE APPLICATION**
God's Visual Aid

Melding these chapters to life.

V. **PRAYER**
Tying these chapters to life with God.

VI. **DEEPER DISCOVERIES**
Historical, geographical, and grammatical enrichment of the commentary.

VII. **TEACHING OUTLINE**
Suggested step-by-step group study of these chapters.

VIII. **ISSUES FOR DISCUSSION**
Zeroing these chapters in on daily life.

"*W*orship is the submission of all our nature to God. To worship is to quicken the conscience by the holiness of God, to feed the mind with the truth of God, to purge the imagination by the beauty of God, to open the heart to the love of God, to devote the will to the purpose of God."

William Temple

BUILDING PROFILE: TEMPLE

The construction of the temple is given more space than any other activity of Solomon's reign (four and one-half chapters). It is obviously seen as a central achievement of his life and is described in four stages:
- The preparation for construction: men and materials (5:1–18)
- The construction of the temple (6:1–7:51)
- The dedication of the temple (8:1–66)
- God's affirmation of the temple (9:1–9)

BUILDING PROFILE: TABERNACLE

- The tabernacle of Moses is the pattern for the temple of Solomon; the essential features are the same
- The tabernacle was portable and fragile; the temple was "permanent" and magnificent
- The plan for the tabernacle was revealed by the Lord to Moses (Exod. 25:8–9); the plan for the temple was revealed to David (1 Chr. 28:11–19)
- The central feature of both tabernacle and temple was a two-part structure containing the Holy Place and the Most Holy Place. Only priests could enter the Holy Place, and only the high priest could enter the Most Holy Place—and this only once a year on the Day of Atonement

- Both tabernacle and temple were built using the resources of Gentiles (the wealth of the Egyptians and the skills of Hiram). Both were to be "a house of prayer for all nations" (Isa. 56:7)

1 Kings 5:1–7:51

IN A NUTSHELL

In his fourth year on the throne, Solomon set out to build a temple worthy of the Lord. These chapters describe his careful preparation for this project as well as the meticulous and extravagant way in which the construction was carried out. The account is interrupted to point to two issues that will become more significant as Solomon's reign unfolds.

A House for God's Name

I. INTRODUCTION

Calling or Career?

An English member of Parliament sat at his desk late one night poring over documents on the slave trade. William Wilberforce was a rising star in English politics, but two years earlier he had become a follower of Christ. Other followers had challenged him to look at British slavery through the lens of Christ. He wasn't naïve. He knew that most of his contemporaries viewed slavery as an ugly and brutal but necessary evil. Almost certainly, opposition to it would bring his career to a screeching halt and earn him the hostility of powerful enemies, including the royal family.

But as Wilberforce studied the facts and God's Word, he became convinced of God's will. On Sunday, October 28, 1787, he wrote these words in his journal: "God Almighty has set before me two great objects: the suppression of the slave trade and the reformation of manners [public morals]."

William Wilberforce already had a career: he was a politician. But on that night, he found his calling, a God-given mission that galvanized his energies for the next fifty years and eventually transformed British society.

Few questions are easier to answer than, What is your career? But if someone asks, "What is your calling?" we tend to stammer and stutter. Christians are called people. We have not only been called *to* Christ; by his grace we have also been called *by* Christ for the furtherance of his purposes in the world. We are people with a calling. That calling may include a career, but it is bigger than that. It is the unique purpose of a holy God for our lives, that special place where our gifts, skills, and experiences connect with the needs of the world and the purposes of God's kingdom.

Solomon had a career; he was the king of a nation that needed to be developed and stabilized. But he also had a calling, a God-given mission not just to rule his people but also to make them a unique nation centered on the living God. Israel was to be like no other nation on earth. When Solomon lived out his calling, his nation flourished. But when he just carried out his career, he made poor choices.

These chapters show Solomon at his best. A major part of the story of his life is directed to his construction of the temple. But behind that project stands a calling: to center his nation on the worship of the living God by building "a house for the name of the L ORD."

II. COMMENTARY

A House for God's Name

> **MAIN IDEA:** The calling of God's people is to center life on honoring God by their commitment to build a house for his Name.

A Preparing for the House (5:1–18)

> **SUPPORTING IDEA:** The recognition of God's special calling in our lives gives us a unique sense of direction and purpose.

5:1–5. David had a dream: He would build a place of worship worthy of his God, so Jerusalem would become not only the political capital but also the spiritual capital of his nation. As he himself described it, "I had it in my heart to build a house for the Name of the LORD my God" (1 Chr. 22:7; see 28:2).

David's desire was grounded in the fact that, through Moses, God had given the nation of Israel a place and pattern of worship that centered on the tabernacle. Israel did not invent its own religious system; God revealed it. But the tabernacle was a portable building, designed to be transported through the wilderness. By David and Solomon's time, the tabernacle was more than four hundred years old. Time and spiritual failure meant that it had become neglected and dilapidated. This aroused a holy desire in David's heart to make things right, to put God's worship at the center of his nation in a building worthy of him.

Worthy as that desire seemed, it was not God's will for David. In one of the most important chapters of the Old Testament (2 Sam. 7), the Lord declared the outworking of his purpose. David was not to build a house, a physical structure, for God; but God would build a house, a living dynasty, for David. The prophet Nathan came to him with the divine declaration that has become known as the Davidic covenant: "The LORD himself will establish a house for you . . . I will raise up your offspring to succeed you. . . . Your house and your kingdom will endure forever before me; your throne will be established forever" (2 Sam. 7:11–16). At the same time the Lord said something more: "Your offspring . . . who will come from your own body . . . he is the one who will build a house for my Name" (2 Sam. 7:12–13). So the temple would be built but not by David. That privilege would go to David's son.

Solomon was that son, and building that house became the defining project of the early years of his reign. The immediate occasion on which Solomon announced his intention was a diplomatic visit by the envoys of **Hiram king of Tyre**. Hiram was the ruler of Phoenicia, one of the great trading nations of the time. He **had always been on friendly terms**, or in a treaty relationship, with David. Such a relationship was advantageous to both parties. The visit from Hiram was thus appropriate royal protocol to honor a new king, and a signal of Hiram's desire to continue the treaty with Israel's new ruler.

Solomon's response to Hiram reveals what was uppermost in Solomon's heart at this point—the construction of the temple. He reminded Hiram of his father David's passion and indicated that he intended to do for his God what his father had not been allowed to do. He would build the temple. Three things stand out in Solomon's reply.

First, the project would be God's house, **a temple** (literally, house) **for the Name of the LORD his God**. This expression occurs three times with variations in these verses, and it will recur as an important description in chapter 8. God's reputation would be bound up with this building; he would own it as his own by placing his name there. God's glory would be revealed there. Solomon knew exactly what the temple was and what it wasn't—a house for God's name, not his person. Only in a figurative way would the Lord "live" in this structure. It would be the house of God only because he graciously chose it, not because he needed it or was bound to it.

Second, Solomon told Hiram this was God's time for such a project: **God has given me rest . . . and there is no adversary or disaster**. David had been a man of war; Solomon would be a man of peace. Israel at this time was the strongest military power in the region. But Solomon would not succumb to the temptation to extend his regime militarily.

The third statement was a declaration of intent. Solomon was God's man for the job: **I intend . . . to build a temple for the Name**. Solomon viewed the temple as God's calling to which he would devote the first of his energy and his fortune. He was not simply doing a task by building a building; he was fulfilling a calling.

5:6–18. The temple may have been a divine calling, but it was also a very human project. It required materials and labor, and that is what the rest of the chapter describes. Lebanon was the region's greatest source of timber, and Solomon wanted Hiram to provide laborers and materials for the project. The place for the temple had been procured by David at the highest point above the city of Jerusalem (1 Chr. 21:1–22:1, esp., 22:1). The design for the temple had been revealed by the Lord to David (1 Chr. 28:11–19). Materials for the temple had been stockpiled by David and the people (1 Chr. 22:14–16; 29:1–9).

First Kings 5:6–12 describes the negotiations between Hiram and Solomon to acquire the timber necessary for the temple. Lebanon was famous for its timber, particularly cedar, and for the skill of its foresters and wood-workers. Although Hiram was a pagan king, he acknowledged the goodness of God in giving Israel a wise king in Solomon. The negotiations proceeded in typical fashion, with Hiram altering Solomon's proposal to conditions more suitable for him. (Solomon would pay him rather than the workers so he would retain control of both the money and the men, and he in turn would provide the workmen.) The final agreement was a blend of both positions. Solomon received the raw materials he required in exchange for agricultural products. The contract was mutually beneficial, and as a result, **there were peaceful relations between Hiram and Solomon, and the two of them made a treaty.**

Solomon's second need was manpower for this huge building project. Verses 13–18 describe the conscription and deployment of the labor force. Thirty thousand able-bodied Israelites (David's census had counted 1.3 million such men; 2 Sam. 24:9) were conscripted to give their time to the project. This was a program that seems to have begun reasonably enough, but it was destined, like many government programs, to expand in numbers and time schedule. In its final form it would arouse great anger in the nation (1 Kgs. 12). A huge force of stonecutters and carriers was enlisted to provide the massive amounts of stone for the building. The author of 2 Chronicles tells us that these were largely Canaanites (2 Chr. 2:17–18). Later 1 Kings will describe the slave labor used by Solomon (1 Kgs. 9:20–22).

There is something sad about a nation that had known the horrors of slave labor in Egypt now reverting to the same pattern. But for the moment the focus was on the preparation for construction: **The craftsmen of Solomon and Hiram and the men of Gebal** (i.e., Phoenicians) **cut and prepared the timber and the stone for the building of the temple.** Solomon was a man on a mission, and his reign was being defined by his sense of God's calling to construct "a house for the Name of the L ORD."

B Building the House (6:1–10,14–38; 7:13–51)

SUPPORTING IDEA: *A sense of God's calling shapes not only what we do but also the way in which we do it.*

These two chapters contain a mass of details, many of them confusing. It is impossible to reconstruct the temple, except in broad outline. The author of 1 Kings wants to help us form in our minds an impression of the glory and splendor of this building that bears the name of the Lord. It is important to realize that the building itself was built following a God-given design. Nothing about this design was accidental. It was richly significant and symbolic of the requirements for approaching a holy God.

6:1. The temple was not an innovation but a culmination. It stands as one of the landmark events of Israel's history, so important that its construction must be dated by the greatest event in Israel's history. The project began **in the four hundred and eightieth year after the Israelites had come out of Egypt, in the fourth year of Solomon's reign.** Since Solomon began his reign about 971 B.C., this gives a date of about 965 B.C., and an apparent date for the exodus of 1446 B.C. (see "Deeper Discoveries"). More significantly, it connects the temple to the exodus. God intended to bring his people out of Egypt into a land of rest, but Israel's sin meant there had been a long delay. Now the nation was at rest, and the temple was to become a reality. God is faithful to his promises.

6:2–10. The building was made of the finest limestone, prepared with the greatest care (v. 7), and roofed with beams and cedar planks (v. 9). The main hall (90' x 30' x 45'; v. 2) had a porch on the front. A three-storied structure of side rooms was attached to the outside of the main hall, rather than built into it, apparently to protect the holiness of the main temple structure. These rooms probably provided storage and office space related to temple business.

6:11–13. *See "C. Interrupting the Story" below.*

6:14–38. Although the building was made of stone, no stone was visible from within. The interior walls were covered with intricately carved **cedar boards** (vv. 15, 18), while the floor of the temple was covered **with planks of pine** (v. 15).

The inner sanctuary, the Holy of Holies, was framed by **cedar** into a perfect cube (vv. 16, 20). Since the building was forty-five feet high, either the ceiling was lowered or the room sat on an interior platform. But no cedar was visible, since it, in turn, was overlaid **with pure gold.** In this room, where the most sacred symbol of Israel's faith—the ark of the covenant—was housed, everything was covered with gold. **The altar of cedar** (the ark of the covenant) was the focal point, overshadowed by a majestic carved and gold-plated **pair of cherubim.** Cherubim were angelic figures who served as guardians of holy places (Gen. 3:24) and the throne of God (e.g., 1 Sam. 4:4; 2 Sam. 6:2). These cherubim dominated the room, standing fifteen feet tall, each with a wingspan of fifteen feet. Intricately carved doors, overlaid by beaten gold, set off the room itself. The outer room, the Holy Place, was also covered with gold.

In fact, that is one of the concerns of the writer of 1 Kings—that we see the gold that covered everything, even the floors and doorjambs. The word *gold* occurs ten times in this passage. The house of God had the finest of stone, the most valued of woods, and the most precious of metals—and it had them in abundance. This was a house for the name of the Lord, a human attempt to show his glory and greatness.

7:1–12. *See "C. Interrupting the Story" below.*

7:13–51. The final stage of the construction is described in these verses, as the temple furnishings were completed. Solomon imported from Tyre a man named **Huram.** A gifted craftsman, Huram prepared the massive amounts of bronze work required for the temple. Some of these required highly developed skill, particularly the large freestanding pillars that stood on the portico (vv. 15–22) and the massive container for water, known as **the Sea** (vv. 23–26). The two massive **bronze pillars**, with the metal sparkling in the brilliant Jerusalem sun, must have been awe-inspiring. They were hollow, with a wall about three inches thick ("four fingers," Jer. 52:21). Eighteen feet in circumference, they stood twenty-seven feet high. But they were topped with a **capital** that added another seven and one-half feet (five cubits, v. 16). Each pillar had a name: **Jakin** ("he establishes") and **Boaz** ("in strength").

These names seem to be part of an inscription that pointed to God's character and his promise to the Davidic dynasty ("He establishes it in his strength"; see "Deeper Discoveries"). **The Sea** was a remarkable feat of metallurgy, with a capacity for 11,500 gallons of water. Water was important in rituals of cleansing and for cleaning the blood from animal sacrifices. Huram was also responsible for the production of other furnishings, all of which were probably used in the outer courtyard, in connection with the altar of sacrifice. Thus we are told of **ten movable stands of bronze** to hold water basins (vv. 27–37), **the ten bronze basins** themselves (vv. 38–39) and a variety of other implements of **burnished bronze** (vv. 40–47).

Solomon himself assumed responsibility for producing the various objects made of gold (vv. 48–50). Solomon was probably the supervisor of this work, not the craftsman. Gold was in such abundance that we read of **gold sockets for the doors** (which must mean gold-plated, since gold itself would not be strong enough).

All of this is intended to leave us breathless with the glory of the temple, a place worthy of the God who would place his name there. Only the finest is worthy of him! Followers of Christ need to remember this glory as we ponder that we, both as congregations (1 Cor. 3:16–17) and as individuals (1 Cor. 6:19–20), are described as "God's temple."

Interrupting the Story (7:1–12; 6:11–13)

SUPPORTING IDEA: *Called people are always in danger of drifting off course and substituting good things for the main thing.*

7:1–12. These verses describe the construction of the royal palace complex. It was a complex of five buildings located next to the temple on what has become known as the Temple Mount. These buildings formed not just the private residence of King Solomon but also the administrative center of his empire. **The Palace of the Forest of Lebanon** (vv. 2–6) took its name from the forty-five massive **cedar beams** on which it was constructed. This building apparently served as an armory and treasury and perhaps as a reception building. Connected to it was the hall of pillars (v. 6), an entry area for **the Hall of Justice** (v. 7). This was the throne room where Solomon dispensed justice and received visitors. The complex also included Solomon's personal residence and **a palace** for Pharaoh's daughter (v. 8), although we are given no details about these buildings.

Only twelve verses are devoted to the palace complex. Clearly the writer of 1 Kings did not consider these buildings as important as the temple. But did Solomon? The description interrupts the description of the temple and sits awkwardly between 6:38 and 7:13. Not only is it an interruption; it is out of sequence chronologically. Solomon didn't build his palace complex until after he had finished the temple (cp. 6:38; 7:1; 9:1,10). Even more significantly, there is a jarring connection between the last verse of chapter 6 and the first verse of chapter 7.

Solomon spent seven years building the temple. But it took him **thirteen years . . . to complete the construction of his palace** (6:38–7:1). Solomon invested almost twice as much time on his royal palace as he did on the house for the name of the Lord. What are we to make of this?

We could explain it on the basis that the palace was a much bigger project than the temple. But that seems inadequate. Why has the writer of 1 Kings chosen to place it here, interrupting the flow of his own story? The evidence is subtle, but are we to see that Solomon was losing sight of his calling? Had his own name become more important than the name of the Lord? Is this another "Solomon loved God, except"? The palace complex was a good and necessary thing. But was it in danger of becoming the main thing, as Solomon drifted off course? Our writer has not given us any answers by his interruption, but he has certainly raised some questions!

6:11–13. The first interruption of the temple construction account comes in a different form, an encounter initiated by God himself. The text says, **The word of the LORD came to Solomon.** In both 3:5 and 9:2 we are told that "the LORD appeared to Solomon," and in both cases a dream or vision was involved. But this was a divine encounter of another kind, as the divine appearance in 9:2 is described as his second appearance to Solomon. Perhaps we are to understand that this message was through an unknown prophet. The emphasis is not on how the message came but on what the Lord said to Solomon, by whatever means. The larger context suggests that this message came after the stone shell of the temple had been completed and before work on the interior of the temple had begun (cp. vv. 9,14).

The way the Lord began his statement leads us to expect that he had something to say to Solomon about the temple itself: **As for this temple you are building.** But that is not where the message takes us. The words that follow are not about the temple at all but rather about Solomon: **If you follow my decrees . . . and keep all my commands and obey them, I will fulfill . . . the promise.** The temple was a magnificent project, undertaken out of a desire to honor God. But it was not a substitute for obedience. God's fulfillment of the promise would have nothing to do with the construction of the temple. In one sense the temple had changed nothing. No amount of money, time, effort, and achievement can earn God's favor or substitute for believing obedience to God's unchanging will. Solomon must not trust the temple; he must trust and obey God.

This was an issue of great importance to a later generation of God's people. They believed that the presence of the temple assured them of God's favor and insulated them from God's judgment. Some of the prophet Jeremiah's most vehement sermons were directed against such a false theology of the temple. The first readers of 1 Kings knew that the temple had not protected them from divine judgment. As they heard these words, the temple itself was a heap of ruins. But they needed to know that trust in the temple had always been wrong. Even before the temple had been completed, God had set out the conditions of blessing. God would bless the temple when it was kept in the proper perspective. But when people used it as a substitute for obedience to him, God would curse the people. That was the message Solomon needed to hear. The temple was not his calling. His calling was to lead his nation in obedience to God and his word.

> **MAIN IDEA REVIEW:** *The calling of God's people is to center life on honoring God by their commitment to build a house for his Name.*

III. CONCLUSION

Building the House of God

Solomon was called by God to build a physical building for the glory of God. He pursued that calling with care and commitment. The description of the project shows us a man who cared passionately about the honor of his God and who spared no expense on the "house for the Name." Everything about the temple spoke of his commitment that God be glorified in his efforts. There was no sense of duty or obligation. This was an act of love, offered to the God he loved. He was not doing a job; he was fulfilling his calling.

In the same way, the Lord Jesus attaches his name to no physical structures. The "house for the Name" is a living body, made up of all those who know the Lord Jesus. It is the growing, living body of believers, ultimately to be formed from those of every tribe and nation who own Jesus as Lord and Savior. We have a God-given calling to expend the best of our energy and resources on what builds the living house of our Lord. Like Solomon we are always in danger of being distracted, of investing more time on our complex than his, or of imagining that we can offer good things as a substitute for the best thing. Called people are people who accept their God-given mission, pursue God-honoring goals, and maintain a God-centered focus.

PRINCIPLES

- Every follower of Christ has a divine calling that links his gifts and skills to the furtherance of God's kingdom.
- Planning and preparation are an indispensable part of doing a work for God.
- God is worthy of our best. His glory must be reflected in all we do.
- We are always in danger of drifting off course and substituting good but secondary things for the main thing.
- There is no priority greater than maintaining a right heart before God in worship and obedience.

APPLICATIONS

- Think beyond your career to your calling, to your God-given mission.
- Embrace your calling with conviction and commitment.
- Act with a passion to exalt your Lord, seeking his glory.
- Evaluate your focus to make sure you are keeping a God-centered focus.

IV. LIFE APPLICATION

God's Visual Aid

Solomon's temple was one of the wonders of the ancient world, perhaps one of the most expensive buildings per square foot ever constructed. It was not intended to be a magnificent piece of architecture but a way of approaching the living God. It demonstrated the same principles as the tabernacle, since it followed the same pattern. The temple has been replaced by the finished work of Christ. We have a "new and living way" into God's presence (Heb. 10:20), and his work is a fulfillment of the great temple principles. The following are some of the most obvious messages:

- The altar at the entrance reminds us that access to God is possible only on the basis of his sacrifice. Our sins must be dealt with. We cannot approach God on the basis of our merits. Christ's sin is the once-for-all perfect sacrifice (Heb. 9:26–28).
- The basins in the inner courtyard tell us that continual cleansing is required when we move into God's holy presence. A priest

could not enter the Holy Place without first washing himself. The Lord Jesus provides the cleansing his people need (Heb. 10:22)

- The Holy Place was open only to priests. It was a place of stunning beauty, reminding us of the wonder of God's presence and the privilege of access. The Israelite priesthood was limited to a privileged few who offered up incense as a symbol of praise in the Holy Place. But now all followers of Christ are priests, invited into God's presence to offer praise to the Lord (Heb. 13:15–16).
- The Most Holy Place could be entered only once a year—and only by the high priest on the Day of Atonement. On the basis of the work of the Lord Jesus, our great High Priest, we are invited into the presence of God (Heb. 10:19–22).

V. PRAYER

Father, you know how easy it is for us to get caught up in the busyness and demands of life. Help us to lift up our eyes to see your calling in our lives and to pursue it with passion and integrity, so we may not only make a living but also serve as your kingdom agents. Amen.

VI. DEEPER DISCOVERIES

A. Four Hundred and Eighty Years (6:1)

The beginning of the construction of the temple, in the fourth year of Solomon's reign (967 B.C.), is dated from one of the most significant dates in Israel's history—the exodus from Egypt. This makes it one of the milestone dates in Israel's history. The significance of the number 480 has been debated. Many interpreters have seen it as a symbolic number, built on the idea that a generation is forty years. The number would thus represent a period of twelve generations. This line of reasoning leads many to suggest a date for the exodus of 1290 to 1250 B.C. This date (the late exodus) is felt by many to account for the archaeological evidence more adequately. Although this understanding is possible, it seems more appropriate to regard it as a real number, which leads to a date for the exodus of about 1447 B.C. (the early exodus).

B. Jakin and Boaz (7:21)

The names of the two massive pillars in Solomon's Temple have aroused much speculation. The word *Jakin* means "he establishes," while *Boaz*, the name of King David's ancestor (Ruth 4:21–22), means "in strength." The two most likely explanations are that it refers to the temple ("it is established in his strength") or to the Davidic dynasty and the Lord's kingdom. In the latter case, the names would probably be catchwords of an inscription on each column: "He will establish [the throne of David forever]" and "In the strength [of the Lord]."

VII. TEACHING OUTLINE

A. INTRODUCTION

1. Lead Story: Calling or Career?

2. Context: Solomon had established himself on the throne by his fourth year. He was now able to devote himself to the special calling with which he had come to the throne—to build the temple for the Lord that his father David had longed to build.

3. Transition: Being a king is a career. But the kind of king Solomon would become depended on his sense of divine calling. The sense that he had come to the throne to accomplish a divine purpose dominated his early activity.

B. COMMENTARY

1. Preparing for the House (5:1–18)

2. Building the House (6:1–10,14–38; 7:13–51)

3. Interrupting the Story (7:1–12; 6:11–13)

C. CONCLUSION: BUILDING THE HOUSE OF GOD

VIII. ISSUES FOR DISCUSSION

1. What do you make of the distinction between calling and career? Spend some time having people talk about their careers and then about their calling. Do you find calling a hard thing or an easy thing to think about?

2. "God will curse as a substitute what he will bless as a substitute." How is this illustrated in God's words to Solomon in 6:11–13? How does that idea apply to other areas of life?

1 Kings 8:1–66

The Path of Revival

I. **INTRODUCTION**
Driven to Our Knees

II. **COMMENTARY**
A verse-by-verse explanation of the chapter.

III. **CONCLUSION**
The Road to Revival:

Able to Hear—Willing to Help

An overview of the principles and application from the chapter.

IV. **LIFE APPLICATION**
God's New Temple

Melding the chapter to life.

V. **PRAYER**
Tying the chapter to life with God.

VI. **DEEPER DISCOVERIES**
Historical, geographical, and grammatical enrichment of the commentary.

VII. **TEACHING OUTLINE**
Suggested step-by-step group study of the chapter.

VIII. **ISSUES FOR DISCUSSION**
Zeroing the chapter in on daily life.

Quote

"*He* who beats his heart, but does not mend his ways, does not remove his sins, but hardens them."

A u g u s t i n e

HISTORICAL PROFILE: TEMPLE

- The first temple was built by Solomon (971–931 B.C.) and continued until it was destroyed by the Babylonians about 587 B.C.
- The second temple was built by those who returned from exile in Babylon, beginning in 538 B.C. The first stage of this construction was begun under Zerubbabel and dedicated in about 515 B.C. (Ezra 1–6). The temple was extensively rebuilt by Herod the Great, a reconstruction that was essentially completed between 20 and 10 B.C. but continued for many years (see John 2:20). The second temple was destroyed by the Romans under Titus in A.D. 70
- The new temple is the temple of the Holy Spirit. In the New Testament there is no physical place of worship, and the need for sacrifices has been done away with in Christ. The dwelling place of God in the present age, his temple, is the body of the individual believer (1 Cor. 6:19), the local church (1 Cor. 3:16), and the church, the body of Christ (Eph. 2:19–22)
- The future temple is apparently described in some passages that speak of such a building in Jerusalem during the tribulation period (Matt. 24:15; 2 Thess. 2:4)
- The millennial temple is a subject of controversy, but some believe that Ezekiel 40–48 describes such a building.

1 Kings 8:1–66

IN A NUTSHELL

*T*he temple had been completed for almost a year when Solomon chose to lead the people in a great national period of dedication. He arranged the bringing of Israel's most sacred piece of furniture, the ark. When God responded by sending his glory into the building, Solomon led the people in the dedication. He began with a sermon describing the building, prayed for its use as God intended, pronounced a blessing over the people, and concluded with a great national celebration.

The Path of Revival

I. INTRODUCTION

Driven to Our Knees

*W*hen terrorists commandeered commercial airplanes and flew them into the World Trade Center in New York and the Pentagon in Washington, D.C., the first response was stunned disbelief. But as those massive buildings crumbled, an instinctive response was prayer. That evening our church auditorium was full. In the days and weeks that followed, churches were crowded and people flocked to special meetings to pray.

Crisis drives us to prayer. Realizing that we have nowhere else to go turns us to God. Sometimes that turn is powerfully transforming. More often, it is only temporary—a short-lived spiritual spasm that passes almost as quickly as the crisis. There is little indication that September 11 has had any lasting spiritual impact on our nation.

Throughout history there have been significant moments of encounter with the living God that we call revivals. From the human side a revival is a time of spiritual awakening when God's people realize their true condition in light of God's awesome holiness and turn to him in repentance and humility. From the divine side a revival is a time when God pours out his Spirit to restore and renew his people. But he does not wait passively for his people. He often brings them into a place of crisis so they will be forced to face their need of him. If God did not intervene, we would drift into apathy or apostasy. Revival is essential because it restores us to a proper relationship with God. But revival must lead to reformation, a deeply rooted transformation of practices and lifestyles.

The temple built by Solomon was intended to serve a variety of purposes. It was first a place of redemption where sin was dealt with by sacrifices that God commanded and by the intercession of God's priests. It was also a place of worship where God's people gathered to sing their praises and celebrate the living God. The temple was also to be a place of prayer, "a house of prayer for all nations" (Isa. 56:7; Matt. 21:13). In this chapter this third function occupied Solomon's attention as he dedicated the temple. What he said has application to all times of prayer, but he was thinking particularly of prayer in a time of crisis, when God's people realize that God alone is the solution to their need.

II. COMMENTARY

The Path of Revival

> **MAIN IDEA:** *The greatest danger for God's people always comes from their own unconfessed sins, not from their external enemies or political circumstances.*

Ⓐ The Procession of the Ark (8:1–13)

> **SUPPORTING IDEA:** *God's presence, not the glory of the architecture, makes the temple uniquely God's temple.*

8:1–9. Solomon had spent seven years and an incredible amount of energy and money to build the temple. Then, as a comparison of 6:38 and 8:2 indicates, he waited for eleven months before he dedicated it (see "Deeper Discoveries"), delaying until **the time of the festival in . . . the seventh month**. The purpose of the delay was probably related to the status of the seventh month on the religious calendar as the holiest month of the year. During this month, Rosh Hoshanah (New Year), Yom Kippur (the Day of Atonement), and Sukkoth (the Festival of Tabernacles) were celebrated. Solomon probably wanted the dedication of the temple to coincide with this time of spiritual celebration.

The presence of God among his people was the distinguishing mark of the nation of Israel (Exod. 33:15–16). It was also the special characteristic of the Mosaic tabernacle (Exod. 40:34–35). The temple may have been impressive, but apart from God's presence it was an empty shell. Therefore, the first order of business was to transport **the ark of the LORD's covenant** from its temporary location in the lower part of Jerusalem, to its new home in the Holy of Holies in Solomon's temple. The ark was Israel's most sacred article, the symbol of God's person, presence, and covenant with his people.

The ark had led Israel through the wilderness to the promised land (Num. 10:33–36; Josh. 3:3). Every year, on the Day of Atonement, it was the central feature in Israel's most solemn ceremony, when the high priest anointed it with sacrificial blood. David had been determined to restore the ark from its years of neglect. He had made it a priority to transfer it to Jerusalem, where it had been housed in a special tent (2 Sam. 6).

Solomon chose the most sacred time of the religious year to transfer the ark to the temple. Having learned from his father's fiasco (2 Sam. 6), he did so with special care. Gathering **the elders of Israel**, along with tribal and family leaders, he made sure that **the priests took up the ark**. In accordance with the law, the Levites carried the rest of the sacred furniture. The sacrificing of animals along the way and the holy procession marked this a solemn occasion. Finally, they brought the ark to **the Most Holy Place** in the temple and put it **beneath the wings of the cherubim**.

The writer of 1 Kings is careful to describe its precise location under the carved golden cherubim and to direct our attention to the fact that the ark contained **the two stone tablets that Moses had placed in it at Horeb**. The presence of the ark in the Holy of Holies is a reminder of the continuity of God's covenant, as well as of the continuity between the temple and the tabernacle of Moses.

8:10–11. The bringing of the ark was a symbolic act on the part of God's people, placing the symbol of God's covenant at the center of their nation. God then responded in a way that put his seal of approval on the temple project. **The cloud**—the same cloud of God's holy presence that had led Israel through the wilderness and which had fallen on the tabernacle (Exod. 40:34–38)—**filled the temple of the LORD**. This cloud was so overwhelming that it forced the priests to retreat from the temple. There is an important truth here: It is God's presence that makes a temple God's temple. Without the presence of God, Solomon's building was nothing but an empty shell.

8:12–13. Solomon recognized the significance of what had happened. His building had now become the dwelling place of God, where he resided in the **dark cloud** of his glory. This expression recalls God's words at Sinai (Exod. 19:9), pointing to the mystery of God's person that lies beyond human comprehension. But nevertheless, God is present among his people. Solomon declared, **I have indeed built a magnificent temple for you**.

⬛ The Sermon of Solomon (8:14–21)

> **SUPPORTING IDEA:** *God does not need the temple, but the temple needs God. When something bears the Lord's name, we must treat it appropriately.*

8:14–21. As all of these events transpired, Solomon's attention had been directed to the temple. But now, as the spiritual leader of his people, he **turned** away from the temple to face the assembled crowd and to address them before his dedicatory prayer. The temple was a new feature of Israel's national life. But the people needed to recognize that it was not just a human innovation. It was grounded in the plan and promise of God. To accomplish this, Solomon directed the people in his brief message to the person of God and the nature of the temple.

Solomon was concerned to honor his God because he was a faithful God who had honored his promises: **Praise be to the LORD . . . who . . . has fulfilled what he promised . . . to my father David**. As we have seen, the Davidic covenant, recorded in 2 Samuel 7, shapes the message of 1 Kings. God had promised not only that David would reign over Israel but also that

David's son would follow him on the throne and that his son would **build the temple for my Name**. Solomon was filled with a gratitude that caused him to repeat himself: **The LORD has kept the promise he made**.

The Solomonic kingdom and the temple of Solomon were not due to his initiative or imagination but to God's purpose and faithfulness. God is also a God who continues his program. While these events were rooted in the recent past—in God's promise to David—they were also rooted in the distant past—in God's deliverance of Israel from Egypt almost five hundred years earlier (see 6:1). The temple dedication was not only a fulfillment of the Davidic covenant but also of the covenant that God made with his people **when he brought them out of Egypt**. The Lord is a God of persistent faithfulness. The temple was the culmination of God's purpose.

Solomon also directed attention to the Lord as a God of grace. David had a passionate longing that the Lord had not permitted him to fulfill: **David had it in his heart to build a temple for the Name of the LORD**. Although the Lord had not granted his desire, he had not ignored his longing. God credited David for his heart's desires! He graciously honors not only the accomplishments of our hands but also the intentions of our heart when they are submitted to his direction.

Solomon also defined the nature of the temple. The temple bore God's name because he claimed ownership of it and identified himself with it. It was his house. He would be known by his association with a particular place. The description was carefully chosen. The temple was not "the house of the Lord," as if he lived there and nowhere else. God cannot be contained in a building.

God doesn't need the temple, but the temple needs God. It is foolish to trust in the temple, as if there were merit in the building itself. This became a troubling issue for the first readers of 1 Kings, who sat in exile in Babylon, aware that the temple had been destroyed. What did that mean for the Lord himself? Had he been defeated or damaged? They needed to recognize that while the temple had contained God's presence in a special way, it had never contained or controlled his person.

The Prayer of Solomon (8:22–53)

> **SUPPORTING IDEA:** *Authentic prayer involves adoration and repentance.*

What follows in this section is a prayer on prayer. As Solomon began his prayer, he "stood before the altar of the L ORD" with his hands "spread out . . . toward heaven" (v. 22). By the end of the prayer, we find him "kneeling with his hands spread out toward heaven" (v. 54). Clearly, this prayer was an outpouring of heart and emotions, not just words.

8:22–26. At the heart of all prayer is a conviction about God. That is why biblical prayer begins with adoration of God. The God to whom we pray is incomparable: **O LORD . . . there is no God like you**. He is unique and incomparable. Therefore, we must pray on the basis of what he has chosen to reveal about himself, not on what we like to think or imagine about him. The God to whom we pray is also loving and faithful. This means that we pray on the basis of his promises. That is why Solomon continually built his prayer around what God had revealed about himself in history and in his Word. In verses 25–26 he prayed God's promises back to him (an excellent model of prayer for every follower of Christ) and also reminded himself that God had set a condition upon the fulfillment of his promises. A condition of answered prayer is that we are in the right condition before God to receive his promise.

8:27–30. Solomon connected prayer to the temple, the unique place on earth where God had placed his glory. The king was under no illusions about the temple. It may have been a glorious building to humans, but God is God—immense beyond imagining. He created space, fills it with his own being, and yet he overflows it. No wonder he asked, **Will God really dwell on earth?** Clearly not, in any literal sense, since **the heavens . . . cannot contain you.** Yet, at the same time, God had given his word: **My Name shall be there.** The omnipresent Lord of the universe had committed himself to the temple.

Solomon's theology was carefully balanced. God's presence was in the temple; his eyes were open to the temple; he heard prayers made in or toward the temple. But he was not, in any way, contained by the temple, and he did not really "hear" in the temple.

Solomon was establishing a pattern of prayer. Prayer would be made either in the temple (**your servant is praying in your presence**) or toward the temple (**hear . . . your people Israel when they pray toward this place**). This pattern of prayer, physically directed toward Jerusalem and the temple, became the standard practice of Jewish piety (see Ps. 138:2; Dan. 6:10). The temple was the house of prayer. Even today pious Jews seek to face toward Jerusalem when they pray. The difference made by the new age of the Spirit introduced by the Lord Jesus is evident here. Followers of Christ pray "in the name of the Lord Jesus" but not "toward the name" in any physical sense.

8:31–53. Solomon presented a series of seven scenarios, both personal and national, in which people would find themselves in need and thus call out toward God in his temple.

1. Conflict, requiring divine resolution (8:31–32).
2. Military defeat, caused by national sin (8:33–34).
3. Drought, caused by national sin (8:35–36).
4. Natural disasters (famine, blight, pestilence, siege, sickness) due to sin (8:37–40).

5. Foreign pilgrims, drawn to the great name of the Lord (8:41–43).
6. Military campaigns on foreign soil (8:44–45).
7. Exile and captivity, under divine judgment (8:46–51).

The last scenario is given the longest treatment since it was of most relevance to the original readers, who were in exactly this situation. The appeal is that God would first **forgive** and then **cause their conquerors to show them mercy.** That this mercy would take the form of return to the land is made clear by the reference to the exodus in verse 51: **For they are your people ... whom you brought out of Egypt.** The relevance of this to the first readers of 1 Kings is evident.

Several observations can be made about this prayer. First, the failure of his people was not a surprise to God. The prayer predicted the problem: **for there is no one who does not sin** (v. 46). Sin permeated everything his people did. Second, God did not take sin lightly. It had certain consequences, and those consequences might be severe. Third, God had prearranged the solution. The temple stood as a dramatic witness to the provision God had made in advance for the failures of his people. Fourth, confession must never be superficial. Repentance involved not only the acknowledgment of sin but also turning from it. Fifth, the situation would never be hopeless because God was a God who heard his people when they came to him as he required. And he would not only hear; he would forgive and restore.

🅓 The Benediction of Solomon (8:54–61)

> **SUPPORTING IDEA:** *God's history of grace and faithfulness to us should motivate us to obedience.*

8:54–61. As Solomon ended his prayer, he turned his attention from the Lord to God's people. He had begun with a short sermon; he ended with a brief blessing. One of God's ancient promises was that he would give his people **rest** in their own land. This was a special promise for a people whose entire history had been marked by pilgrimage, captivity, wandering, and warfare. This rest meant they would not only possess a land of their own, but they would have peace within it. That vision was a reality in the time of Solomon: **Praise be to the LORD, who has given rest to his people.** In fact, Solomon borrowed words from the Book of Joshua (21:45; 23:14–15) to celebrate God's blessing and faithfulness: **Not one word has failed of all the good promises he gave.**

Solomon's final words took the form of a benediction-petition. There are two requests in the Hebrew text: that God would dwell with his people so his people would live lives of obedience (vv. 57–58) and that God would hear Solomon's prayer so Israel's lifestyle would cause pagan nations to know that the Lord alone is God (vv. 59–60). Solomon concluded his message with an appeal to the people: **live by God's decrees and obey his commands**. Ironically, this was precisely what Solomon himself would show himself unable to do.

E The Celebration of the People (8:62–66)

SUPPORTING IDEA: *When God is appropriately honored, his people are blessed.*

8:62–66. Solomon was determined to make this a day that his people would never forget. Earlier he had offered sacrifices in honor of the procession of the ark to the temple (v. 5). Now he offered an immense number of sacrifices to mark the dedication of the temple itself. The sheer magnitude of the celebration boggles the mind. And it continued beyond the traditional seven days of the Festival of Booths into an additional week. The result was a genuine time of national renewal and celebration. Solomon had prayed about the ongoing conditions of revival. He had also brought about a major time of spiritual blessing for his nation. The people returned home, full of praise for Solomon. They rejoiced **for all the good things the LORD had done for . . . his people Israel.**

MAIN IDEA REVIEW: *The greatest danger for God's people always comes from their own unrepented sins, not from their external enemies or political circumstances.*

III. CONCLUSION

The Road of Revival

Able to Hear—Willing to Help

The most striking thing about this chapter is that God is not surprised by our sin. In fact, he expects our failure, "for there is no one who does not sin" (8:46). But sin must never be taken lightly. Sin has consequences, and deliverance comes only as we confess our sin and turn to our gracious God in heartfelt repentance. If our failure is never a surprise to God, it is also true that our confession must never be superficial before him. Whatever the situation, he is not only able to hear but also willing to help.

Second Chronicles 6–7 conveys the same story in almost identical terms. But in that context the Lord responded to Solomon's prayers with words that gave God's people great hope: "If my people, who are called by my name, will humble themselves and pray and seek my face and turn from their wicked ways, then will I hear from heaven and will forgive their sin and will heal their land" (2 Chr. 7:14).

PRINCIPLES

- Our greatest danger does not come from outside but from within.
- It is God's presence, not splendid architecture, that makes a building the temple of God.
- God's heart is committed to the place where he has placed his name.
- God's presence is not limited to any physical place, but he graciously reveals himself in special ways in his "house."
- Whatever our circumstances due to sin, we can turn to God in heartfelt repentance.
- When God is appropriately honored, his people are blessed.

APPLICATIONS

- Value the people of God (the church) as highly as Israel valued the temple.
- Cultivate a worthy view of God so your prayers will be appropriate.
- Avoid the guilt-driven fear that your sins are so awful that you cannot come to God. That is precisely when you must come.
- Beware of mechanical prayer and shallow repentance.

IV. LIFE APPLICATION

God's New Temple

Traveling in the Middle East, you quickly become aware that Muslims are careful to pray toward Mecca and Jews are careful to face toward Jerusalem. But followers of Christ have no such concerns. There is a profound difference that is directly related to this passage.

In John 4, a woman asked Jesus a significant question about worship, about whether Jerusalem or Samaria was the place of worship. The Lord responded, "A time is coming and has now come when the true worshipers will worship the Father in spirit and truth, for they are the kind of worshipers the Father seeks" (John 4:23). There is no physical altar to which we bring our sacrifices; no geographical direction to which we turn in prayer; no central building in which we worship because God's presence is uniquely present there.

When the Lord Jesus died and rose again, he rendered the temple obsolete, as the Book of Hebrews says. This is not to say that there is no temple. Individual believers (1 Cor. 6:19–20), local congregations (1 Cor. 3:16), and the universal church (Eph. 2:19–22) are all spoken of as the temple of the

Lord. Church buildings never are. There is no special physical dwelling place of God on earth in the present age. God's temple consists of the followers of Christ who bear his name before a watching world—and that is an awesome responsibility.

The need to seek God's renewing, reviving presence is no less significant than it was for Israel. We do not pray toward a physical temple on earth but toward the One who is seated at the Father's right hand. We approach the throne of grace in boldness. Yet, at the same time, unless there is the heartfelt confession of and turning from sin that we see described by Solomon, we will not experience the renewing, reviving work of God.

V. PRAYER

Father, thank you that in spite of my sin, you always invite me to come into your presence in my brokenness and shame. Thank you that you invite me to face you, not some physical building, and that I am never out of your presence. Amen.

VI. DEEPER DISCOVERIES

A. "In the Month of Ethanim, the Seventh Month" (8:2)

The temple had been completed "in the month of Bul, the eighth month" (6:38). It is surprising to read that it was dedicated in the seventh month (8:2). It is simplistic to dismiss this as an error, due to the author's carelessness. Others have suggested that the temple was dedicated a month before it was completed. However, 7:51 is explicit that the temple was finished and furnished, and only then does the author describe the events of the bringing of the ark (8:1). The conclusion seems inevitable that Solomon delayed the dedication for eleven months. The dedication at the time of the celebration of the Feast of Booths was, therefore, intentional, not coincidental. This was the most important and most popular festival in the life of ancient Israel. It represented the fulfillment of God's promise of rest in the promised land (see 8:56), and it was a major time of covenant renewal every seven years (Deut. 31:9–13). These were important theological themes that Solomon wanted to reinforce on this occasion.

B. The Posture of Prayer (8:22,54)

There is no prescribed posture of prayer in the Bible. The most common position seemed to be standing—as Solomon did in verse 22 (see Mark 11:25; Luke 18:11,13)—with one's gaze directed toward heaven (see Mark 6:41; John 11:41; 17:1). Solomon ended his prayer kneeling, probably an indication of submission and worship. A common feature of either posture was to have one's hand spread toward heaven, as Solomon did in both verses 22 and

54. This was a posture of appeal, worship, and surrender. Our physical posture for prayer is significant because it indicates our attitude of reverence. But the emphasis of the Bible is on the posture of our heart before God.

VII. TEACHING OUTLINE

A. INTRODUCTION

1. Lead Story: Driven to Our Knees

2. Context: After completing the temple, Solomon determined to dedicate it in a way that would bring the approval of God, teach the people its importance, and create an atmosphere of praise and celebration.

3. Transition: One of the most important principles in life is to do first things first. Solomon was determined that the new temple not only begin to function but that from the very beginning it should fill the need intended by God.

B. COMMENTARY

1. The Procession of the Ark (8:1–13)

2. The Sermon of Solomon (8:14–21)

3. The Prayer of Solomon (8:22–53)

4. The Benediction of Solomon (8:54–61)

5. The Celebration of the People (8:62–66)

C. CONCLUSION: THE ROAD OF REVIVAL

VIII. ISSUES FOR DISCUSSION

1. As you consider the state of the church in your community, what are the sins we are blind to before God?

2. What false views about God that would keep us from experiencing true spiritual renewal are addressed in this chapter?

3. It has become customary to speak about a particular part of a church building as a "sanctuary" and to call a building a "church." Is there any danger in this? How do the Old Testament and the New Testament differ on this issue?

1 Kings 9:1–10:29

Halftime

Quote

"*There* is nothing wrong with success, but it becomes an addiction when our desire to win causes us not to have enough time for our God, our wives, our families and friends—or to put something meaningful back into our communities. . . . While it is more socially acceptable to be addicted to success, it can be just as dangerous as alcohol, drugs or mistresses."

Bob Buford

1 Kings 9:1–10:29

IN A NUTSHELL

Solomon's age was the golden age of glory, which is described in detail in this passage. But before that glory is described, we observe the Lord's appearance to Solomon at the halfway mark of his reign. The Lord passes by the completion of the temple to remind Solomon of the priority of a life of obedience and spiritual imitation of his father David's commitment to the Lord. There is a disturbing sense that, beneath the glittering appearance of Solomon's reign, something has gone wrong.

Halftime

I. INTRODUCTION

Success or Significance?

*B*ob Buford was the president and CEO of a large cable communications company based in Tyler, Texas. By the time he was forty-four years old, he had reached all his career goals—the home he'd always wanted, a marriage he deeply valued, more money than he needed, a young adult son who was everything he'd hoped for, and a company growing at a rate of 25 percent annually. Still he found himself with a gnawing question, "How could I be so successful, so fortunate, and yet so unfulfilled?" Later he was to call it "success panic." He didn't know how much was enough; he was worried that he was becoming addicted to success, and he didn't know what came after he reached all his goals.

Bob is a follower of Christ, and he found himself wrestling with the place of his Lord in all of this. Tragically, in the middle of his confusion, his son drowned in a swimming accident. Bob had built an empire to pass on to his son, but now there was no one to give it to. He found himself at "halftime." The first half of his life had been about success, about how to make a living. Now he faced a choice: what would the second half be about? In his helpful book *Halftime*, he tells the story of a personal paradigm shift, about leveraging his success for a new goal of significance.

Halftime is an incredibly important time in any game. Much has happened, but the game isn't over yet, no matter the score. More than a few teams have squandered big leads or battled back from seemingly impossible deficits. I've been on both sides of that equation. No matter what the score, there are always adjustments to be made. No game is really over at the half. What happens in the second half determines the outcome. Life operates on the same rules.

Solomon had enjoyed an amazingly successful first half. Twenty years into his reign, he had accomplished all his goals, both personally and nationally. He had achieved unimaginable glory and prosperity, and so had his nation. But it was only halftime, and, sadly, the way Solomon chose to play the second half undermined all his first-half achievements.

II. COMMENTARY

Halftime

> **MAIN IDEA:** *Unless we shift from a mind-set of success to one of significance, our successes will turn into failures.*

A Solomon's Glory (9:1; 10:1–13)

> **SUPPORTING IDEA:** *The Lord often gives us the privilege of significant success at the midway point of life's journey.*

9:1. The time frame of this verse is significant: **Solomon had finished building the temple** and the royal palace. The project had begun in the fourth year of his reign (6:1), and it took twenty years to complete (9:10). Solomon was therefore at the twenty-four-year mark of his forty-year reign (11:42). He had probably been about twenty years of age when he came to the throne, so he was in his early forties at this point, slightly more than halfway through his reign, at the prime of his life, and at the top of his game as a man and as a king.

- He had completed the temple and established a spiritual center for the worship of God.
- He had completed the palace complex, which not only housed his family but also served as the administrative and judicial hub of his large empire.
- He had solidified his kingdom and extended his influence (4:21,24).
- He had achieved international stature (4:29–34).
- He had brought peace, prosperity, and blessing to the people of his nation (4:20,25).
- He had led his nation spiritually and focused them on the Lord (8:65–66).

As Solomon came to halftime, he was in the rare and enviable position of knowing that he had achieved **all he had desired to do**. At the age of forty-four, he was the golden boy who had brought his nation into its golden age. He would go down in history as one of his nation's most successful kings. Nothing makes the extent of his accomplishments more evident that the account of the visit of the queen of Sheba, recorded in 10:1–13. Jumping to that account enables us to frame a picture of Solomon at the height of his glory.

10:1–13. Although the location of **Sheba** is not certain, most scholars locate it in the area of modern Yemen, a journey of about fifteen hundred miles overland to Israel. Sheba was a well-watered and fertile part of the Arabian Peninsula, strategically located at the confluence of the Red Sea and the Indian Ocean. This location made it a prosperous center of trade, linking the regions to the north to Africa and India by sea. Sheba was famous for its spices, incense, gold, and precious stones. Solomon had formed a trading alliance with Hiram of Phoenicia (9:26–28) that made him an increasingly important player in the region.

The visit of **the queen of Sheba** was inspired by Solomon's growing reputation on the international stage. Even at such a distance, she had heard about Solomon's fame **and his relation to the name of the LORD**. Solomon's fame was not just personal; it was linked to his God. It is unlikely that the queen was moved just by personal curiosity; she was obviously a dynamic, venturous leader of her nation, and her visit was intended as a prelude to a trade relationship with this powerful new regional power. The gifts she brought with her—spices, large quantities of gold, and precious stones—indicate that her visit was more than personal. She desired to measure Solomon as a potential partner and ally. So she came **to test him with hard questions**.

The ancient world delighted in elaborate riddles, proverbs, and wisdom puzzles. There were apparently "wisdom games" in which leaders and sages engaged. Games of this type were apparently part of her encounter with Solomon. It is also likely that she and Solomon engaged in discussion of the kind of administrative, diplomatic, legal, and ethical questions that would concern ancient heads of state. They discussed **all that she had on her mind**, and Solomon displayed his intellect and shrewdness, answering **all her questions**.

Solomon's wisdom had already become famous. Now the queen saw for herself **all the wisdom**. In the life of the royal court, it had taken visible form, and **she was overwhelmed**. Her words conveyed not only her astonishment at the display of wealth and wisdom all around her but also her praise to the Lord for Solomon. She could hardly find words to express her amazement: **In wisdom and wealth you have far exceeded the report I heard**.

But this pagan queen attributed the glory she saw to God as the underlying cause. She probably had a very limited idea of who God was. She may have understood him as little more than the national god of Israel. Nevertheless, she had caught sight of the distinctive nature of the God of Israel—that he was a God of **eternal love** who established **justice and righteousness**.

The queen of Sheba and Solomon exchanged extravagant gifts. The queen gave Solomon **120 talents of gold** (about four and one-half tons!), as well as **large quantities of spices and precious stones**. In turn, Solomon gave the queen **all she desired and asked for**. This probably included tangible gifts and perhaps involved a formal trade agreement. But Solomon really didn't need the queen's gifts. Verses 11–12 describe the massive influx of wealth that came through his normal enterprises, linked to his partnership with Hiram, king of Phoenicia.

B The Lord's Appearance (9:2–9)

SUPPORTING IDEA: *No matter how spectacular our success, fundamental spiritual principles always apply.*

9:2. In light of Solomon's glittering success at halftime, this was the precise time when the Lord appeared to him a second time, **as he had appeared to him at Gibeon**. The Gibeon experience had happened twenty years earlier (3:4–15). Both occasions were dreams or visions, dramatic encounters with the living God, who was mysteriously present in the dream experience. These were not just the subconscious projections of Solomon's desires but authentic engagements with the Lord.

9:3. The dedication of the temple had taken place before the building of Solomon's royal complex was completed. On that occasion God had sent his glory into the Holy of Holies in the temple (8:10–11). The writer of 2 Chronicles indicates that, following Solomon's prayer, the Lord sent fire from heaven to consume the sacrifices that had been placed on the altar, and God's glory once again filled the temple (2 Chr. 7:1–4). These two events were the Lord's visual display of his acceptance of the temple.

On this occasion, God spoke to indicate his acceptance of the temple. Solomon had dedicated the temple by setting it apart to the Lord. But what made the temple unique among all the places of worship on earth was God's relation to it. He himself had **consecrated** it (made it holy) by placing his **Name there forever**. It was not simply that Solomon had attached the Lord's name to the building. The temple was a house for God's name because he had put his name there. In so doing he claimed ownership of it and identified himself with it.

9:4–5. While the Lord accepted the temple in a few brief words, he had much more to say about Solomon himself. Building the temple had been a great accomplishment, but Solomon needed to realize that constructing the temple was not the basis of his relationship with God. The words of 9:4–5 are familiar—we have heard them earlier from David (2:2–4) and the Lord himself (3:14; 6:11–13). In one sense, the completion of the temple had changed nothing, in terms of Solomon's relation to his Lord. His achievements were no substitute for obedience.

God had made a covenant with David that promised him an enduring dynasty: **You shall never fail to have a man on the throne of Israel**. There would always be a potential Davidic king. But no king in the line of David could assume that he or his son would be the one to enjoy that promise. From the beginning, God made clear that the blessing of each generation was conditioned on obedience: "When he does wrong, I will punish him with the rod of men, with floggings inflicted by men" (2 Sam. 7:14). Therefore, Solomon must continue in the path of obedience.

The terms of the promise were significant—inward **integrity of heart** and external conformity to God's standard. The first was particularly characteristic of David. He was anything but perfect. He was capable of great sin. But he had a repentant heart, and David never flirted with idolatry or allegiance to a false god.

At the height of Solomon's success, the Lord was challenging him to examine his own heart. Twenty years earlier God had summoned him to "walk in my ways and obey my statutes and commands as David your father did" (1 Kgs. 3:14). Success had followed upon success, but at halftime, Solomon needed to know that none of the basics had changed. The building and dedication of the temple was a great accomplishment, but it had changed nothing about the fundamentals of his relationship with God.

9:6–9. The Lord wanted Solomon to have no illusions that the game was over. Successful as he had been so far, there was still danger of defection. This would happen if he or his sons turned away from the one true God **to serve other gods**. This was a warning, not a threat, addressed not only to Solomon but to all who would follow him. At this point in his life, Solomon may have thought that such a warning was unnecessary. How could the man who built the glorious temple of the Lord turn away to serve other gods? But this is exactly where Solomon eventually failed.

There would be consequences to rebellion. God would **cut off Israel from the land** he had given them. God also declared that he would **reject this temple**. It was unthinkable that he could turn his back on such a glorious building, one that had cost so much in money and in manpower. Furthermore, Israel would become **a byword and an object of ridicule**. A "byword" conjures up associations of failure or evil or disgrace. Past blessing was no guarantee of spiritual blessing, particularly if the people forsook the Lord their God and **embraced other gods**.

One of the reasons the Book of 1 Kings was written was to answer the question for the Jews in exile in Babylon, How did we get here? These words to Solomon would have hit with tremendous force four hundred years after they were first spoken to Solomon. Here was the history of the nation in a nutshell! They were a people exiled from their land, lamenting the destruction of their magnificent temple, and enduring deep national disgrace, exactly as God had predicted. And the process of destruction had begun with Solomon in the second half of his life.

C The Seeds of Destruction (9:10–28; 10:14–29)

SUPPORTING IDEA: *What looks like continuing success may, in fact, be accelerating decay.*

9:10–14,26–28. In these verses, Solomon's international relations are in focus, especially his profitable alliance with **Hiram king of Tyre**, the ruler of the

Phoenicians. This period found Phoenicia rising to dominance in the Mediterranean area as a powerful marine nation. It was a period of commercial and political expansion because of Phoenicia's entrepreneurial energy and technological skill. This made Hiram a valuable ally. Solomon and Hiram initially had worked together in the building of the temple and royal complex in Jerusalem (5:1–18). This alliance had proven to be mutually beneficial, and it led to other projects. Phoenicia dominated the eastern Mediterranean sailing industry. Israel, under Solomon, controlled the overland trade routes to the east. This made the two nations a powerful force, and they were even stronger when they engaged in a joint venture to develop maritime trade to the south and east (9:26–28).

Ezion Geber was on Israel's southern boundary, on the Gulf of Elath, with access to the Red Sea and the Indian Ocean. Solomon **built ships** there, almost certainly with the assistance of Hiram, who, in turn, **sent his men— sailors who knew the sea—to serve in the fleet with Solomon's men.** Historically, Israel was not a seafaring people, but now under Solomon's leadership, they developed a navy capable of venturing down the east coast of Africa (**Ophir**) and perhaps as far east as India. In 10:22, Solomon's ships are described as "trading ships" (literally, "ships of Tarshish").

Since Tarshish was in Spain, the expression describes "ocean-going vessels" that were capable of making three-year expeditions. The cargo is described in 10:22 as "gold, silver and ivory, and apes and baboons." The partnership thrived: **they sailed to Ophir and brought back 420 talents** (about 16 tons) **of gold.**

Solomon, perhaps strapped for cash because of the massive cost of his building projects, exchanged **twenty towns in Galilee** for **120 talents of gold.** It is disconcerting to think of a king selling people's homes for cash! It is not clear whether this was a sale (like the Louisiana or Alaska Purchase) or a mortgage-like arrangement. But when Hiram saw what he had received for his money, **he was not pleased.** He called the region **Cabul**, a term meaning "worthless, good-for-nothing." Perhaps Solomon had cheated his partner and gotten away with it. Turning a huge profit on relatively worthless land may be shrewd business, but it is hardly worthy of God's king.

9:15–25. These verses describe Solomon's building projects. In addition to the temple and the palace complex, he reengineered the region of the city (**the supporting terraces**) and built **the wall of Jerusalem**, probably for defense purposes. Although he never led the nation into war, he invested heavily in military protection, building a series of regional fortress cities: **Hazor** in the north, **Megiddo** in the central region, and **Gezer** in the south. There was a host of other projects. With this flurry of construction Solomon reshaped his nation.

But such projects were not without cost. Solomon needed a lot of money and manpower to fulfill his ambitions. One source of manpower consisted of the descendants of the original inhabitants of the land, **the Amorites, Hittites, Perizzites, Hivites and Jebusites**. Israel's failure to obey God in the time of the conquest by wiping out the Canaanites meant that they remained as a continual source of trouble for the Israelites. But Solomon turned them into **his slave labor force**. Slaves were a cheap labor force.

Slave labor alone was not an adequate source of manpower. So Solomon conscripted his fellow citizens. They were required to serve in positions of oversight and leadership. Many Israelites were required to give one month out of every three to Solomon's projects. This situation would explode into rebellion of the northern tribes after Solomon's death. Solomon's personal ambitions were crushing his people.

10:14–25. In these verses we are overpowered with the account of Solomon's wealth. **Gold** is mentioned nine times in these verses, and it is present in massive amounts. Much of this wealth was used for trivial purposes. He made **two hundred large shields of hammered gold**. These shields were purely ceremonial. There were also **three hundred small shields**, each made of gold.

That was only the beginning. Solomon's great throne was **inlaid with ivory and overlaid with fine gold**. This conspicuous splendor extended to the smallest details. **All his goblets were gold, and all the household articles in the Palace of the Forest of Lebanon were pure gold**. In fact, gold was so abundant that silver was deflated in value. Solomon filled his palace with the splendid, the exotic, and the extravagant.

God had promised Solomon that he would give him "both riches and honor—so that in your lifetime you will have no equal among kings" (3:13). The Lord had been faithful to his promises. Solomon was the epitome of success by any earthly measurement. But there is no indication that the people shared this wealth. Solomon's gold seems to have gone to self-indulgent decorations and to extravagant displays of royal wealth. He was doing very well, but this prosperity was not reaching the average citizens of his nation.

10:26–29. The final verses of this section point us to Solomon's participation in raising and trading horses. This was not recreational but military. The chariot was the greatest weapon of its day. Horses were used for pulling chariots. Solomon rarely, if ever, used his army. Nevertheless, he **accumulated chariots and horses**, building special chariot cities and stationing some chariots in the capital city. He not only accumulated horses; he had them **imported from Egypt and from Kue** (a region famed for its horses in southern Turkey). He then exported horses to nations to the north, **the kings of the Hittites and of the Arameans**.

This description looks innocent enough until it is put against the background of Deuteronomy 17:16: "The king, moreover, must not acquire great numbers of horses for himself or make the people return to Egypt to get more of them." Suddenly the double reference to Egypt in 1 Kings 10:28–29 takes on deeper significance. Solomon's booming import-export business in horses and his personal accumulation of horses and chariots may have been successful in business and military terms, but it represented defiance of the standards of God.

> **MAIN IDEA REVIEW:** *Unless we shift from a mind-set of success to one of significance, our "successes" will turn into failures.*

III. CONCLUSION

Addicted to Success

At halftime Solomon's life was, by all apparent standards, a success. He "had achieved all he had desired to do" (9:1). But he never made a shift from success to significance. The second half of his life was all about more—of everything. But Solomon was not a success. His kingdom was impressive but very superficial. It had no staying power. In the process of his success, he made compromises with God's standards that proved to have devastating long-term consequences.

Solomon's situation tells us three things. First, success can become an addiction. Solomon accumulated more and more "stuff." But there was no compelling purpose and no compelling game plan for the future, just more and more of the same, in a lifestyle of self-serving excess. Second, success can become a deception. It may mask our true condition. All of the gold that surrounded Solomon masked the fact that his heart was turning to stone, as he revealed in Ecclesiastes with his heartbreaking cry, "Meaningless! Meaningless! . . . Utterly meaningless! Everything is meaningless!" (Eccl. 1:2). More money, more buildings, more fame, more women—none of these could substitute for the relationship with God that he lost in the process. Third, success can be an illusion. No one coming to the end of chapter 10 of 1 Kings would believe that nearly all of this glittering success would disappear within a few short years. But it did.

Halftime, especially during a time of great success, is very important. Choices made then will determine how the game ends. This is the lesson we must learn from Solomon.

PRINCIPLES

- Apparent success can blind us to genuine success, if we do not measure by God's standards.
- Genuine success can be measured only in the long run, not the short run.

- The indispensable requirement in success is a proper relationship to God and his requirements.
- Successful people are in danger of living insignificant lives if they become addicted to success.
- Earthly accomplishments are no substitute for a lifestyle of obedience to the Lord.

APPLICATIONS

- Make an intentional choice to move from a success mind-set to a significance mind-set.
- Guard your heart against the seduction of success and its addictive nature.
- Follow the standards of God's Word with integrity and passion.
- Recognize that your lifestyle can become an idol that turns you away from faithfulness to the Lord.

IV. LIFE APPLICATION

All That Glitters

Enron was on top of the world. Sixteen years after it had been formed by the merger of two companies, it was ranked as the seventh largest company in America. An influential business magazine listed it as the second most admired company in America for "quality of management," and first as the most innovative company. Its growth rate had been stunning, and its chairman boasted, "We will do it again next decade."

It was not to be. Before 2001 ended, Enron applied for bankruptcy protection—the largest bankruptcy in American history. Almost seventy billion dollars of equity vanished, with devastating effects on many investors and employees.

Investigators will spend years uncovering the full story. But it appeared to be a failure of integrity. Losses had been hidden, profits had been overstated, and debts had been camouflaged. There had been real success in the past, but that had led to an addiction to success. The company was committed to looking a lot better on paper than it was in fact. But truth finally won out, although at a terrible cost to many innocent people.

The danger of living for short-range success rather than long-term significance in God's sight is a temptation for all of us as well as corporate executives. A significant life may not be as impressive as the Enron tower. But it is far more enduring.

V. PRAYER

Father, you know how I am tempted to measure my life by a false standard of success. Help me to pursue what is truly significant in your eyes. Amen.

VI. DEEPER DISCOVERIES

A. Solomon the Builder (9:15–18,24)

The temple and the royal palace complex in Jerusalem were the most important projects undertaken by Solomon. But connected to them were two other major projects in Jerusalem. The phrase "supporting terraces" is the translation of a Hebrew word (*millo*), which means "filling." Since the city was built on a hill, this refers to the filled-in area, the supporting terraces built so the population of the city could be enlarged. This would primarily be the area between the narrow ridge of the city of David and the higher region of Mount Zion, where Solomon had built the temple complex. This was a major engineering feat. The city wall was also extended to the north to enclose the new areas of the city constructed by Solomon. Jerusalem was always most vulnerable to attack from the north.

King Solomon also engaged in major military building, placing fortified towns in strategic places, guarding the main road to the north (Hazor), a strategic pass to the coastal plain (Megiddo), and the vulnerable southern approaches from Egypt (Gezer). The location of some of the other towns is less certain. But the extent of Solomon's activities, constructing store cities, fortifications, and towns, is indicated by the comment that he built "whatever he desired to build in Jerusalem, in Lebanon and throughout all the territory he ruled" (9:19).

B. Solomon's Labor Force (9:20–23)

The author of 1 Kings distinguishes between Solomon's Canaanite slave laborers and the Israelite workers. He is clear to say that Solomon "did not make slaves of any of the Israelites." They were given the responsibility to serve in the army and to supervise the Canaanite labor force. But in 5:13, we are told that Solomon conscripted thirty thousand Israelite workers, who were placed under Adoniram. They are described as forced labor, rather than slave labor, because their duty was temporary rather than permanent (5:14). It is likely these workers were not paid for this compulsory civic duty. This labor policy became an oppressive burden for the northern tribes, leading to the ultimatum made to Solomon's son (12:3–4).

VII. TEACHING OUTLINE

A. INTRODUCTION
1. Lead Story: Success or Significance?
2. Context: Solomon, at the halfway mark of his reign, has an encounter with the Lord that reminds him of the need to finish his reign well.
3. Transition: This is a time of great success for Solomon. But success is not final. He will finish his reign as a success only if he makes some fundamental adjustments. Some disturbing things are already present in his life.

B. COMMENTARY
1. Solomon's Glory (9:1; 10:1–13)
2. The Lord's Appearance (9:2–9)
3. The Seeds of Destruction (9:10–28; 10:14–29)

C. CONCLUSION: ADDICTED TO SUCCESS

VIII. ISSUES FOR DISCUSSION
1. How would you define the difference between living for success and living for significance?
2. Solomon is famous as the great man of wisdom. What marks of wisdom do you see in this section? What marks of foolishness? What is the link between wisdom and integrity of heart?

1 Kings 11:1–43

Self-Inflicted Wounds

I. INTRODUCTION
Our Own Worst Enemy

II. COMMENTARY
A verse-by-verse explanation of the chapter.

III. CONCLUSION
How Big Is Your God?

An overview of the principles and application from the chapter.

IV. LIFE APPLICATION
Setting the Standard

Melding the chapter to life.

V. PRAYER
Tying the chapter to life with God.

VI. DEEPER DISCOVERIES
Historical, geographical, and grammatical enrichment of the commentary.

VII. TEACHING OUTLINE
Suggested step-by-step group study of the chapter.

VIII. ISSUES FOR DISCUSSION
Zeroing the chapter in on daily life.

Quote

"*What* makes resisting temptation difficult for many people is that they don't want to discourage it entirely."

F r a n k l i n   J o n e s

1 Kings 11:1–43

I N   A   N U T S H E L L

Chapter 11 brings us to the end of Solomon's life and reign. As king, he had sown seeds of self-indulgence that produced an ignominious end. Solomon ends his life in spiritual rebellion, under the judgment of God, with his kingdom beginning to unravel. His failure will haunt the nation for the rest of its history.

Self-Inflicted Wounds

I. INTRODUCTION

Our Own Worst Enemy

*F*or five years George Stephanopoulos served as a senior adviser for President Clinton, first in his campaign and then in the White House. He left after Mr. Clinton's reelection in 1996 and, two years later, set out to write his memoirs about the man who had dominated his life for five years. It was to be the story of how "an ambitious and idealistic president of uncertain personal character grew in office." But the Monica Lewinsky affair intruded, and the book took a very different turn. As he writes, "I'm still mystified by the Clinton paradox: How could a president so intelligent, so compassionate, so public-spirited, and so conscious of his place in history act in such a stupid, selfish, and self-destructive manner?" (*All Too Human: A Political Education*, Little, Brown, 1999, p. 4).

Bill Clinton had many political enemies. But in the long run, it wasn't his enemies but his own character and choices that caused him the most trouble.

He's not alone. On the other side of the political spectrum, Newt Gingrich in 1994 led the Republicans to a sweeping victory in the House of Representatives. This gave him high position and great influence. Only four years later he was forced to step down as speaker of the house, damaged not only by political failures and misjudgments but especially by the inconsistency between his strident attacks on the president and his own moral misbehavior. The sad fact is that our greatest enemy is most often ourselves, and our most painful wounds are self-inflicted.

No one illustrates this truth better than King Solomon. He rose faster and flew higher than anyone in his generation. When he was at the zenith of his power, his contemporaries must have imagined that his kingdom would last for a thousand years! But he fell. Although he had never faced a significant enemy on the battlefield, he lost his biggest battle—the one with himself. He inflicted permanent damage on his kingdom and left a legacy of suffering for those who came after. He is living proof that a gifted mind is no substitute for an obedient heart.

We are vulnerable in exactly the same way Solomon was. It is foolish and even arrogant to imagine that we are immune to the forces that caused his downfall. Solomon's story forces us to face some powerful temptations in our own lives.

II. COMMENTARY

Self-Inflicted Wounds

> **MAIN IDEA:** *When we compromise our relationship with God, we set in motion a course of events that destroys what we value and incurs the judgment of God.*

🅐 Solomon's Sin (11:1–8)

> **SUPPORTING IDEA:** *When we do not guard our hearts by obedience to God, we are capable of great evil and foolishness.*

11:1–2. Solomon's first step downward came when he disobeyed God's clear standards: He **loved many foreign women**. This statement reminds us of the earlier description, "Solomon loved the Lord" (see 3:3). These are clearly incompatible loves, since God had given his people an unmistakable command: The people of Israel were not to intermarry with pagan foreigners **because they will surely turn your hearts after their gods**. The strongest form of the command is found in Deuteronomy 7:1–4:

> When the LORD your God brings you into the land you are entering to possess and drives out before you many nations—the Hittites, Girgashites, Amorites, Canaanites, Perizzites, Hivites and Jebusites, seven nations larger and stronger than you—and when the L ORD your God has delivered them over to you and you have defeated them, then you must destroy them totally. Make no treaty with them, and show them no mercy. Do not intermarry with them. Do not give your daughters to their sons or take their daughters for your sons, for they will turn your sons away from following me to serve other gods, and the LORD's anger will burn against you and will quickly destroy you.

Solomon chose his wives from the very nations that God had prohibited, probably to form alliances with local chiefs and clan leaders. He probably rationalized it as a means of national security, but it was an act of rebellion and defiance against God. Good relations with his pagan neighbors became more important to Solomon than a good relation with his Lord. And Solomon not only broke the law against foreign wives; he also shattered God's commands against multiple wives in Deuteronomy 17:17: "He must not take many wives, or his heart will be led astray."

11:3. Solomon not only defied God's standards; he practiced sensual indulgence as well. Although we are told that he loved many foreign women, it is impossible for one man to love **seven hundred wives of royal birth and three hundred concubines**. They were like his collection of gold—never enough. These women were trophies, used to enhance his status and power. It is probable that he was addicted to sexual indulgence, but at some point this was no longer about status or sex but about a sickness of the soul.

11:4–8. The end result was that Solomon abandoned God. It is almost impossible to recognize in these verses the man who prayed the great dedicatory prayer at the beginning of his reign. This defection began when Solomon tolerated the presence of false gods. He did not insist that his pagan wives leave their pagan gods in their homeland and worship the Lord alone. Whether for what he felt was political necessity or because of a misguided tolerance, he permitted the presence of pagan gods in Jerusalem. He imported his wives, and they in turn imported their gods. One compromise inevitably led to another in a process of creeping idolatry. He then sponsored the presence of these pagan gods: **Solomon built a high place for Chemosh the detestable god of Moab, and for Molech the detestable god of the Ammonites. He did the same for all his foreign wives, who burned incense and offered sacrifices to their gods**. The place where these pagan altars were built would become known as "the Hill of Corruption." It lasted until it was destroyed by King Josiah more than three hundred years later (2 Kgs. 23:13).

But Solomon's sin did not stop at toleration or sponsorship. He actually bowed in worship to false gods, offering sacrifices to them. His heart had been **turned . . . after other gods**. Even in terms of the paganism of the time, this made little sense. Solomon was the dominant power in the region. His "God" had conquered the gods of the other nations. Why bow at the shrine of a less powerful god? Since the worship of most of these gods was associated with sensuality and immorality, it seems clear that they appealed to something in Solomon's fallen heart.

The only way Solomon could do what he did was to adjust his view of God. He did not abandon the worship of the Lord. He continued to patronize the temple and probably did many things in God's name. But the God he now served was, in fact, a lesser God. Solomon adjusted his view of the God of glory downward to accommodate his new lifestyle: **He did not follow the LORD completely, as David his father had done**. Solomon was only the first of a long line of kings of Israel and Judah of whom it would be said, "He did evil in the eyes of the Lord." No matter how successful Solomon appeared, this is the epitaph of ultimate failure in the part of life that matters most.

B God's Justice (11:9–13)

SUPPORTING IDEA: *Although God is always gracious, he will not allow his people to continue to sin.*

11:9–10. God was not an indifferent observer as the king led his nation into spiritual rebellion. He was outraged by Solomon's defection. Two things made Solomon's sin particularly outrageous. First, Solomon had enjoyed unique privileges: the God of Israel **had appeared to him twice**. Solomon had experienced direct encounters with God himself and had felt his love and power firsthand. He could not offer the excuse that God was a distant reality whom he had known only through his father David or some prophet. Second, Solomon could not claim that he was ignorant of God's requirements. Through the written Word, his father's instruction, and God's direct intervention, he had received God's standards. But all of these did not keep Solomon on course.

11:11–13. Solomon once again met God. But this time the experience was different. God would not allow himself to be trifled with. He charged Solomon with covenant unfaithfulness: **you have not kept my covenant**. The king had a rebellious attitude. The Lord had repeatedly reminded Solomon that while the Davidic covenant was unconditional, covenant blessing was contingent on obedience (2:2–4; 3:13–14; 6:11–13; 9:4–9). Now Solomon confronted the fact that God would not allow his people to continue to sin. Judgment was certain: **I will . . . tear the kingdom away from you and give it to one of your subordinates**. "Tear away" indicated that the removal would be forceful and even violent.

But God's covenant promise to David was inviolable, and even Solomon could find shelter under it. Although judgment was certain, it would be deferred: **for the sake of David your father, I will not do it during your lifetime**. Even as drastic a sin as Solomon's did not draw immediate judgment, "for the sake of David." This is a note that will reappear not only in this chapter (vv. 13,32,34,36) but also throughout the history of the kings (1 Kgs. 15:4; 2 Kgs. 19:34; 20:6). The Davidic covenant was inviolable, and it would move relentlessly to its fulfillment in the person of the Lord Jesus, the Son of David (Matt. 1:1). But Solomon had the knowledge that his own son would pay the price of his failure: **I will tear it out of the hand of your son**. Yet, for David's sake, judgment would be mitigated.

One tribe, the tribe of Judah, would form the basis of a new, reduced nation. Solomon's sin and rebellion had not annulled God's promise to his father David. David's dynasty remained the chosen line of royalty, and Jerusalem remained God's chosen city. The concept of God acting for the sake of the chosen city of Jerusalem is a theme that will recur throughout 1 and 2 Kings (1 Kgs. 11:32; 14:31; 2 Kgs. 19:34; 20:6; 23:27). No matter what was ahead for the nation, Judah—the Davidic dynasty—and Jerusalem would survive.

ⓒ Solomon's Enemies (11:14–43)

SUPPORTING IDEA: *While we can control our sinful choices, we cannot control the consequences.*

11:14–22. The first source of trouble for Solomon came from one of Israel's ancient enemies, **Edom**, a desert people who lived on Israel's south-eastern border at the southern end of the Dead Sea. In David's time Joab had led the army on a six-month campaign into Edom. There had been a massive destruction of the Edomite army, but the young prince, **Hadad the Edomite, from the royal line**, had managed to escape into Egypt.

Egypt had good reasons to cultivate warm relations with their Arab neighbors, so Hadad was treated with kindness. The pharaoh, a successor to Solomon's father-in-law, gave him a house, land, and food. Hadad not only was given asylum; he was allowed to marry into the royal family. The son of this union, **Genubath**, was **brought up in the royal palace**. All of this is written to remind us of Moses, a refugee from another land who found respite in Egypt, and a foreign child taken into the royal household. This association is made even stronger by Hadad's words to Pharaoh, on hearing of David's death: **Let me go, that I may return to my own country**. This appeal echoed that of Moses as he pleaded with Pharaoh to "let my people go" (see Exod. 5:1; 7:16; 8:1,20; 9:1,13; 10:3).

Hadad's return is not described, nor are we told the form that his opposition to Solomon took. He probably returned with a burning resentment at what Israel had done to his nation. It was probably only later in Solomon's reign that he was able to be a source of aggravation for Solomon, probably as the leader of a nationalistic guerilla band. Divine irony was at work. Solomon's defection had begun with a marriage alliance made with Pharaoh. His first troubles began with an adversary who had been sheltered by another Pharaoh.

11:23–25. The second enemy to rise against Solomon emerged in the northeast, in the region of **Aram** (Syria). Once again the seeds of the problem were planted during the time of David. Zobah was an Aramean kingdom north of Damascus. David had campaigned in the area and defeated **the forces of Zobah**. But before David's victory a man named **Rezon** had broken away from King Hadadezer of Zobah, gathered a group of disgruntled men, and become the leader of a band of rebels. They made Damascus their base of operations, and here they exercised increasing control. Although the region was nominally under Israelite control, Rezon became its *de facto* leader. The local people were increasingly loyal to him.

If Hadad brought memories of Moses, Rezon, the guerilla leader of Zobah, was reminiscent of David. His emergence in the strategic territory of Damascus must have caused great difficulty for Solomon in the movement of troops, tribute, and trade. This trouble along the northern border of Israel was the first visible evidence that God had turned his hand against Solomon.

11:26–39. Solomon's greatest problem, however, was not to be external but internal. His policies had created conditions ripe for rebellion. All that was needed was an individual around whom opposition could coalesce. That person proved to be **Jeroboam son of Nebat**, a man from the tribe of

Ephraim, the largest and most influential of the northern tribes. He is introduced as **one of Solomon's officials**. This translation in the NIV obscures an important connection. The phrase is literally "a servant of Solomon," and is meant to recall God's statement that he would give Solomon's kingdom "to one of your subordinates" (v. 11, where "subordinates" is the word "servants"). The phrase then has an ominous note. This was the man who would not only bring great harm to Solomon but great harm to his kingdom.

Jeroboam was promoted by Solomon himself to the very position where he could do the most damage! He was **a man of standing**, a term that describes his ability more than his status. When Solomon saw how well the young man Jeroboam did his work, he put him in charge of the whole labor force of the house of Jacob (the two tribes descended from Jacob, Ephraim, and Manasseh). The labor force would become the issue that led the northern tribes to break away from Judah. Trouble and discontent were already present, but Jeroboam was in a natural position to become the magnet for the disgruntled. As he, a northerner, dealt with the grievances and complaints of his fellow tribesman, they increasingly came to value his abilities and to recognize his potential for leadership.

At this point God intervened directly by means of **the prophet of Shiloh named Ahijah**. He was the first of the prophets who would become such significant figures throughout the history of the kings. His encounter with Jeroboam was carefully staged for the greatest impact. As Jeroboam was in the countryside, away from Jerusalem, Ahijah suddenly met him, **wearing a new cloak**. He dramatically removed it, **tore it into twelve pieces**, and gave ten of them to Jeroboam. The tearing of the cloak was reminiscent of the encounter between Saul and Samuel in 1 Samuel 15, when Samuel used a torn robe to inform Saul that "the L ORD has torn the kingdom of Israel from you today and has given it to one of your neighbors—to one better than you" (1 Sam. 15:28).

God had two things to tell Jeroboam through Ahijah. The Lord would **tear the kingdom out of Solomon's hand and give** Jeroboam **ten tribes**. Judgment had come because they (the nation, not just Solomon) had forsaken God, worshiped pagan gods, and failed to keep his statutes and laws. But God's covenant with David was not being terminated. God would continue to guide his people **for the sake of David my servant**. God also declared that he would leave one tribe for Solomon and his descendants: **I will give one tribe to his son so that David my servant may always have a lamp before me in Jerusalem**. This promise must have been a source of hope for the exiles in Babylon as they heard these words.

The second major part of the message was directed to Jeroboam himself. He received from God a promise similar to the one he gave to David in 2 Samuel 7: **You will be king over Israel**. Jeroboam was not only promised kingship but also a dynasty **as enduring as the one I built for David**. But this promise of a perpetual dynasty was conditioned on Jeroboam's obedience of the Lord. This was exactly the same condition that God had impressed upon Solomon. God also suggested that things would not turn out well for Jeroboam: **I will humble David's descendants because of this, but not forever**. The ten tribes would not be removed forever from David's line. One day they would be returned to the dynasty of David, a hope that would be realized in the reign of the Messiah.

11:40. Earlier we were told that "Jeroboam son of Nebat rebelled against the king" (vv. 26–27). We are nowhere told what form that rebellion took, but now we are told that **Solomon tried to kill Jeroboam**. Jeroboam obviously represented a significant threat to the king. Realizing his peril, Jeroboam fled to Shishak, king of Egypt, and stayed there until Solomon's death. Once again Egypt was the refuge for Solomon's enemies.

11:41–43. These verses tell us that Solomon reigned for forty years and was succeeded by his son Rehoboam. Solomon's reign had seemed so enduring. But he had put his glory before the glory of the Lord. Soon his kingdom would be only a shadow of its former self.

MAIN IDEA REVIEW: *When we compromise the integrity of our relationship with God, we set in motion a course of events that destroys what we value and incurs the judgment of God.*

III. CONCLUSION

How Big Is Your God?

Solomon's life ended in tragedy, and the wounds were self-inflicted. His unwillingness to keep a pure heart before God, along with his refusal to discipline his appetites, led him to commit sins that would have been unimaginable at an earlier point in his life. The great temple builder became a pathetic idol worshiper, bowing before the very idols he had contracted someone to build.

The only way that Solomon could sustain his moral lifestyle was to shrink his view of God. Immorality always partners with idolatry. Solomon not only invented a God who would tolerate his behavior; he also bowed down before the fraudulent creations of human imagination. He turned his back on the true God to grovel before false gods. What a tragic ending for a king who began so well.

PRINCIPLES

- There is no substitute for a heart that is submissive and obedient to God.
- Our view of God is the most important thing about us.
- The first steps of compromise place us on a slippery slope that leads to defection.
- Great sins grow from small compromises.
- Our greatest enemy is within us, in the depravity of our own hearts. All of us are capable of great evil.
- Precisely because he is a God who loves us, the Lord will not allow us to continue to sin.
- God is faithful to his promises of grace, in spite of the failures of his people.
- All human accomplishments, no matter how impressive, are fragile.

APPLICATIONS

- Guard your integrity and allow yourself no moral or spiritual compromise.
- Submit to God's discipline in repentance and reformation.
- Value God's grace, but do not presume upon it.
- Value leaders of godly character and integrity.

IV. LIFE APPLICATION

Setting the Standard

Almost hidden in the words of this chapter is a significant insight. God spoke to Jeroboam through Ahijah: "They have forsaken me and worshiped Ashtoreth the goddess of the Sidonians, Chemosh the god of the Moabites, and Molech the god of the Ammonites" (11:33). But in verses 5 and 7, these were the sins of Solomon. The people had become like their king. This is a recurring theme of 1 Kings. The people became like those whom they followed. Leaders set the standard for better or for worse.

Unfortunately, Solomon wasn't a safe leader to follow. His wisdom was unsurpassed. His competence was undeniable. But he gave away his heart to sinful things, and he devastated his nation. Solomon was not a safe leader because he did not guard his heart. His glory became more important than God's glory; his pleasures became more urgent than God's will; his wisdom became more determinative than God's truth; his search for security became more reliable than God's promises.

What should we look for in a leader? Would you rather be in a church led by people of moderate skills who have unquestioned integrity? Or do you prefer a church led by those with great ability who are immature spiritually? We must be careful whom we follow. Leaders set the standard.

V. PRAYER

Father, give me a heart that is ruthless with the impulses to go its own way and to do its own thing. Teach me to love your pleasure more than my own and to value your glory and honor above all things. Amen.

VI. DEEPER DISCOVERIES

A. Solomon's Royal Wives (11:3)

The NIV translation "seven hundred wives of royal birth" is possible but unlikely. It is more likely that the phrase refers to "seven hundred wives of royal standing," referring to their status after marriage rather than before. A good number of Solomon's wives would have been "of royal birth," so their marriages represented an alliance between Solomon and their fathers. Many would have been daughters of petty chieftains or clan leaders and some of more prestigious figures. A marriage to a person of the stature of Pharaoh's daughter was unique. Solomon entered into these marriages to secure good relations with the surrounding states.

B. Ten and One Make Twelve (11:30–32)

The arithmetic of Ahijah seems flawed. He tore his cloak into twelve pieces, gave ten to Jeroboam, and told him that Solomon would keep only one tribe. What happened to the twelfth? The answer is that the tribe of Benjamin, the tribe of King Saul (and the apostle Paul, Phil. 3:5), lay on the border of Israel and Judah and was divided by the northern secession. For example, Bethel, which was part of Benjamin, became the center for the northern false cult. But the majority of Benjamin seems to have been incorporated into Judah. Verses 31 and 35 are the only time the expression "ten tribes" occurs in the Old Testament.

C. David's Lamp (11:36)

A lamp gives light in the darkness. It thus became a fitting symbol of the Davidic covenant as the hope of the nation. Even in the darkness of Solomon's apostasy, the light may flicker, but it will not fail. The term was first used of David as the hope of the nation by his soldiers in 2 Samuel 21:17. The symbol will appear again in some of the nation's darkest hours (1 Kgs. 15:4; 2 Kgs. 8:19; 2 Chr. 21:7; Ps. 132:17).

VII. TEACHING OUTLINE

A. INTRODUCTION
1. Lead Story: Our Own Worst Enemy
2. Context: Solomon is coming to the end of his life. By all indications his was a life of fame and success. But seeds he had planted along the way now yield a harvest. His kingdom, once so impressive, will dissolve under the hand of God because of his sins.
3. Transition: Few people illustrate the truth that a good beginning does not guarantee a good ending more than Solomon. As an old man, he reaped the consequences of his self-destructive choices.

B. COMMENTARY
1. Solomon's Sin (11:1–8)
2. God's Justice (11:9–13)
3. Solomon's Enemies (11:14–43)

C. CONCLUSION: HOW BIG IS YOUR GOD?

VIII. ISSUES FOR DISCUSSION
1. Trace the course of Solomon's defection. What steps did he take that led him astray? His downfall appeared to be sudden. Do you think it was?
2. Was Solomon a success or a failure as a king? At what point can you make the most accurate evaluation? What should this tell us about how we should measure such things?
3. Looking back over the life of Solomon, what major lessons are evident to you?

1 Kings 12:1–24; 14:21–31

The March of Folly

I. **INTRODUCTION**
Mistakes Leaders Make

II. **COMMENTARY**
A verse-by-verse explanation of these passages.

III. **CONCLUSION**
To Serve or to Be Served
An overview of the principles and application from these passages.

IV. **LIFE APPLICATION**
Fighting to the Better End
Melding these passages to life.

V. **PRAYER**
Tying these passages to life with God.

VI. **DEEPER DISCOVERIES**
Historical, geographical, and grammatical enrichment of the commentary.

VII. **TEACHING OUTLINE**
Suggested step-by-step group study of these passages.

VIII. **ISSUES FOR DISCUSSION**
Zeroing these passages in on daily life.

Quote

"*O*utside of Christ, you love to lead; in Christ,

you lead to love."

Howard Butt

BIOGRAPHICAL PROFILE: REHOBOAM

- Forty-one years old when he came to the throne
- Son of an Ammonite woman named Naamah
- At the start of his reign, the nation permanently divided
- Ruled from 931 to 913 B.C. as the first king of the diminished nation of Judah
- Invaded by Shishak, the ruler of Egypt, in 926 B.C. He bought relief by looting the temple and giving its treasure to Shishak
- Under his leadership the nation engaged in widespread pagan worship
- The first of nineteen kings descended from David who would reign over Judah in its 345 years of existence

IN A NUTSHELL

*T*he Lord had already announced to both Solomon and Jeroboam that judgment would fall on the house of David because of Solomon's failures. Ten tribes will break away from the Davidic line. That judgment, announced from heaven, is now carried out on earth because of the foolish and ungodly choices of Solomon's son, Rehoboam.

The March of Folly

I. INTRODUCTION

Mistakes Leaders Make

*K*ing George III did not intend to lose America. Quite the opposite. It was his most important colonial possession. America was important to the British government for a host of reasons. It gave them great strategic advantage in the global balance of power, especially in the ongoing conflicts with England's ancient enemies, France and Spain. It was significant economically. The colonies were not only a major source of raw materials for English industries; they were an important market for their finished products. Culturally, there were strong ties between the old world and the new. Personally, George had no desire to be remembered as the king who lost a major part of England's empire that was so vital to her prosperity and prestige.

But lose her he did. The English king and his advisers pursued policies that seemed determined to drive the colonies into rebellion. They treated the Americans with an arrogance that suggested they knew what was best and that they did not need to listen to the concerns or suggestions of the people they ruled. They combined that with an ignorance of the situation in the New World, dismissing their grievances and mocking their willingness or ability to put up a fight against English armies. In the process they stirred up such deep resentment that once-loyal subjects were driven to take up arms against the very king they had once willingly followed.

If King George and his advisers had deliberately set out to act against their own best interests, they could hardly have devised a better way to do so. Once America was gone, it was gone forever. And this is not an isolated example. The noted American historian Barbara Tuchman titled her study of such events *The March of Folly*. She describes folly as the pursuit of policies that are contrary to a nation's own welfare and best interests, even though appropriate options exist. Behind that, she contends, is a stubbornness that clings to preconceived ideas, fails to learn from experience, and thrives in self-deception.

Foolish leaders cause terrible damage, whether they work their mischief in nations, churches, businesses, or families. What their foolishness loses can often never be regained. On the other hand, wise leaders can build in a way that leaves a legacy of blessing. The leaders of the American Revolution were not perfect, but more than two hundred years later, we benefit from their wisdom.

Rehoboam did not intend to lose the larger part of his nation. But lose it he did. It is ironic that the epitome of foolish leadership in the Book of 1 Kings is the son of the king whose reign began with a prayer for wisdom, whose early years showed so much of it, and whose proverbs, given to his son, speak so much about wisdom and foolishness. Following a leader like Solomon would have been a challenging task for the wisest of men. His forty-year reign had been marked by brilliance, but his later years of apostasy had planted land mines that could only be avoided with great care. But Rehoboam, Solomon's foolish son, plunged recklessly into the minefield. He set off an explosion that split his nation. In fact, Tuchman finds in Rehoboam her first example of "the march of folly."

In 1 Kings 11, God has given us, through the prophet Ahijah, the why of the nation's division. It was God's judgment on the sin of Solomon. Here in chapter 12, we have the how, as we see the mistakes of a foolish leader. Probably no one who reads these words will ever be a king. But each of us has areas where we are responsible to give leadership. Rehoboam is a case study in mistakes leaders cannot afford to make.

II. COMMENTARY

The March of Folly

> **MAIN IDEA:** *Wise and godly leaders recognize that they are entrusted with leadership to bring benefit to God's people on God's behalf. Foolish leaders lead for their own benefit.*

A Rehoboam's Confrontation (12:1–15)

> **SUPPORTING IDEA:** *When leaders protect and promote themselves, they destroy the foundations of their leadership.*

12:1. Since he had seven hundred wives and three hundred concubines, Solomon must have had many sons. There is no indication that there was any doubt or dissension over the succession of **Rehoboam** to the kingship. Almost certainly he was the clear choice of Solomon. We learn in 14:21 that he was the son of an Ammonite woman named Naamah and that he was forty-one years old when he came to the throne. Since Solomon reigned for forty years, Rehoboam was born before the death of David. His spiritually divided upbringing is another evidence of his father's divided legacy.

It is significant that Rehoboam's coronation was not held in the capital, Jerusalem, but in **Shechem**. It was a city notable for its connection to Abraham and Jacob (Gen. 12:6–7; 33:18) and as the place where Joshua led the nation in a renewal of their covenant with God (Josh. 24). More significantly, it was in northern territory. Rehoboam's venture north for his coronation shows that he recognized the northern tribes needed to be placated. Their grievances had to be heard, although they came to the assembly with the expectation that they were gathering **to make him king**.

12:2–5. Events took an ominous turn against Rehoboam with the arrival of **Jeroboam**. Although Jeroboam had received the prophecy that the Lord had appointed him to be Israel's king, he did not appear to be the prime mover of the events. He remained in Egypt until he was summoned by his fellow Israelites, who obviously valued him as a leader. He then joined, and perhaps led, the delegation appointed to declare the north's grievances to the king. They wanted relief from the policies of Solomon that had become increasingly oppressive. Those policies had favored Solomon's own tribe of Judah. There was resentment over **the heavy yoke** with which he had bound them, a yoke that primarily describes **the harsh labor** required for the construction of Solomon's buildings (5:13–17), particularly those in Jerusalem (11:27). Although this was not the slave labor imposed on the Canaanites (9:20–23), it was compulsory and oppressive.

In addition, the heavy yoke involved an oppressive tax burden to sustain the extravagance of the royal court (4:7). Their resentment was deep-seated. At the same time, their request was not unreasonable. They did not demand the removal of all those burdens, but only that the king would make them lighter. They were prepared to serve him, but he needed to show that he had their interests at heart, not just his own.

The request from the northern tribes had implications for Rehoboam. It would call for a downsizing of his government and lifestyle. It would mean that he would have to accept a lesser glory than his father. But the crisis also represented an opportunity for Rehoboam to act in a way that would ensure the loyalty of disgruntled subjects. Rehoboam recognized there was a lot at stake in their request, so he asked for three days to think about his response.

12:6–11. Rehoboam turned first to the veterans who had advised his father, men of experience. They recognized the explosiveness of the situation. The new king needed to win the trust of the people. The best way to do this was by convincing them he was sensitive to their plight and committed to serving their needs. People will follow leaders whom they trust and who will not exploit them for selfish reasons. If Rehoboam chose to serve them, he would not lose authority; he would gain credibility and earn their loyalty.

This is a fundamental principle of effective leadership. Leadership is built on trust, and trust is built by serving the best interests of others. In the New Testament the concept of servanthood is the basic principle of the kingdom. Jesus declared to his followers, "Whoever wants to become great among you must be your servant" (Matt. 20:26).

Rehoboam was not interested in this kind of greatness. He was interested only in the greatness of power and privilege. He had already made up his mind about the kind of answer he intended to give. He **rejected the advice the elders gave him** and turned to his peers. They were **the young men who had grown up with him.** But the writer of 1 Kings actually uses a term that means "children" to indicate his disrespect for these advisers. These were immature men, impressed by their position and power. They also knew Rehoboam well enough to anticipate the answer he wanted to give them. They believed in intimidation and domination, not servant leadership. They had no interest in acknowledging the peoples' concerns or lightening Solomon's oppression. Instead they celebrated Solomon's hardships and mocked the people's requests. They advised Rehoboam to tell the disgruntled northern tribes: **My father scourged you with whips; I will scourge you with scorpions** (apparently a stinging whip).

Note that Rehoboam sought the counsel of veterans and peers but not of the Lord. There is no mention of prayer or of seeking the input of a prophet or a priest.

12:12–15. After hearing the advice that mirrored his intentions, Rehoboam summoned the northern leaders to declare his policy. The people had complained that Solomon had treated them harshly. Solomon's son now answered them **harshly.** Rehoboam had become like Israel's ancient enemy Pharaoh, who responded to the Israelites' complaints by increasing his oppression (Exod. 5:1–21). He borrowed the words of his young advisers and promised the northern tribes that they could expect greater burdens. This is a case study in how not to escalate conflict. Rehoboam abused his position by answering harshly; he thought win-lose, rather than win-win, by refusing negotiation or compromise; he chose inflammatory language; he used threats; and he **did not listen to the people.**

This last phrase takes on special significance when we remember that the heart of Solomon's prayer for wisdom in 3:9 was that he would have a "discerning" (or listening) heart. Twice we are told that Rehoboam did not listen to the people, and neither did he listen to God. This was the essence of Rehoboam's foolishness.

Up to this point, we have seen men acting on the basis of their sinful desires and characters. The hand of God has been unseen, but it has not been absent: **This turn of events was . . . to fulfill the word the LORD had spoken to Jeroboam** (see 11:29–39). God was not coercing the action. Rehoboam was acting freely, but his actions accomplished the sovereign purpose of God. On a human level these events were the result of human maneuverings, character flaws, and factional disputes. But behind the political maneuverings stood the certain purpose of God. God is sovereign, and his sovereignty is carried out in a marvelous creativity, which never overrides human accountability.

B Rehoboam's Civil War (12:16–24)

SUPPORTING IDEA: *It is easier to break up what God intends to be together than it is to put together what sin has broken.*

12:16–17. It is much easier to tear down than to build up. One bad decision tore apart what had taken more than a century to put together. It is relatively simple to break apart a nation, a church, or a family. But it is almost impossible to put it together again. This fact should make us weigh our actions carefully.

The nation of Israel had been a single nation under one king for 120 years—during the reigns of Saul, David, and Solomon. But there were hostilities between the tribes that went back many years into Israel's history. These were like a hidden fault line along which the nation now split. Most of the hostility was petty; some was justified by the marginalizing of the ten tribes and the favoritism shown to the tribe of Judah by Solomon. The fault line could not withstand the pressure of Rehoboam's foolish pronouncement.

The effect was instantaneous. The northern tribes borrowed a slogan that a man named Sheba had used earlier to instigate a rebellion by the northern tribes against King David: **What share do we have in David, what part in Jesse's son? To your tents, O Israel!** (see 2 Sam. 20:1). This must have been a traditional rallying cry for the northern tribes. The last phrase, added here by the northern tribes, was a repudiation of the Davidic royal family: **Look after your own house, O David!** This was a repudiation of any attempt at reconciliation. The die was cast. Israel (the term now becomes a description of the ten northern tribes) retreated to its tents, ready to do battle if required. The nation had split.

12:18–19. Rehoboam's aide, **Adoniram**, who was in charge of forced labor, was the worst choice imaginable to try to appeal to the northern tribes. The embodiment of all the grievances of the northern tribes, Adoniram was sent either to negotiate or to coerce compliance. His presence so infuriated the northern tribes that they rose up to stone him. Rehoboam, realizing he was in enemy territory, fled to Jerusalem. He had left for Shechem, certain of his throne and authority. He returned as the king of a greatly diminished kingdom.

12:20. Jeroboam was crowned king of the northern confederacy. He had not been the person who shaped the actions to this point. He was a figure of great importance whom we will meet in the next chapters. From this point on, there are two nations: **all Israel** and **Judah**.

12:21–24. Rehoboam was not willing to concede the loss of his kingdom. He prepared to invade Israel with a huge army of 180,000 soldiers. The futility of dealing with the problem with force should have been obvious. But before Rehoboam could launch his attack, he was intercepted by a man of

God, **Shemaiah**. The prophet's message was clear. The Lord forbade military attack on his **brothers, the Israelites**. Once again we see the hand of God. The division of the nation was not just the result of the foolishness of human leaders. God declared: **This is my doing**. God was working out his sovereign purposes in fulfillment of his prophetic word. This time the people were obedient to the word of God.

Ⓒ Rehoboam's Legacy (14:21–31)

SUPPORTING IDEA: *Sin leaves us with cheap substitutes for the blessings of God.*

14:21. We jump over the intervening chapters that deal with Jeroboam to conclude the life of Rehoboam at the end of chapter 14. It is part of the pattern of 1 Kings that the author follows the career of the king he is discussing, then switches to the other kingdom to consider the king of the other nation. It is like watching a split-screen television. Events in Israel are frozen while we watch unfolding events in Judah.

The reign of each Judean king is recounted in the same way: the king's name, his father's name, the length of his reign, his age when he came to the throne, his mother's name, and usually a comparison to King David (which is not given here). Rehoboam came to the throne of Judah at the age of forty-one, and he reigned for seventeen years, from 931 to 913 B.C. We are told twice in this section (vv. 21,31) that his mother was **Naamah** and that **she was an Ammonite**.

14:22–24. While Rehoboam was king, Judah not only lost most of its territory; it also lost its spiritual integrity. The people of Judah became more like the Canaanites around them than the people of God they were called to be. Jerusalem may have been "the city the LORD had chosen out of all the tribes of Israel in which to put his Name" (14:21), but possession of Solomon's temple did not keep the people from falling into paganism: **By the sins they committed they stirred up** [the Lord's] **jealous anger**. God's jealousy is his zeal for his own glory and for the exclusive loyalty of his own people. He will not allow his people to continue to sin.

The catalogue of the people's sins will recur over and over in 1 Kings. Here they involved participation in the idolatry and immorality of the Canaanite religions around them. Jeroboam introduced a syncretistic worship of God into Israel. Judah was involved in paganism. This did not go unnoticed by the Lord. These were **the detestable practices of the nations the LORD had driven out before the Israelites**. If a righteous God drove out pagans for their sins, how could he tolerate such practices among his own people? The original readers of 1 Kings would hear in these words an explanation of why they were in exile in Babylon. We need to hear them as ominous reminders of the holiness of God, who will not let his people defile his name.

14:25–28. God's immediate judgment arrived in the person of the Egyptian pharaoh, Shishak. Known as Shehonq I (945–924 B.C.), he invaded the area of Palestine to reassert Egyptian control of the region. He overran numerous cities (150 are listed in a temple relief in Karnak). This was the first successful attack on the region by a foreign power since David was king. Rehoboam's folly left him without the resources to resist Shishak, so he bought him off, using the wealth of the temple. Shishak **carried off the treasures of the temple of the LORD and the treasures of the royal palace.** This shows how far Rehoboam had fallen from the glory days of Solomon.

But Rehoboam was not willing to face reality. He provided cheap substitutes (**bronze shields**) to replace what was taken. He protected them with great pomp and ceremony. But no one was fooled. The glory of the nation has been degraded by human sin and pagan worship. The golden age was over. The bronze age mocked the past. Here was a people in moral, spiritual, political, economic, and military decline. The cost of sin was great indeed.

14:29–31. Rehoboam passed off the scene, leaving a legacy of conflict and decline. His reign had been a march of folly.

> **MAIN IDEA REVIEW:** *Wise and godly leaders recognize that they are entrusted with leadership to bring benefit to God's people on God's behalf. Foolish leaders lead for their own benefit.*

III. CONCLUSION

To Serve or to Be Served

Rehoboam did not cause the problems that led to his downfall. He inherited them from his father. But he took a difficult situation and made it worse. The fact of the conflict was not in his control; the form the conflict took was. Because he chose to listen only to his own desires and to promote his own short-term interests, he set in motion a series of events that permanently divided his nation. The twelve tribes were never reunited.

Rehoboam faced a fundamental choice—whether he would see his leadership as an opportunity to serve or to be served. He chose being served, and he lost those whom he expected to serve him. He chose to listen only to his own desires and to those who told him what he wanted to hear. He chose not to listen either to the people or to God. As a result he chose the way of folly.

Wise leaders are good listeners. They first listen to the Lord and follow his standards of leadership. That was the mark of David. He was a man who listened to God. Then they listen to those whom they lead, concerned about their best interests, not their own.

PRINCIPLES

- Wise leaders understand that they are called to be servants in the best interests of those whom they lead.
- Wise leaders listen: to those they lead, to qualified advisers, and to the Lord most of all.
- Wise leaders realize that they must earn the support of followers, not demand or coerce it.
- Wise leaders focus on the long-range benefits, not the short-term costs of their actions.

APPLICATIONS

- Listen carefully to those whom you lead. Are their concerns legitimate?
- Choose wisely those from whom you seek counsel. Are you seeking people who will have the wisdom and courage to challenge your viewpoints?
- Evaluate your motives honestly. Are you leading to get your will done, or God's?
- Think deeply about your goals. What legacy are you leaving by your present choices? Are you thinking short-term or long-term?

IV. LIFE APPLICATION

Fighting to the Better End

A national magazine carried the photograph of the fossil remains of two saber-tooth tigers locked in combat. The caption described it like this: "One had bitten deep into the leg bone of the other, a thrust that trapped both in a common fate. The cause of the death of the two cats is as clear as the causes of their extinction as a species is unclear."

Conflict is an inevitable part of life in a fallen world. Disagreements arise in the most loving of homes, and in the most healthy of churches, as well as in the most dysfunctional. The way a leader deals with conflict will determine the future health of those whom he leads.

Experts suggest that there are six responses to conflict: *avoidance* (nobody wins); *antagonism* (if I lose, you're going to lose); *capitulation* (I lose; you win); *competition* (I win; you lose); *compromise* (we both win a bit and lose a bit); and *cooperation* (we both win).

It is not always possible to have a win-win solution to a problem when sinful people are involved. But it was certainly possible in Rehoboam's situation and probably in most of the conflicts that arise in our homes and churches. We need to recognize that our immediate response may lead us down a path toward destructive conflict unless we seek the mind of Christ.

V. PRAYER

Father, when I am challenged or criticized, help me to remember the command of your Word to be quick to listen, slow to speak and slow to get angry, remembering that human anger does not bring about your righteousness (Jas. 1:19–20). Teach me, when I lack wisdom, to ask it of you (Jas. 1:5). Amen.

VI. DEEPER DISCOVERIES

A. Human Responsibility and God's Sovereignty (12:15)

When we read that "the king did not listen to the people, for this turn of events was from the LORD," we are not to think that God coerced the stubbornness of Rehoboam against his will. Rehoboam acted freely, but in such a way that he advanced God's hidden purposes. The Lord's hand is hidden, but he is at work. The greatest evidence that human freedom and divine sovereignty work compatibly is found in the crucifixion of our Lord Jesus, as described in Acts 2:23; 4:27–28.

B. Only the House of Judah (12:21)

The arithmetic of this section is interesting. In chapter 11, Ahijah tore his garment in twelve pieces and told Jeroboam that he would rule ten tribes and Rehoboam one tribe (11:30–32). What happened to the twelfth? In 12:20, we are told that "only the tribe of Judah remained loyal to the house of David." But the very next verse indicates that Rehoboam mustered "the whole house of Judah and the tribe of Benjamin." Benjamin was on the border between Judah and Israel. The tribe itself was divided between the two nations, although most of the tribe was incorporated into Judah, a much larger and more powerful tribe.

C. Shemaiah, the Man of God (12:22)

The term "man of God" is used in 1 and 2 Kings as a synonym for "prophet." It apparently emphasizes the prophet's status as a person who represents God as his spokesman. Because the Lord has revealed his truth to him, his message comes with divine authority: "This is what the Lord says."

VII. TEACHING OUTLINE

A. INTRODUCTION
1. Lead Story: Mistakes Leaders Make
2. Context: The death of Solomon brought about a critical moment for the Israelites. During his reign, grievances had arisen that his son Rehoboam had to address.
3. Transition: Every conflict presents both opportunity and danger. The path of wisdom will solidify the nation. The path of foolishness will inflict irreparable damage. Either path is available to Rehoboam at this moment.

B. COMMENTARY
1. Rehoboam's Confrontation (12:1–15)
2. Rehoboam's Civil War (12:16–24)
3. Rehoboam's Legacy (14:21–31)

C. CONCLUSION: TO SERVE OR TO BE SERVED

VIII. ISSUES FOR DISCUSSION
1. What can you learn from Rehoboam's example in terms of leadership and conflict in your local church and in your family?
2. Does a servant leader always do what those whom he leads want him to do? Is the supreme loyalty of a servant leader to his followers or to his Lord?
3. What should be the characteristics of those whom you seek out for counsel in a conflict situation?

1 Kings 12:25–13:34

Accept No Substitutes!

"*W*hat comes into our minds when we think about God is the most important thing about us. . . . Perverted notions about God soon rot the religion in which they appear."

A . W . T o z e r

BIOGRAPHICAL PROFILE: JEROBOAM I OF ISRAEL

- First came to prominence as an official of Solomon, supervising the northern labor force in a building project in Jerusalem (11:26–28)
- Involved in a rebellion against Solomon. When Solomon attempted to have him killed, he fled to Egypt (11:26a,40)
- Upon Solomon's death, his fellow Israelites summoned him back to Israel to help lead in the presentation of grievances to Rehoboam (12:2–3)
- Crowned king of Israel when the nation split
- Reigned in Israel from 931 to 909 B.C. over the new kingdom composed of the ten northern tribes
- His sin in setting up the golden calves was the defining moment in the history of the Northern Kingdom and ultimately resulted in the nation's destruction
- The fifth most-mentioned king in the Bible (after David, Saul, Solomon, and Hezekiah), but his influence was consistently negative

I N A N U T S H E L L

*A*s a new king over a new nation, Jeroboam faces the problem of how he can consolidate his kingdom. How can he keep his nation together when its religious system is focused outside of its borders in Jerusalem? The way Jeroboam resolves that problem leads his nation into a sin from which it never recovers.

Accept No Substitutes!

I. INTRODUCTION

Too Good to Be True?

A major tax preparation company launched a promotion to draw customers to use its services by giving walk-in customers the opportunity to participate in a drawing for one million dollars. A couple in New Jersey entered their names and thought no more about it. In fact, when the company representative phoned them at their home in Sewell, New Jersey, to inform them that they had won, Glen and Gloria Sims dismissed it as a practical joke.

The company persisted. They made further contact by mail and by phone, but the couple remained unconvinced. They now thought it was a scam, so they hung up the phone or threw the notices in the trash. After several weeks the company made one last attempt. They told the couple that the deadline for accepting their million dollars was drawing near. If they refused, the story of their refusal to accept the prize would be featured on NBC's *Today* show.

That got Glen Sims's attention. A few days later he appeared on the *Today* show to tell how he and his wife had finally believed the news and collected their million-dollar prize. The problem had never been with the company or the good faith of its offer but with their ability to believe their good fortune. "From the time this has been going on," he said, "H&R Block explained that they wanted a happy ending to all this. They were ecstatic that we finally accepted the prize."

Some news seems just too good to be true. In fact, that is the major problem many people have with the gospel of salvation. It seems too good to be true that everything we need to be right with God has already been done through the saving death and resurrection of the Lord Jesus and that all we need to do is to trust in him. Surely we need to earn it on our own, to take our salvation into our own hands, and to do it ourselves! The good news of God's grace is that salvation comes to us as God's free gift. All we need to do is to trust his promise.

The story in our present chapter is about a man who had received an amazing promise from God. God had given his word to Jeroboam that if he would only trust and obey him, the Lord would establish Jeroboam's family as a dynasty in Israel, as secure as David's dynasty in Judah. But such a promise seemed too good to be true. Jeroboam faced some major political problems that seemed to threaten his kingdom unless he took matters into his own hands. He did not really know or trust the Lord; therefore, he could not take God at his word. When he took matters into his own hands by doing what seemed politically expedient, he distorted and denied God's promise, launching a program that spelled disaster for him and his nation.

II. COMMENTARY

Accept No Subsitutes!

> **MAIN IDEA:** *When we fail to trust God and his promises and take matters into our own hands, we bring disaster upon ourselves and others.*

Jeroboam's Golden Calves (12:25–33)

> **SUPPORTING IDEA:** *When we doubt the God of the Word, we will distort the Word of God.*

12:25. Shechem was the city where the rebellion against the house of David had taken place. It now became the first capital of the new nation, as Jeroboam acted quickly to solidify his power. The city was strategically located in the hill country, commanding major roads. Shechem had spiritual significance because of its association with Abraham (Gen. 12:6) and Jacob (Gen. 33:18). Jereboam also moved across the Jordan River into the region of Gilead to fortify **Peniel** as a royal base in the area of Transjordan. This was also a place with rich patriarchal associations, the place where Jacob had wrestled with God (Gen. 32:30).

Jeroboam's kingdom was in its infancy. Every decision he made had great significance. As he came to the throne of the Northern Kingdom, Jeroboam had two priceless assets: an amazing promise from God himself through his prophet and a profound experience of God's faithfulness to his word. As we have seen, the Lord sent his prophet Ahijah to announce to Jeroboam that he was tearing ten tribes from the rule of Solomon and giving them to Jeroboam (1 Kgs. 11:29–39). Jeroboam did not earn his kingship; he received it as a gift of God's grace. He had become king not by political maneuvering but by the grace of God. He had seen God fulfill his promise to him, and he had every reason to believe that God would honor his promises.

12:26–27. The tragedy is that Jeroboam chose not to trust the Lord. He did have an obvious political problem. Although he had established a new capital and could build all the other institutions that an independent nation requires, Israel's worship of God centered in the temple in Jerusalem. The people in Jeroboam's kingdom in the north would be drawn back into the nation of Judah when they went to offer sacrifices or to celebrate God's festivals.

This seemed to Jeroboam, as he **thought to himself**, to be a political impossibility. It seemed inevitable that if the people continued to journey to Jerusalem, they would **again give their allegiance to their lord, Rehoboam**. In fact, Jeroboam feared that the people would rebel, assassinate him, and return to the house of David. He did not trust anyone—the people who crowned him and especially the God who made him king.

Jeroboam's lack of trust contradicted God's promise. The Lord had pledged to secure his throne if Jeroboam would walk in obedience before him. He had become king not by his own efforts but by God's grace. He had been protected from military attack not by his defenses but by God's intervention. Jeroboam chose not to trust God but to trust himself. He would protect his throne by actions which seemed sensible politically, but which took him into direct violation of the word of God.

12:28–33. Jeroboam's solution to his political problem was a substitute religion that violated every principle of God's law. If his goal was to flaunt God's law, he could hardly have succeeded more dramatically. Like Rehoboam he turned to the wrong advisors and established a new religion built around four innovations.

First, Jeroboam changed the object of worship by making **two golden calves**. This was a stunning act, seemingly done in direct imitation of Aaron's actions, recorded in Exodus 32. In fact, Jeroboam used almost precisely the words Aaron did when he displayed his idol: **Here are your gods, O Israel**. Jeroboam's words suggest that there was more than one god. This was not the worship of Baal but of the Lord. But it was a deviant, distorted, and paganized understanding of God. The calf or bull was a prominent fertility symbol in the Canaanite worship of Baal. Scholars have debated whether the calves represent an actual idol or a pedestal for the Lord (see "Deeper Discoveries"). These calves would suggest to the average Israelite that his "God" was a localized, paganized being, little different than those worshiped by the surrounding peoples.

Second, Jeroboam changed the place of worship. He built one shrine at Bethel, just north of the Judah-Israel border, and the second in the far north at Dan. His goal was to divert the people from Jerusalem. The two locations were intended to appeal to the people's desire for convenience and accessibility. Bethel, with its powerful associations with Jacob as "the house of God" (Gen. 28:17) and its geographical centrality, eventually became the central site. But it was in Jerusalem that God had placed his name and his glory. God's law prohibited multiplying places of worship (Deut. 12:4–14).

Third, Jeroboam changed the personnel of worship by appointing **priests from all sorts of people, even though they were not Levites**. In fact, the writer of 2 Chronicles indicates that Jeroboam specifically excluded the

Levites (2 Chr. 11:14). This again was a defiance of the law of God (Exod. 29:9; Num. 1:51; 3:10).

Jeroboam's fourth innovation was a change in the calendar of worship. He instituted a festival in **the eighth month, a month of his own choosing**. This involved moving the Feast of Tabernacles (also known as Booths or Sukkoth), from its divinely intended location in the seventh month (Lev. 23:33–44). This change seemed to be for no reason other than to make Jeroboam's religion distinctive.

The king's advisers probably hailed each of these changes as pragmatically necessary and politically shrewd. Jeroboam was a decisive leader and decision maker who was willing to do what was necessary, as he understood it, for the well-being of his nation. But God's verdict was very different: **this thing became a sin**. We will read of the sin of Jeroboam twenty-two times in 1 and 2 Kings, always with reference to his deviant worship of God. Jeroboam did not turn away from the Lord to worship Baal, although he mixed features of Baal worship into his system. Instead, he chose to worship the true God in a false way. God simply will not accept worship that distorts who he is, worship that is the product of human creativity or political expediency.

Jeroboam's religion was very popular. It was accepted immediately by the vast majority of the people, and it lasted as long as the nation of Israel did. But it was an abomination in the eyes of God. The true God must be worshiped in truth.

B Jeroboam's Condemned Altar (13:1–10)

SUPPORTING IDEA: *When we obey God's Word, we experience the power of God's Word.*

13:1. Jeroboam defied the word of God by his actions in chapter 12. But he did not escape the consequences. The first words of chapter 13 introduce us to the key phrase in the chapter, one that occurs seven times: **by the word of the LORD**. God sent an unnamed prophet, **a man of God from Judah**, with a message for Jeroboam. It was not the king who was determining the future, or even the prophet, but the word of God. God's word confronted Jeroboam in the act of his false worship, as he **was standing by the altar to make an offering**.

13:2–3. God's spokesman did not address the king. He ignored Jeroboam and spoke directly to the altar, the symbol of his counterfeit religion. It is a remarkable prediction that a king who would not live for more than three hundred years (although neither he nor Jeroboam could know this), **Josiah** of Judah, would desecrate the counterfeit altar by burning the bones of false priests on the false altar. This prophecy, whose fulfillment is recorded in 2 Kings 23:15–18, told Jeroboam two things: his religious system stood under divine condemnation, and the house of David would continue. God delivered a thundering no to the king's new religion.

13:4–6. Jeroboam acted to defend his cult against this threat to his regime. But he was powerless against the word of God. Not only was his hand **shriveled up** in instantaneous paralysis; he had to watch helplessly as the altar collapsed in front of him, in fulfillment of **the word of the LORD**. Jeroboam was forced to recognize the authority of God's messenger, and he pleaded with him to pray for the healing of his arm. Clearly Jeroboam was not in control of events; God was.

13:7–10. Jeroboam was not ready to concede defeat. He invited the man of God to share a meal with him. There was probably much more than a dinner invitation involved. Hospitality was a sign of fellowship in the ancient world. If the man of God were to accept the invitation, this would be seen as a public sign of approval and a virtual withdrawal of the words of judgment. But the man of God would have nothing to do with it. He was under divine orders, and he refused the dinner invitation.

C A Prophet's Sad Ending (13:11–32)

SUPPORTING IDEA: *When we disobey God's Word, we suffer the consequences.*

13:11. If the story had ended there, we would have been impressed by the man of God and his commitment to God's word. But the last section of the story is one of the most unusual in the Old Testament. We suddenly encounter **a certain old prophet living in Bethel**. His association with Bethel makes it likely that he was not only *in* Bethel but also *of* Bethel, loyal to Jeroboam's new regime. Apparently, he saw the man of God as a threat to the new religion, and he intended to harm him. But we are never explicitly told his motives. With his appearance, events take an unexpected turn.

13:12–19. The old prophet was determined to encounter the man of God. He found him sitting under an oak tree by the road he was taking back to Judah. We may wonder what the man of God was doing, sitting by the side of the road, since the implication of his God-given orders was that he was not to stop on his way home. The old prophet invited the man of God home to share a meal. Once again the man of God stated his orders clearly: he was to return home without delay. He knew what he was supposed to do.

The old prophet attempted to trump the orders of the man of God: **I too am a prophet . . . an angel said to me . . . "Bring him back with you."** There was no truth to this claim. But the man of God did not know that, so he accepted the prophet's claim as true and went with him.

13:20–22. When they had settled in the old prophet's home, the man of God received an authentic message from God: **You have . . . not kept the**

command the LORD **. . . gave you**. His disobedience brought judgment. The man of God would not reach home safely. He would die a violent death away from home and not be buried in the family tomb.

13:23–32. Events unfolded as the old prophet had said they would. The man of God set off for home, only to be attacked and killed by a lion. But the lion didn't follow its instincts. He stood by the body, protecting rather than devouring it, and the man's donkey stood beside it. This was a remarkable indication of God's supernatural oversight. When the old prophet heard the news, he rushed to get the body and buried him in his family tomb. In the last words he spoke we hear the message the story is intended to drive home: **The message he declared by the word of the** LORD **. . . will certainly come true**.

God's spokesman may fail; God's word will not! And if prophets cannot escape, neither can kings or ordinary people. The old prophet had set out to nullify God's word against the altar in Bethel. In the end he was forced to bear witness to its enduring power.

D Jeroboam's Determination (13:33–34)

SUPPORTING IDEA: *A person may know he is sinning and choose not to repent. The greater knowledge a person has, the more severe God's judgment when he fails to act on that knowledge.*

13:33–34. Jeroboam would have heard the story of the strange death of the man of God who had confronted him so boldly at the altar in Bethel. He had seen evidence of the power of God's word firsthand and heard about it from others. But having turned his back on God, he paid no attention. He **did not change his evil ways** but only reinforced his God-condemned religion. He would not repent. Jeroboam would not escape the consequences of his sin any more than the man of God did. Neither would his house or his nation because they persisted in his sin.

MAIN IDEA REVIEW: *When we fail to trust God and his promises and take matters into our own hands, we bring disaster upon ourselves and others.*

III. CONCLUSION

The Legacy of Distrust

The central issue in life is our view of God. If we know him as all-powerful, all-wise, and all-loving, we will trust his word, even when circumstances seem to defy the possibility that he will do what he said. We will also hold on to what he has revealed, not yielding to other people's claims to have revelation that replaces what God has clearly said. Nothing is more important for us as followers of Christ than to think thoughts of God that are worthy of him and to order our lives accordingly.

Jeroboam failed because he would not trust God. He trusted himself and his own solutions. He invented a god in his own image. This corrupted him as well as all who came after him. Distrust leaves a destructive legacy.

The man of God knew and witnessed the power of God's word. But in a time of crisis, he turned from what he knew, allowing someone else to intimidate him or impress him. He defied the word of God by taking matters into his own hands, and he experienced dire consequences. This reminds us of our need to live with great respect for the God of the Word and for the Word of God.

PRINCIPLES

- Our view of God will determine our confidence in the promises of his Word.
- God's Word has great power, even when people distrust it, distort it, or disobey it.
- There is a great difference between common sense and "God sense." Pragmatism can bring short-term gains with long-term pains.
- Claims to revelation from God need to be tested, and the standard of testing is God's Word.
- The person who delivers God's Word is not exempt from obeying God's Word. We stand under Scripture, not over it.

APPLICATIONS

- Cultivate a view of God that is worthy of him.
- Examine your life to determine whether you are taking matters into your own hands and out of God's hands.
- Be diligent in the study and application of God's Word to every area of your life.

IV. LIFE APPLICATION

The God Who Is There

The leader of the interfaith council of a major American city explained the ground rules of their events. Participants must avoid any specific references to deity. Rather than praying in the name of Jesus, Allah, or Shiva, they were to use such terms as Sustainer, Creator, God, or Lord. "There is a sense we are all worshiping the same God," he said. "We are sharing our various lenses of God, so we can grow and deepen our understanding."

Such a perspective is increasingly prevalent in our culture. But it stands in direct contrast to what we have seen in this passage. The living God was not willing to be seen through the lens of Jeroboam. He insisted on being seen as he had revealed himself. What he reveals about himself is far more important than what we want to think about him.

Modern pluralism seems polite, but it is an insult to God and destructive to people. It is also intellectual nonsense, since various religions are not worshiping the same God. In many cases religions contain incompatible understandings. Confusion about the character of God will always produce confusion about life and obscurity about God's salvation. All paths do not lead to heaven. The story of Jeroboam is a powerful reminder that the false worship of the true God is a sin that God will judge.

V. PRAYER

Father, help me to know you as you truly are. May the thoughts I think of you be controlled by your truth that is found in your Word. Build within me the kind of confidence that causes me to trust in you with my whole heart and not to lean on my own understanding (Prov. 3:5). Amen.

VI. DEEPER DISCOVERIES

A. Jeroboam's Golden Calves (12:28)

Jeroboam's golden calves, or bulls, were modeled on those made by Aaron (Exod. 32:4). Some scholars insist that Jeroboam's calves did not represent the Lord, but they were pedestals upon which the Lord sat. This may be true. But it is clear that they became an object of worship that the Lord calls an idol in Exodus 32:8. Hosea referred to them in the same way (Hos. 10:5). The association of the bull with the pagan fertility cult and its religiously sanctioned immorality made the new religion more pernicious. At best, the golden calves misled and confused the people. At worst, they blasphemed the true God.

B. The Sin of Idolatry (12:29; 13:34)

Israel was guilty of many sins, but from the perspective of 1 Kings, its worst sin was idolatry. This is clearly prohibited in the second commandment (Exod. 20:4–6; Deut. 5:8–10). Biblical worship is not based on human imagination but on divine revelation. A self-made god is a substitute, counterfeit god. Any idol distorts God's character, demeans God's glory, and subverts

God's authority. Ultimately, it debases our humanity because we become like the God we worship or imagine. An idol is anything that becomes a substitute for the living God. We need to avoid idols of the mind, as surely as we avoid idols of stone or gold.

C. "By the Word of the LORD" (13:1)

The repetition of this phrase seven times in this chapter (vv. 1–2,5,9,17–18,32) indicates that this is a major concern of the author of 1 Kings. The phrase "the word of the L ORD" also occurs four times (vv. 20–21,26[twice]). It is the word of God, not the power of the king or even the person of the prophet, that shapes events in the nation. The author wanted his readers in Babylon to sense the significance of God's word.

VII. TEACHING OUTLINE

A. INTRODUCTION

1. Lead Story: Too Good to Be True?
2. Context: The united kingdom has come to an abrupt end. The rebellion of the northern tribes has brought two new nations into being. Jeroboam, the newly crowned king of the Northern Kingdom, faces the challenge of making Israel a viable nation.
3. Transition: Jeroboam has received great promises from God about his kingdom. But now political reality seems to demand that he deal with the problem of the temple in Jerusalem.

B. COMMENTARY

1. Jeroboam's Golden Calves (12:25–33)
2. Jeroboam's Condemned Altar (13:1–10)
3. A Prophet's Sad Ending (13:11–32)
4. Jeroboam's Determination (13:33–34)

C. CONCLUSION: LEGACY OF DISTRUST

VIII. ISSUES FOR DISCUSSION

1. Most of us do not face the temptation to substitute physical idols for the true God. What can become golden calves in our lives?
2. We live in an age in which all views of God are considered equally valid. But the Bible makes clear that there is such a thing as false religion. What are the marks of the false and the true?

3. God does not deal with all acts of disobedience as he did with the man of God. How do we deal with those people who claim that they have a special word from God for us to follow?

1 Kings 14:1–16:28

The Law of the Harvest

I. **INTRODUCTION**
A State of Decay

II. **COMMENTARY**
A verse-by-verse explanation of these chapters.

III. **CONCLUSION**
"It's the Economy, Stupid!"

An overview of the principles and application from these chapters.

IV. **LIFE APPLICATION**
Faster in the Wrong Direction

Melding these chapters to life.

V. **PRAYER**
Tying these chapters to life with God.

VI. **DEEPER DISCOVERIES**
Historical, geographical, and grammatical enrichment of the commentary.

VII. **TEACHING OUTLINE**
Suggested step-by-step group study of these chapters.

VIII. **ISSUES FOR DISCUSSION**
Zeroing these chapters in on daily life.

| Q u o t e |

"*S*ooner or later everybody sits down

to a banquet of consequences."

R o b e r t   L o u i s   S t e v e n s o n

1 Kings 14:1–16:28

I N   A   N U T S H E L L

*T*he unfolding history of Judah and Israel reveals a disturbing pattern. The kings of both nations, with the exception of Asa, perpetuate the founder's sins, in spite of the clear warnings of God given through his prophets. The nations are reaping the consequences of their sins and are in a state of decay.

The Law of the Harvest

I. INTRODUCTION

A State of Decay

A friend of mine tells me that when he was transferred to California to take up a new responsibility, the company for which he worked was one of the strongest in the nation, an industry leader. Two decades later it no longer exists. Changing market conditions had something to do with that, but it is equally clear that conditions inside the company kept it from adapting to new conditions. The decay was not instantaneous, but it was terminal. The same can be said for churches, nations, and families. Death may be slow, but it is certain.

By this point in their histories, both Israel and Judah were in a state of decay. The glory days seemed far in the past, although only a few decades had passed. But the seeds sown by Solomon, Jeroboam, and Rehoboam were producing their ugly fruit. The leaders of both nations seemed to be locked into a pattern, repeating the same sinful actions over and over. Almost no one was willing to take the drastic action necessary to turn conditions around. The consequences were bitter, but they were inevitable. The most profound commentary on this passage is the declaration by the apostle Paul: "Do not be deceived: God cannot be mocked. A man reaps what he sows" (Gal. 6:7).

II. COMMENTARY

The Law of the Harvest

> **MAIN IDEA:** *What we sow in our lives will determine what we harvest.*

The Wages of Sin (14:1–20)

> **SUPPORTING IDEA:** *Sinful choices produce devastating consequences that begin at home and spread outwards.*

14:1–5. At some unspecified time in his reign, Jeroboam's young son **Abijah** became ill. The boy's name means "My father is Yahweh" and indicates that Jeroboam continued to see himself as a worshiper of God. He kept the externals of the faith, even though he had corrupted its essence. The unidentified illness was severe enough that Jeroboam worried for the life of his son. He told his wife to **disguise** herself in order to travel unrecognized to **Ahijah the prophet** at **Shiloh**. His directions suggested that Jeroboam had been estranged from **the one who told me I would be king over this people**. Jeroboam's idolatry had drawn the fiery anger of God's spokesman.

But King Jeroboam recognized Ahijah's authentic spiritual power and intended to manipulate him into a promise of healing for his son. If he could manipulate God's prophet, perhaps he could coerce God into acting on his behalf—a viewpoint that betrayed the depth of his pagan worldview. Jeroboam sent his wife with a modest gift for the prophet, one that would not give away her royal identity.

But Jeroboam had underestimated both God and his prophet. **Ahijah could not see; his sight was gone because of his age**. If Jeroboam had known of the prophet's blindness, he would have recognized the futility of a disguise. You don't need a disguise to fool a blind man! More significantly, he had underestimated the Lord, who had revealed Jeroboam's plan to his prophet. Ahijah wasn't dependent on his physical senses but on God's revelation. Human disguises are of no value before an all-seeing, all-knowing God!

14:6–16. Ahijah's greeting of Jeroboam's wife made clear that he had a source of information unrestricted by blind eyes: **Come in. . . . Why this pretense?** Ahijah delivered his message in the strongest of language, which reflected the anger of a righteous God against Jeroboam. He had only **bad news** for the rebellious king and his hapless wife. His message defined Jeroboam's sin (vv. 7–9) and declared God's inescapable judgment (vv. 10–16).

There were many sins for which God could have brought judgment upon his people. But the central issue throughout the history of the nation was always obedience to the first and second commandments: that the Lord alone must be worshiped and that he must be worshiped in truth without the evil of idolatry (Exod. 20:1–7). Failure to obey these simple requirements was a display of disrespect and ingratitude for the abundant goodness of God to his people.

That had certainly been the case with Jeroboam. God had graciously **raised** him up and made him the ruler of the kingdom he had torn away from David. **I gave it to you** was a reminder to Jeroboam that his elevation had been a display of sheer grace, but Jeroboam had responded in a very different way than David, **who kept my commands**. In fact, Jeroboam had made for himself **other gods**. This provoked God to anger.

Such sin would not go unpunished. Ahijah announced that divine judgment would take three forms. First, Jeroboam's sin would destroy his legacy (vv. 10–11). God had promised him "a dynasty as enduring as the one I built for David" (11:38) on the condition of obedience and spiritual loyalty. The condition had not been met. Instead of dynasty, there would be **disaster**—for Jeroboam and for **every last male** in his lineage. Every human trace of Jeroboam was to be removed from the nation. Jeroboam's family would become a pile of **dung**. They would die violent deaths in disgrace and would be unburied and unlamented.

Second, Jeroboam's sin would devastate his family. His son would not recover (vv. 12–13). Jeroboam's wife was given the awful news: **When you set foot in your city, the boy will die**. The king's sin would break a mother's heart and cost a young boy's life. But the boy's death would be different from that of other members of the family; he would be mourned, and he alone of Jeroboam's descendants would be buried. It would have seemed small consolation to the grieving mother that, through premature death, Abijah would escape the disaster that Jeroboam's sin was about to bring down upon the family.

Third, Jeroboam's sin would damage his nation (vv. 14–16). The end of Jeroboam's dynasty would not mark the end of his nation: **The LORD will raise up for himself a king over Israel**. But his sin had introduced two certainties into the history of his nation: instability and exile. The former was to be the permanent character of the Northern Kingdom: there would be nineteen kings in 210 years, with a series of assassinations and coups. The latter, exile, became reality in 722 B.C. when Israel ceased to exist as a political entity. It was scattered among the nations **beyond the** (Euphrates) **River**. The poison of idolatry, one form of which was **Asherah poles**, would have its deadly effect. God would reject Israel because of the sins Jeroboam had committed and had caused Israel to commit.

14:17–18. The journey home must have been long and terrifying for Jeroboam's wife. If the prophet were correct, her arrival home would bring death to her son. Events turned out just **as the LORD had said**. The boy died, was mourned, and was buried. It was the word of God that was shaping events. The rest of 1 Kings will show that Ahijah's warnings of instability and exile would come true.

14:19–20. No further information is given about Jeroboam's reign, other than its duration of **twenty-two years**. Secular historians would regard much about the career of Jeroboam as a success. The biblical writer sees him only as a failure. He was one of his nation's most important kings, but his influence was entirely negative. Every single northern king would perpetuate the sin of Jeroboam until God finally declared "enough" and terminated the nation's existence. His was a sad story of what might have been—but was not, because of sin.

B A Vicious Cycle (14:21–15:24)

SUPPORTING IDEA: *A godly response to sin can reverse a course of destruction.*

Verse 21 introduces a pattern that will become familiar through much of the rest of 1 Kings. The writer of 1 Kings is now telling the story of two kingdoms,

Israel and Judah. He does so one kingdom at a time. The history of Israel is now frozen by the writer at the death of Jeroboam, and he directs attention to events in Judah, which will take us through 15:24. He will then return to Israel. This period of history, so soon after the national disruption, was a time of conflict, especially over the mutual border. Irritations were inevitable, since Bethel and Jerusalem were only ten miles apart.

Judah's history, for the most part, would be marked by political stability. There would always be a Davidic king, except for the six-year usurpation of wicked queen Athaliah (2 Kgs. 11). But there would not be spiritual stability. Judah would often find itself on a moral and spiritual downward spiral. But God would occasionally raise up a godly king, a man with the heart of David who would stop the decline by initiating godly reforms. In the Northern Kingdom, God's agents were godly prophets. In the Southern Kingdom, they were godly kings. That pattern becomes evident in this initial portrayal of events in Judah.

14:21–31. We have already considered these verses. For our present purposes, we need to note that the spiritual influence of Judah's first king, Rehoboam (reigned 930–913 B.C.), was little different from that of Israel's first king, Jeroboam. Rehoboam did not pollute worship in the temple, but he did introduce Canaanite perversions into the land. As a result, Judah sinned by turning to **high places, sacred stones and Asherah poles**. There were even **shrine prostitutes** in the land. In 14:15, we are told that Israel "provoked the LORD to anger." Now we read that by the sins Judah committed they stirred up the Lord's **jealous anger**. Rehoboam was only marginally better than Jeroboam. He also set his nation on a path toward national disaster.

15:1–8. Rehoboam was succeeded on the throne by his son **Abijah** (reigned 913–910 B.C.). Sadly, he was his father's son both physically and spiritually, committing **all the sins his father had done**. His reign was short, only **three years**. Although we are not told the cause of his death, we are given a diagnosis of his spiritual problem: **His heart was not fully devoted to the LORD . . . as the heart of David . . . had been.** This expression in 1 Kings points to a lack of exclusive loyalty to God, because of idolatry and involvement at the high places. The course was downward. Solomon had divided his heart, and those who followed him also rejected the way of exclusive loyalty to the Lord.

The defining difference between Judah and Israel was the enduring legacy of David. He had lived with a heart of devotion to his Lord and had done what was right, **except in the case of Uriah the Hittite** (both his adultery with Uriah's wife and his arrangement of Uriah's death). However, it was not David's merit but God's covenant of grace to David that set Judah apart. The Lord had promised David **a lamp in Jerusalem**, an heir (1 Kgs. 11:36; 2 Kgs. 8:19). God had already acted **for David's sake** (1 Kgs. 11:12–13,32,34), and he will do so again throughout 1 Kings. The promise of Messiah, the son of David, was central, not only to Judah's history but to all of salvation history, leading to the Lord Jesus Christ. He is not only "the lamp of David"; he is "the light of the world" (John 8:12).

15:9–24. Abijah's son **Asa** (reigned 910–869 B.C.) was a person of different character. He reigned over the nation of Judah longer than anyone before him. During his forty-one-year regime, six different kings sat on the throne of the sister nation Israel. What set Asa apart was not the duration of his reign but his devotion. He **did what was right in the eyes of the LORD, as his father David had done.** He was one of Judah's few good kings, ranking with Jehoshaphat, Hezekiah, and Josiah. His devotion went beyond the personal. He attacked the spiritual vices that had plagued his nation from the time of Solomon. Three specific reforms were conducted during Asa's reign.

He removed the Canaanite cult **prostitutes** with whom worshipers had sexual relations to induce agricultural or personal fertility. He also destroyed pagan **idols**, another action that must have aroused the anger of dedicated idolaters. Finally, he **deposed his grandmother Maacah**, who held the important court position of **queen mother**. She not only was involved in pagan fertility worship; she had sponsored an **Asherah pole**. Asa dealt with the pole as well, cutting it down and burning it. His reformation was not perfect: he did not **remove the high places.** Sadly, this will be said of the Judean kings until the time of Josiah (2 Kgs. 23).

Nevertheless, **Asa's heart was fully committed to the LORD all his life**. A further evidence of his commitment to God was his desire to enrich the temple. Apparently, his father had begun to set aside **silver and gold and** special **articles**. Asa not only added to their number; he brought them into the temple, which had been stripped of its treasures to buy off Shishak in the time of Rehoboam (14:25–28). Abijah's interest in the project was unexpected; Asa's was consistent with his lifestyle of devotion to the Lord.

Asa's main military and political concerns revolved around the border with Israel. Israel's king, **Baasha** (see 15:27), fortified **Ramah**, a city five miles north of Jerusalem. This blockaded Asa in his capital, prevented movement between the two nations, and restricted trade. The situation was untenable, but Asa felt unable to deal with it on his own. So he enlisted the help of **Ben-Hadad**, king of Aram (Syria). He emptied the palace and temple treasures and sent them to Damascus with the plea that Ben-Hadad break his **treaty** with Israel, form an alliance with Asa, and force Baasha to withdraw.

Ben-Hadad accepted the bribe. He then marched against Israel from the northwest. The attack was focused on upper Galilee, and Baasha was forced to withdraw his troops from his southern border to fortify his capital city of Tirzah. When he withdrew, Asa seized the opportunity to dismantle the fortifications. He then conscripted the entire nation to tear down the barriers and, using the same materials, fortified two other border towns, **Geba** and **Mizpah**. This pushed the border several miles north, providing a larger defensive buffer zone for his capital city.

But this came at a cost. This was the first appearance of Syria as an active player in the region. Asa's treaty whetted Syria's appetite for more military advances in the region. More importantly, Asa's actions violated his commitment to God. He had looked to Syria rather than to God for relief, an action that received a biting indictment from the prophet Hanani (2 Chr. 16:7–10). Asa had committed himself to enrich the temple of the Lord. But this treaty forced him to take **all the silver and gold** left in the temple. This should have indicated that he was on the wrong course.

Asa reigned for a long time and died in old age, perhaps from complications related to the fact that **his feet became diseased**. He had not been a perfect king, but he was one of Judah's best. Only Hezekiah and Josiah receive higher praise. He stopped the movement of his nation into deeper departure from obedience to God. A godly king determined to obey his God had made a significant difference. Such kings, rare though they were, set Judah apart from Israel.

"A Reed Swaying in the Water" (15:25–16:28)

SUPPORTING IDEA: *Sin causes a descending spiral that destabilizes life.*

15:25–32. The author of 1 Kings now "freeze-frames" the story of Judah and returns to Israel. The North will be in our focus almost to the end of 1 Kings (see 22:41). Jeroboam had been told by God's prophet that his dynasty would not endure (14:10–11). That judgment now fell on his son **Nadab** (reigned 909–908 B.C.). In spite of the prophetic warning to his father, there was no sign of repentance or reform. Nadab was no Asa! He was his father's son, **walking in the ways of his father and in his sin**. This is the constant refrain used for Israel's kings.

Nadab's reign was brought to an abrupt end after only two years when he was assassinated by **Baasha**, a citizen of the tribe of **Issachar** (we met him in 14:16). Choosing a time when Nadab was in the field with his army, Baasha struck the king down **at Gibbethon**, a Philistine city. The fact that Baasha could carry off his coup when Nadab was surrounded by his army and could then take over military command reveals that there was widespread unhappiness with Nadab's leadership.

The violence did not stop with the king. Baasha **killed Jeroboam's whole family**. This not only solidified Baasha's position by eliminating all claimants to the throne; it fulfilled the prophecy of the prophet **Ahijah the Shilonite** (14:10–16). Once again the writer strikes the note of the fulfillment of the prophetic word, a consistent theme throughout 1 Kings. Israel's kings did not call the nation back to God, but the Lord continually raised up prophets who did.

15:33–16:7. Baasha (reigned 908–886 B.C.) moved quickly to consolidate his power. He was to remain on the throne for twenty-four years, the third longest reign in Israel's history. He may have replaced the family of Jeroboam politically. But he continued in his spiritual tradition of sin and rebellion: He walked **in the ways of Jeroboam and in his sin**. Baasha had not come to the throne as a spiritual reformer but only for personal power. As a result, we are told nothing of his reign other than his spiritual rebellion. The writer of 1 Kings is not concerned about **what he did and his achievements**. They are not important, in light of the fact that he provoked the Lord **to anger by the things he did**. This provocation of the Lord was so characteristic of the man that it is repeated twice in the nine verses that summarize his life.

Once again a prophet came to the forefront. God raised up **Jehu son of Hanani** to pronounce his judgment. Baasha had been God's agent, lifted up from obscurity by the Lord to become **leader** in Israel. But his continuance of the sins of Jeroboam had provoked God to anger. As a result, he would establish no dynasty, and his family would die violently in disgrace and dishonor.

16:8–22. The descent of Israel into instability now accelerated. Baasha's son **Elah** (reigned 886–885 B.C.) reigned only for **two years**. In fulfillment of Jehu's prophecy, he became the victim of one of his military commanders, **Zimri** (reigned 885 B.C.). The circumstances of his death were less than honorable. While a major portion of his army was in the field, Elah was in the capital city of Tirzah, **getting drunk** in the home of a palace official. Zimri assassinated the king, seized power, and then slaughtered the royal family. This ruthlessness was intended to remove every potential claimant to the throne, but it served to fulfill **the word of the LORD spoken against Baasha**.

But Zimri had overreached. He had no base of support. When news of his coup reached the army encamped near Gibbethon, the response was immediate. Omri, commander of the army, was proclaimed king over Israel. Zimri's coup had no chance of success against such military opposition. Omri pulled the army away from Gibbethon and attacked Zimri at Tirzah. Zimri, realizing that his cause was hopeless, committed suicide. He had royal power for only seven days.

But Omri's victory over Zimri did not bring stability to the nation. Israel split into two factions; one-half supported Tibni for king, and the other half supported Omri. The nature of this division is not clarified. We do not know which part of the nation was loyal to Tibni, or why. This situation apparently lasted for four years. All we know is that the followers of Omri were **stronger than those of Tibni**. The cryptic statement **so Tibni died** does not indicate whether his death was natural or violent. Regardless, Omri finally emerged as the unrivalled king of the nation, the sixth king in forty-five years, from four different families. The nation had become what the prophet had predicted: "a reed swaying in the water" (14:15).

16:23–28. With the emergence of Omri (reigned 885–874 B.C.), everything changed. He was the first to establish a dynasty in Israel, one that would last for four kings (Omri, Ahab, Ahaziah, and Jehoram) and forty-five years. The Omride kings were leaders of significant ability, but they were a spiritual disaster, bringing Israel to its greatest spiritual crisis. Once again God would address their apostasy through prophets, in this case two of his greatest—Elijah and Elisha. The ministry of both men would be devoted to opposing the Omride kings and their Baal-worshiping ways.

Omri did not need to slaughter any rivals when he came to the throne, since Zimri had already accomplished that. He was a man of great ability and skill. His twelve-year reign included the period of conflict with Tibni. Nevertheless, he managed to reunite his nation and to establish a new national capital at **Samaria**. He chose a central site that could be easily defended. For the remainder of the history of the nation, Samaria was its capital. Under the Omrides it became a city of great beauty and prosperity. Omri also apparently ended the incessant conflict with Judah and made a strategic alliance with Phoenicia by the marriage of his son Ahab to the Phoenician princess Jezebel. He became an international figure. For years afterward the Assyrian Chronicles referred to Israel as "the land of Omri."

In secular terms Omri was a great and successful king. In biblical terms he was the worst of kings since Jeroboam. He increased the momentum of paganism, paving the way for the importation of Baal worship in the time of his son Ahab.

MAIN IDEA REVIEW: *What we sow in our lives will determine what we harvest.*

III. CONCLUSION

"It's the Economy, Stupid!"

The first presidential campaign of Bill Clinton was conducted around the premise that the only issue of real importance to the voters was the condition of the economy. Whatever issues might emerge, the one the Clintonians returned to again and again was the need to turn around the economy and to restore Americans to prosperity. The tactic worked, and Clinton was elected. But reducing a campaign to economics alone elevates the important to the primary. Authentic and effective leadership must be about much more than money. Some of the kings judged by God as abject failures presided over times of prosperity, but the Lord repudiated them.

The writer of 1 Kings saw things in a different way. "It's loyalty to God and his word," he tells us. Leaders are responsible for their own moral and spiritual integrity, lived out through exclusive commitment to God and his commands. There can be no compromise with competing gods, no playing with his commands, no subverting of his standards. When loyalty to God is compromised, the only hope is repentance and reform. In the absence of these, a nation begins to reap the consequences of the sin it has sown. God will not be mocked.

PRINCIPLES

- Sinful choices have significant consequences not only for us, but also for those who follow us.
- God's judgment is not always postponed to a future time.
- God will not tolerate anything less than exclusive loyalty to him.
- God is faithful to his promises, even in the midst of human failure.
- A godly son can come from an ungodly father. Sadly, the reverse is also true. We are the product of our choices, not just our parents.
- God's measure of success is different from that of the world.

APPLICATIONS

- Take sin in your life seriously, not deceiving yourself that you can get away with it.
- Guard your heart against all loyalties that compete with your loyalty to the triune God.
- Accept responsibility for your own life, refusing to see yourself as a victim of others' choices.
- Live in the belief that your life can make an impact for good.
- Measure your life by God's standards, and reject the shallow perspective of culture.

IV. LIFE APPLICATION

Faster in the Wrong Direction

I was late and, although I wouldn't admit it, I was lost. I increased my speed, but none of the landmarks I had expected were in view. But I pressed on, convinced that if I just kept going, I would find myself where I wanted to be. Finally, reason and the persistent voice of my wife caused me to turn around.

Going faster in the wrong direction will never get you to your destination. The only way forward is to go back where you went wrong and to head in the right direction. That was precisely the need of both Judah and Israel. Judah had gone wrong when Solomon permitted worship at the high places even after the temple had been completed. His son had compounded his problem by permitting pagan worship in his nation. Israel's wrong turn had been taken by Jeroboam, by his introduction of the golden calves and the polluting of genuine worship. But no king of Israel was willing to deal with the Bethel and Dan cults. Each one of them followed in the steps of Jeroboam. And no king in Judah before Josiah was deeply committed to attacking the problem of the high places. They all kept going faster in the wrong direction.

It is an issue we need to face honestly in our own lives. If we make a wrong turn, there is no way we can get to our destination until we turn around and deal with it in the presence of God. Anything else is simply moving faster in the wrong direction.

V. PRAYER

Father, give me a repentant heart which responds quickly to your Spirit's conviction. Give me the wisdom to see my sin and the humility to confess it in your presence. Amen.

VI. DEEPER DISCOVERIES

A. Seventeen or Eighteen Years? (14:21; 15:1)

A comparison of these two verses raises a question about how long Rehoboam reigned (seventeen or eighteen years). The solution is interesting because it illustrates some of the challenges of chronology in the books of 1 and 2 Kings. Judah followed the accession year method, in which the first year of a king began only with the first day of the next calendar year. Any time before that was considered an accession year. On the other hand, Israel used the non-accession year system, which began counting as soon as the king came to the throne. To make matters even more complex, both nations switched their methods at later times. Another factor is that Israel's calendar began in the spring (Nisan), Judah's in the fall (Tishri). In this context the difference in numbers (seventeen or eighteen) represents a difference in the ways of computing regnal years. Rehoboam reigned for seventeen actual years.

B. The Asherah (14:23; 15:13)

Asherah was a Canaanite goddess, the consort of the god El and also of Baal. Often depicted naked, she was the mother goddess of the Canaanite fertility cult, one of the major figures in the pagan pantheon. The Asherah pole was a wooden object associated with the cult of the goddess. There seemed to be strong sexual overtones to her worship. The mention of male shrine prostitutes indicates that immorality was linked with the idolatry. The Asherah cult was very resilient, persisting until the time of the Babylonian captivity (2 Kgs. 21:3,7; 23:4,13,15).

C. Ben-Hadad of Aram

This is a throne name for three Aramean (Syrian) kings who are mentioned in Israel's history. The name means "Son of Hadad," Hadad being the name of a Syrian god, "the thunderer," the equivalent of Baal. *Aram* is an ethnic term that describes a people (their language was Aramaic), while *Syria* is a geographical term that identifies a region, with Damascus as its capital. Their treaty with Asa was the first entry of the Arameans of Damascus into Israel and Judah's life. They eventually became a major rival in the region.

VII. TEACHING OUTLINE

A. INTRODUCTION

1. Lead Story: A State of Decay
2. Context: As the first generation leaders of Judah and Israel pass off the scene, the new kings have the opportunity to maintain the past or to turn back to God. Sadly, most of them decide to keep going in the wrong direction, even though the Lord makes clear that they are headed the wrong way.
3. Transition: We have seen both Jeroboam and Rehoboam lead their nations in disastrous directions. We return to see how they ended their tenure in this section and how this influenced those who followed them.

B. COMMENTARY

1. The Wages of Sin (14:1–20)
2. A Vicious Cycle (14:21–15:24)
3. "A Reed Swaying in the Water" (15:25–16:28)

C. CONCLUSION: "IT'S THE ECONOMY, STUPID!"

VIII. ISSUES FOR DISCUSSION

1. Asa is one of the few examples of a godly king in Judah, although he was not without defects. What positive qualities do you see in his life?

2. Prophets play an important role in this section. Is there a pattern to their ministry?
3. Omri was a great success in secular terms, an abject failure in biblical terms. Discuss the difference and its relevance for modern life.

1 Kings 16:29–17:24

God's Man for the Times

I. **INTRODUCTION**
Standing in the Gap

II. **COMMENTARY**
A verse-by-verse explanation of these passages.

III. **CONCLUSION**
He's All I Need

An overview of the principles and application from these passages.

IV. **LIFE APPLICATION**
At His Best

Melding these passages to life.

V. **PRAYER**
Tying these passages to life with God.

VI. **DEEPER DISCOVERIES**
Historical, geographical, and grammatical enrichment of the commentary.

VII. **TEACHING OUTLINE**
Suggested step-by-step group study of these passages.

VIII. **ISSUES FOR DISCUSSION**
Zeroing these passages in on daily life.

Q u o t e

"*God* fits the man for the hour and the hour for the man. There is a voice for the hour and an hour for the voice."

C h a r l e s   S p u r g e o n

(d e s c r i b i n g   J o h n   W y c l i f f e)

BIOGRAPHICAL PROFILE: AHAB

- A son of Omri, he reigned for twenty-two years in Israel (874–853 B.C.)
- Married Jezebel, the daughter of Ethbaal, the king-priest of Phoenicia
- Fortified Israelite cities (22:39) and did extensive construction in the capital city of Samaria, especially an elaborate ivory-inlaid palace (22:39)
- His reign coincided with that of Jehoshaphat of Judah (872–848 B.C.), with whom he had both a military (1 Kgs. 22) and marital alliance (2 Kgs. 8:18,26)
- Went to war with Aram (Syria) under Ben-Hadad (20:1–43; 22:1–38)
- His promotion of Baal worship and his refusal to do anything about Jezebel's slaughter of true followers of the Lord marked him as the worst of Israel's kings (16:30,33; Mic. 6:16)
- Clashed with the prophet Elijah
- Died in battle against Syria, as prophesied by the prophet Micaiah (22:17,23,37–38)

1 Kings 16:29–17:24

IN A NUTSHELL

After years of instability, Israel finally has a stable government. But it is also a rebellious kingdom, as Ahab and Jezebel work to rebuild the nation on a foundation of Baal worship. The Lord raises up his prophet Elijah to challenge this departure of Israel from its roots and from its covenant commitment to the only true God.

God's Man for the Times

I. INTRODUCTION

Standing in the Gap

*W*hen I was in high school, one of my heroes was a young man named Jim Elliot, an acquaintance of my parents. He and his four companions had been killed while trying to reach a jungle tribe in Ecuador, then known as the Aucas, with the gospel of Christ. His wife's book about his brief life, *Shadow of the Almighty,* had a profound effect upon me. In it, she recorded a journal entry Jim Elliot had made as a student at Wheaton College in 1948: "Father, make of me a crisis man. Bring those I contact to decision. Let me not be a milepost on a single road. Make me a fork that people may turn one way or another on facing Christ in me."

That longing to make a difference for the sake of the kingdom was richly answered. The deaths of those five young men profoundly affected their generation of Christians. Now, in a new millennium and a vastly changed culture, the need is still the same—for followers of Christ who will commit themselves to make a difference for the glory of God.

One of the attributes needed for this task is courage. The terrorist atrocities against the United States on September 11, 2001, gave a new appreciation for the virtue of courage and a new gratitude for those who put their lives on the line for the public good.

Courage of a spiritual variety is what comes to mind when we think about the prophet Elijah. One of the great laments of Scripture is found in Ezekiel 22:30: "I looked for a man among them who would build up the wall and stand before me in the gap on behalf of the land so I would not have to destroy it, but I found none." That could not be said in Elijah's time. At a time of desperate spiritual need in his nation, he stood in the gap, virtually alone, for the cause of the Lord. His world was very different from ours, but the issues that called him to stand with courage and conviction are relevant to the twenty-first century.

II. COMMENTARY

God's Man for the Times

MAIN IDEA: *Spiritual courage, the capacity to stand for the Lord, comes from commitment to the Word of God.*

A Ahab's Spiritual Rebellion (16:29–34)

SUPPORTING IDEA: *Each generation faces a distinct attack on the truth of God.*

16:29. Charles Dickens's novel *A Tale of Two Cities* begins with a famous sentence: "It was the best of times, it was the worst of times." The same could be said about the reign of **Omri** and his son **Ahab**. With the coming to power of the house of Omri, Israel entered a time of peace with its neighbor Judah. It was also a time of increasing regional power, international prominence, and economic prosperity. Archaeologists suggest that the craftsmanship discovered in the Samaria of Ahab's day was unequalled in quality. During the **twenty-two years** of Ahab's reign (874–853 B.C.) he consolidated and expanded his father's achievements. His military was a force to be reckoned with. He put two thousand chariots and ten thousand troops in the field at the Battle of Qarqar in 853 when he joined Syria to resist the emerging regional superpower, Assyria. The Assyrians claimed victory, but it then withdrew its armies from the region for a time. A secular historian would be inclined to speak well of the accomplishments of Ahab.

16:30–33. But the Bible has a different perspective. It was indeed the worst of times: **Ahab . . . did more evil . . . than any . . . before him**. It would have been bad enough if Ahab had just followed his father and all the previous kings and **considered it trivial to commit the sins of Jeroboam son of Nebat**. But Ahab did not repudiate the perverted worship of the Lord through the idolatrous worship of the golden calves instituted by Jeroboam. Ahab considered himself a follower of the Lord. But he also **began to serve Baal and worship him**. Polytheism—the worship of many gods—had come to Israel.

The most powerful influence in Ahab's life was his wife **Jezebel**. Her father Ethbaal ruled Sidon and the entire region of Phoenicia for thirty-three years. He was not just a king but a king-priest, serving the god Baal Melqart. His daughter was a fervent follower of Baal. She was determined not only to worship Baal personally but also to make Baal worship the state religion of Israel. Her influence enticed her husband to Baal worship, and **he set up an altar for Baal . . . in Samaria**. She also supported the prophets of Baal from the royal table (18:19) and set out to execute all the followers of God who insisted that the first commandment still applied and that the Lord alone was to be worshiped in Israel (18:4,13). Under Ahab and Jezebel, Baal worship became the official state religion of Israel.

Baal was the storm god, the "rider of the clouds" who exercised control over rain, wind, and clouds. As the fertility god, he became the most significant deity, since life depended on rain and harvest. The stories of the gods were full of violence, cruelty, rape, and seduction. Baal worship was characterized by idolatry and immorality that went along with cult prostitution. The mother goddess **Asherah** was sometimes depicted as Baal's enemy—but more often as his consort. Often depicted as the naked goddess, the goddess of fertility, she was honored by a wooden pole or a stone pillar, which probably had sexual implications.

Ahab and Jezebel did not reject the worship of God (in its corrupted form at Bethel) or insist that everyone worship Baal only. Polytheism tolerated the worship of any god. The insistence of the Lord that he alone was the true God and that he only was to be worshiped, served, and obeyed was intolerable to Jezebel. She hated the God of Moses and Elijah—the one who insisted on exclusive loyalty. The names of the gods have changed, but this is the central issue of our time. Everyone is happy, as long as we speak of spirituality and a generic deity. But when we insist on the finality of Jesus' claims, "I am the way, the truth and the life; no one comes to the Father except by me," battle lines are drawn!

16:34. A curious note ends this chapter. We are told that **Hiel of Bethel** (the center of the Jeroboam cult) **rebuilt Jericho**. He could not have done so without the permission of Ahab. But his project was at the cost of two of his sons, **in accordance with the word of the LORD spoken by Joshua.** Joshua had placed a curse on anyone who attempted to rebuild the city of Jericho (Josh. 6:26). Ahab and Hiel defied this curse, and it cost Hiel two sons. It is not known whether the pagan Hiel offered his two sons as sacrifices or whether two terrible accidents occurred. What is important is that this was precisely what Joshua had prophesied more than five hundred years earlier. God's promise will not fail, no matter how long it takes. Ahab's defiance of God could not succeed because God's word was acting against it.

B Elijah's Declaration (17:1)

SUPPORTING IDEA: *Spiritual courage calls us to fight for the glory of God, standing alone, if necessary, against the false gods of our generation.*

17:1. The word of God entered the scene in dramatic fashion. Out of nowhere God's prophet burst on the scene to confront the king, who was at the height of his power. The writer of 1 Kings has done nothing to prepare us for this moment: **Now Elijah the Tishbite, from Tishbe in Gilead, said to Ahab**. The location of Tishbe is uncertain, and there is much we do not know about this man. His name was significant because it conveyed his message. *Elijah* means "my God is Yahweh," a name that shouted defiance to Ahab while declaring allegiance to the Lord. The author of 1 Kings at this point makes a significant change. From 1 Kings 17 to 2 Kings 9, the central figures in his history will not be kings but two prophets, Elijah and Elisha. God did not raise up an army or an organization to oppose the power of an evil king or the spread of baalism. Rather, he used two men who were armed with the word of the Lord.

Elijah's message to Ahab was brief, but it went like an arrow to the central issue: **There will be neither dew nor rain in the next few years, except at my word**. And with those brief words, the prophet was gone. He had defined the issue and drawn the battle lines. Elijah was convinced that the Lord, in contrast to Baal, was the living God. Canaanite mythology talked about Baal dying each year and coming back to life to bring the rains. Elijah knew that such a belief was nonsense, since Baal was a fraud. The Lord alone was the living God. Furthermore, he was the sovereign God who claimed the nation as his own, "the God of Israel" who would tolerate no rivals.

Elijah attacked Baal at his strongest point. Baal claimed to be "the rider of the clouds," the storm god who controlled the rains and the crops. Very well, then, "there will be neither dew nor rain." The Lord would demonstrate that he is the God of all things, including rain and storm.

Elijah's Training Camp (17:2–24)

SUPPORTING IDEA: *Spiritual courage is sustained only as we are trained to know him better and to trust him more.*

Elijah emerged from nowhere to confront Ahab with the word of the Lord. Then he disappeared from the public arena for three years while the drought took hold and the nation felt the effects of God's judgment. Those three years were silent years in terms of public ministry, but they were significant years as Elijah was prepared for the great battle on Mount Carmel, recorded in chapter 18.

17:2–7. Elijah's confrontation with King Ahab was followed by a divine command. The reference to **the word of the LORD** introduces an important theme of this chapter (vv. 5,8,16,24). Elijah lived his life under the authority of God's word, whether he was obeying it or proclaiming it. Elijah was to leave the area **and hide in the Kerith Ravine** in an isolated area. Here he would be protected from the wrath of Ahab and Jezebel. It would also serve as a place of preparation for Elijah. This command from God was accompanied by a promise, which was also a call to faith: **drink from the brook, and . . .**

the ravens [will] **feed you there**. This demanded faith because the brook that ran through the Kidron was a wadi, a stream that flowed only during the rainy season—hardly a long-term source of water when a drought was on the way. And ravens were untamed scavengers, not providers. How could they serve as a food source?

Nevertheless, Elijah followed God's instructions. He made his way to the wadi Kerith, where he spent a period of time. It was a place of total dependence upon God, and the Lord demonstrated his sufficiency by providing food and water for Elijah. In the midst of the drought, God demonstrated that he, not Baal, was the God of nature who could provide all the resources that Elijah required. This was crucial training for the later event at Mount Carmel. Elijah was learning the absolute reliability of the Lord.

But there was another challenge to Elijah's faith: **some time later the brook dried up**. The irony was that God was answering Elijah's prayer that there would be neither dew nor rain (17:1), and Elijah was experiencing the consequences of his own prayer being answered! Nevertheless, he did not leave the place where God had sent him until the Lord said he could. He was submissive to the Lord's timing, and he waited for the Lord to communicate the next step. Kerith was Elijah's "boot camp" where he learned that God, not Baal, was the Lord of creation, the God of rain and crops.

17:8–16. The next divine instruction was even more remarkable than the first. God told Elijah to go **to Zarephath of Sidon and stay there**. Zarephath was located eight miles south of Sidon, the very region where Jezebel's father Ethbaal ruled. This was the heartland of Baal worship, Baal's home territory, a remarkable place for the prophet of God to be protected! Was this a place where the Lord's power could be seen? God also told the prophet that he directed **a widow in that place to supply you with food**. Widows were marginalized in ancient society, the first to suffer in times of drought and famine. Most widows were dependent on the charity of others. This was hardly the place a person would look for help.

In spite of the strangeness of this command and promise, Elijah obeyed. He went to Zarephath, traveling through the heart of his own country. At the town gate, he saw a widow, probably identifiable by her characteristic widow's black dress, **gathering sticks**. This was hardly a person with significant resources that could be placed at Elijah's disposal. But Elijah recognized in her the widow God intended to meet his needs, so he entered into a dialogue with her. Relying upon cultural traditions that made hospitality and kindness to strangers a duty, he asked her for **a little water in a jar**. He added a second request: **bring me, please, a piece of bread**.

The prophet's request had trapped the woman between the demands of hospitality and her own desperate condition: **I don't have any bread—only a handful of flour in a jar and a little oil in a jug. I am gathering a few sticks**

to take home and make a meal for myself and my son, that we may eat it—
and die. The drought that Elijah's words had brought on Israel was devastating Phoenicia as well.

The situation must have been startling to Elijah. The Lord had said that
he had commanded a widow to supply him with food, but this couldn't have
been the way he expected it to happen. Nevertheless, the prophet had learned
to trust God, and he invited the widow to trust him as well. The woman was
to make a small cake of bread, first for Elijah and then for herself and her son.
This was an audacious request for a stranger to make, but it was followed by
an even more remarkable promise: The jar of flour will not be used up and
the jug of oil will not run dry until the day the LORD gives rain on the land.

Something about Elijah stirred a remarkable faith in the widow. She had
been called to risk her last meal and to rely on the promise of a "foreign
God." But she went away and did as Elijah had told her. As a result, she
experienced God's supernatural provision, not just on that occasion but for
an extended period of time. There is no suggestion that the Lord allowed the
provision to be stored in advance. God was consistently faithful, meeting the
need just in time every day. The widow and her son were forced to rely on the
Provider, not the provision. In the process God revealed that he alone, and
not Baal, was the Lord of enemy territory.

17:17–24. But Elijah's training was not finished. In the mysterious providence of God, the widow's son became ill and died. The heartbroken mother
lashed out in grief at Elijah, complaining that the presence of the prophet, the
man of God, had directed God's attention to her family, reminded God of her
sin, and drawn divine retribution. This was the language both of grief and of
pagan concepts of God, but Elijah was in no mood to defend God. He was
also perplexed with this turn of events. Why would God allow this to happen
to the woman who had spared him from death?

The prophet took the boy from his mother, carried him into his special
room, and poured out his confusion to the Lord. But Elijah had also learned
by now that there was no realm in which the Lord was not present with
power. He stretched himself over the boy three times and then prayed as no
one in previous biblical history had prayed: O LORD . . . let this boy's life
return to him!

What followed was the first recorded restoration to life in the Bible. The
writer of 1 Kings is careful to attribute the miracle not to Elijah but to God:
The LORD heard Elijah's cry, and the boy's life returned to him. In the heart
of Baal territory, God had displayed his incomparable power. In the Baal
myths, Baal was subject to the laws of nature; he died each year during the
dry season. But God is not subject to death; he is Lord over it.

In the widow's eyes the miracle proved that Elijah was God's true prophet.
It also served to authenticate the message that he gave as the true word of the

Lord: **the word of the** LORD **from your mouth is the truth.** We are not told the effect of the miracle upon Elijah, but it must have given him an even deeper sense of confidence in God as the Lord of life and death, a confidence born in the midst of enemy territory. His courage to stand alone for God was born in these profound experiences of the glory and greatness of the Lord. He was now ready for the next step.

MAIN IDEA REVIEW: *Spiritual courage, the capacity to stand for the Lord, comes from commitment to the Word of God.*

III. CONCLUSION

He's All I Need

Elijah lived at a time when the most cherished truths and values of his nation were under attack. He was part of a small minority, with the power of the king and the establishment sponsoring the attack on God's truth. But aroused by the word of God, he determined to stand against his age, knowing his life was in peril. He was a man of unquestioned loyalty to God, and he was willing to confront the king with a challenge that struck at the very heart of baalism. His name was his message: "My God is Yahweh."

The prophet was able to confront the king. But to take the next step, he needed to deepen his confidence in God's power and availability. The Lord took him out of the public eye to build within him an unshakable confidence in God. The Lord trained Elijah for the most important moment in his life—the great challenge at Mount Carmel.

PRINCIPLES

- Each generation faces the battle to live out their loyalty to the Lord Jesus.
- People who are conscious that they stand primarily before God will have the courage to stand before evil kings.
- Our greatest calling is to declare God's will faithfully and fearlessly to our times.
- God not only works *through* us; he works *in* us to prepare us for his next great purpose.
- Faith grows as we trust God's word and see his faithfulness to his promises.
- The difficult places of life are God's training ground.

APPLICATIONS

- Be alert to the central places where God's truth is being challenged in our time.

- Listen carefully to God's Word, so you can understand the message he is calling you to proclaim.

- Obey God, even when his directions may seem strange or unusual.

- Let God work through your life to accomplish his will.

IV. LIFE APPLICATION

At His Best

In 1936 the reigning king of England, Edward VIII, announced that he intended to marry the woman he loved—a twice-divorced American woman named Wallis Simpson. Because of the traditional and constitutional relation of the monarchy to the Church of England, a constitutional crisis occurred, and Edward was required to abdicate the throne and relinquish his regal claims. On one level the story read like a tragic romance, but on a deeper level it unveiled a self-indulgence in Edward that became increasingly evident as World War II drew near.

I have never forgotten the way Alistair Cooke summarized the life of this man: "The most damning epitaph you can compose for Edward—as a Prince, as a King, as a Man—is one that all comfortable people should cower from deserving: he was at his best only when the going was good!"

This is certainly not an epitaph that can be applied to Elijah! He served his God in one of the most dangerous periods in history. The issues of syncretism and pluralism, so significant in Elijah's day, are with us today in somewhat different form. These are times when followers of Christ need to be at their best.

V. PRAYER

Lord, give me eyes to see where the crucial battles are being waged in my time; give me the wisdom see your truth; give me the courage to speak your word as I must; and give me the patience to allow you to shape me into a person who can be an effective servant for your glory. Amen.

VI. DEEPER DISCOVERIES

A. Elijah and the New Testament

Elijah left a mark on the New Testament as well as his own time. The last prophecy of the Old Testament predicted the coming of Elijah "before that great and dreadful day of the L ORD comes. He will turn the hearts of the fathers to their children, and the hearts of the children to their fathers" (Mal. 4:5–6). John the Baptist came "in the spirit and power of Elijah, to turn the hearts of the fathers to their children" (Luke 1:17), and there was open discussion about the relation of John the Baptist to the original Elijah (John 1:21; Matt. 11:14; 17:10–13). Elijah was present with Moses, the great Old Testament figures representing the law and the prophets, at the transfiguration of the Lord Jesus (Matt. 17:1–9). The two witnesses who appear at the time of the tribulation (Rev. 11:1–14) are Elijah-like. Some interpreters have speculated that they are Moses and Elijah returned.

B. The Next Few Years (17:1)

Elijah did not specify the length of time the drought would last. But 18:1 indicates that the Lord called him to return to confront Ahab in the third year. The New Testament twice refers to the drought as lasting for three and one-half years (Luke 4:25; Jas. 5:17). The rainy season begins in Israel in October and extends to April. It is unlikely that Elijah would prophesy drought as the dry season was beginning. He would do so in October, when rain was expected. However, the land had already been dry for six months and would remain so for three more years. Thus, the three years is the period between Elijah's prophecy and rain; the three and one-half years is the total length of time without rainfall.

C. Elijah, the Widow, and the Lord Jesus

In Luke's account of the ministry of the Lord Jesus, he set his message in the synagogue of his hometown of Nazareth as the manifesto of his ministry (Luke 4:16–30). His words were heard well at first, as "gracious words." But then, speaking of Israel's history of rejecting God's prophets, he referred to this story of the widow: "Elijah was not sent to any [widow in Israel], but to a widow in Zarephath in the region of Sidon." The people were enraged and attempted to kill Jesus. They were furious that he suggested they were like the generation of Ahab and also at the picture of God's grace being extended to Gentiles outside the boundaries of Israel. This offended their exclusivistic pride, but God's grace was always intended to flow out *from* his people, not just *into* them.

Those closest to God's blessing have no right to it, and it will go else-where, even to Gentiles, if his people reject it. This obviously had great importance to the Lord's ministry but also the wider salvation history of the church, planted among the Gentiles. The widow was a harbinger of God's saving purpose.

VII. TEACHING OUTLINE

A. INTRODUCTION

1. Lead Story: Standing in the Gap

2. Context: Israel has reached a crisis point in its history. Under Ahab and Jezebel, the nation has repudiated God as its covenant Lord and adopted a pagan religion. God will not allow such a condition to exist unchallenged, and his instrument is a lone prophet, Elijah.

3. Transition: To understand the urgency of the crisis, we need to understand what has happened with the accession of Omri and his son Ahab to the throne. The nation is in a time of great prosperity and spiritual laxity.

B. COMMENTARY

1. Ahab's Spiritual Rebellion (16:29–34)

2. Elijah's Declaration (17:1)

3. Elijah's Training Camp (17:2–24)

C. CONCLUSION: HE'S ALL I NEED

VIII. ISSUES FOR DISCUSSION

1. What parallels do you see between the times in which Elijah lived and our own? What issues would an "Elijah" feel compelled to address today?

2. Elijah's confrontational style was God's will for him. Is it always the right way or even the best way?

3. If you were at Kerith and the water started to fail, how do you think you would have responded? Are there parallels in our experience today?

1 Kings 18:1–46

A Time to Choose

I. INTRODUCTION
No Middle Ground

II. COMMENTARY
A verse-by-verse explanation of the chapter.

III. CONCLUSION
Wavering Between Opinions

An overview of the principles and application from the chapter.

IV. LIFE APPLICATION
Living in a Democracy

Melding the chapter to life.

V. PRAYER
Tying the chapter to life with God.

VI. DEEPER DISCOVERIES
Historical, geographical, and grammatical enrichment of the commentary.

VII. TEACHING OUTLINE
Suggested step-by-step group study of the chapter.

VIII. ISSUES FOR DISCUSSION
Zeroing the chapter in on daily life.

Quote

"If God has really done something in Christ on which

the salvation of the world depends, and if He has made it

known, then it is a Christian duty to be intolerant of every-

thing which ignores, denies, or explains it."

J a m e s   D e n n e y

BIOGRAPHICAL PROFILE: ELIJAH

- Probably emerged around 860 B.C. when the reign of Ahab (874–853 B.C.) was well established
- Ministered in the Northern Kingdom
- Stood for obedience to the first and second commandments, requiring exclusive loyalty to God uncontaminated by idolatry, in a time when the worship of Baal had become entrenched in Israel
- Was a speaking prophet rather than a writing prophet, with the exception of the letter recorded in 2 Chronicles 21:12–15
- Appointed Elisha as his servant and successor (1 Kgs. 19:15–21)
- Gathered around him several groups loyal to God known as the company of the prophets (1 Kgs. 20:35; 2 Kgs. 2:3,5,7)
- Departed from life supernaturally, without death, early in the reign of Jehoram of Israel (852–841)

1 Kings 18:1–46

IN A NUTSHELL

*A*fter three years of drought, God summons Elijah to press the issue of whether his people Israel will follow him or continue worshiping the false god Baal. Elijah first summons a private follower of God to declare his allegiance to the king. Then he confronts the king, the nation, and the false prophets of Baal with a contest between the two gods. When God demonstrates his superiority by fire, the people proclaim their commitment to him and eradicate the Baal prophets. Then the Lord sends rain, proving that he is superior to Baal.

A Time to Choose

I. INTRODUCTION

No Middle Ground

A young, redheaded lawyer stood in a church in Richmond, Virginia, on March 23, 1775. Angry and agitated by what seemed to him to be an endless debate about the next response the colonists should take in their conflict with King George and Great Britain, Patrick Henry could contain himself no longer. His impassioned speech ended with the words: "Is life so dear or peace so sweet as to be purchased at the price of chains and slavery? Forbid it, Almighty God! I know not what course others may take, but as for me, give me liberty or give me death!"

Seventy years later, as the tensions that would explode into the Civil War increased, the poet James Russell Lowell described what he called *The Present Crisis:*

> Once to every man and nation comes
> the moment to decide,
> In the strife of Truth and Falsehood,
> for the good or evil side.

Ours is a society that does not feel very comfortable with "either-or" choices. A postmodern culture embraces a "both-and" mind-set. We want to multiply options, to insist that we can blend different traditions and perspectives. We celebrate diversity and tolerance, embrace ambiguity and uncertainty, and insist on individual autonomy. We must value all viewpoints, and it is arrogant to question someone else's beliefs. It is intolerant to call someone to choose or commit rather than to validate opposites and to respect all ways. Ours is an age that celebrates pluralism, relativism, openness, inclusivism, and mutual respect.

In many areas of life, these are valuable and desirable attributes. But they confront one major obstacle: the living God, the Lord of heaven and earth, revealed in his Son, the Lord Jesus Christ, is not satisfied with respect. He insists not only on our loyalty but on our *exclusive* loyalty. He will not allow himself to be reduced to one possibility in a cafeteria of spiritual options. He forces us to decide. There is no middle ground.

Few Old Testament stories are as well-known as the story of Elijah on Mount Carmel doing battle with the prophets of Baal. And few stories are as relevant to the modern world we live in.

II. COMMENTARY

A Time to Choose

> **MAIN IDEA:** *The evidence that the Lord alone is the true God compels our undivided loyalty to him.*

A Going Public (18:1–15)

> **SUPPORTING IDEA:** *The choice of whether we live by fear or by faith is linked to our certainty that the Lord is the living God.*

18:1–2. Elijah **was sustained by the Lord** at Kerith and Zarephath for **a long time, into the third year.** By that time the effect of the drought had reached catastrophic proportions. Life for many people in Israel was stretched to the breaking point. Elijah had not acted on his own initiative but at the direction of God. That was true on this occasion as well. Once again he received divine direction in the form of a command and a promise: **present yourself to Ahab, and I will send rain on the land.** Through the drought God had demonstrated the weakness of Baal, the so-called rain god, and he had revealed his anger at the nation's sin. Now through the sending of rain, he would show that he alone was the living God of creation whom the people must worship and obey.

18:3–6. In these verses we are introduced to an Israelite civil servant named **Obadiah,** whose name means "servant of Yahweh." He was **a devout believer in the LORD,** but he also had an important position in the court of Ahab. That he was **in charge of his palace** suggests that he was the king's chief domestic servant. He was a man caught between a rock and a hard place. His commitment to God was real. Jezebel had sought to purge loyal prophets of God from the land. But while she was executing them, Obadiah risked his life in order to hide and feed one hundred of them. Yet he was also committed to the service of an evil king.

Obadiah was trying to balance loyalties, and that balancing act could not continue forever. He had kept his faith private, and he had apparently kept it with integrity. But events were soon to force him to choose sides.

The drought was getting worse and worse. So was the spiritual situation in the land, as Jezebel's determined purge of faithful followers of the Lord advanced. Ahab was not concerned that **Jezebel was killing off the LORD's prophets.** What concerned him most were his **horses and mules** because these were the basis of his military strength. He was determined to commandeer food for them, whatever the effects might be on his civilian population. It was of such high priority to Ahab that he gave the responsibility to himself and his chief official.

18:7–15. In the course of these duties, **as Obadiah was walking along, Elijah met him**. Obadiah recognized and honored God's prophet, but Elijah's response turned Obadiah's world upside down: **tell your master, "Elijah is here."** Obadiah knew that Ahab had made Elijah public enemy number one and had mounted a massive search-and-destroy mission against the prophet. Ahab believed that Elijah was the cause of his problems, perhaps because he had insulted Baal. If he could control the prophet, he could find a way to overturn the disaster that afflicted his land.

Knowing the king's hatred of Elijah, Obadiah feared that he might be suspected of complicity in his three-year disappearance if he reported he had seen Elijah. This might lead to the discovery of his secret support of the prophets of the Lord. That would put him in mortal danger from both Ahab and Jezebel. Obadiah protested Elijah's instructions and found several reasons not to take his message to Ahab. But Elijah would not back down; it was time for him to come out of hiding to face Ahab. It was also time for Obadiah to come out of secret loyalty to the Lord to open commitment. It was time to choose.

Obadiah was a man of faith, but he was also a man of fear. His protection of the prophets had been costly and courageous. But if he identified himself before the king as a worshiper of God, it could cost him his life! His fear of Ahab and Jezebel was much greater than his loyalty to God.

🅱 Taking Sides (18:16–25)

SUPPORTING IDEA: *The stark differences between God and Baal show there is no middle ground between them.*

After an intense inner struggle, Obadiah complied with Elijah's directions and arranged a meeting between the prophet and the king. Elijah delivered a set of three challenges, involving the king, the people, and the false prophets. At every point Elijah was careful to give Baal the upper hand.

18:16–19. Ahab met Elijah with an accusation: **Is that you, you troubler of Israel?** There was a significant accusation bound up in the word **troubler**. Ahab's accusation was that Elijah was to blame for Israel's judgment, and only his death could remove the curse from the nation. He was attempting to shift the blame and to frighten Elijah.

But God's prophet was not intimidated by Ahab's attack. He rejected Ahab's charge and laid the blame where it belonged—at the feet of Ahab's family. The nation's problem was not lack of rain but lack of loyalty and obedience to God. Their sin and rebellion had drawn the divine judgment.

Elijah's purpose was not to accuse Ahab but to call the nation back to national repentance. So he challenged Ahab to **summon the people from all over Israel to meet me on Mount Carmel**. Mount Carmel was a high ridge that rose out of the Mediterranean Sea to a height of about seventeen hundred feet, stretching for about thirty miles to the southern region of Phoenicia. It was an area often claimed by pagans as a home of the gods and had long been associated with the worship of Baal. In other words Elijah was giving the Baal worshipers a home-field advantage by choosing this location.

Ahab was to **bring the four hundred and fifty prophets of Baal and the four hundred prophets of Asherah, who eat at Jezebel's table**. This is the first mention of these prophets. It demonstrates how deeply Baal worship had embedded itself in Israel under Ahab and Jezebel. The false prophets lived at state expense, sanctioned and supported by the king, while loyal prophets of the Lord who survived the queen's purge were hiding in caves.

18:20–24. Ahab assembled his prophets and the general population on Mount Carmel, as Elijah had requested. The prophet then issued his second challenge, addressed to the people. It was a time to decide: **How long will you waver between two opinions? If the LORD is God, follow him; but if Baal is God, follow him**. The phrase translated "waver between two opinions" is an unusual expression that means "to limp or hobble between two boughs (sticks or crutches?)." The verb is translated "dance" in verse 26, where it refers to the shuffling, ritual dance of the Baal prophets. Elijah's message was clear. The people were trying to hold together two mutually exclusive loyalties. But this was impossible. It was time to choose. The Lord and Baal could not both be the true God. Syncretism was not an option. The two loyalties were mutually exclusive.

But Elijah's challenge drew no response: **the people said nothing**. They felt no need or desire to choose. In spite of what Elijah said, they wanted both Baal and God. Each had something to offer. Baalism did not require a choice. You could be a faithful follower of Baal and still follow God. Why couldn't God be equally accommodating? Besides, Baal was the storm god, necessary for fertility. Who wanted to take the chance of offending him? If there was truth in both religions, why not blend them together in a new, inclusive faith?

God's claims are absolute. If the Lord was God, Baal could not be. And if Baal really was an option, the faith of God was based on a fallacy. So Elijah issued a second challenge—a way to test the truth claims of each of these deities. The people were to acquire **two bulls** to use as sacrifices, and Baal's **four hundred and fifty prophets** would be given their choice of animals. They would then kill the bull, prepare it for sacrifice, and place it on an altar. Elijah would do the same. Then the Baal prophets would call on Baal, and Elijah would call on the Lord. **The god who answers by fire**, Elijah declared, **he is God**.

Once again Elijah seemed to have played into the hands of Baal. They were in "Baal territory," and Elijah was outnumbered, so the Baal prophets could seemingly bring much more "spiritual power" to the contest. But most of all, Baal was known to be the storm god, the god of fire and lightning. This was his realm. But God also had manifested himself by fire in Old Testament times (Lev. 9:24; 10:2; Num. 16:35). The people recognized the fairness of Elijah's challenge: **What you say is good**.

18:25. The final challenge was addressed to the Baal prophets. They were to prepare their sacrifice **first, since there are so many of you**. Once again Elijah was giving them the advantage. Going first allowed them to take as much time as they needed. And if their sacrifice did catch on fire, God had lost, no matter what happened when Elijah prayed. Elijah was not contending for the Lord's equal position alongside Baal but for God's exclusivity and uniqueness. Elijah was not only confident of God's existence; he was certain of Baal's nonexistence. With the challenge issued and accepted, the battle of Mount Carmel began.

Undeniable Proof (18:26–46)

SUPPORTING IDEA: *Undivided loyalty to God rests on convincing proof that he alone is the living and true God.*

18:26–29. The Baal priests began their attempts in the morning, perhaps around nine o'clock. **They took the bull given them and prepared** it and began their ritual prayers. Their prayers amounted to a repeated shout of **O Baal, answer us!** These shouts were accompanied by a ritual dance, done with hobbled, limping steps around the altar. Their rituals continued until noon, but the silence was deafening: **there was no response; no one answered**. There was no one there to answer. Baal was a no-god.

After about three hours Elijah began to **taunt** the Baal prophets. His mockery was designed to show his contempt for the empty claims of the Baal prophets. But it also served to agitate the Baal prophets, to spur them on to continued activity. He did not want them to quit until the futility of their actions had been displayed. So he goaded them: **Shout louder! . . . Perhaps he is deep in thought, or busy, or traveling**. A god who would be distracted by such things would be no god at all! Such a god was a joke, not a god worthy of worship and service.

Elijah's taunts spurred the Baalists to greater effort. In an attempt to gain Baal's attention and sympathy, they raised their intensity, shouting louder and slashing themselves with swords and spears. Such frenzy was a common part of pagan religion, an attempt to enter a heightened state in which they could influence the god or arouse his pity. But it was all in vain. By **the time for the evening sacrifice** (around 3:00 P.M.), they had expended six hours of frantic effort, **but there was no response**. Baal was silent and unresponsive. There was no response because there was no Baal.

18:30–35. Finally, Elijah seized center stage. His delay made it impossible for the Baal prophets to claim that they had not been given a fair opportunity. He summoned the people to gather around an abandoned **altar of the LORD**. Perhaps this was an altar destroyed during the Jezebel purge. Elijah chose **twelve stones** to reconstruct the altar, a reminder of God's original formation of the nation of Israel, **one for each of the tribes descended from Jacob**. This connection with Jacob and God's covenant with the original nation was an important statement. It showed the Lord's claim on the nation as well as its present defective condition because of its division and rebellion against God.

Having **built an altar in the name of the LORD**, Elijah prepared it for the sacrifice. His instructions must have seemed bizarre to the onlookers. First, he dug a large trench around the altar, the size of which is uncertain (two seahs is about five gallons; see "Deeper Discoveries"). Then he arranged wood on the altar, butchered the bull, and spread the sacrificial pieces on the altar. Apparently, some people had stepped forward to act as his assistants. He instructed then to **fill four large jars with water and pour it on the offering and on the wood**. The process was repeated three times. Water drenched the altar and filled the trench. Elijah was removing all possible claims of trickery. He was making the miracle seem as difficult as possible for the Lord.

18:36–38. Elijah's prayer contrasted sharply with the frantic and pro-longed activities of the Baal prophets. It was brief and simple, without any of the elaborate antics of the Baalists. He was a man of prayer, not a worker of magic who needed to manipulate a reluctant god by formulas or actions. He was not coaxing the Lord or seeking to convince him. Rather, in complete confidence, he addressed his prayer to the covenant God: **O LORD, God of Abraham, Isaac and Israel**. It was a prayer motivated by a passion for the glory of God among his people. He had shown that Baal was dead, but now he needed to show that God was alive. He called upon the Lord to answer him **so these people will know that you, O LORD, are God**.

The prophet had two secondary requests. He wanted the people to know that he was God's **servant** and had done all these things at God's **command**. He had been accused of being the "troubler of Israel" (18:17). He would now be confirmed as the servant of God. A second concern was that the people, having seen the authenticity of God, would know that he was **turning their hearts back again**. The purpose of the miracle was to be conversion—the return of the people to the Lord, the living and true God.

God's answer came at once. No sooner were the words out of Elijah's mouth than **the fire of the LORD . . . burned up the sacrifice, the wood, the stones and the soil, and also licked up the water in the trench**. This fire fell out of a clear sky, as the following verses make clear. The Lord alone was God.

18:39–40. When God's fire fell, so did the people: **they fell prostrate and cried, "The LORD—he is God!"** This confession was a response not only to Elijah's challenge but also to the miracle they had just witnessed. They were affirming that the Lord, and he alone, was God, and therefore Baal was no God. As sole God, the Lord had sole claim upon them.

Elijah immediately issued the orders: **Seize the prophets of Baal.** They were a cancer that had to be removed from the nation. This was also retribution for the part they had played in Jezebel's execution of true followers of the Lord. Therefore the Baalists were seized, **and Elijah had them brought down to the Kishon Valley and slaughtered there.** This was not murder but a commanded purging of moral and spiritual evil. It also served as a powerful reminder that there was no middle ground between God and Baal. It was time to choose! All traces of Baal must go.

18:41–46. The Lord next revealed himself as the God of rain. He had promised Elijah in 18:1, "Present yourself to Ahab, and I will send rain on the land." With the coming of rain, the defeat of Baal would be complete. His claims would be shown to be bankrupt and God's claims to be authentic.

Elijah's confidence in the Lord was revealed by his instructions to Ahab: **Go, eat and drink, for there is the sound of a heavy rain.** While Ahab went to eat, Elijah climbed to a high point on the mountain where he could look westward toward the Mediterranean Sea, the direction from which a storm would come. Elijah took a position of humility and concentration, **bent down** with **his face between his knees,** and began to pray for rain. He used his servant as a lookout, to peer out into the cloudless sky over the Mediterranean. Elijah's prayer for rain was based not only on God's promise in 18:1 but also on God's covenant promise for repentance in Deuteronomy 28:12.

Six times the prophet sent his servant and received the report that there was no sign of rain. Still he continued to pray, and the seventh time he received the report that **a cloud as small as a man's hand is rising from the sea.** Elijah's confidence that God would answer his prayer was so great that this was all the evidence he needed. He sent the servant to advise Ahab to head for home as quickly as possible, before the storm overtook him. Torrential rain after a drought presented the likelihood of swollen streams, mudslides, and flash floods that would make charioteering dangerous.

The rain that followed was not just much-anticipated drought relief; it was visible evidence that God, not Baal, was sovereign over nature and life. Once again, **the power of the LORD came upon Elijah,** enabling him to run the seventeen miles back to Jezreel, arriving ahead of Ahab (see "Deeper Discoveries").

MAIN IDEA REVIEW: *The evidence that the Lord alone is the living and true God compels our undivided loyalty to him.*

III. CONCLUSION

Wavering Between Opinions

The central question of this chapter appears in verse 21: "How long will you waver between two opinions?" That was the challenge Obadiah faced, as he was pulled between his loyalty to Ahab and his commitment to God. There was a time to choose, when he could no longer try to find middle ground.

This was also the question faced by the nation of Israel. The people were trying to reconcile the irreconcilable—worship of Baal and worship of God. The only way they could do that was to distort the truth of who the Lord was, and to deny the reality of who Baal was—a false god. Truth demanded a choice, and God made the truth evident through his dramatic intervention.

It is the issue we face continually. We face it theologically in an attempt to appease the modern insistence on pluralism, when we deny the exclusive reality of the Lord Jesus Christ. We do it morally when we try to blend an unbiblical lifestyle with a profession of faith in Christ. We do it spiritually when we allow anything to take the place of the Lord Jesus Christ. Wavering between opinions has become philosophically respectable and even politically correct, but it is spiritually impossible and intellectually untenable. Truth calls for a choice. There is no middle ground. If Jesus is Lord and Savior, follow him!

PRINCIPLES

- We will obey God's commands to the degree that we believe his promises.
- There comes a time when private faith must become public loyalty.
- Whether we live by fear or by faith is determined by our certainty that the Lord is the living God.
- There is no middle ground between loyalty to God and commitment to any other rival.
- Spiritual commitment must rest on convincing proof, not personal preference.

APPLICATIONS

- Decide who your real master is so you won't become a prisoner of fear who is torn between loyalties.

- "Spiritual questions" are often a symptom of your desire to find middle ground and to have it both ways. Examine your heart honestly.
- Ground your trust in Christ in God's convincing proofs of who he is, not just your personal feelings.
- Face the implications of Elijah's question: What is keeping you from unqualified loyalty to Christ?
- Deal ruthlessly with competitive loyalties in your life.

IV. LIFE APPLICATION

Living in a Democracy

Western democracies are not theocracies, as ancient Israel was. We value freedom of religion and recognize that God established his church not as an extension of the state but as a community of believers who are joined by personal faith in Christ—not by nationality, ethnicity, social class, or gender. We are loyal citizens, but our supreme loyalty is to Christ. And the rights we desire for ourselves, we defend for others. We may disagree passionately with their viewpoint, but we respect their civil rights. At the same time we pray for them and pray for every opportunity to persuade them of the truth found only in Christ.

Our modern culture has responded to religious diversity by insisting that all differences are only apparent, that all religious beliefs are equally true (or untrue), that all beliefs are at core the same, and that all claims to absolute truth are not only arrogant but also dangerous and tyrannical. There is, we are told, unity at the point of a generic spirituality and a vague deity. But we must minimize, so our culture says, any specific claims about Jesus, about salvation and lostness, and about heaven or hell.

At this point we are back on Mount Carmel because Elijah's challenge will not go away: "If the Lord is God, worship him." The central challenge of our time is how we declare the inescapable claims of the Lord Jesus Christ. The gospel is wonderfully *inclusive*: it is for all people in all places. We are not proclaiming some local deity or Western god. He is Lord of all. But the gospel is also relentlessly *exclusive*. Jesus is not *a* way but *the* way.

V. PRAYER

Lord, show me what it means to live with total loyalty to you in my generation. Give me a gracious heart that respects those who do not know you. But give me as well a passionate longing to represent you, so they will see that you alone are God and will bow the knee before you. Amen.

VI. DEEPER DISCOVERIES

A. Elijah's Altar (18:30–32)

The altar Elijah rebuilt on Mount Carmel had apparently been used by loyal followers of the Lord. It was clearly irregular, but since Jeroboam had corrupted the worship of God at Bethel and Dan, any altar to him was better than a Baal altar. Almost certainly, fervent Baalists had destroyed the altar. Elijah rebuilt it for the occasion, and the Lord's fire destroyed it so it could not become an alternative shrine. The twelve stones Elijah used not only symbolized the twelve tribes; they also recalled the twelve stone pillars that Moses set up by the altar when God's covenant with Israel was established by sacrifice (Exod. 24:1–8). The size of the trench is difficult to determine since it could describe volume (large enough to hold two measures of seed, about seven gallons) or area (the amount of land that could be sown with two measures of seed). The former seems more likely.

B. Twelve Large Jars of Water (18:33–34)

Although we are not sure how much water was poured on the altar, we must ask where the people could have acquired such a large amount of water after a long drought. Water was precious but apparently not absent. There are several possibilities. There may have been a well or spring in the area, which was one of the highest precipitation regions in the area. Underground supplies may have been available. The tens of thousands of people present would have brought their own water. People may have contributed what they had. The site was near the Mediterranean Sea. It would have been possible to get sea water that, although not drinkable, was suitable for drenching an altar.

C. Elijah's Race to Jezreel (18:45–46)

Elijah's seventeen-mile run from Carmel to Jezreel was an amazing physical feat at the end of a long day. The fact that he ran ahead of Ahab's chariot may have been partially due to his ability to run straight across country. Ahab's chariot would have maneuvered through ground cracked by the drought. But there was another factor involved in Elijah's speed: "The power of the LORD came upon him." Tucking or tying up one's robe in one's belt was typical preparation for such activity.

VII. TEACHING OUTLINE

A. INTRODUCTION

1. Lead Story: No Middle Ground

2. Context: Through Elijah, the Lord had created a crisis in the nation of Israel. The nation had turned to worship the rain god Baal. But the drought had put Baal's claims in question. It was time for a "battle of the gods," which would force the nation to choose between God and Baal.

3. Transition: For three years God had not only been depriving the land of rain; he had also been developing his prophet for the greatest moment of his life and one of the most significant in his nation's history.

B. COMMENTARY

1. Going Public (18:1–15)
2. Taking Sides (18:16–25)
3. Undeniable Proof (18:26–46)

C. CONCLUSION: WAVERING BETWEEN OPINIONS

VIII. ISSUES FOR DISCUSSION

1. Consider the situation of Obadiah. His genuine faith is not questioned, but he was deeply conflicted. Are there parallels today? Do you ever find yourself torn between loyalty to "Ahab" and to the Lord? Should a follower of Christ avoid all such situations? If not, what advice would you give an "Obadiah"?

2. Elijah accused the Israelites of attempting to do the impossible—wavering between the Lord and Baal. What similar temptations occur in our world? How does our cultural promotion of nonjudgmental tolerance, relativism, and pluralism impact followers of Christ today? Are there any parallels to Elijah's world and Elijah's challenge?

1 Kings 19:1–21

When Dreams Die

"*The* occupational hazard of Christian discipleship and

ministry is discouragement."

J o h n   S t o t t

1 Kings 19:1–21

I N   A   N U T S H E L L

We would have expected the great victory of Mount Carmel to lead to a sweeping reformation of the entire nation. But it does not. Instead, in the face of a death threat from Queen Jezebel, Elijah flees in fear to another country out of the reach of the queen. There, in great despair, he attempts to resign his prophetic ministry and even asks that his life be taken. But God not only does not grant his wish; he graciously restores him to ministry in a special encounter on Mount Sinai. By the end of the chapter, Elijah responds obediently to God's call by anointing his successor Elisha.

When Dreams Die

I. INTRODUCTION

The Battle with Burnout

$\mathcal{F}$ew men have had the impact for Christ that Charles Haddon Spurgeon did. Known as "the prince of preachers," he was the best-known preacher in London by the age of twenty-two. The congregation outgrew its building, and the Metropolitan Tabernacle was built to seat six thousand people. Every Sunday, from 1861 to his death in 1892, it was filled as people gathered to hear Spurgeon's powerful biblical teaching. He spoke to an estimated ten million people in his lifetime, and millions more around the world read his published sermons. His was a God-blessed life. Yet he also carried on a lifelong battle with discouragement.

"I know by most painful experience what deep depression of spirit means," he told his students, "being visited therewith at seasons by no means few or far between." On another occasion he wrote a friend, "I have never lost my calm faith in God, but at times I have been so depressed that the cable has been strained to the limit."

Spurgeon's depression probably had some medical causes, but at least part of what he was struggling with was what we know as burnout. Researchers have observed that those who are involved in people-helping activities are particularly prone to physical and emotional exhaustion when their idealism hits the stubborn truths of human nature. People disappoint us. They start well and finish badly. They make promises and do not keep them. These things make working with people incredibly draining. Helping people is hard work, especially when our hopes for people collide with their depravity. Given those realities, burnout is a very real possibility.

This has a special relevance for followers of Christ, since the Lord Jesus called us to be in the people-helping business. When he commissioned us to "go and make disciples of all nations" (Matt. 28:19), he called us to invest our lives in others. And people do not always respond in the way or at the pace we desire.

Sometimes we imagine that the great figures of the Bible were superheroes, exempt from the pressures and frailties felt by ordinary people like us. It would be foolish to deny the uniqueness of Elijah. At the same time he was "a man just like us" (Jas. 5:17). Nowhere is this more evident than in the episode that immediately followed his great victory on Mount Carmel. On the very next day he turned and ran, overwhelmed with fear. How could that be?

Elijah's weakness can teach us some important truths about the struggles of all faithful servants of the Lord.

II. COMMENTARY

When Dreams Die

> **MAIN IDEA:** *When times of discouragement and burnout overwhelm us, the path to recovery involves a new and deeper understanding of God's purpose.*

A Elijah on the Run (19:1–8)

> **SUPPORTING IDEA:** *Even the strongest people are subject to discouragement and failure.*

19:1–2. Elijah's victory on Mount Carmel was one of the glorious moments in Israel's history. The Lord had revealed himself in dramatic fashion, in fire and in rain, and the people had responded in a massive confession of faith, apparently returning to their covenant loyalty to God. Only good things could follow from such an event!

However, this is not what happened. Ahab and Elijah had arrived back at Jezreel, where Ahab's queen, Jezebel, would have eagerly awaited his account. **Ahab told Jezebel everything Elijah had done and how he had killed all the prophets.** We should not miss the fact that Ahab's report was not about what God had done but about the deeds of Elijah. He had been impressed, but he had not been changed. Ahab the king was no closer to the Lord than before. He remained blind to spiritual reality.

Jezebel was as committed to Baal as Elijah was to God. The Carmel events did not lead her to repentance but to fury. She was not prepared to admit either that Baal was a fraud or that the Lord alone was God. She would deal with Elijah, so she sent out a threat against his life. Her track record of killing the prophets of God (18:4,13) made clear that these were not idle words.

19:3–4. Suddenly, Elijah **was afraid** (see "Deeper Discoveries"). We can only guess at the reasons. Perhaps he had convinced himself that the battle was over and that Jezebel would give up before the power of God. After all, Baal had been exposed and humiliated. Or perhaps Elijah realized that the people followed the king, and the king had not changed. Whatever the reason, this man of great faith was suddenly overwhelmed by fear **and ran for his life.** Accompanied by an unidentified servant (see 18:43–44), he fled southward out of the political jurisdiction of Ahab and Jezebel into the kingdom of Judah.

Elijah paused in **Beersheba**, the southern limit of Judah, about ninety miles from his starting point in Jezreel. Then he left his servant there and headed off another **day's journey** (about fifteen miles) into the desert. He had abandoned his opportunity and discredited his ministry out of fear for his own safety.

As Elijah **sat down** in an isolated spot, exhausted, he was a portrait of despair. In an outburst he gave voice to his brokenness: **I have had enough, LORD.** This stated his intention to resign his prophetic office. He was through! And he wanted to resign from life itself. **Take my life** was an appeal for death. He truly wanted to die, although he did not want it to be at the hand of Jezebel! He was in utter despair at his failure: **I am no better than my ancestors.** His ancestors were his prophetic predecessors. They had not made any significant difference in the spiritual life of his nation, and neither had he. Things should have been so much different! He should have been able to do so much more!

Three things should be said about Elijah at this point. First, *he was exhausted.* Mount Carmel had taken a tremendous physical and emotional toll, and he had added to it by his race from Carmel to Jezreel and his hundred-mile flight from Jezebel. He had depleted his resources and was suffering from a kind of "combat exhaustion." Not even the great prophets were exempt from the physical and emotional laws of life.

Second, *Elijah was disillusioned.* He had expected things to turn out differently. Disillusionment is always the child of illusion. Elijah's illusion had been that one great victory would produce permanent change and that Jezebel would give up. The fact was that, while Carmel had been a breakthrough, it was not the end of the battle. Jezebel was tenacious and resilient. He had also imagined that he had what it took to change his nation. Depression now told him the opposite lie—that all his actions had been futile.

Third, *Elijah's perspective was distorted.* His despair led him to ignore what had happened on Carmel. Focused on the negative and forgetful of the positive, he sank deeper and deeper into the swamp of despair. Jezebel had become very large and God very small. When people get big and the Lord gets small, we are headed for trouble!

19:5-8. The Lord's response to Elijah was remarkable. He did not rebuke his despairing servant but allowed him to sleep. After a time he provided refreshment: **an angel touched him and said, "Get up and eat."** If Elijah needed rest, he also needed food. He found set before him food intended not only to refresh him but also to remind him: **a cake of bread baked over hot coals, and a jar of water.** This was the same food provided through the widow of Zarephath (17:13). The Lord was reminding Elijah of his past faithfulness and his mighty power. The Lord then permitted further sleep and another provision of food. This second provision was for a coming journey: **Get up and eat, for the journey is too much for you.** Elijah was headed for **Horeb, the mountain of God,** also known as Mount Sinai, where God had revealed himself to the nation of Israel in Moses' time (see "Deeper Discoveries").

This was a destination chosen by Elijah, and he traveled forty days and forty nights to reach it. Since the distance of about 250 miles would have normally taken only two weeks, Elijah was in no hurry. The Lord was giving him time to himself, before a significant encounter at Sinai.

B Elijah on the Rebound (19:9–18)

SUPPORTING IDEA: *God ministers to our despair by giving us a new understanding of his person and his purpose for us.*

19:9–12. When Elijah finally reached Mount Horeb, **he went into a cave and spent the night.** The Hebrew text says that he went into *the* cave. Some interpreters have suggested that this was the same "cleft in the rock" that Moses had used (Exod. 33:22). This is possible but unprovable. But it is clear that Elijah was on Horeb because it was a holy place, linked to Moses and his profound experience of God (see "Deeper Discoveries"). In the region of Horeb Moses had encountered God in the burning bush (Exod. 3). Here he had received the Ten Commandments (Exod. 31:18) and had encountered the glory and greatness of God (Exod. 33–34). But Elijah had not come to Sinai to experience more of God. He had come to the holy place of God's covenant to express his complaint to God and to resign his prophetic commission.

The Lord's word came to Elijah as a challenge: **What are you doing here, Elijah?** This could be taken as asking, "What are you doing here on Sinai and not back in the place where I sent you, Israel and Samaria?" Or perhaps God was asking why Elijah had chosen Sinai for this encounter. But the Lord was not seeking information from Elijah. He knew his heart better than Elijah himself did. He was challenging Elijah to speak his mind and to make his case.

Elijah had not made much progress in the forty days that had elapsed on his journey. He was still in the depths of discouragement. He began by declaring his own rightness, teetering on the edge of pride: **I have been very zealous for the LORD.** His zeal was not just enthusiastic commitment to God above all other gods but a passionate commitment to the truth of the first commandment. The Lord alone was God, and he alone was to be worshiped.

The prophet followed his self-description with an indictment of Israel for its sins. It was not just Ahab and Jezebel who had sinned. The nation itself was guilty of three great spiritual crimes: covenant violation by their worship of Baal, altar desecration, and the murder of God's messengers. Elijah's analysis was correct as far as it went. Israel was guilty of the worst kind of sin and rebellion against its covenant Lord. But it was as if Mount Carmel had never taken place. Not once did Elijah mention the events of that remarkable day. Certainly, it had only been a beginning. But much of value had taken place. God's altar had been rebuilt; the people had confessed God as their covenant Lord; and the prophets of Baal had been executed.

Elijah's third complaint exposed his despair: **I am the only one left, and now they are trying to kill me too**. Once again Elijah's grief had distorted his perspective. He had indeed stood absolutely alone for the Lord. They were seeking his life. On the other hand, Obadiah had revealed the existence of at least a hundred other prophets of God (18:4,13), and the Lord had faithfully protected the life of Elijah during the previous three years, when they had been trying to kill him. The prophet was speaking out of his deep disappointment and sense of isolation. But there was a profound difference between his feelings and reality. He had lost sight of the nature of his God. As a result his vision was distorted. At the bottom of his complaint was a complaint about God himself. The Lord had not treated him well by allowing him to experience such things. Despair had made Elijah self-centered.

God did not respond verbally to Elijah or try to argue him out of his perspective. Instead, he summoned him to an encounter with him that had direct parallels to the experience of Moses in that same place: **stand on the mountain in the presence of the LORD, for the LORD is about to pass by**. The Lord had said to Moses, "There is a place near me where you may stand on a rock. When my glory passes by, I will put you in a cleft in the rock and cover you with my hand until I have passed by" (Exod. 33:21–22). Once again the Lord would reveal himself in a special way to one of his special servants.

God's revelation of himself to Elijah began with well-known signs of the power and presence of the living God. The first sign was a great and powerful wind, strong enough to tear the mountains and shatter rocks. **But the LORD was not in the wind**. Then came an earthquake, but again, **the LORD was not in the earthquake**. Finally, there came a fire (lightning?), **but the LORD was not in the fire**. These dramatic acts of power were reminiscent of God's presence on Mount Sinai (Exod. 19:16–19), while the fire and the wind clearly recalled Mount Carmel (1 Kgs. 18:38,45). Such displays of power could show the presence of an awesome, powerful God. But not on this occasion. The Lord was not limited to such things, and he did not always work in the same way.

After these dramatic signs there came **a gentle whisper**. This expression is difficult to translate—"the sound of total silence," or "a still, small voice." We are not specifically told that the Lord was in the gentle whisper, but Elijah's response of covering his face in holy reverence showed that he knew God was in this voice. We are not told what, if anything, Elijah heard or what the gentle whisper said. The message seemed to be in the *form* of the message. God was not always present in the powerful and the dramatic. He did not always work through the sensational or the overpowering. This was not to deny or minimize his presence on Mount Carmel. It was to insist that the spectacular was not God's *only* way of working. There was more to God than wind and fire. Elijah needed to realize that his God was instituting a process to deal with baalism.

19:13–18. Elijah's first need was a new vision of God. But he did not grasp immediately what God was saying to him. This became evident when the Lord repeated the question of verse 9: **What are you doing here, Elijah?** Elijah's response was exactly the same as it had been in verse 10; he had not moved forward in his emotions or his understanding. He seemed to be stuck in his gloom. But this time the Lord responded in a different way. He did not accept Elijah's complaint or even address it. Instead, he gave him a new commission. He would not relieve Elijah of his prophetic responsibility. Instead, he sent him back into the fight against Baal: **Go back the way you came.** The Lord did not coddle Elijah's fear or discouragement; he sent him back into the battle. There comes a time when we need to realize that the only way to overcome our discouragement is to get back into the work to which the Lord has called us.

Until now Elijah had served the Lord on his own. This time he was sent back by the Lord with a specific commission to enlist others in the work of God. Elijah would not be the one to complete the victory over Baal. Rather, he would initiate a process that would accomplish God's purpose. His call was to appoint three men who would complete the elimination of Baal worship in Israel.

Elijah's first task was to **anoint Hazael king over Aram.** Since Hazael was not a member of the royal family in Syria, this amounted to prophetic incitement to revolution in a foreign country (the story will be told in 2 Kgs. 9). His second task was to **anoint Jehu son of Nimshi king over Israel.** Jehu also was an outsider, not a member of the royal family, so this also amounted to a call to revolution. The Lord was calling Elijah to dangerous activity, which the ruling kings of Israel and Syria could only consider treasonous. Elijah's third responsibility was to **anoint Elisha . . . to succeed you as prophet.** In each of these cases, "anoint" seems to have a weakened sense of "designate as successor," since only Jehu was formally anointed with oil (2 Kgs. 9:6). Elijah himself would only directly appoint one of these—Elisha (1 Kgs. 19:19–21). But Elijah's authority stood behind each appointment.

Then Elijah was told of God's plan: **Jehu will put to death any who escape the sword of Hazael, and Elisha will put to death any who escape the sword of Jehu.** The statement was cryptic, but Elijah would have understood that the Lord was promising the removal of baalism. It would not take the form of a prophetic challenge to repentance, but the physical elimination of Ahab's family as well as Baal worshipers. This would occur through the unlikely means of the combined efforts of a pagan king, a new dynasty in Israel, and his successor prophet, Elisha. Elijah would only begin the process; others would finish what he began.

The Lord dealt with Elijah's discouragement by giving him an important new perspective on ministry. Elijah needed to know that, although he was a part of God's plan, he wasn't the plan itself. He was important, but he was not indispensable. The Lord would use him not to finish the project of eliminating baalism but to initiate the process that would accomplish that purpose. Elijah also needed to understand that ministry success did not necessarily mean achieving the final result; it did mean completing his God-given assignment. He needed to adjust his expectations so he could rejoice in what God had accomplished through him. Rebound in ministry occurs when we refocus our energies around the calling of God.

The Lord had one more piece of information for Elijah. The prophet felt isolated, telling God, "I am the only one left." But he wasn't. God told him that he had seven thousand followers in Israel **whose knees have not bowed down to Baal**. Elijah needed to know that God had his faithful few who were deeply loyal, even if not highly visible. The Lord was at work, even though Elijah could not always see the evidence.

Elijah's pain and depression had made him self-centered and myopic. Seven thousand in a nation of more than a million was hardly a power bloc! It was only a remnant, but increasingly in the Old Testament we will see in the faithful remnant the true hope of the nation (see Rom. 11:1–16). God was at work, and Elijah needed to move away from the somewhat egotistical sense that he was God's last and only hope. His complaint that he was alone represented arrogance rather than reality.

Ⓒ Elijah's Return to Action (19:19–21)

SUPPORTING IDEA: *The road to recovery is the road of obedience.*

19:19–21. In the words **so Elijah went from there**, we see once again his characteristic obedience. Whatever he may have felt, he did what God had commanded and **found Elisha son of Shaphat**. Elijah had been told in verse 16 that Elisha was from Abel Meholah, a community in the Jordan Valley about twenty miles south of the Sea of Galilee. This required a return of hundreds of miles by Elijah, back into the heart of Ahab's nation. Even though about two months would have passed since Jezebel's death threat, her animosity was not likely to have disappeared.

We are not told whether Elijah had previous knowledge of Elisha, although Elisha seems to have recognized Elijah immediately. Elisha was working in the fields, **plowing with twelve yoke of oxen**. This suggests that

Elisha came from a prosperous family, since a single yoke of oxen would have been much more common. Elijah's actions seem bizarre. Approaching Elisha, he threw his cloak around him, then walked away. The cloak must have been an immediately recognizable symbol, either of Elijah himself, or of the prophetic office. The act of "robing" was probably a symbol of appointment to office.

Elisha recognized that he had been called by Elijah to be his disciple. He pursued Elijah with a declaration of his intention to follow this startling calling: **Let me kiss my father and mother good-by . . . and then I will come with you**. Elijah's response is puzzling: **What have I done to you?** Apparently this meant something like, "It's up to you. You have to decide what my act means to you."

Elisha did take the time to bring an appropriate conclusion to the way of life he was leaving behind. He took his yoke and slaughtered the oxen. This was a dramatic way of putting the past behind him. He then turned the occasion into a celebration: **He burned the plowing equipment to cook the meat and gave it to the people, and they ate**. It would take a number of hours to butcher and roast the meal. Elisha was wise enough to celebrate the past but also to set it firmly behind him as he entered into the new call of God on his life.

Elisha **set out to follow Elijah and became his attendant**. Just as Joshua was the attendant of Moses (Exod. 33:11; Num. 11:28; Josh. 1:1), Elisha was to spend the next years serving the needs of Elijah and serving alongside him, learning the things that would launch him into the ministry the Lord had for him. This ministry was to last for more than fifty years and is the major subject of 2 Kings 2–9. This also marked a major transition for Elijah. For the first time he had a companion to share the burden of ministry.

> **MAIN IDEA REVIEW:** *When times of discouragement and burnout overwhelm us, the path to recovery involves a new and deeper understanding of God's purpose.*

III. CONCLUSION

Grace for the Journey

Times of shattered dreams and broken spirits come to the most unexpected people in the most unexpected ways at the most unexpected times. The strong are not always strong; the brave are not always brave; the trusting are not always free of fear and doubt. The experience of Elijah is a vivid illustration of this. There is encouragement in recognizing that the discouragement and burnout with which we battle is not something new or unusual. It is a product of our own frailty and the challenge of being involved with people who do not respond in the way we desire.

Elijah's problem is simple to diagnose: Jezebel had become bigger to him than God. This was not true on an intellectual level. Elijah would have denied any such perspective. But it had become true on a personal level. At his most vulnerable moment of physical, spiritual, and emotional exhaustion, a person had become big, and God had become small. It is a battle we all fight.

God's ways of grace in the life of Elijah are full of significance for us. First, he gave him a new experience of his loving care and practical provision, ministering to his need for rest and refreshment. He also gave him new insight into his nature, helping Elijah see his God with a new depth. He then called Elijah to a fresh commitment to play the part God called him to fulfill. He also gave him a new companion who would share in this ministry.

We live in a different time than Elijah did, but God's escape route from times of discouragement or burnout will follow the same path that put Elijah back into service.

PRINCIPLES

- Our physical and emotional condition impacts our spiritual life.
- Even the strongest people can be driven by fear rather than being sustained by faith.
- When people and problems become too large, we can allow God to seem too small.
- Our feelings are not a reliable guide to reality.
- Victory in one battle does not mean that the war is over.
- Our greatest need is not an answer to our arguments but a new understanding of God's purpose.
- The road to recovery is the way of obedience.

APPLICATIONS

- Beware of illusions about the Christian life. Biblical realism is the best antidote to disillusionment.
- Remind yourself that God is often much more patient with you than you are with yourself.
- Beware of isolation. Elijah did himself no favors by trying to go it on his own.
- Withdraw from ministry when you need to renew your sense of God's person and purpose.
- Reengage in ministry. Mount Carmel may be a place of retreat, but the path to recovery always takes you back into the battle.

IV. LIFE APPLICATION

Measuring Success

What does success look like? Most of us have fairly clear ideas because we have paraded before us people who claim to be successful. In Christian ministry we inevitably measure this with numbers: bodies, buildings, and bucks. How many people, what new building projects, how large the budget? And we are told that if we are faithful to the Lord, he will do great things through us. But what about the pastor who faithfully pastors a small church? What about the godly leader who challenges the ungodly lives of church members? He sees the size of his congregation shrink, but some of his hearers take the message to heart and experience significant growth in Christ. What about the missionary who buries herself in an unresponsive people group, consistently sharing Christ?

One of Elijah's greatest problems was a faulty view of success. He saw it in terms of a dramatic event that would end all resistance to the Lord. When that did not happen, he was plunged into despair. He saw success in terms of large numbers. When he could not see the multitudes, he missed the remnant. He saw success in terms of being better than his predecessors rather than being faithful to God. One of the things the Lord taught the prophet on Horeb was the need to define success in a different way. The reality was that Israel was already headed for judgment. Any victory would be only temporary. The Lord was not asking Elijah to change his nation. He was asking him to accomplish his God-given mission. His call had not been to be successful, measuring success by numbers. He would be successful by being godly and faithful. This is always God's measure of success.

V. PRAYER

Lord, you know I am prone to make others big and to make you small. Help me to keep you in the center of my vision. Teach me to deal with the creeping invasion of self-pity and discouragement. Amen.

VI. DEEPER DISCOVERIES

A. Elijah Was Afraid (19:3)

The Hebrew text reads "and he saw," but it is difficult to understand what that means. Exactly the same consonants in Hebrew give the translation "and he was afraid." This is the reading of the Greek translators and is the most likely original reading of the Hebrew text as well.

B. Horeb, the Mountain of God (19:8)

The words *Horeb* and *Sinai* are used interchangeably in the Old Testament to describe the same location—a mountain in the Sinai Desert that played a crucial role at the time of Israel's exodus from Egypt and the establishment of the Mosaic covenant. The region of Horeb was where God revealed himself to Moses as "I Am" when he commissioned Moses to return to Egypt to deliver his people from slavery (Exod. 3:1). The people camped before Mount Sinai following the exodus (Exod. 19:1–2); Moses made several trips up the mountain to meet with God (Exod. 20:21; 24:9; 32:31). It was on Mount Sinai that the Lord twice gave the Ten Commandments, inscribed on two stone tablets and symbolizing the covenant (Exod. 31:18; 34:28). It was before the mountain that God formally ratified the Mosaic covenant (Exod. 24:1–8).

C. Elijah and Moses (19:8)

The central concern of Elijah's ministry was the first commandment of the Mosaic Law: "You shall have no other gods before me" (Exod. 20:3). The connection to Moses is suggested by the forty days and forty nights it took Elijah to reach Horeb. Horeb was, of course, closely linked to Moses, and the number *forty* is connected to Moses both by the forty days he spent on Mount Sinai (Exod. 24:18; 34:28) and by the forty years he led the people through the wilderness (Exod. 16:35). Elijah's experience on Sinai is strikingly similar to that of Moses on the mountain (Exod. 33:17–34:9).

VII. TEACHING OUTLINE

A. INTRODUCTION

1. Lead Story: The Battle with Burnout
2. Context: On the very next day after the great Mount Carmel encounter, Elijah received a death threat from Jezebel. He panicked and fled from his area of ministry.
3. Transition: We think of the great heroes of faith as always strong and victorious. But this episode gives us insight into areas of weakness against which we must be on guard.

B. COMMENTARY

1. Elijah on the Run (19:1–8)
2. Elijah on the Rebound (19:9–18)
3. Elijah's Return to Action (19:19–21)

C. CONCLUSION: GRACE FOR THE JOURNEY

VIII. ISSUES FOR DISCUSSION

1. Discuss John Stott's comment at the beginning of this chapter that discouragement is the occupational hazard of Christian discipleship. Do you think this is true? Has it been an issue for you?
2. In your opinion, what were the main factors that made Elijah run? What things have this effect on you?
3. What are the main lessons you see in the way the Lord dealt with Elijah?
4. How should we as followers of Christ measure success?

1 Kings 20:1–21:29

Judgment Day

"*G*od has resolved to be everyman's Judge, rewarding every man according to his works. Retribution is the inescapable moral law of creation; God will see that each man sooner or later receives what he deserves—if not here, then hereafter. This is one of the basic laws of life. And, being made in God's image, we all know in our hearts that this is right."

J a m e s   I .   P a c k e r

GEOGRAPHICAL PROFILE: ARAM (SYRIA)

- Its capital was Damascus
- Ruled at this stage by Ben-Hadad, a name meaning "son of Hadad," the Syrian storm god, equivalent to Baal. A Ben-Hadad (900?–875? B.C.) had been king in the time of Asa (15:18). But the evidence suggests that he was succeeded by his son, who had the same name. The king of Syria who collided with Ahab was thus Ben-Hadad II, who ruled from about 875–843 B.C.
- Because Assyria dominated upper Mesopotamia, Syria pushed south against Israel, seeking territory and access to the important coastal trade routes. This caused continual conflict with Israel, under Ahab and his sons

GEOGRAPHICAL PROFILE: ASSYRIA

- Under Ashurbanipal II (883–859 B.C.) and his son Shalmeneser III (859–824 B.C.), Assyria reached new military heights. They were known for the brutality of their campaigns
- Shalmeneser moved westward into the region of Syria. In 853 B.C. he encountered an alliance of twelve western kings at Qarqar on the Orontes River, in northern Syria. This battle is not mentioned

in the Bible, but the Assyrian inscriptions list Hadadezer of Syria and "Ahab the Israelite" as the leaders of the opponents

- Shalmeneser claimed in his annals that he had won a great victory. But since he advanced no further and retreated to the east, his claim is dubious

1 Kings 20:1–21:29

IN A NUTSHELL

*A*hab has declared himself an enemy of Elijah, the prophet of the Lord. He now displays his attitude toward God himself by twice setting his desires above the standards and purposes of God. In the first case he spares a pagan king whom the Lord had delivered into his hand, ignoring God's call to holy war. In the second case he allows his wife to flout God's law and commit murder so he can fulfill his desire for a vegetable garden. Both acts call down God's judgment.

Judgment Day

I. INTRODUCTION

The Point of No Return

*Y*ears ago, when my wife and I were flying from Hawaii to Australia, our plane unexpectedly hit "clear air turbulence." I had just returned from walking around the plane and had not had the time to buckle my seat belt when the plane suddenly dropped. Instantly I was thrown to the ceiling, where my head smashed the light and air panel. Elizabeth was thrown into the air and actually came down on the other side of the aisle. Our injuries were not significant, but those of some other people were. Several were transported to the hospital when we finally reached Sydney.

In the first moments after the episode, conditions in the cabin were chaotic. I worried about the condition of the airplane. Would we crash? Would we need to find a place to land? Were we past the point of no return, that point at which it would be necessary to press on to our destination because turning back was no longer an option? Where, in the South Pacific, were there other options? As it turned out, our plane had suffered no damage, and we were in no danger. But at that moment, "the point of no return" was no longer an abstract concept. I suddenly understood in a new way what it meant to be committed to a course from which there was no turning back.

Ahab had chosen a course of rebellion against God. Still, by God's grace, there remained the possibility of turning back. Through Elijah and other prophets, God set before him the opportunity of repentance. But Ahab refused to change course. Even then the Lord did not strike out in holy anger. Both Israel and Ahab were the continuing beneficiaries of the restraint of a holy God, who "is patient with you, not wanting anyone to perish, but everyone to come to repentance" (2 Pet. 3:9).

But choices have consequences, and consequences become inevitable. That is the situation in 1 Kings 20–21. In both of these chapters, Ahab is the main figure, as he interacts with his nation's enemies, his own citizens, and God's prophets. In both chapters God's guilty verdict is pronounced upon him, in the first case by an anonymous prophet and in the second by his nemesis, the prophet Elijah. Judgment day has arrived.

II. COMMENTARY

Judgment Day

> **MAIN IDEA:** *We are accountable to a holy God, who will certainly judge us for our sins.*

A War Against Syria (20:1–30)

> **SUPPORTING IDEA:** *The Lord delights to show his people who trust him and follow his word that he is the one true God.*

20:1–12. Israel did not live in isolation from surrounding nations. One of the major regional powers was the nation of **Aram** (or Syria), with Damascus as its capital. Syria has entered the history of 1 Kings to this point only when they were hired by King Asa of Judah to harass Baasha of Israel about twenty years earlier (15:18–22). Elijah was also told by the Lord that Hazael, a future Syrian king, would be part of God's plan for eradicating the house of Ahab (19:15–17). For the next century, conflict between Syria and Israel would be a recurring theme. Syria was a growing regional power, desiring to extend its control to the southwest, toward Israel and Judah. This was caused by the emergence of Assyria as an expansionist superpower to its northeast. Syria could expand only to the southwest, and it needed to secure its southern flank to avoid a two-front war. This led to a series of battles with Israel, under King Ahab, two of which are described in this chapter and a third in chapter 22.

Ben-Hadad II, also known as Hadadezer, had succeeded his father on the throne of Damascus. At an unspecified time, he chose to invade his neighbor in force, at the head of an alliance of **thirty-two kings**, most of whom were probably tribal chiefs and heads of minor states. They **besieged Samaria**, Ahab's capital, although it was not a tight siege, since Ahab was able to move people and troops in and out of the city.

Ben-Hadad's apparent intention was intimidation, not attack. But a series of three diplomatic exchanges escalated into violence. In the first encounter, Ben-Hadad insisted that Ahab submit and acknowledge his status as Ben-Hadad's vassal: **Your silver and gold are mine, and the best of your wives and children are mine**. We have no indication what had brought Ahab to such a lowly position, but he submitted with the degrading acknowledgment: **I and all I have are yours**. This humiliating confession only served to feed Ben-Hadad's arrogance. He escalated his demand, insisting that within twenty-four hours Ahab should allow the Syrians to **seize everything you value**, whether people or treasures, **and carry it away**. This demand for surrender was a virtual declaration of war, and Ahab recognized it as such.

Gathering his nation's leaders, Ahab sought to rally their support, pointing out the Syrian intent: **See how this man is looking for trouble!** The nation's leaders agreed with Ahab that submission was untenable. They would fight rather than surrender. Ahab sent back his bold refusal, knowing the effect it would have. War was now inevitable, made more so by Ben-Hadad's threat to reduce Samaria to **dust**. This was both an arrogant boast and a reminder to Ahab of Syria's numerical superiority. Ahab had many faults, but cowardice was not one of them. He responded with the ancient equivalent of "Don't count your chickens before they hatch": **One who puts on his armor should not boast like one who takes it off.**

At that response Ben-Hadad issued the order: **Prepare to attack.** But it was a sign of his arrogant overconfidence that the order was issued **while he and the kings were drinking in their tents.** In his eyes Israel was not an enemy to be taken seriously.

20:13–14. Because of Ahab's past relationships with Elijah and God, it would not be surprising to read that he had been abandoned by God to face Syria on his own. Instead, **a prophet came to Ahab the king** with good news from the Lord: **this vast army . . . I will give . . . into your hand.** This victory would not be about Ahab but about the Lord's ability to reveal his glory and to demonstrate his reality to Ahab. The king would be forced to declare that the Lord was God (a theme repeated in v. 28). God was gracious and patient even with a defiant, rebellious man like Ahab.

The prophet not only promised victory; he also provided military counsel: the attack was to be initiated by Ahab and led by **the young officers.** The identity of this group is debated. Some see this as an elite force, but the term simply means "young men" and seems to refer to untrained fighters. If so, this would reinforce the fact that it was God alone who would be responsible for the victory. God, not Ahab, was Israel's true defender and deliverer.

20:15–21. The Lord fulfilled his promise. Ahab summoned his troops and attacked **at noon.** This was a strange time to launch an attack since there was no opportunity for surprise. But **Ben-Hadad and the 32 kings allied with him were in their tents getting drunk.** This led to the foolish order to take the Israelite troops alive, a command that made a Syrian counterattack almost impossible. The Israelites quickly routed the enemy, so **that the Arameans fled, with the Israelites in pursuit.** Israel had won a great victory, because it had followed God's prophet. The battle of Samaria was over, and the weaker army had won.

20:22–25. In the aftermath of battle, both sides prepared for the inevitable return engagement. **The prophet** who had previously come with the divine promise of victory now came with a warning to prepare for another attack the next spring. Ahab's victory had not put an end to the ambitions of Syria.

Preparations on the Syrian side took a different form. The king's military advisers attributed the Israelite victory to the fact that **their gods are gods of the hills,** and that is where the battle had been waged. Their tactical planning involved three components: an attack on **the plains,** where their chariots and their gods would be **stronger;** the replacement of petty kings with trained military **officers;** and the rebuilding of the army to its former strength, **horse for horse and chariot for chariot.** The advice was militarily sound, but it had one fatal weakness. It was blasphemy against the Lord of heaven and earth, reducing him to a local hill deity.

20:26–30. Ben-Hadad followed the counsel of his advisors, rebuilding his army and marching out to a city on the plains, **Aphek,** to confront Israel. This would be a full military engagement. Aphek, located on the east side of the Sea of Galilee, provided the kind of terrain where Syria's chariots could operate effectively. The manpower advantage was overwhelming. Israel's situation seemed hopeless.

But Ben-Hadad faced an adversary greater than he could imagine. Once again the prophet, **the man of God,** brought a message from the Lord to the king. Ahab would have a further lesson in God's greatness, and Syria would learn the consequences of demeaning and defaming the God of Israel: **I will deliver this vast army into your hands, and you will know that I am the LORD.** This was no ordinary military engagement: the glory and honor of God were at stake.

The battle itself is not described. The two nations **camped opposite each other** for seven days. When the battle was over, Israel had won a stunning victory. Syrian casualties numbered in the thousands. When the survivors fled for refuge in Aphek, thousands more died when the city walls collapsed on them. Ben-Hadad, the great king, was reduced to hiding **in an inner room.** Once again, when the nation and king had listened to God's prophet and followed his word, they had experienced the Lord's victory.

B Sparing Ben-Hadad (20:31–43)

> **SUPPORTING IDEA:** *When we substitute our desires for God's will, we bring ourselves under God's judgment.*

20:31–34. After his previous defeat, Ben-Hadad had been able to escape. This time his advisers suggested that they cast themselves on the mercy of Ahab, since Israel's kings had a reputation for being **merciful.** Wearing symbols of submission (**sackcloth**) and surrender (**ropes**), they approached the enemy king. Their carefully chosen words echoed the vassal language Ahab had been forced to use in verse 4: **Your servant Ben-Hadad.** Ahab's response told them all they needed to know: **Is he still alive? He is my brother.**

This was not the language of anger or revenge. It may have been common diplomatic language, but it revealed that Ahab did not view Ben-Hadad as a hated enemy or a vassal. His language emphasized their mutual standing as kings. Ahab was more aware of his royal status than his national responsibility. Syria's negotiators were quick to catch the nuance of Ahab's words, and they offered to bring Ben-Hadad to Ahab. When he arrived, **Ahab had him come up into his chariot**, a sign of honor. Often captured kings were forced to put their shoulders to the wheel of a chariot, to symbolize submission and defeat. Ahab had chosen to honor, not humiliate, a defeated enemy.

Ahab then entered into negotiations with Ben-Hadad. The Syrian king was forced into significant concessions. He agreed to return the Israelite cities they had taken and to permit Ahab to **set up . . . market areas in Damascus**. This had the status of a **treaty**, not just a gentlemen's agreement. On its basis, Ahab set Ben-Hadad free. Ahab was politically shrewd. He had won a great victory, he made significant commercial and territorial gains, but he had not alienated a potential ally against Assyria. But the victory over Syria had been God's doing, not Ahab's. He was acting as if the victory was his. He made no effort to consult the prophet whose direction had been so decisive.

20:35–38. The author of 1 Kings suddenly shifts the scene to a remarkable encounter between two members of **the sons of the prophets**. It is a strange story. One prophet, obviously speaking under divine direction, demanded that another prophet attack him with a **weapon**. When the man refused, the first prophet pronounced a divine judgment: **as soon as you leave me a lion will kill you**. That indeed happened, a striking reminder of the events of 1 Kings 13:23–26. Not even a prophet was exempt from the requirements of obedience. A second prophet then struck the prophet, wounding him. The wounded prophet then made his way to the road the king would travel, disguising himself so his identity would be hidden.

20:39–40. When the king appeared, the disguised prophet made use of the custom that any citizen could appeal to the king as the court of final resort. He presented his problem: he had been given responsibility to guard someone else's prisoner. But he had been warned that if the man escaped, he must pay a huge penalty. The scenario must reflect an ancient cultural practice of caring for prisoners. But the man had failed his duty. He had become distracted, and his prisoner had escaped. Ahab didn't even wait for the question before he delivered his verdict: "You are responsible for allowing the man to escape. You must pay the penalty."

20:41–43. The story had been a prophetic setup, like Nathan's famous confrontation with David in 2 Samuel 12. Ahab had pronounced his own sentence. The prophet removed his disguise and declared God's judgment: **You have set free a man I had determined should die**. Ahab had violated the rules of holy war. He did not have the right to treat Ben-Hadad as he pleased.

His treatment of Ben-Hadad may have seemed shrewd and humane, but it was, in God's eyes, spiritual rebellion. He had not won the victory; God had. The life of Syria's king was not his to deal with as he chose. At the very least, Ahab should have consulted the Lord's prophet about the matter.

Therefore, the sentence of death now fell on Ahab: **it is your life for his life, your people for his people.** The judgment would fall not only on Ahab but also on his family. For the first time Ahab stood under the divine sentence of death. He was not repentant, but **sullen and angry.** Not even God's remarkable display of his power had softened his heart.

Murdering Naboth (21:1–16)

SUPPORTING IDEA: *When God's law is ignored, the powerful corrupt the system to further their interests.*

21:1–4. Ahab had failed at Aphek because he had done what he pleased to get what he wanted without any concern for the will of God. The next episode also finds its origins in Ahab's desires. He had a winter palace in **Jezreel.** One of his neighbors, a man named **Naboth,** had a **vineyard** near the palace. Ahab wanted **a vegetable garden,** and Naboth's property seemed like the ideal location. So he approached Naboth and made an offer: **I will give you a better vineyard or . . . I will pay you whatever it is worth.** There is no indication that the offer was not sincere or fair. This was a simple real estate transaction. Ahab, as the king, was accustomed to getting what he wanted under such conditions.

Ahab was not prepared for Naboth's emphatic refusal to sell. His opening words indicated that he saw such a sale as an affront to God himself. Behind his refusal was a conviction about the nature of land and inheritance laws in Israel. The land was seen as belonging to the Lord, not to the people (Lev. 25:23). After the conquest each family had received an allotment. This was **the inheritance of my fathers** to which Naboth referred. There were complicated laws that kept the poor from losing their rights to ancestral lands and prevented the elite from accumulating more and more land at the cost of the poor (see "Deeper Discoveries"). Naboth's land, therefore, was not his to sell to the king or anyone else. He was a man of integrity who would not violate his conscience, even at the risk of offending the king.

Ahab was not pleased, but he had no recourse. **Sullen and angry,** he returned home like a petulant child.

21:5–10. For the first time in 1 Kings, **Jezebel** steps front and center. We have only heard about her indirectly, but now we see an aggressive, determined, and energetic woman in action. She was the native of a country where the king made the law and considered himself above the law. In the ancient world the king's rights and powers were absolute. Might made right. When she heard the story of why Ahab had become sullen and withdrawn, her question was, **Is this how you act as king over Israel?** She would show Ahab how a king acted: **Cheer up. I'll get you the vineyard.**

If the pagan world believed that the king was the law and made the law, the biblical view was very different. The law was rooted in the nature and character of God, and the king must be submissive to it. The law in Deuteronomy 17:14–20 mandated that a king was to write for himself his own copy of the law and to read it daily "so that he may learn to revere the Lord his God and follow carefully all the words of this law and these decrees and not consider himself better than his brothers and turn from the law to the right or to the left."

Ahab stepped back and allowed his wife to do "whatever it took." He was aware of her character, and she could not have used **his seal** without his permission. But the plan and the process were clearly hers. Her intention was to have Naboth executed on false charges, in such a way that neither she nor Ahab were directly involved. She used her royal authority to issue instructions to the city leaders of Jezreel. The plan was a shrewd combination of ruthlessness and religiosity. The entire affair was couched in the cloak of Hebrew religion: a **fast** mourning a public offense against God; the use of **two** witnesses (Deut. 17:6); the biblical accusation of blasphemy (**cursed**) against God and the king (Exod. 22:28; Lev. 24:10–16); and the stoning outside the city (Num. 15:36).

Her ruthlessness was seen in her coercion of city leaders who knew the power of the queen to punish them, the putting of Naboth in a position of prominence to make his offense seem even more serious, the suborning of perjury by **two scoundrels**, and the sheer audacity of the entire plot. The corruption of Israel under Ahab and Jezebel is revealed by the willingness of the most prominent citizens of Jezreel to be involved in the extermination of a man whom they knew to be innocent.

21:11–16. Jezebel's plan was carried out precisely. The civic leaders did as they were told and reported to Jezebel that the deed had been accomplished: **Naboth has been stoned and is dead.** The letters may have been sealed with Ahab's seal, but the leaders realized this was Jezebel's plan.

All that remained was for Jezebel to present her gift to her husband. Her words echo her earlier words to Ahab in verse 7: **take possession of the vineyard of Naboth . . . He is no longer alive, but dead.** It is possible that Hebrew law specified that the land of an executed criminal reverted to the king. We are told in 2 Kings 9:26 that Naboth's sons were also killed at this time. Whatever the legal niceties, Ahab did not ask any questions. He went **to take possession of Naboth's vineyard.**

An innocent man and his sons lay dead; a wicked king and queen had made a mockery of justice; responsible citizens had engaged in great evil. And

God had not intervened to prevent this from taking place. Evil appeared to have spoken the last word. But although God's judgment is not always immediate, it is always inevitable.

D Meeting the God of Justice (21:17–29)

SUPPORTING IDEA: *We may try to ignore God's law, but we will not escape it.*

21:17–19. At the very moment that Ahab and Jezebel believed that their word was the last word in Israel, **the word of the LORD came to Elijah**. The prophet was called by God to confront Ahab, in the very place of his apparent success. The story must end where it began, in **Naboth's vineyard**. His mission was to pronounce God's verdict on his actions. Ahab was held accountable for the actions of his wife. He could not escape God's justice by pleading ignorance. So a judgment would fall upon him that fit the crime: **dogs will lick up your blood**. Just as Naboth had died a violent death, so would Ahab.

21:20–26. The text shifts from commission to encounter. Ahab greeted Elijah with an insult: **So you have found me, my enemy!** Elijah denounced Ahab for his sin. The murder of Naboth may have been the immediate cause of the Lord's anger, but Ahab's guilt was far greater than one act. Elijah did not use the normal prophetic formula, "This is what the Lord says." Instead, he spoke directly in the voice of the Lord: **I am going to bring disaster**. Ahab would experience God's anger.

The unnamed prophet of chapter 20 had already told Ahab of the violent death that would fall on him (20:42). Elijah now indicated the scope of that judgment. It would fall upon Ahab personally. It would also fall on his descendants, so that **every last male** would meet a violent death. As a result, the dynasty of Omri and Ahab would be obliterated, just as the preceding dynasties of **Jeroboam** and **Baasha** had been. This amounted to a prediction of a coup. Jezebel would also meet a violent death in Jezreel, in retribution for her part in Naboth's murder. Her death would be violent and dishonorable: **Dogs will devour Jezebel**.

In a final statement that summarized the brutal finality of the judgment that was to fall upon this powerful king, Elijah declared, **Dogs will eat those belonging to Ahab who die in the city, and the birds of the air will feed on those who die in the country**. Dogs were the ancient scavengers of the city, and birds were the scavengers of the country. The family of this proud king, who was enjoying the vineyard stolen from an innocent man, would be turned into dog food! The graphic language was a way of indicating the violent, dishonorable deaths that would befall them.

Ahab and Jezebel were a vile couple who deserved all they were to receive at the hands of the Lord. **By going after idols**, they had committed greater sins than even Jeroboam had.

21:27–29. For the first time Ahab responded to a message from God's prophet: **He tore his clothes, put on sackcloth and fasted**. He gave immediate, visible expression of his humbling before the Lord. We are not told of any public acts that Ahab did to confirm his repentance. But the Lord did not treat his response with contempt. The Lord announced to Elijah the delay of judgment on Ahab's house and wife. Judgment would still fall, but not until after Ahab's death. His self-humbling had granted his dynasty one more generation. It is a vivid illustration that God is patient, not wanting anyone (even Ahab) to perish, but everyone to come "to repentance" (2 Pet. 3:9). But even this belated repentance would not cancel the judgment that had been announced.

MAIN IDEA REVIEW: *We are accountable to a holy God, who will certainly judge us for our sins.*

III. CONCLUSION

Here Comes the Judge!

A major newspaper recently featured a front-page article pointing out that mention of hell, even from evangelical pulpits, is at an all-time low. It is, they claimed, an indication of the impact both of secularism and of a consumer mind-set that wants to avoid the negative and the unpopular. Downplaying damnation has become fashionable.

But one of the most common themes of the Bible is that God is the judge to whom everyone will give an account. His judgment on our sins may not be immediate, but it is inevitable. Evil may seem to be triumphant for a time. But a righteous and holy God will bring it to account, perhaps in this life—and certainly in the next. At the height of his power, in the moment of military victory over his greatest enemy, and in a moment of celebration when he had acquired a piece of land that his heart desired, Ahab's enjoyment was interrupted by a message from a holy God. He was not the all-powerful king who could do as he pleased. He was a weak human being, accountable to a holy God for his actions. He was a man about to face the wrath of a holy God.

And so are we. The only escape is through the Lord Jesus Christ, who has taken the guilt and judgment of those who put their faith in him. "Therefore, there is now no condemnation for those who are in Christ Jesus" (Rom. 8:1). By grace, Ahab experienced a *postponement* of judgment. Through the cross we experience a *cancellation* of God's judgment.

PRINCIPLES

- God is gracious to his undeserving people.
- When we trust and follow God's Word, we experience God's blessing.
- When we minimize the living God and reduce him to the status of other "gods," we are guilty of blasphemy.
- When we treat God's enemy as our friend, we defy God.
- Law must be grounded in the character of God, not the arbitrary standards of humans or the desires of the powerful.
- God cares about social justice and acts to protect the poor and the powerless.
- God will judge our sin.

APPLICATIONS

- Cultivate gratitude for God's grace, and beware of spiritual presumption.
- Trust God's Word and act on his promises.
- Discipline your desires to be sure that you do not elevate them above his Word.
- Ground your understanding of right and wrong in absolute standards.
- Become aware of your sin and God's judgment and respond with repentance rather than despair or denial.

IV. LIFE APPLICATION

The God of Social Justice

One of the themes of chapter 21 is the relation of God and his people to a world in which evil seems to triumph and injustice is rampant. Although God did not intervene to stop the actions of Ahab and Jezebel, he did send his prophet to declare and confront the evil. It is sad that no one in Jezreel had the courage to declare the evil of what Jezebel intended to do.

What is our response in view of oppression and injustice if we are followers of Christ? We are called to be salt and light (Matt. 5:13–16). What does this involve?

We are not surprised. We are deeply realistic about the nature of life in a fallen world.

We must not be seduced. We refuse to go along to get ahead. We are committed to God's standards.

We cannot be silent. We are called to represent the standards of the Lord and to serve as his spokespeople. We must speak his truth in a way that represents the grace and truth of Christ rather than our anger and self-righteousness, even when to speak such truth may be costly.

We will not be stopped. We are to "stand firm. Let nothing move you. Always give yourselves fully to the work of the Lord, because you know that your labor in the Lord is not in vain" (1 Cor. 15:58).

V. PRAYER

Father, remind me that you are a holy God who hates sin and will not clear the guilty. Help me to take my own sin seriously. Help me to understand the wonder of the cross and the work of the Savior on my behalf. Give me an urgency to share the gospel as I think about others who are not ready to meet their Judge. Amen.

VI. DEEPER DISCOVERIES

A. "You Will Know That I Am the LORD" (20:13,28)

The purpose of the victory that God would give over the Syrians would not be to protect Israel or to relieve Ahab. It would be to promote the glory of the Lord and to demonstrate his status as the unique, sovereign God. This is language borrowed from the exodus, where the Lord revealed his glory to both Israel and Egypt (see Exod. 6:7; 7:5; 10:2; 14:4)

B. The Inheritance of My Fathers (21:3)

The law of land inheritance in Israel was built around two institutions recorded in Leviticus 25. The sabbatical year meant that every seven years the land was to rest, debts were cancelled, and slaves were set free. The year of Jubilee was a super-sabbatical, when all land outside walled cities was returned to their original families. Land tenure was related to the year of Jubilee: "The land must not be sold permanently, because the land is mine and you are but aliens and my tenants" (Lev. 25:23). There were three guiding principles that provided the basis of a biblical social justice system.

First, the land was the Lord's and was to be treated as a trust to be handled with care, not a possession to be spoiled. Second, the poor must have the opportunity for a new beginning. Third, limits must be placed on the ability of the few to accumulate land and wealth at the expense of the many. The Bible did not attempt to eliminate poverty or wealth because of the nature of the human heart and the difference in personal abilities. But it did place limits and mandate opportunities.

VII. TEACHING OUTLINE

A. INTRODUCTION
1. Lead Story: The Point of No Return
2. Context: The previous three chapters have shown the conflict between God and Baal, primarily through the battle between Elijah and Baal. Elijah has been the main figure. Now Ahab is the main figure, and we see him headed for divine judgment as he puts his own desires before the will of God.
3. Transition: The nation of Israel found itself under military attack from its more powerful neighbor, Syria. God chose not to abandon his rebellious people but once again to display his glory to them—a glory that does not touch the hard heart of Ahab.

B. COMMENTARY
1. War Against Syria (20:1–30)
2. Sparing Ben-Hadad (20:31–43)
3. Murdering Naboth (21:1–16)
4. Meeting the God of Justice (21:17–29)

C. CONCLUSION: HERE COMES THE JUDGE!

VIII. ISSUES FOR DISCUSSION
1. Ahab chose to put his desires above the word of God. Is that a temptation you face? How do you avoid the kind of pragmatic reasoning of an Ahab or a Jezebel?
2. The modern church doesn't talk very much about God's judgment. Is that biblical? Is it wise? How much emphasis should be placed on the doctrine of hell and final judgment?
3. God cares about social justice and the abuse of power, as 1 Kings 21 makes clear. How well do evangelical Christians show that concern?

1 Kings 22:1–
2 Kings 1:18

Playing with Fire

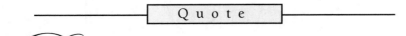

"*D*efend the Bible? I would as soon defend a lion!

Unchain it and it will defend itself."

C h a r l e s   H a d d o n   S p u r g e o n

BIOGRAPHICAL PROFILE: JEHOSHAPHAT OF JUDAH

- Sixth king in the line of David, he ruled Judah from about 873 to 848 B.C. For the first three years of his reign, he was co-regent with his father Asa
- Allied with Israel by the marriage of his son Joram to Ahab's daughter Athaliah. He joined in at least two military campaigns with Israel, with Ahab (1 Kgs. 22) and with Jehoram (2 Kgs. 3)
- The Book of 2 Chronicles devotes four chapters to him (2 Chr. 17–20), emphasizing his commitment to have God's law taught to his people, his reform of the nation around obedience to the Lord, and a divine deliverance from a military invasion
- He was a king approved by God, although the approval is qualified by his tolerance of the high places

BIOGRAPHICAL PROFILE: AHAZIAH OF ISRAEL

- Oldest son of Ahab, he followed his father on the throne but reigned only briefly (853–852 B.C.), dying as the result of injuries suffered in a fall
- Spiritual successor of his father, he was a Baal worshiper who treated the prophet Elijah as his enemy
- Died childless and was succeeded by his brother Jehoram

1 Kings 22:1–
2 Kings 1:18

IN A NUTSHELL

The Lord has been gracious and patient toward Ahab in spite of the depth of his sin and rebellion. But it is now time for the announced judgment to come, both upon him and his oldest son. The reason for God's judgment becomes obvious by their arrogant response to the word of God, communicated through his prophets Micaiah and Elijah.

Playing with Fire

I. INTRODUCTION

Trifling with the Word of God

*O*n November 14, 1874, the American evangelist D. L. Moody stood up to speak to a hall filled with students at Oxford University in England. Moody was a powerful speaker, but he was uneducated, and he spoke with what the British considered a hopeless American accent. He had just come from Cambridge University, where the students had mocked his grammar, laughed at his accent, and done everything they could to disrupt his meetings. But God's Spirit had moved in a powerful way, and hundreds of students had come to Christ.

The students at Oxford had no intention of being outdone by their rivals at Cambridge. They would put this uncouth American in his place. When Moody got up to read the Bible, they began to stomp and shout. Moody closed his Bible, leaned over the pulpit, and said, "You jeered at the hymns and I said nothing. You jeered at the prayers and I said nothing. But now you jeer at the Word of God. I would rather play with forked lightning or meddle with the most deadly disease than trifle with the Word of God."

Moody was absolutely right. Playing with the Word of God is playing with fire, and the trouble with playing with fire is that you inevitably get burned! There are all kinds of ways we can trifle with the Word of God. We can ridicule it and pass judgment upon it; we can ignore it; we can turn from it to some kind of substitute; or we can undermine it with faint praise, reducing it to the status of one among many "good books." But the one thing we cannot do is escape it. The day will come when our lives will be measured by God's Word. That is what Ahab and his son discovered.

II. COMMENTARY

Playing with Fire

> **MAIN IDEA:** *We may ignore God's Word or fight it, but we cannot evade it or defeat it.*

A The Death of Ahab (22:1–40)

> **SUPPORTING IDEA:** *The Word of God cannot be outwitted or subverted by human ingenuity.*

22:1–4. In the middle of the ninth century B.C., Assyria was the superpower that threatened the stability of life in the biblical regions. Under

Shalmeneser (858–824 B.C.), it was pushing west. While Syria was the nation most directly under threat, other nations in the region felt the pressure. In 853 Assyria had pushed to Qarqar, a city on the Orontes River, about one hundred miles from Damascus. Assyrian records indicate that the Assyrians encountered here a large coalition of armies led by Ben-Hadad and including Ahab. Shalmeneser claimed victory in the ensuing battle, but it is more significant that he did not advance further but withdrew from the region.

It is most probably in the light of these events that we are to understand the statement that **for three years there was no war between Aram and Israel**. Assyria had made them allies for a time. But Assyria's retreat to the east removed the threat temporarily, making it possible for the weaker states to pursue their smaller ambitions.

Apparently not long after the battle of Qarqar, **Jehoshaphat king of Judah** made a state visit to **the king of Israel** (this title or "king" is used twenty-seven times in the chapter, and we do not learn that Ahab is meant until verse 20). This is Jehoshaphat's first appearance in 1 Kings, although by this time he had been on the throne of Judah for almost twenty years (his reign will be summarized in 22:41–50). We will discover as the story of 1 and 2 Kings unfolds that Ahab and Jehoshaphat had made an alliance of peace, sealed by the marriage of Ahab's daughter Athaliah to Jehoshaphat's son Jehoram (see 2 Kgs. 8:18,26). This marriage was to prove disastrous to Judah, infecting the nation with the corruption of baalism and almost resulting in the extermination of the Davidic dynasty (2 Kgs. 11).

Jehoshaphat and Ahab were a spiritual "odd couple," as can by seen by a comparison of their evaluations in 1 Kings 21:25–26 and 22:43. Jehoshaphat was a good and godly king who initiated reform and renewal in the Southern Kingdom (2 Chr. 17). But his alliance with Ahab, while economically successful and militarily shrewd (it allowed both nations to focus on the greater threat of Syria), was a compromise that would cost his nation dearly.

Ahab took the opportunity of Jehoshaphat's visit to propose a joint military venture against the Syrians. Although Ben-Hadad had promised to return captured cities to Israel (1 Kgs. 20:34), he had failed to return the strategic border town of **Ramoth Gilead**. Ahab asked the king of Judah to join him in a campaign to take the city by force, and Jehoshaphat agreed: **I am as you are, my people as your people**. Jehoshaphat made this commitment publicly before seeking guidance from the Lord. The compromise with Ahab had made it difficult to resist further involvement. Perhaps he assumed that if God had previously blessed Israel in battle against Syria, he would do so again. He was wrong, as the prophet Jehu would make clear to him on his return from this battle: "Should you help the wicked and love those who hate the LORD?" (2 Chr. 19:2).

22:5–12. Having made his commitment to the battle, Jehoshaphat remembered the need to **seek the counsel of the LORD** on such matters. But he was now seeking confirmation rather than direction. Because he had made up his mind, he was deaf to the Lord's voice. Ahab was more than willing to oblige. He brought together an impressive number of court-sponsored prophets who endorsed Ahab's project: **Go . . . for the LORD will give it into the king's hand.** Jehoshaphat detected the absence of an authentic messenger of God: **Is there not a prophet of the LORD here?** Ahab's response revealed both his attitude toward the Lord and his true prophets: **There is still one man . . . but . . . he never prophesies anything good about me.**

The pattern of one true prophet against many false prophets and the authentic prophet's opposition to Ahab are familiar from the Elijah stories. There were two kinds of prophets: prophets of Ahab and prophets of God. The situation should have been reason enough for Jehoshaphat to return to Judah as quickly as possible. This genuine prophet was a man known only from this episode— **Micaiah son of Imlah.** It is another confirmation that Elijah was not "the only one left" (19:10,14,18).

While Micaiah was being brought to the kings, the false prophets put on a display for two rulers. It was a formal occasion, with the kings **dressed in their royal robes** and **sitting on their thrones,** in the large open public space just outside the city gates. Before them, a prophet named **Zedekiah** used **iron horns** as a symbol of military might. He probably mimicked the goring actions of an ox or bull as he and his companions proclaimed the certainty of Syria's destruction and Israel's victory. The prophets were carrying out their duty: furthering the aspirations of the state and the king. But there was no authentic word of God, in spite of all the action and noise. The show may have been impressive, but it was empty.

22:13–28. The royal official sent to bring Micaiah had some advice for the prophet as they made their way back to the royal audience. In his view, a prophet's task was to support whatever project the king desired. Since the prophets were unanimously **predicting success for the king,** Micaiah should not suggest anything different. His advice was straightforward and probably conveyed an unspoken threat: **speak favorably.** But he had misread Micaiah. This prophet was not for sale, and he had no interest in impressing the powers-that-be. He was willing to stand alone, if that was what the Lord required. Micaiah was a prophet in the tradition of Elijah.

But Micaiah took the king by surprise. When he stood before Ahab and was questioned about whether they should go to war, his answer mimicked that of the court prophets: **be victorious . . . for the LORD will give it into the king's hand.** It may have been his sarcastic tone, his nonverbal behavior, or even the answer itself, but Ahab detected that Micaiah was mocking him. Ahab was also alert to the fact that Micaiah had not spoken in the name of

God. His rebuttal was direct but ironic, perhaps designed to impress Jehoshaphat: **How many times must I make you swear to tell me nothing but the truth in the name of the LORD?**

Micaiah then delivered the message he had received from God. If the two kings went to war, all Israel would be **scattered on the hills like sheep without a shepherd**. A shepherd was a common image for a king. This statement predicted the death of Ahab and the departure of his army. Since they were the attacking army, withdrawal meant the failure of their mission. Ahab responded by complaining that this negativism was typical of Micaiah.

Micaiah was not finished. He needed to explain the prophecy of the rival prophets. He made clear that the Lord was intent on Ahab's death. A divine death sentence had been passed on the king, and all that remained was for it to be carried out. Ahab would be enticed **into attacking Ramoth Gilead and going to his death**. The prophecies of the false prophets were evidence that God had allowed a deceiving spirit to operate, so that he would be enticed (see "Deeper Discoveries").

There is a cost to faithfulness. **Zedekiah**, the apparent leader of the court prophets who had been exposed as false by Micaiah's revelation, **slapped Micaiah in the face**. The violent insult was followed by a denial that Micaiah was speaking by prophetic inspiration. Ahab's response was to imprison God's prophet and order him to be put on a diet of **bread and water** until his return from the battle. Micaiah met these acts with a God-given confidence. The test of a true prophet was whether his words came to pass (Deut. 18:21–22). Thus Zedekiah would learn the truth when he hid in fear in an inner room because of the outcome of battle, and Ahab would never return. Micaiah was confident of vindication because he had spoken the message of God.

22:29–38. It is not surprising that Ahab went into battle; it is more surprising that Jehoshaphat did. Surely he should have detected the truth of Micaiah's words! Perhaps he had become more concerned about losing face by going back on the commitment he had made to Israel. So Ahab went to battle, proclaiming his confidence in his safe return. But his underlying anxiety was betrayed by his behavior. Kings often wore royal robes in battle to provide a rallying point for their soldiers. But it also made them obvious targets for the enemy. Ahab's proposal to Jehoshaphat was, **I will enter the battle in disguise**. Ahab knew he would be a target. But he felt confident he could outwit the enemy by his disguise.

You can flout God's word, but you cannot defeat it. The Syrian king had commanded his soldiers to target Ahab, since his death would deprive the armies of their most forceful leader. However, Jehoshaphat was the only soldier in royal robes, and he soon found himself in peril. **But when Jehoshaphat cried out**, the enemy saw that he was not Ahab and withdrew.

The writer of 2 Chronicles informs us that his cry was a prayer (2 Chr. 18:31).

The death of Ahab was full of irony. The man who thought he could outwit God died because **someone drew his bow at random**, and the arrow hit Ahab **between the sections of his armor**. There was nothing random about the arrow. It was a divinely guided missile. Ahab recognized the severity of his injuries, and he ordered his chariot driver out of the battle. But the press of the battle made withdrawal impossible. He spent the day **propped up in his chariot facing the Arameans**, while his life slipped away. He began the battle by trying to disguise his identity; he ended it by trying to disguise his death. But neither was successful. He died, was transported to his capital, and was buried.

The writer of 1 Kings ends the account of Ahab's life in dramatic fashion: **They washed the chariot at a pool in Samaria . . . and the dogs licked up his blood**. This recalls Elijah's prophecy in 21:19. God always has the last word. You can deny God's word, reject God's word, attempt to outwit God's word, but you can never escape it. Ahab's death was not a military accident but a divine act of justice.

22:39–40. The writer of 1 Kings directs his readers to what could be known about Ahab from other sources and alludes to other accomplishments—a luxurious **palace . . . inlaid with ivory** and **cities he fortified**. But as significant as those achievements may have been to a secular historian, they were meaningless because of the spiritual evil that Ahab inflicted on his nation.

B The Reign of Jehoshaphat of Judah (22:41–50)

SUPPORTING IDEA: *The Word of God obeyed produces a life that receives divine approval.*

22:41–50. The "split-screen" method of the writer of 1 Kings means that the history of either Judah or Israel is frozen, while the other nation's history is followed. Since 15:25 we have been following events in the Northern Kingdom, with a special focus on the events surrounding the conflict between Ahab and Elijah, Baal and God, for the soul of the nation. First Kings is more than a record of history. It is a historical sermon, intended to direct its readers to a divine perspective of events so future generations will not follow the sins and failures of their predecessors.

We return in 22:41 to the history of Judah. It is a brief interlude, since in 22:51 the writer will return to the Northern Kingdom, and **Jehoshaphat** will be Judah's king of record until 2 Kings 8:16. Jehoshaphat came to the throne at the age of **thirty-five** in 872 B.C., serving with **his father Asa**, a basically good king, for the first three years as co-regent. He reigned for **twenty-five**

years, from 872 to 848 B.C., sharing the last five years with his son Jehoram as co-regent. The writer of 2 Chronicles devotes four chapters to Jehoshaphat, most of which focuses on his role in leading his nation in reform, renewal, and trust in God (2 Chr. 17–20). The writer of 1 Kings spends only nine verses on his life.

One of the most significant things about Jehoshaphat was that he was **at peace with the king of Israel**. This peace was forged by a marriage alliance and expressed by joint military ventures. There is passing reference to his military exploits, his control of **Edom**, and a failed attempt to renew the glory of Solomon's navy. Although he had allied with Ahab's son, Ahaziah, in the beginning of this project, he **refused** Ahaziah's suggestion that they jointly man the ships.

What is most important to the writer of 1 Kings is the evaluation of Jehoshaphat: **in everything he walked in the ways of his father Asa and did not stray from them.** This falls one step short of the highest accolade of the author—that a king walked in the ways of David—but it places him among the good kings of Judah, behind only Hezekiah and Josiah: **He did what was right in the eyes of the LORD.** Jehoshaphat was a good king because he governed his rule by the standards of God's word.

C The Death of Ahaziah of Israel (1 Kgs. 22:51–53; 2 Kgs. 1:1–18)

SUPPORTING IDEA: *The Word of God cannot be controlled or defeated by human opposition.*

1 Kings 22:51–53. In these verses we are plunged back into the moral and spiritual quagmire of the Northern Kingdom. Ahab's son had a name that spoke of the God whose faith Ahab had spent a lifetime perverting. **Ahaziah** means "held by Yahweh." But his heart was held by Baal. He came to the throne in 853 B.C. and reigned into 852 B.C., a reign counted as two years but probably considerably less than twenty-four months. He continued the pattern of his parents. He had learned nothing from the display of Baal's impotence on Mount Carmel or from the tragic death of his father. Nor was he deterred by the divine pronouncement of disaster that had been pronounced on him by Elijah (21:20–24). By his Baal worship he **provoked the LORD . . . to anger, just as his father had done.**

2 Kings 1:1–2. The division between 1 and 2 Kings is purely artificial. It was not part of the original form of the book but occurred at the time of its translation into Greek (the Septuagint), the division apparently coming at the point where a standard scroll was full. Here it is disruptive, interrupting the account of Ahaziah. The rebellion of **Moab**, Israel's vassal state, will be discussed in greater length in chapter 3 of 2 Kings.

Ahaziah suffered a life-threatening injury when he fell **through the lattice of his upper room in Samaria**, his capital. Such a room was commonly on the flat roof of a house. The lattice provided shelter, shade, and privacy while allowing the breezes to have their cooling effect. His fall may have been an accident or the result of drunkenness. But the injuries he suffered were serious.

In his crisis, Ahaziah turned to Baal as his "god of choice." The specific attributes of the local manifestation of the Baal in the Philistine town of **Ekron** are not known to us. Perhaps he was a god known for his healing powers. His name was **Baal-Zebub**, meaning "lord of the flies." It was to this pagan god that Ahaziah turned for help. He dispatched messengers to make the forty-five-mile journey to Ekron to confer with this god about the possibility of his recovery.

2 Kings 1:3–8. Ahaziah would not be allowed to proceed any further in his rebellion. While Ahaziah's messengers were on the way to Ekron, God sent his messenger (**the angel of the LORD**) to Elijah. The message he brought to Elijah is repeated precisely three times in the chapter (vv. 3–4,6,16), like the clanging of a bell. The first part of the message was that the living God would tolerate no rivals. God would not tolerate syncretism, and he would no longer permit the sin and rebellion of Ahab's family to go unpunished. Ahaziah would know the full weight of God's righteous judgment: **You will certainly die!**

Elijah's encounter with Ahaziah's messengers is not recorded. But it was powerful enough that these men failed to complete their mission. They returned immediately to the palace. They repeated to the king the words they had heard from a powerful but unrecognized messenger they had met in the course of their journey. When Ahaziah asked for his characteristics, he was told that **he was a man with a garment of hair and with a leather belt around his waist**. Ahaziah recognized his father's nemesis: **Elijah the Tishbite**.

2 Kings 1:9–17a. Ahaziah now displayed another way in which he was like his father. He had the word of God from God's prophet. But he would not repent before it. Rather, he would try to defeat it or to bring it under his power. Apparently he believed that if he could capture Elijah, he could change his message. He sent a military squadron to seize the prophet. The confrontation turned into a battle of authority: the man with the power of the king looking up at a solitary, unarmed man **sitting on the top of a hill**. His command conveyed the arrogance of power, as if he were the one determining the course of events: **Man of God, the king says, "Come down!"**

But the king and the people had to realize that trifling with God's word was playing with fire. **If I am a man of God**, Elijah replied, **may fire come down from heaven and consume you and your fifty men!** Although the fire did indeed fall, neither Ahaziah nor the second captain whom he sent were deterred. The second captain's demand was even more arrogant: **Come down at once!** But once again, the fire of God came down.

The third captain came with a humble heart and profound respect for God's prophet. Falling to his knees, he pleaded, **please have respect for my life and the lives of these fifty men**. But Elijah was a man under orders. The decision was not his to make, but the Lord's. **The angel of the LORD** gave Elijah permission to go down with the captain, where he once again confronted the king with the message of God. There was no softening of the word of God. Elijah declared once again the divine verdict to Ahaziah: **You will certainly die!** So Ahaziah died, as Elijah had predicted.

2 Kings 1:17b–18. The death of Ahaziah did not mark the end of the family of Ahab. The bloody end predicted by Elijah in 1 Kings 21:20–24 was still in the future. Ahaziah's brother **Joram** now took his place on the throne, **in the second year of Jehoram . . . king of Judah**. Joram and Jehoram would rule at the same time. The two nations would become virtually indistinguishable spiritually in this period, as Judah adopted the Baal worship that had plagued the north.

> **MAIN IDEA REVIEW:** *We may ignore God's Word or fight it, but we cannot evade it or defeat it.*

III. CONCLUSION

Four Men and the Bible

The four major figures of this section teach us something about our relation to the Word of God.

Ahab shows us that we cannot outwit or outmaneuver the word of God. He first tried to counterfeit it, providing four hundred false teachers who would supply an imitation of God's word and give the message he wanted to hear. But when he could not avoid the authentic word of God, he chose to believe he could outwit it. A clever disguise gave no protection against God's word. In the end, dogs licked the blood of Ahab "as the word of the LORD had declared" (1 Kgs. 22:38).

Micaiah challenges us to stand for the word of God courageously, whatever the cost. He is a powerful example of a prophet determined to proclaim God's truth fearlessly, even though his audience did not want to hear it.

Jehoshaphat is a reminder that we must listen to God's word first, not second. He was a king who loved the Lord, but his pragmatism lured him into a compromising relationship that did great damage to his nation. He fell into the trap of first making his decision and then consulting God. When he heard

God's word, he was unwilling to admit his mistake and to follow God's direction.

Ahaziah thought he could control God's word, that human power could force the word of God to adjust to him. But like his father, he learned that God's word always has the last word. His epitaph is significant: "So he died, according to the word of the LORD that Elijah had spoken" (2 Kgs. 1:17).

These four men and their response give us a pattern or model by which we can measure our response to the word of God. For them, that word came from the lips of a prophet. For us, it is primarily to be found in God's written Word, the Bible.

PRINCIPLES

- Small compromises inevitably lead to larger ones.
- Truth is found in those who listen to God's Word, not in the majority whose words are designed to please their hearers.
- To choose a voice other than God's voice is to choose deception.
- We cannot outwit the Word of God. He does exactly what he says he will do.
- God honors those who are committed to do what is right in his eyes.
- When we pursue substitutes for God, we pursue our own destruction.
- God resists the proud and arrogant.

APPLICATIONS

- Resist the temptation to compromise your spiritual convictions.
- Seek God's will as the beginning of your decision making, not as an afterthought.
- Be careful to hear God's word; do not just go along with the majority.
- Pursue exclusive loyalty to the Lord.
- Cultivate a humble heart before God and his Word.

IV. LIFE APPLICATION

When the Fire Falls

One day, as Jesus and his disciples were making their way through Samaria, the locals refused to welcome them because of the animosity between the Jews and the Samaritans. James and John reacted with anger: "Lord, do you want us to call fire down from heaven to destroy them?" (Luke

9:54). Jesus rebuked his followers, not the Samaritans (Luke 9:55). During his trial the Lord Jesus received the utmost in disrespect and dishonor. The indignities heaped upon him were indescribable, but he did not call upon the angels to deliver him or to devastate his enemies (Matt. 26:53). Rather, he prayed for their forgiveness (Luke 23:34).

The model of the Lord Jesus was different from that of Elijah, and he sets the pattern for our response to our enemies (Matt. 5:43–48). But we would be wrong to imagine that Elijah misrepresented the character of God. The Lord Jesus clearly taught the existence of hell. He tells us that it is personal (Luke 12:4–5), painful (Luke 16:19–31), and eternal (Matt. 25:41). The Bible warns us that "it is a dreadful thing to fall into the hands of the living God" (Heb. 10:31) because "God is a consuming fire" (Heb. 12:29). For those who have not trusted Christ as Lord and Savior, "no sacrifice of sins is left, but only a fearful expectation of judgment and of raging fire that will consume the enemies of God" (Heb. 10:26–27).

Elijah's calling down of fire on enemy soldiers is not a denial of God's character but a window into the seriousness of disrespect for the person of God. Sin kills, and it kills eternally. But our Savior has already taken the fire of divine judgment "that whoever believes in him shall not perish but have eternal life" (John 3:16).

V. PRAYER

Lord, help us not to trifle with your word. Cause us to seek it first, and teach us to humble ourselves before it. When we receive it, help us to stand for it courageously and to do it thoroughly, whatever the cost. Amen.

VI. DEEPER DISCOVERIES

A. "The LORD Has Put a Lying Spirit" (1 Kgs. 22:23)

Micaiah's vision of the heavenly court depicts the Lord sending a lying spirit to deceive Ahab's false prophets. It may be questioned whether the vision is intended to describe what actually happened. It is more likely a dramatic way of describing the fact that the false prophets were both the victims and the agents of deception. It is consistent with other biblical passages to suggest that the Lord judicially permitted a demonic lying spirit to inspire the false prophets (see 2 Thess. 2:11). The punishment fit the crime: Ahab had chosen the false god, so he would receive falsehood.

The bottom line is that Ahab was not deceived. Through the prophet Micaiah, he was clearly told that his prophets were deceiving him and that he would meet his death in the battle. His problem was not that he did not know what God had said but that he would not obey what God wanted. He chose to follow the false prophets because this was what he wanted to do.

B. Jehoshaphat (1 Kgs. 22:43)

The evaluation of the writer of 1 Kings that Jehoshaphat "did what was right in the eyes of the LORD" (1 Kgs. 22:43) is confirmed by the material in 2 Chronicles 17–20. Three things stand out. First, Jehoshaphat was a person with a passionate personal commitment to God: he "sought the God of his father. . . . His heart was devoted to the ways of the LORD" (2 Chr. 17:4,6). Second, Jehoshaphat was committed to the centrality to the word of God, so that he ordered his reign around it (2 Chr. 17:7–9; 19:4–11). Third, he was a man determined to trust the Lord. His trust moved him to pray and to act as God directed. His rallying point for his nation is expressed in 2 Chronicles 20:20: "Have faith in the LORD your God and you will be upheld; have faith in his prophets and you will be successful."

These three characteristics of Jehoshaphat are the indispensable qualities of a life that God approves, whatever our calling in life.

C. Baal-Zebub (2 Kgs. 1:2)

This name, meaning "lord of the flies," was probably a Hebrew parody of an original "Baal-Zebul," which meant "lord prince." In the Gospels the Pharisees mention "Beelzebub, the prince of demons" (Matt. 12:24). Jesus also spoke of Beelzebub (Matt. 10:25; 12:27), and it seems to have become a synonym for Satan.

VII. TEACHING OUTLINE

A. INTRODUCTION

1. Lead Story: Trifling with the Word of God
2. Context: Judgment has been pronounced by God's prophets on Ahab and his family. God's word has been declared; now it will begin to be fulfilled.
3. Transition: Once again Israel is in conflict with Syria. But previous victories are not a guarantee of future victories.

B. COMMENTARY

1. The Death of Ahab (1 Kgs. 22:1–40)
2. The Reign of Jehoshaphat of Judah (1 Kgs. 22:41–50)
3. The Death of Ahaziah of Israel (1 Kgs. 22:51–53; 2 Kgs. 1:1–18)

C. CONCLUSION: FOUR MEN AND THE BIBLE

VIII. ISSUES FOR DISCUSSION

1. Are there times when you have made a decision and then decided you should consult the Lord? What have you found helpful in making good and godly decisions?
2. What are some ways in which we trifle with the word of God?
3. In crisis Ahaziah instinctively turned to an idol. Are there ways in which we can do the same?
4. Elijah called down fire from heaven against his enemies. How do you understand the judgment of God on human sin? How seriously should we take the idea of hell? Does it make a difference that Jesus was the one who spoke most about it?

2 Kings 2:1–3:27

Taking the Mantle

I. INTRODUCTION
When a Leader Leaves

II. COMMENTARY
A verse-by-verse explanation of these chapters.

III. CONCLUSION
Raised Up by the Lord

An overview of the principles and application from these chapters.

IV. LIFE APPLICATION
Facing the Tests of Leadership

Melding these chapters to life.

V. PRAYER
Tying these chapters to life with God.

VI. DEEPER DISCOVERIES
Historical, geographical, and grammatical enrichment of the commentary.

VII. TEACHING OUTLINE
Suggested step-by-step group study of these chapters.

VIII. ISSUES FOR DISCUSSION
Zeroing these chapters in on daily life.

"*S*piritual leaders are not made by election or appointment, by men or any combination of men, nor by conferences or synods. Only God can make them. Simply holding a position of importance does not constitute one a leader, nor do taking courses in leadership, or resolving to be a leader. . . . Spiritual leadership is a thing of the Spirit and it is conferred by God alone."

J . O s w a l d S a n d e r s

2 Kings 2:1–3:27

I N A N U T S H E L L

*I*n the sovereign purposes of God, it was time for Elisha to succeed Elijah. The transition takes place in the most remarkable of ways, as Elijah is supernaturally removed from the earth. Elisha is supernaturally empowered to carry on Elijah's ministry—a succession made evident by the miracles of blessing and judgment he is empowered to do, and the rescue of his nation's army that he prophesies.

Taking the Mantle

I. INTRODUCTION

When a Leader Leaves

On April 12, 1945, Harry Truman received a message asking him to come to the White House "as quickly and as quietly as you can." Truman left immediately, thinking that the president had a special job for him to do. To his surprise, when he arrived he was ushered into Mrs. Roosevelt's sitting room. She got up, put her arm on his shoulder, and said, "Harry, the president is dead."

Truman was too stunned to speak. Finally, he managed to say to Mrs. Roosevelt, "Is there anything I can do for you?"

"No, Harry," she said. "Is there anything we can do for *you?* You're the one in trouble now."

It is hard enough to become president at any time, but this happened in the middle of World War II. President Roosevelt had been the longest-serving president in American history—a controversial but dominating leader. The war was going well, but there were big decisions to be made—about Hitler, Japan, and Joseph Stalin's obvious maneuvering to dominate the postwar world. All the responsibility of leading his nation and the free world was suddenly on Truman's shoulders. The next day he said, "I felt like the moon, the stars, and all the planets had fallen on me."

Few assignments are more difficult than following a great and gifted leader, whether it is a president or a parent. But leaders, no matter how good or godly, don't last forever. Change is inevitable. Good people die or depart; new problems emerge; new opportunities arise. Sometimes we would love to clone the past, but life doesn't work that way. And all of us face times in the relay of life when the baton is in our hands, and the next lap is ours.

When a leader is taken, we tend to look for a substitute, a replacement—someone to fill the position. But the Lord doesn't recycle the past. Our need isn't that person or another just like him but the God of that person. The critical truth is this: *when God's leader is removed, everything of God remains.* Transition times are times to refocus on the unchanging God.

Elisha was given the formidable task of following one of the most powerful figures of Old Testament times—Elijah. He was wise enough to recognize that the real question wasn't "Where is Elijah?" but "Where is the God of Elijah?" He would serve God in a context very similar to that of Elijah, but his Lord would lead him to a distinctive ministry. He would finish what Elijah began, but in a way that reflected his unique design.

II. COMMENTARY

Taking the Mantle

> **MAIN IDEA:** When God's leader is removed, everything of God remains.

A The Launching of a Leader (2:1–14)

> **SUPPORTING IDEA:** Our need is not just being appointed by God to a position but being anointed by him to carry out our assignment.

The Lord had made clear to Elijah on Mount Horeb that Elisha was the man who would finish what he had begun in the battle against Baal and the followers of Ahab (1 Kgs. 19:15–18). We have no way of knowing how long Elisha accompanied Elijah as his servant and protégé, but now the time had come for the transition to occur.

2:1–6. The opening words of the chapter announce the dramatic event that was about to occur: the Lord was about to **take Elijah up to heaven in a whirlwind**. With the possible exception of Enoch, no such thing had ever occurred. But a surprising number of people were aware that something dramatic was about to take place that would remove Elijah from them. The passage is organized around a journey. Beginning at **Gilgal**, Elijah and Elisha proceeded to **Bethel** and **Jericho**. At each stop Elijah made an effort to deter Elisha: **Stay here, Elisha**. But Elijah's efforts seemed rather halfhearted. He never insisted that Elisha remain where he was. He seemed to be testing the younger man's loyalty and determination, rather than trying to stop him. Elisha's response was the same each time: **I will not leave you**.

This was a strong oath of refusal which reflected Elisha's determination to stay with Elijah, wherever he went. Elisha was aware that this was a momentous day, and he would not be diverted or distracted. In two of the towns, the two were met by **the company of the prophets** (see "Deeper Discoveries"), and the course of the journey was determined by Elijah's desire to meet with these men. Twice they had the same message for Elisha: **the LORD is going to take your master from you today**. Apparently the Lord had revealed this information to them as well as to Elisha. But he refused to discuss the matter since that would change nothing and would only intensify Elisha's grief.

The journey began at **Gilgal**, a name of importance when Joshua led Israel into the promised land (Josh. 5). But since Gilgal was near Jericho and would require a climb to Bethel, it was apparently another town of the same name. They **went down to Bethel**, a place associated with Jacob's remarkable encounter with God (Gen. 28:10–22) but also the center of the pagan Jeroboam cult. A **company of the prophets** was there, and Elijah and Elisha met with them. From there Elijah led them to **Jericho**, following the Lord's direction. This was the location of Joshua's first great victory in the conquest (Josh. 6) and also the locale of another **company of the prophets**. From there they journeyed to the west bank of the Jordan River, where a group of "fifty men of the company of the prophets" (v. 7) had gathered to witness what was to happen.

2:7–12. The Jordan was both the border of the nation and a place of rich biblical significance. It was the boundary Moses had not been allowed by God to cross, so that Joshua led the people into the land, finishing what Moses had started. This would be true of Elijah and Elisha as well. **Elijah took his cloak, rolled it up and struck the water with it**. The parallel to Moses at the Red Sea (Exod. 14:15–22) is obvious. Moses had raised his staff, the symbol of his shepherd leadership, over the water, while Elijah struck it with his cloak, the symbol of his prophetic office. In a reprise of the exodus, **the water divided . . . and the two of them crossed over on dry ground**. They were now outside the land, in Moab, where Moses had died.

The reason for Elisha's persistence now became evident. A dying man would traditionally pronounce a blessing over his successors. That custom led Elijah to ask, **What can I do for you before I am taken from you?** This was the moment for which Elisha had been waiting. He replied, **Let me inherit a double portion of your spirit**. "Double portion" is a Hebrew idiom. It does not mean "twice as much" but "the firstborn's share" (Deut. 21:17; see "Deeper Discoveries"). Elisha knew that he had been appointed to be Elijah's successor (1 Kgs. 19:19–21). But he recognized his need of divine empowerment. He would inherit Elijah's role; he needed Elijah's God-given equipping for the task.

Elisha recognized that a position without God-given power was an impossible assignment. But God's Spirit is God's Spirit. He was not under the control even of an Elijah. Elijah could not guarantee the request, but he could give a sign that God had granted it: **if you see me when I am taken from you, it will be yours—otherwise not**.

The departure of Elijah into heaven was filled with divine symbolism. In the course of their walking and talking, **a chariot of fire . . . appeared and separated the two of them**. Chariots and horses were military symbols; they represented God himself as the ultimate protection of his people (Deut. 20:1; see 2 Kgs. 6:15–17). But in a nation riddled with Baal worship, they were a refutation of the false claim that Baal was the "rider of the clouds." God alone "rides on the heavens to help you and on the clouds in his majesty" (Deut. 33:26). **Elijah went up to heaven in a whirlwind**, not in the chariot, another indication of the emptiness of the claims of Baal, the so-called storm god. It was the Lord who controlled the storm and God's prophet who rode it into his presence. Ahab and Jezebel's deaths would be associated with dogs; Elijah's departure happened through supernatural intervention.

Elisha's response was a spontaneous cry of grief which honored Elijah and captured his sorrow: **My father! My father! The chariots and horsemen of Israel!** Elijah had been his mentor ("my father"), and Elisha knew him to be God's true military defense of the nation ("the chariots and horsemen of Israel," a description later used of Elisha in 2 Kgs. 13:14). God's prophet had been the guarantee of Israel's divine protection. But now he was gone. Elisha **took hold of his own clothes and tore them apart**—a vivid expression of grief for himself and his nation. Something precious and valuable had departed with Elijah.

2:13–14. Elisha met Elijah's condition. God had enabled him to witness the departure of his mentor. The evidence of that was **the cloak that had fallen from Elijah**, the symbol of his prophetic office and of his divine empowerment. Elisha picked up the cloak and returned to the banks of the Jordan River. He was a "Joshua" about to demonstrate that he was his master's legitimate successor. Elisha's cry was both a plea and a petition for God to authenticate him: **Where now is the LORD, the God of Elijah?** The answer came when Elisha **took the cloak . . . and struck the water with it**, and the water divided.

It is significant that in the Baal mythology the river and the sea were the enemy of Baal which he struggled to control. The river represented no challenge to the Lord, its maker. While Elijah may have departed, everything of God remained. Israel's need was not Elijah but the Lord. Elisha's focus was on the God of the man, not the man. He had been given not only Elijah's position but his power as well.

𝔹 The Testing of a Leader (2:15–25)

SUPPORTING IDEA: *The evidence that we have been called by God is what his Spirit does through our lives.*

2:15–18. The fifty men of the company of the prophets had been watching from a distance, but how much they had seen is not clear. Almost certainly they had not seen Elijah's remarkable departure, but they had seen Elisha divide the river and return to the land. They recognized that the spirit of Elijah was **resting on Elisha.** Meeting him, they **bowed to the ground before him.** They were willing to accept his God-given empowerment and his leadership. But they were much less willing to let go of Elijah. Concerned about him, they wanted to launch a search: **Perhaps the Spirit of the LORD has . . . set him down on some mountain.**

Did they expect to find Elijah's corpse and desire to bury it? Or did they expect to find him wandering, lost, and confused in some remote location?

Their confusion and dedication to Elijah was understandable. No one had ever departed life in such a way!

Elisha attempted to dissuade them, knowing their search would be futile. But their persistence made him **ashamed to refuse**, an idiomatic way of referring to the fact that their search went on for a long time. They were submissive to Elisha's leadership, but they felt a need to get closure about Elijah. Elisha finally relented, allowed them to search for their beloved leader, and reminded them of his warnings when they returned empty-handed. The whole story is a very human insight into how hard it is to let go of a beloved leader and to move on to the next part of God's purposes.

2:19–22. Elijah's name meant, "My God is Yahweh," a name descriptive of his ministry. Elisha means, "My God saves," a name also capturing his unique ministry. Elisha's life would be notable for the significant number of miracles, almost all saving or delivering individuals from personal problems. His first miracle (excluding the dividing of the Jordan River) showed his credentials as God's prophet and set the pattern of his ministry.

The city where the miracle transpired is not named, but both the location near the Jordan and the tradition that persists to this day about Elisha's water show that Jericho is meant. It was certainly a place of which it could be said, **this town is well situated**, nestled as it was in an oasis in the Jordan Valley. The city had been rebuilt under Joshua's curse (see 1 Kgs. 16:34), and this may account for the problem of the water: **the water is bad and the land is unproductive**. The last phrase is literally, "the land suffers miscarriages." This may refer to a predominance of miscarriages in the area, a situation far worse than poor crops.

Whatever the exact problem, Elisha's solution was remarkable. Taking a new bowl filled with salt, **he went out to the spring and threw the salt into it**. This was obviously not a scientific solution but a miraculous cure. It was not Elisha or the salt that "healed" the water but God. Elisha's actions had power because of the underlying power of God.

2:23–25. God's word also comes in judgment upon those who resist and reject it. Retracing their journey, **Elisha went up to Bethel**. This had become the center of Jeroboam's pagan cult, a place where the Lord was mocked with golden calves and where God's faithful prophets were mocked (2 Chr. 36:15–16). The story must be read against its wider context. **Some youths** of the city, a large group of at least forty-two young men in their early teen years (see "Deeper Discoveries"), recognized Elisha and **jeered at him**. Their words were more than the childish taunts of young boys. They were full of deep spiritual animosity: **Go on up, you baldhead!**

"Go on up" is best read as a mockery of the story of Elijah's departure. "Baldhead" was a personal insult, directed at Elisha's lack of hair. But in a society where the young were expected to respect their elders, it was a hate-filled insult of God's prophet. They knew who Elisha was, and they were ridiculing him and the God he served.

In response, Elisha **called down a curse on them in the name of the LORD**. To ridicule God's prophet was to ridicule his God. To mock God's prophet was to mock God. Elisha's curse was not intemperate language but a call for divine judgment, to which the Lord responded by the unexpected appearance of **two bears** that **mauled forty-two of the youths**. The message was clear: don't mess with God's prophet! Most of his miracles would be miracles of blessing, but this was a warning: if the nation persisted in its rebellion against the Lord, it was headed for disaster. In a rebellious age God would speak in a way that could not be ignored.

Elisha retraced Elijah's steps all the way to **Mount Carmel**, the scene of his great battle with the Baal prophets. But from there he **returned to Samaria**. This was significant. Elijah had spent most of his ministry in isolation. Elisha took up residence in Ahab's capital city and represented God there. He would complete the ministry of Elijah but not as an imitator of his great mentor. He was God's unique man, not a shadow of Elijah.

The Emergence of a Leader (3:1–27)

> **SUPPORTING IDEA:** *When we are available to the Lord, he will provide his platform for our ministry.*

3:1–3. For a time we appear to leave Elisha behind and to move to the stage of international affairs. **Joram son of Ahab** (reigned 852–841 B.C.) had become king of Israel upon the death of his brother Ahaziah (1:17–18). His actual name was Jehoram, but the NIV translators have chosen to call him "Joram," to avoid confusion with Jehoshaphat's son, also named Jehoram (8:16). Joram was a son slightly better than his father Ahab (**he did evil in the eyes of the LORD, but not as his father and mother had done**). He moderated their Baal worship: **he got rid of the sacred stone of Baal**. He apparently did not destroy this stone, since it reappeared later (10:26–27). Although he tolerated baalism, he apparently did not participate in it personally. **Nevertheless he clung to the sins of Jeroboam**. Things had changed for the better, but only marginally.

3:4–12. We were informed of the rebellion of Moab in 2 Kings 1:1. Ahaziah had done nothing to deal with the situation, and the responsibility now fell upon King Joram. The rebellion of Moab under **Mesha king of Moab** represented a huge economic loss for Israel. The size of the yearly tribute had been immense: **a hundred thousand lambs and . . . the wool of a hundred thousand rams**. The death of Ahab was an opportune time to break free of such an oppressive burden. So Mesha had **rebelled**. Joram determined to crush the rebellion, so he summoned his ally, King Jehoshaphat of Judah, to join the campaign. Jehoshaphat's response echoed his earlier response to Ahab (1 Kgs. 22:4): **I will go with you . . . I am as you are**. After the disastrous conclusion of that former venture, one would think there would have been some restraint or prayerfulness on Jehoshaphat's part. But not so.

The plan of attack was unconventional. Because the northern approach to Moab was well defended, the allies, joined by Judah's vassal, **the king of Edom**, circled south through the desert to attack from an unexpected, undefended direction. The plan, devised by King Joram with no divine input, was creative and clever. But a serious problem soon emerged: the march took longer than expected, and the armies found themselves stranded in the desert without adequate water.

Joram's response was audacious and predictable for a son of Ahab: he blamed God: **Has the LORD called us three kings together only to hand us over to Moab?** Where was any indication that God had called them? It is amazing how quickly people who ignore God attack him when their plans go wrong! Jehoshaphat ignored this attack on God, but did ask, **Is there no prophet of the LORD here, that we may inquire of the LORD through him?** He learned that Elisha was with the army. Elisha was unknown to both kings, so a servant described him by his relation to Elijah: **Elisha . . . used to pour water on the hands of Elijah** (as his servant).

That association was sufficient for Jehoshaphat. Because of the urgency of the situation, the kings did not follow the normal pattern of summoning the prophet. The three of them **went down to him**.

3:13–19. This was Elisha's first engagement in political affairs, but he did not receive his three royal visitors with any sense of inferiority. Quite the opposite. His words to Joram were biting: **Go to the prophets of your father and the prophets of your mother**. His disrespect for the family of Ahab was clear. King Joram persisted in his attack on the character of God, claiming that the calamity was due to the Lord's misdirection. Elisha ignored this, declaring that only the presence of Jehoshaphat would lead him to seek a message from his Lord. Elisha was like Elijah, a man not given to deference or flattery of the rich and powerful. He was a man totally committed to the Lord.

But Elisha did agree to consult the Lord. He asked for **a harpist**, probably to quiet his spirit because of the inner turmoil caused by his confrontation of King Joram. **The hand of the LORD** came upon Elisha, and he brought God's promise to the kings. The Lord would provide water in abundance, although there would be no visible storm (**wind nor rain**) to supply it. The water would be sufficient to supply the needs of the soldiers as well as **your cattle and your other animals**, even though they were in a desert place. In addition, the Lord would give them victory over Moab, in spite of their precarious situation.

3:20–26. At dawn the next morning (**the time for offering the sacrifice**), the prophecy began to be fulfilled. A flash flood, with water coming from an unseen storm on higher ground in the west (from **Edom**), supplied all the water the kings needed. It also threw Moab into confusion. Mesha had mobilized the entire nation, but they were camped west of the alliance army. So when they arose and looked directly into the rising sun, they saw it reflecting **red—like blood**—off the water and the red soil (the words *red, Edom,* and *blood* sound alike in Hebrew). They jumped to the conclusion that the red was the blood of enemies, who had turned on one another and charged toward **the camp of Israel**. Their reckless charge was met by an assault of the alliance army, which slaughtered the Moabites and then invaded the land.

The remaining Moabites were forced to retreat to their capital at **Kir Hareseth**. The city was surrounded. When Mesha realized that the situation was desperate, he made a final attempt **to break through to the king of Edom**, presumably because he was the weakest of the three armies or because Moab and Edom had been allies on occasion. The attempt failed, and Moab's destruction seemed inevitable. God had miraculously provided the water, as his prophet had declared he would, and Israel had won a crushing victory. Elisha had demonstrated that he was Elijah's true successor and that the Lord spoke through him.

3:27. But the story does not end the way we would expect. The pagan king turned to his god, Chemosh. He took the crown prince, **his firstborn son, who was to succeed him as king, and offered him as a sacrifice on the city wall**, where the act could be seen by his enemies. This brutal act leads to a statement that has proven extremely difficult to interpret (see "Deeper Discoveries"): **the fury against Israel was great**. This cannot be the fury of Chemosh, since he, like all pagan gods, was a fraud. Nor would the Lord respond to such an act. The fury must be either the aroused fury of the Moabites or the indignation of the Israelites at such an act that terminated any will to continue the battle: **they withdrew and returned to their own land**.

This strange ending meant that the fulfillment of Elisha's prophecy had taken an unexpected turn. His word had rescued the nation and predicted the events. He had been authenticated as the Lord's prophet, God's new man for the times. Elijah would be missed, but God was just as present with his people as he had always been. Israel's spiritual state, however, kept the nation from receiving all that God had promised.

MAIN IDEA REVIEW: *When God's leader is removed, everything of God remains.*

III. CONCLUSION

Raised Up by the Lord

Elisha had not chosen to be Elijah's successor. In many ways it was a position to avoid, not to seek. His was a call to conflict, controversy, and opposition. But he was God's man for the times, called to stand for the authority of the Lord in the nation of Israel.

Elisha did not become Elijah's successor because he had sought the role, because Elijah had trained him for the role, or because the companies of the prophets had selected him for the role. He was Elijah's successor because he had been named by the Lord years before on Mount Carmel. Undoubtedly the years of serving Elijah and observing him closely had been formative. He was certainly a gifted individual in his own right. But the passage makes clear that a spiritual leader must be called by God, empowered by God, and confirmed by God through the presence of God's Spirit in his life.

Elisha was a unique servant of the Lord, called to do a special task in a special time. But the lessons contained in this transition of leadership are timeless. At each passing of the baton, our question must be, "Where is the God of Elijah?" Leaders come and go; "Jesus Christ is the same yesterday and today and forever" (Heb. 13:8).

PRINCIPLES

- Wise leaders test the commitment of their followers.
- We need more than God's appointment for a position; we need to be anointed through his Spirit.
- We need to focus on the God of the man, not the man of God.
- God's calling and empowering is made evident to others through what he does in us.
- Before the Lord uses us, he will test us to refine us.
- The Lord will open doors of ministry for his servants as they are available and sensitive to him.

APPLICATIONS

- Spiritual condition is more important than your ministry position. Position without power is a burden, not a blessing.
- Value people who have gone before you, but let your trust and focus be on the Lord alone.
- Expect times of testing and refining.

- When God opens a door of opportunity, let your primary concern be integrity and faithfulness to the Lord, not the impression you are making on others.

IV. LIFE APPLICATION

Facing the Tests of Leadership

As Elisha walked through the Jordan River, he knew he had been called and empowered by God for whatever lay ahead. What may not have been so clear was the challenges that lay ahead. Spiritual leaders are raised up by the Lord—called, empowered, and confirmed by his work in their lives. But leaders are also refined and developed by the challenges and opportunities they face. The four tests that Elisha faced are significant for every leader.

1. *The test of nostalgia.* The company of the prophets recognized God's call, but they needed some time before they could let go of the past. Leaders are called to serve in the present by moving toward the future. But the way they deal with the past will determine whether it is an anchor or a rudder. Elisha's followers had an enduring tie to the past and an inadequate view of God. That was a test that he could not avoid.

2. *The test of need.* The situation in Jericho was beyond human ability to solve. Almost every leader will discover that his predecessor, no matter how godly or gifted, has not solved every problem or met every need. He must face the tough problems with the highest of human resources as well as the deepest of spiritual dependence.

3. *The test of opposition and criticism.* Most leaders do not face the opposition of forty-two teenagers, shouting their taunts of God and his Spirit. But all leaders face the test of criticism. People who are committed to lead for the glory of the Lord will not always please people or make popular decisions. At such times one is tempted to resort to Elisha's bears! But a more appropriate model is that of our Lord Jesus: "When they hurled their insults at him, he did not retaliate; when he suffered, he made no threats. Instead, he entrusted himself to him who judges justly" (1 Pet. 2:23).

4. *The test of success.* Suddenly, Elisha had three kings who had sought him out and were waiting on his help and direction. He had not sought this recognition, but the Lord had graciously given it. Few things are harder to deal with than success. We become proud or self-sufficient, or, out of sin or insecurity, we begin to bend the rules to maximize our opportunities or ensure our position.

Elisha dealt with these tests well, by the grace of God, and went on to establish a track record of sixty years of faithful service to the Lord. This is a good path to follow!

V. PRAYER

Father, help us never to forget that apart from you and your enabling power, nothing that we attempt will have any lasting value. God of Elijah, show yourself alive in and through us to those around us, for their good and your glory! Amen.

VI. DEEPER DISCOVERIES

A. The Company of the Prophets (2:3,5)

The first use of this term (literally, "the sons of the prophets") occurs in 1 Kings 20:35, when one from their company confronted Ahab because he had spared Ben-Hadad. A "band of prophets" appeared in the time of Samuel (1 Sam. 10:5,10; 19:20, where Samuel was presiding over them). The company of the prophets appeared in the time of Elijah and Elisha (1 Kgs. 20:35; 2 Kgs. 2:3,5,7,15; 4:1,38; 5:22; 6:1; 9:1). They appear to be a loosely organized group, committed to exclusive worship of the Lord, which coalesced around Elijah and Elisha, then faded from the scene. They seemed to possess the gift of prophecy and to look to the two great prophets as their teachers and leaders.

B. Moses and Elijah (2:7)

The parallels between Moses and Elijah seem more than accidental. The writer of 2 Kings is establishing a pattern. Both divided bodies of water (the Red Sea; the Jordan River); both had fire from heaven come down upon a sacrifice (see Lev. 9:22–24); both met the Lord on Mount Sinai; both experienced miraculous provisions of food; both ended their earthly lives in remarkable ways, so that their bodies could not be located (see Deut. 34:5–6); both had important successors who furthered the work the Lord had given them to do (Joshua, Elisha). The two of them are associated with each other on the Mount of Transfiguration (Matt. 17:4).

C. A Double Portion of Your Spirit (2:9)

The English expression causes us to think that Elisha was asking for twice as much as Elijah had. But it is obvious that a spirit—and ultimately this is a reference to God's Spirit (v. 16)—is not an object to be divided and parceled out. There were many "sons of the prophets," and fifty of them were waiting on the other side of the Jordan River. But Elisha was to be the "firstborn son," the heir of Elijah. Therefore, he asked under the terms of Israelite inheritance law (Deut. 21:17) for the oldest son's portion of the divine empowerment.

D. Elisha, the Boys, and the Bears (2:23–25)

Few stories have proven as troubling to people as this. We find it hard to deal with stories of divine judgment, but that is not a sign of our maturity or our righteousness. It is a sign of our sinfulness, so that we do not see the awesomeness of God's holiness and the offensiveness of sin. However, it is important to read this story carefully. It is not the story of harmless, foolish, and rude children mocking a bald man in good-natured fun. It was a gang of young men representing a city whose religion rejected God's standards that mocked the spokesman of God. Their jeering represented disrespect, not only for Elisha but also for the Lord. The judgment upon them was a vivid message from God himself that people would pay the price for their blatant disrespect of him and his messengers.

D. "The Fury Against Israel Was Great" (3:27)

The exact meaning of this text remains a mystery. It is foolish to interpret it in a way that contradicts everything else taught by the books of 1 and 2 Kings. It cannot mean that Chemosh, who like Baal did not exist, responded in fury against Israel. Nor can it mean that the Lord responded to a pagan sacrifice which he prohibited for his people (Lev. 18:21). Determining what it does mean is more difficult. It is interesting that the fury was directed against Israel, which in this context refers to the Northern Kingdom and not the entire alliance. The Israelites were a paganized people, under the leadership of Ahab and his sons. The fear may have been their superstitious dread of Chemosh's retaliation, since many of them believed he really did exist.

VII. TEACHING OUTLINE

A. INTRODUCTION

1. Lead Story: When a Leader Leaves
2. Context: The Lord is replacing Elijah with Elisha as the one through whom he will remove the influences of Ahab and Baal from Israel. It is a critical moment of transition.
3. Transition: When there is a change of leadership, we can look too fondly to the past or believe that the new person is all we need. But God alone is the unchanging power.

B. COMMENTARY

1. The Launching of a Leader (2:1–14)

2. The Testing of a Leader (2:15–25)
3. The Emergence of a Leader (3:1–27)

C. CONCLUSION: RAISED UP BY THE LORD

VIII. ISSUES FOR DISCUSSION

1. When gifted leaders move on, we are tempted to yearn for the past or to burden the new leader with impossible expectations. What does this story suggest about what we should look for in leaders and how we should view them?

2. King Joram's response to crisis was to blame God (3:10), even though he had totally ignored him until that time. Do you see people doing that today?

2 Kings 4:1–6:7

A Heart of Compassion

I. INTRODUCTION
The Cause of the Weak

II. COMMENTARY
A verse-by-verse explanation of these verses.

III. CONCLUSION
No Respecter of Persons

An overview of the principles and application from these verses.

IV. LIFE APPLICATION
Pictures of Salvation

Melding these verses to life.

V. PRAYER
Tying these verses to life with God.

VI. DEEPER DISCOVERIES
Historical, geographical, and grammatical enrichment of the commentary.

VII. TEACHING OUTLINE
Suggested step-by-step group study of these verses.

VIII. ISSUES FOR DISCUSSION
Zeroing these verses in on daily life.

"Our calling and purpose as followers of Christ is to love God completely, to love self correctly, and to love others compassionately."

K e n n e t h   B o a

BIOGRAPHICAL PROFILE: ELISHA

The ministry of Elisha was remarkable for his miracles. Most were performed for individuals in need. There are striking parallels with some of the miracles of Jesus.

- The parting of the Jordan River (2:14)
- The cleansing of Jericho's water (2:21)
- The curse on the youths and the two bears (2:24)
- Water and victory in Moab (3:20)
- The widow's oil (4:6)
- The Shunammite's son (4:15)
- The raising of the Shunammite's son (4:35)
- The purifying of the stew (4:41)
- The multiplying of food (4:44)
- The healing of Naaman (5:14)
- The striking of Gehazi with leprosy (5:27)
- The floating ax head (6:6)
- The blinding of Aram's soldiers (6:18)
- The stampede of Aram's army (7:6–7)

2 Kings 4:1–6:7

IN A NUTSHELL

Although Elisha's ministry involved him in a struggle for the soul of the nation against the royal family and the Baal priests, much of his ministry took the form of miracles that showed God's love and compassion to those who trusted him in their need, people of all classes and even non-Israelites. A series of miracles is described in this section.

A Heart of Compassion

I. INTRODUCTION

The Cause of the Weak

*I*n the heart of London, in Piccadilly Circus, there is a monument with a golden-winged archer on the top. Tour guides declare it to be a monument to Eros, the god of love, but there is more to the story. It was first erected in 1893 to honor Ashley Cooper (1801–1885), the seventh Earl of Shaftesbury.

Cooper was brought up in an aristocratic but dysfunctional and debt-ridden home. But a housekeeper named Maria Millis led him to Christ, and a series of events led him as a young politician to "devote whatever advantages He might have bestowed . . . in the cause of the weak, the helpless, both man and beast, and those who had none to help him." With his gifts and connections, he could have reached the highest offices in the land, but he chose to pursue another course—the service of Christ and the cause of the poor.

What Cooper accomplished in sixty years of public life was remarkable. He changed the treatment of the mentally ill; improved working conditions in factories, mines, and agriculture; provided housing for the poor; worked to ensure sewage systems and clean water; and fought the exploitation of women. His special concern was children who were exploited as workers in mines or factories, as chimney sweeps, or as child prostitutes. He also pioneered a public school system, known as the "Ragged Schools." A list of his accomplishments would cover page after page—all of them done in the name of Christ.

When Cooper died, tens of thousands of London's poorest stood hatless in the rain, showing their love for the man who had spent sixty years fighting for their cause. Eight years later the Shaftesbury Monument was dedicated in Piccadilly Circus, with an inscription by then Prime Minister William Gladstone: "During a public life of half a century he devoted the influence of his station, the strong sympathies of his heart, and the great powers of his mind to honouring God by serving his fellow-men, an example of his order, a blessing to his people, and a name to be by them ever gratefully remembered."

Those are powerful words to describe a man whose life proved to be a window on the heart of God, which beats with compassion and grace for those in need.

The Lord uses different people to display different aspects of his character. Elijah, a flamboyant man of action, crusaded for the truth of God against the falsehood of Baal. Elisha, no less committed to the Lord, displayed God's love and compassion for individuals. That is particularly on display in this passage, which consists of a series of miracles for people in need.

II. COMMENTARY

A Heart of Compassion

MAIN IDEA: *The Lord works through his people to show his compassion for all kinds of people with all kinds of needs.*

A God Cares for the Desperate (4:1–7)

SUPPORTING IDEA: *God's compassion reaches those without position or power.*

4:1–7. Widows were always in a very vulnerable situation in the ancient world. We know little about the living arrangements of **the company of the prophets.** This passage makes clear that some were married, had children, and had personal debts. The widow of one such man came in desperation to Elisha. She had already lost her husband; now she was in danger of losing her sons: **his creditor is coming to take my two boys as his slaves.** Slavery was the way debt was worked off in biblical times (Exod. 21:2–4), and the creditor was fully within his rights. Such "slaves" would be set free when the debt was paid or in the Jubilee Year (Lev. 25:39–43), but that would be small consolation to a mother's heart.

Elisha could do nothing for the woman legally since the creditor was within his rights. He could provide an alternative solution. Discovering that the widow's only resource was **a little oil** (an important commodity for both cooking and light), he instructed her to borrow as many jars from her neighbors as she could. She was then to fill the jars with the oil. This was clearly a test of faith, both in asking for a large number of jars when her own supply was so paltry and in acting in the absence of the prophet. This miracle would be about trust in God, not confidence in Elisha.

After meeting these conditions, the widow began to pour the oil into these jars. She **kept pouring** until her son told her, **There is not a jar left.** She had enough oil to fill every jar she had collected. She reported this remarkable provision to Elisha. He commanded her to **sell the oil and pay your debts** and **live on what is left.** God had provided for a private need in a private way. He had paid the debts the impoverished widow could not pay and redeemed her sons from slavery.

B God Cares for the Heartbroken (4:8–37)

SUPPORTING IDEA: *God's compassion reaches those with hidden heartbreaks.*

4:8–17. The woman who was the recipient of the next two miracles was a person at the opposite end of the social scale from the widow. She was **well-to-do,** literally a "great woman," a person of standing and status who lived in the village of **Shunem** (see "Deeper Discoveries"). Located just north of Jezreel, this was in an area much traveled by Elisha. On one occasion the woman urged him to stay for a meal. That led to a habit of hospitality for the prophet, whom she recognized as **a holy man of God**. Finally, she approached her husband with a suggestion: **Let's make a small room on the roof**. The prophet could lodge there when he was in the area.

Elisha was grateful for this woman's kindness. **One day** (notice the repetition in vv. 8,11,18) he sent **his servant Gehazi**, who appears here for the first time, to summon the **Shunammite**. He then asked how he could repay this woman's kindness. Was there a problem or a desire that he could present on her behalf **to the king or the commander of the army**? The woman's response was an emphatic no. She had no interest in or desire for reward: **I have a home among my own people**. Apparently content with her life, she needed nothing from the prophet.

But things are not always as they seem. This secure, self-confident woman had a secret heartbreak that was exposed by a simple observation of Gehazi: **she has no son and her husband is old**. Infertility has always been a heavy burden for many women. In this situation it was compounded by the stigma of the culture, the reality of her husband's age, and the deep desire in Hebrew society for every family to have a son. She had closed a door on hope. But Elisha, led by God's Spirit, recalled her and made a stunning promise: **About this time next year . . . you will hold a son in your arms**.

That possibility, although wonderful, was too painful for her even to consider: **No, my lord . . . Don't mislead your servant**. Her longing for a child was a hurt too deep to admit, a longing too painful to reopen. Her wealth and her status had not shielded her from the raw hurts of life. Her needs were different from the destitute widow's, but her heart was just as fragile. And God graciously gave her heart's desire: **the next year about that same time she gave birth to a son**. The word of God's prophet could be trusted.

4:18–37. The writer of 2 Kings takes us from the delight of unexpected life to the horror of unexpected death. The boy had grown to the age where he was able to be in the fields with his father. One day out in the fields, he suddenly cried out, **My head! My head!** His father sent him home to his mother. Her despair is not recorded, but as she cradled him in her arms, **he died**. What loss is harder than the loss of a child? The heartbreak of infertility had given way to the even more devastating heartbreak of bereavement.

The woman refused to accept the finality of death, at least until the prophet who was responsible for the boy's life had spoken. Her actions reveal her determination to get to the man of God as quickly as possible and to keep the boy's death a secret until then. She first concealed the boy's body **on the bed of the man of God**; then she requested that her husband provide a donkey **so I can go to the man of God quickly**.

The journey to **Carmel** was about twenty-five miles, but even when she reached the vicinity of Elisha, she refused to be deflected. Dismissing **Gehazi** and his polite queries with another **everything is all right**, she finally reached Elisha, threw herself to the ground, and **took hold of his feet**. Only then would she spell out her agony: **Did I ask you for a son? . . . Didn't I tell you, "Don't raise my hopes"?** But she had not come this far just to complain; she had come to see her son restored to life. Perhaps she had heard of what Elijah had done for the widow of Zarephath (1 Kgs. 17:17–24).

Elisha responded by sending Gehazi to the boy, taking Elisha's staff. He was to travel with such urgency that he must avoid the normal courtesy of greeting fellow travelers. But the Shunammite would not accept anything less than the presence of God's prophet: **As surely as the Lord lives . . . I will not leave you.** Her faith in the Lord was expressed by faith in God's prophet.

When Gehazi arrived, his actions proved futile: **there was no sound or response**. Gehazi told Elisha: **The boy has not awakened.** There was no question of the boy's death. For hours the body had remained untended in the upper room.

The miracle itself is described in the briefest of terms. Alone in the room with the dead boy, Elisha prayed to the Lord. He then spread himself on the body, **mouth to mouth**. When the boy's body grew warm, Elisha stepped away for a time, then returned to stretch out on the body again. **The boy sneezed seven times and opened his eyes.** No explanation is given for some of these actions or why there were seven sneezes. But the miracle was not the result of Elisha's technique; it happened because of God's intervention. The Lord had worked through Elisha, just as he had through Elijah, to restore a dead boy to life.

The climax of the story came when Elisha called the woman and presented her with a living son. Her emotions can only be imagined! But before she took the boy, she **fell at his feet and bowed to the ground**, in joyful gratitude for God's work through his prophet. God in his grace had touched a heartbroken woman by overcoming her infertility and raising the dead.

ℂ God Cares for the Hungry (4:38–44)

SUPPORTING IDEA: *God's compassion extends to the basic needs of life.*

4:38–41. After the wonder of the Shunammite woman's experience, almost any other miracle would seem anticlimactic. The first of the two food stories takes us back to the context of **the company of the prophets**, who had gathered to meet with Elisha in the vicinity of **Gilgal**. These prophets were almost certainly poor, and **there was a famine in that region**. This was a subsistence level economy, in which food was always precious, but much more so in a time of famine. When Elisha gave the instruction to **cook some stew**

for these men, some of the prophets went into the nearby fields to forage for food. One of them gathered some **herbs** and also **a wild vine**. Unaware of the toxic effects of the gourds from this vine, he put them in the stew.

When the stew was first tasted, the tasters cried out in alarm: **there is death in the pot**, probably referring to its bitter taste. The eaters were apparently not in immediate danger; Elisha did nothing for them. But food was precious in a time of famine. Rather than dumping out the stew, Elisha commanded bystanders to **get some flour**, which he threw into the pot. As a result, **there was nothing harmful in the pot**. The flour did not bring about the change; this was a miracle from God.

4:42–44. Few details are given about the events surrounding the next miracle. Perhaps it also happened during a time of famine. A man came with **twenty loaves of barley bread baked from the first ripe grain.** The offering of firstfruits was to be taken to the priests (Num. 18:13; Deut. 18:4–5). But there were no authentic Aaronic priests in Israel, so this man brought the offering to the Lord's servant Elisha, who ordered that this offering be set before **a hundred men.** However generous the gift, it was inadequate for such a large group. But Elisha had a revelation from the Lord: **They will eat and have some left over.** He was a man of faith, acting on the word of God. When the others did as he said, they discovered that God's promise was reliable: **they ate and had some left over.**

It is impossible to read this account without seeing in it a smaller version of two great events in the life of the Lord Jesus, the feeding of the five thousand (Matt. 14:13–21) and the feeding of the four thousand (Matt. 15:32–39).

Ⓓ God Gives Grace to the Humble (5:1–27)

SUPPORTING IDEA: *God's compassion flows to those who follow his word, but he resists those who disrespect it.*

5:1–7. The scene shifts again, from Israel to Syria, and from Israelites to a Syrian general. Everything about **Naaman** indicates that he was an exceptional person. His name, which means "pleasantness," suggests that he had a pleasant personality. As **commander of the army of the king of Aram** (Syria), he carried a heavy responsibility. The terms used about him indicate that his reputation was impeccable: **a great man . . . highly regarded . . . a valiant soldier.** He was a pagan, yet even his relation to the Lord is unusual: **through him the LORD had given victory to Aram.** The specific victory intended is not indicated, but God is the Lord of the nations, not just Israel.

In spite of all these attributes, Naaman **had leprosy.** Although the term was used of a variety of illnesses and does not correspond to a modern clinical term (see "Deeper Discoveries"), leprosy was an extremely serious condition. The disease was progressive, and Naaman was clearly in the early stages, since he could still move about in public. It was, however, terminal, with no known cure. Most of all, this disease was isolating. It bore a stigma and aroused fear, as AIDS does in many places today.

Serving in the home of Naaman was **a young girl from Israel**, the victim of one of Syria's raiding parties into Israel. She was everything Naaman wasn't: a slave, a girl, a Hebrew, and a believer in God. She was probably in her early teens. Learning of her master's illness, she responded with compassion for him and with confidence in God's prophet: **If only my master would see the prophet who is in Samaria! He would cure him of his leprosy.**

Desperately ill people are willing to do desperate things. On the basis of a foreign girl's wish, Naaman was willing to approach the king, who apparently already knew of his condition. The king valued Naaman enough to approve and authorize the expedition, going so far as to write **a letter to the king of Israel**. So Naaman set out, equipped with two things that would assure him of healing.

First, he would buy what he wanted from Israel's God, with his gift of **ten talents of silver** (about 750 pounds), **six thousand shekels of gold** (about 150 pounds), and **ten sets of clothing**. This was a huge amount of money. Naaman could hire the prophet to do what he wanted. His second resource was power and position, in the form of a letter from the king. Kings generally got what they wanted. The king of Syria made his desires clear: **I am sending my servant Naaman to you so that you may cure him of his leprosy.**

In the presence of such a demand, the unnamed **king of Israel** came unglued. The last thing he would think of was to call upon the Lord or his prophet. All he could read in the letter was a pretense for war: **See how he is trying to pick a quarrel with me.** He was totally out of touch with what was happening and was blind to the hand of God.

5:8–19a. Elisha, on the other hand, knew God and his purposes. What the king could not do, he could. He told the king of Israel to send Naaman to him, and Naaman came, **with his horses and chariots.** Samaria was not a large city; a retinue like this would stand out like a presidential motorcade in a middle-class neighborhood. But Naaman did not get down from his chariot. He stopped at the door of Elisha's house. A great man like him deserved respect and deference. But Elisha sent a messenger to tell him, **Go, wash yourself seven times in the Jordan, and your flesh will be restored.**

Naaman was enraged by such treatment. He pulled away from the prophet's home, only to pour out his anger to his men: **I thought that he would surely come out to me.** Naaman was actually saying, "Doesn't this guy know who I am?" He also betrayed his expectation that healing was all about a prophet's special technique, not his God: **I thought that he would . . . wave his hand over the spot and cure me of my leprosy.** And there was also a matter of national pride: **Are not Abana and Pharpar, the rivers of Damascus,** better than any of the waters of Israel? Couldn't I wash in them and be cleansed? It would have been hard to argue with Naaman. The Jordan River was muddy and unimpressive.

Naaman was the epitome of a man who knew what he wanted from God, but he thought it was a business arrangement that could be purchased or a mechanical arrangement that could be manipulated. The thought that his healing involved humble submission to God, on his terms alone, did not occur to him. The way of God was too simple and too silly: "dip seven times in the Jordan."

Fortunately, Naaman's men read him like a book. They challenged his foolish response. Their appeal cut through his bluster: **if the prophet had told you to do some great thing, would you not have done it? How much more, then, when he tells you, "Wash and be cleansed!"** They were telling him, "What have you got to lose, except a little pride?" Their words pierced the general's armor. He made the twenty-five-mile journey to the river and **dipped himself in the Jordan seven times**. The effect was instantaneous. **His flesh was restored and became clean like that of a young boy.** Following the word of God's prophet brought the healing he had longed for.

Naaman did not return directly to Damascus to display his healing but to the prophet in Samaria to confess his faith. He had a new relation to the Lord, declared in a grand confession of faith: **There is no God in all the world except in Israel**. The miracle, done in Elisha's absence, had pointed him to Elisha's God. Naaman was not just saying the right thing. A few moments later he would insist on the depth of his transformed view of reality: **your servant will never again make burnt offerings and sacrifices to any other god but the LORD**. This is the language of conversion. He also had a new relation to God's prophet. Earlier he had stormed at Elisha's failure to defer to him. Now he called himself, the formerly arrogant general, **your servant**.

Naaman offered a gift to express his appreciation, but Elisha rejected it. This was about God and his glory: **As surely as the LORD lives . . . I will not accept a thing**.

Naaman suddenly had a new set of values. Hours before he had despised the muddy Jordan River. Now the most valuable thing he could imagine was **as much earth as a pair of mules can carry**. He apparently intended to build an altar on soil from God's land, where he would worship the Lord. His theology was obviously immature, with a faulty understanding of God, the Lord of all nations. He linked God to the physical land of Israel. Faulty as his theology was, his desire to honor the Lord was honorable.

Naaman also had a new sensitivity to his responsibilities. As the right-hand man of the king of Syria, there would be ceremonial occasions when he would be expected to accompany his master into the temple of the god, **Rimmon**, the Syrian equivalent of Baal. He recognized the inappropriateness of such an action (**may the LORD forgive your servant for this one thing**, repeated twice, showing his distress). He would bow alongside the king, but his heart would be given to God. He would be there out of loyalty to his king, not his king's god.

5:19b–27. It is possible to be close to the work of God and to the people of God but to be far from the heart of God. As Elisha's servant **Gehazi** saw Naaman depart, all he could see was a lost opportunity for personal enrichment. He was blind to the glory of what had taken place. His greed stood in stark contrast to Elisha's generosity and Naaman's gratitude. He determined to seize the opportunity to enrich himself.

Gehazi's plan was simple and shrewd. Hurrying after Naaman, he caught him and spun a story, in Elisha's name, of unexpected visitors and a sudden need for provisions: **Please give them a talent of silver and two sets of clothing**. His shrewdness was seen both in the plausibility of the story and the limited request. At the same time the transformation that had taken place in Naaman was shown by his willingness to dismount to greet a servant and his offer of more than Gehazi requested. He even supplied several of his servants to help transport the provisions back to Elisha. But Gehazi **took the things from the servants and put them away in the house**. As Naaman's servants headed toward Syria, Gehazi knew that no one in Israel knew anything about his secret deal. He had committed the "perfect crime," and no one had been harmed.

Or so it seemed until he met Elisha. Gehazi had underestimated the prophet of God. By divine revelation Elisha knew all that had taken place, and he made clear to Gehazi that his disrespect for God and his word had been found out. It was futile to try to deceive a man who was getting his information from a divine source. Even more, it was God's glory that was being tarnished. To enrich oneself by cashing in on an act of God was reprehensible. And Gehazi would pay the price: **Naaman's leprosy will cling to you and to your descendants forever**.

As the story comes to an end, Naaman and Gehazi have traded places. The pagan who humbled himself to submit to God's word through his prophet had found healing. The servant of the prophet who had disrespected God's word had tasted the bitterness of judgment. The God of compassion who heals the trusting is also the God of justice who will clear the guilty. "God opposes the proud, but gives grace to the humble" (1 Pet. 5:5).

E God Cares for the Careless (6:1–7)

> **SUPPORTING IDEA:** *No need is too trivial for a compassionate Lord's concern.*

6:1–7. Once again we are with **the company of the prophets** in an undisclosed location. They had outgrown the place where they customarily met with Elisha, so they proposed to their leader a new structure, apparently with a simple lodge-pole construction. Since trees suitable for such poles could be found by **the Jordan**, Elisha agreed to the plan to make a trip to the river to acquire the needed materials. In the course of events, one of the men was chopping a tree on the banks of the muddy Jordan River, when **the iron axhead** slipped off the handle and splashed into the river, hopelessly lost. The young prophet turned to Elisha with the cry, **Oh, my lord . . . it was borrowed!** Iron was expensive, and the situation was like borrowing a friend's car and totaling it.

Elisha's response was not to berate the man for his carelessness. Instead, he asked where the iron had landed. Then he **cut a stick and threw it** into the water at that spot, and miraculously **made the iron float**. Our God is a God who rules over his own laws of nature. Elisha then commanded the man to take it out of the water.

Of all the miracles, this was surely the most "trivial." But that is probably the point. Even the trivial issues of life, even things brought on by our own carelessness or things we label as accidents, are not outside of God's care. He does not promise to float all lost ax heads or to locate all lost keys. But he does invite us to "cast all your anxiety on him because he cares for you" (1 Pet. 5:7).

> **MAIN IDEA REVIEW:** The Lord works through his people to show his compassion for all kinds of people with all kinds of needs.

III. CONCLUSION

No Respecter of Persons

The miracles of Elisha show that God cares for the poor and needy, especially those who follow him in faith. Four of the miracles are directed toward people connected to the companies of the prophets. But whether it was a widow in desperate straits, people sharing the common struggle to survive in a famine, or a somewhat careless borrower of a friend's ax, each is the object of God's special care.

But he is not only the God of the poor and needy. The God who cares for the disadvantaged also cares for the advantaged and the affluent whose heartbreaks may be hidden from view. He was the God of compassion to the Shunammite woman as well as the prophet's widow.

But God's love and compassion is not restricted to Israel. He is the God of compassion to Naaman, the pagan leper, who humbled himself before him. Naaman could not buy God's love, or demand it by his power, or merit it by his reputation or his achievements. But he could receive it freely by obeying his word through his prophet.

PRINCIPLES

- God's grace and power are available to those who trust in him, whatever their need or station in life.
- Faith is acting on the word of God.
- God's grace is available to all who will come to him in humble faith.
- We must do nothing that would detract from the glory that belongs to God alone.

APPLICATIONS

- What need do you have that seems trivial and insignificant? Bring it to God in simple trust.
- What need do you have that seems too large for God? Bring it to him with boldness.
- No merits you have can impress God or put him in your debt; come to him in humility.
- God has made himself and his ways known through his word. Listen to him.
- God's glory is supreme and beyond our understanding. Protect it.

IV. LIFE APPLICATION

Pictures of Salvation

Two of the miracles we have considered provide marvelous pictures of what God does for us in the Lord Jesus Christ. The widow, hopelessly enslaved in debt, was delivered from bondage because the Lord paid her debts. He provided for her what she was unable to provide for herself. The Lord himself was her redeemer. It is a small picture of the provision the redeemer God made for us when his Son paid the price of our redemption. But she needed to believe and act upon the word of the prophet who brought God's way of deliverance to her.

The story of Naaman reminds us that God resists the proud but gives grace to the humble. Naaman set out to Israel believing he could demand deliverance from his illness because of the power of the king, that he could buy it with the massive fortune he brought with him, or that he could achieve it by some great act the prophet told him to do. Instead he received the word of God. It was not going to come because the king demanded it or because he paid for it or because he earned it. God's gift would not cost Naaman anything, except his pride. He must humble himself and follow the word of God through the prophet of God. When he submitted to the word of God, he experienced the healing power of God.

V. PRAYER

Father, thank you that you care about every situation in our lives, whether large or great, and that we can come boldly to "the throne of grace" at all times. Teach us to come on the basis of what you have taught in your Word, with humility about who we are and confidence about who you are. Thank you for your great grace. Amen.

VI. DEEPER DISCOVERIES

A. The Meaning of Miracles

Miracles are significant throughout the Bible, but a careful evaluation shows that many of them are clustered in three major periods—the exodus and conquest (Moses and Joshua), Elijah and Elisha, and the New Testament period (Jesus and the apostles). In the first case, God's covenant people are being established in a special way; in the second, the covenant is under attack by baalism; in the third, the new covenant community is being born. Miracles were given to authenticate the messenger and the message of God. They are almost never mere displays of divine power, but they serve as signs and pointers to something beyond themselves. They also reveal the heart of God, by putting his character on display. In one sense, they are also glimpses of the kingdom, since they are a window into what God intended apart from the effects of sin.

B. Shunem (4:8)

Shunem was a town on the southwestern slope of the Hill of Moreh, a few miles south of Nazareth. In the time of Jesus, a village called Nain was located a few miles away on the slopes of the same hill. What unites the two is more than geography. Elisha raised a dead boy to life in Shunem. The Lord Jesus interrupted a funeral by raising a widow's son to life in the village of Nain (Luke 7:11–15). Several of Elisha's miracles point to those of the Savior, most notably the feeding of a hundred (2 Kgs. 4:42–44) and the healing of a leper (2 Kgs. 5:1–19).

C. Leprosy

In our modern world we associate the term *leprosy* with Hansen's disease. It is debated whether this specific condition existed in ancient Israel. The biblical term is described in some detail in Leviticus 13, where it covers a variety of skin conditions. Although we cannot be sure of the exact nature of Naaman's condition, it is obvious that it was regarded as serious, probably fatal, and socially isolating for the victim in its advanced stages.

VII. TEACHING OUTLINE

A. INTRODUCTION

1. Lead Story: The Cause of the Weak

2. Context: Although Elisha was called to be a prophet to the nation, he spent much of his time with the poor, the weak, and the needy, showing them the love and compassion of his Lord. But God's grace also flowed to the strong and the wealthy who humbled themselves in faith.

3. Transition: Having been in the presence of kings and armies in chapter 3, we now move to the world of individuals, those who are often weak and needy.

B. COMMENTARY

1. God Cares for the Desperate (4:1–7)

2. God Cares for the Heartbroken (4:8–37)

3. God Cares for the Hungry (4:38–44)

4. God Gives Grace to the Humble (5:1–27)

5. God Cares for the Careless (6:1–7)

C. CONCLUSION: NO RESPECTER OF PERSONS

VIII. ISSUES FOR DISCUSSION

1. The miracles in this section display God's compassion for people of all backgrounds—the poor and needy, the well-to-do and affluent, and the powerful foreigner. How do we in our local churches display the compassion of our God, who is not a respecter of persons?

2. Naaman's pride almost kept him from experiencing healing and conversion. How big an issue do you think pride is in keeping people from experiencing God's blessing in their lives? How does pride manifest itself in your life?

2 Kings 6:8–8:29

God's Secret Agent

I. **INTRODUCTION**
Conspiracy Theory

II. **COMMENTARY**
A verse-by-verse explanation of these verses.

III. **CONCLUSION**
Person of the Year

An overview of the principles and application from these verses.

IV. **LIFE APPLICATION**
No Place to Hide

Melding these verses to life.

V. **PRAYER**
Tying these verses to life with God.

VI. **DEEPER DISCOVERIES**
Historical, geographical, and grammatical enrichment of the commentary.

VII. **TEACHING OUTLINE**
Suggested step-by-step group study of these verses.

VIII. **ISSUES FOR DISCUSSION**
Zeroing these verses in on daily life.

| Q u o t e |

"*I*f you read history, you will discover that the Christians who did most for the present world were just those who thought most of the next. . . . They all left their mark on Earth, precisely because their minds were occupied with Heaven. It is since Christians have largely ceased to think of the other world that they have become so ineffective in this. Aim at heaven and you will get earth 'thrown in'; aim at earth and you get neither."

C . S . L e w i s

BIOGRAPHICAL PROFILE: HAZAEL OF SYRIA (ARAM)

- He ruled Aram (Syria) from about 843–801 B.C. (the date of his death is uncertain), following Ben-Hadad
- He is named in the Assyrian annals, where he is described as "a son of a nobody," meaning that he was a commoner
- He was besieged and defeated by the Assyrian Shalmeneser III in 841 B.C. and was attacked again by him unsuccessfully in 838 B.C.
- He engaged in military conflicts against Joram, Jehu, and Jehoahaz of Israel. His attacks on Israel usually coincided with times of Assyrian withdrawal from the region (837–805 B.C.)
- He is described in the Assyrian annals as a vassal of Adad-Nirari III (806–798 B.C.)

2 Kings 6:8–8:29

IN A NUTSHELL

*E*lisha was a prophet whose life touched people in their need. But the Lord also put him in a position where he influenced the affairs of nations.

God's Secret Agent

I. INTRODUCTION

Conspiracy Theory

*W*hen we lived in Dallas, one of the places we invariably took out-of-town visitors was the Sixth Floor Museum in the old Texas Schoolbook Depository Building. This was the place where Lee Harvey Oswald squatted, rifle in hand, waiting for the limousine carrying President John Kennedy to enter Dealey Plaza. The floor has been turned into a museum, enabling visitors to relive the events of that day, to gain an understanding of the criminal investigation, and to stand in the corner window from which the shots that killed the president were fired on November 22, 1963. I always came away from that display with my memories of that terrible day refreshed and my emotions stirred.

Then we would often walk a few hundred yards to the West End Market Place for something to eat. As we walked around the shops, we would invariably stop at a store that offered an entirely different perspective on the Kennedy assassination: that the official explanation was a complete cover-up. We would often find people engaged in noisy debate over various theories of the Kennedy assassination, accusing the Cubans, the Mafia, the CIA, the KGB, or some combination of the above. Even decades after the event, passions run high.

Conspiracy theories abound. Many people in the Muslim world claimed that the Jews, seeking to discredit Islam and the Palestinians, engineered the attacks on the World Trade Center in New York City. Other people contend that Princess Diana was murdered, or that the moon landing was faked, or that the government is the puppet of a mysterious group of businessmen or Communists. While conspiracies and cover-ups undoubtedly do exist, most of the theories are a product of overactive imaginations or paranoia. Humans have a need to make sense of events that seem to defy rational explanation.

It is true that there may be an explanation for some events that lies far deeper than the visible. History seems to be shaped by kings, governments, and armies. But God often has his agents at work; they are the true shapers of events. A historian would see the events of these chapters in a different way from a person viewing life through the lens of divine revelation. It was not the kings but the prophet of God, Elisha, who was the determinative figure of his time. He saw what others didn't because he saw with eyes opened by his God. He was the one through whom victory came and by whom kings were set up and pulled down. History is in the hands of a sovereign God.

II. COMMENTARY

God's Secret Agent

> **MAIN IDEA:** *Because God's prophet was his spokesman, people's response to his prophet determines blessing or judgment.*

🅐 Syria's Attack on Dothan (6:8–23)

> **SUPPORTING IDEA:** *When God's people follow God's prophet, they experience divine protection.*

6:8–14. The previous section of 2 Kings had shown Elisha involved with people of many different backgrounds, working miracles to meet their needs. The scene now shifts to the national and the international, with God's prophet as the pivotal player. The last recorded encounter between Syria and Israel was the time when Ahab attempted to retake Ramoth Gilead, only to lose his life (1 Kgs. 22). Once again the nations found themselves in conflict. Although we are told that **the king of Aram was at war with Israel**, it becomes evident that this took the form of raiding parties by Syria into Israelite territory (6:23) rather than full-scale warfare. Neither the king of Aram nor the king of Israel is mentioned by name in this episode. Presumably they were Ben-Hadad and Jehoram, although we cannot be certain. The absence of names serves to put the spotlight more squarely on **the man of God**, Elisha, God's secret agent.

The king of Syria would develop his plan for quick-strike forays into Israel, but before he could deploy his troops, Elisha would send word to the king of Israel: **Beware . . . because the Arameans are going down there**. The king listened to God's prophet. As a result, the raids of the Syrians were repulsed **time and again**.

The king of Syria drew the only reasonable conclusion: **one of his officers** was a spy. Enraged, he demanded that the guilty party confess. Somehow his men knew the truth of the situation: **Elisha . . . tells the king of Israel the very words you speak in your bedroom**. This was not because Elisha had a network of informers in Syria but because of God's revelation. Syria's problem was not a king or an army but one prophet. The solution was obvious: find him and bring him under control! When his intelligence agents discovered that Elisha was in **Dothan**, a town about ten miles north of Israel's capital of Samaria, the king of Syria ordered an invasion to capture the prophet. Surely military might could deal with such a small problem!

6:15–17. We are not told why Elisha was at Dothan, since his home was in Samaria. But when his servant ventured outside early in the morning, he discovered that **an army . . . had surrounded the city**. He recognized that the army was Syrian, that they were there with hostile intent, and that the city was defenseless. His only recourse was to cry out to Elisha: **what shall we do?**

Elisha answered, **Don't be afraid. . . . Those who are with us are more than those who are with them.** It was a call to faith, because the presence of God changed the equation. Nevertheless, the servant must have wondered what Elisha meant by this statement. The numerical superiority of the Syrians was clear. The answer came with the prayer of Elisha: **O LORD, open his eyes so he may see.** Then the Lord opened the eyes of Elisha's servant, and he saw **horses and chariots of fire all around Elisha**. These invisible resources were reminiscent of the chariot and horses at the translation of Elijah (2:11). They represented the angelic forces made available for the protection of God's servant.

The significant thing is that the invisible army had been present all along. Elisha's prayer was not that they arrive but that their presence be revealed to the servant. Before anyone had known of the need, God's protection had been in place. What the servant now saw changed his perception of the balance of power. The enemy's superiority had only been an illusion. They thought they were in control. But real power lay elsewhere.

6:18–23. The presence of the invisible army did not cause the Syrians to go away. They came toward Elisha with hostile intent, and he countered their attack by prayer. He did not just count on the presence of the heavenly army; he prayed, **Strike these people with blindness**. The Syrians were reduced to helplessness and foolishness. Elisha, the one-man intelligence service (6:8–10), now became a one-man security force as he led the helpless Syrians on a ten-mile march to the national capital. When they were within the walls of Samaria, he prayed that God would restore their sight. The frustration of the proud forces of Syria when they discovered they were helpless prisoners of one man can only be imagined. They could only hope for a speedy death.

That was exactly what Israel's king intended: **Shall I kill them?** Elisha reminded him that prisoners of war were not killed and they were not the king's prisoners. They were to be treated as guests and sent home without being harmed. Once again, the king followed Elisha's directions. Elisha did not play the game by the usual rules. He was God's man, and he chose to humble his enemies with kindness.

The result was a temporary stop of hostilities: **so the bands from Aram stopped raiding Israel's territory**. More significantly, an important principle had been made clear. Because God's invisible army is more powerful than any human army, those who follow the word of God through his prophet experience the blessing of God.

B Syria's Siege of Samaria (6:24–7:20)

SUPPORTING IDEA: *When God's people trust God's word through his prophet, they experience divine provision.*

6:24–7:2. The cessation of hostilities between Syria and Israel did not last long. Some time later King Ben-Hadad of Aram mobilized his **army and marched up and laid siege to Samaria**. No explanation for this eruption of total war is given. Siege warfare was all-out war. A chokehold was placed on everyone who lived in a city, civilians and soldiers alike. The effect was gradual, but after a time there was a great famine in the city. Chaos and confusion mounted, and as food supplies dwindled, profiteers took advantage of people's desperation. Even virtually inedible things, normally discarded as trash, sold for exorbitant prices.

A donkey's head, unclean and unappetizing, **sold for eighty shekels of silver** (about two pounds). The term the NIV translates as **seed pods** literally means "dove's dung" or "pigeon droppings." The suggestion that it was seed pods is due to a feeling that the desperation could not have reached such depths. But, whatever the material, **a quarter of a cab** (a cab is about 1.2 liters) sold **for five shekels** (about two ounces of silver).

But inflated prices for worthless food was hardly the worst of it. **As the king of Israel was passing by on the wall**, probably reviewing the position of the Syrian forces and observing life within the city, a woman made an appeal to him as the judge of last resort: **Help me, my lord the king**. The king is unnamed, but it was probably Jehoram. His anger and frustration at God was evident. He replied, **If the LORD does not help you, where can I get help for you? From the threshing floor? From the winepress?** The sarcasm of his words could not mask his sense of hopelessness or his anger at God. The famine, in his mind, was caused by God's failure. This was a repetition of his accusation in the Moab crisis (3:10,13). The king's instinct in trouble was to blame God!

The woman's appeal made clear that conditions were even worse than the king imagined. She and another woman had made an agreement to kill and cannibalize their children. Nothing worse can be imagined than mothers trying to survive at the expense of their children. They had eaten the complainant's son, but when time came to eat the second child, **she had hidden him**. The woman had no sense of shame about her actions; she had a sense of outrage about the unfairness of the other woman. She expected the king to take her side and to defend her right to eat the other child!

The king reacted with horror. Tearing his robes, he revealed that hidden underneath **he had sackcloth on his body**. He had the signs of repentance, but he kept it private, and his heart showed no genuine repentance before God. This was not a king leading his people in public repentance. The atrocity of cannibalism was a clear sign of divine judgment for covenant rebellion, predicted in Deuteronomy 28:53–57. A holy God was not inspiring such atrocities. But he had removed his restraint on evil and allowed human depravity to take its ugly course.

The king exploded in anger, not at Baal, not at the evil introduced into the nation by his parents, not at the Jeroboam cult, not at the evil hearts of people—but at Elisha: **May God deal with me . . . severely, if the head of Elisha . . . remains on his shoulders today!** The response would be laughable, were it not so tragic. What had Elisha had to do with this? At most he had spoken the truth: that the famine was God's judgment on the nation's sin. Elisha was a convenient scapegoat! It was easier to kill the messenger than to listen to his message.

Elisha was not exempt from the suffering of his people. He had remained in the city and, by divine revelation, was aware of the king's threat. He was sitting in his house, and the elders were sitting with him, when he suddenly exposed the king's intention: **this murderer is sending someone to cut off my head.** The messenger did arrive, followed by the king himself, who poured out his animosity against God: **This disaster is from the LORD. Why should I wait for the LORD any longer?** In a sense, he was right. The disaster was God's hand of judgment on the nation.

But God had not abandoned his people. Elisha spoke in the most formal language of a prophet: **About this time tomorrow, a seah of flour** (about 7.3 liters) **will sell for a shekel and two seahs of barley for a shekel at the gate of Samaria.** The idea that there would be quality food at low prices within twenty-four hours at the city gates was, by any normal reckoning, absurd. That was the immediate reaction of one of the king's officers. There was no conceivable way for such a thing to come to pass. But this was not the predictions of a person, but the promise of a prophet, speaking in the name of the Lord. To make that point clear, Elisha pronounced a judgment on the cynic: **You will see it with your own eyes . . . but you will not eat any of it!** In the midst of the chaos and confusion of a city under siege, Elisha modeled a deep-seated confidence in God.

7:3–15. God keeps his promises, but he does so in the most unexpected ways. During a famine people on the edge of society such as lepers were the most vulnerable. They were not allowed to enter the city, but even if they did, only death awaited them. If they remained outside, they would be the victims of famine or of the first attacks of the enemy. Since they had nothing to lose, the lepers of the city decided to defect to the enemy.

But at almost the very moment they set out for the enemy camp, the Lord was intervening. He **caused the Arameans to hear the sound of chariots and horses and a great army.** The Syrians jumped to the conclusion that the Israelites had hired an army from the south (the Egyptians) and from the north (the Hittites) to catch them in a pincher movement. It was **dusk**, when hazy shapes were hard to make out. In the panic of the moment, the Syrians abandoned their tents, leaving behind everything that would hinder their flight—**horses and donkeys** and, most importantly, food.

When the lepers reached the Syrian camp, they found it abandoned and a vast treasure trove available to them. They had no way of knowing what had happened, but they began to loot the tents and to satisfy their hunger. But a guilty sense of responsibility came upon them. **Let's go at once**, they declared, **and report this to the royal palace.**

The king had gone to bed, obviously having given no credence to Elisha's promise. So he could only greet the report with skepticism, believing it to be a clever tactic of the Syrians. His unbelief was deep-seated, and only an appeal by one of his officers could budge him. The officer reasoned like the lepers did: "We have nothing to lose. We should take men and two chariots. If they stay in the city, they're going to die; if the report is wrong, the Syrians will kill them. But if the report is right, we all may live." His argument carried the day. The teams were sent out. They discovered the evidence of the Syrian's flight and followed it **as far as the Jordan** (about twenty-five miles). Then they **returned and reported to the king** that the Syrian army had vanished.

7:16–20. The conclusion of the story emphasizes the fulfillment of God's word through his prophet: **just as the man of God had foretold.** The Lord had kept his promise. The inhabitants of the famished city rushed out **and plundered the camp of the Arameans.** The Lord had fulfilled his promise; entrepreneurs brought food back to the city gate and sold high-quality food for low prices, precisely as Elisha had predicted. God had also kept his word of judgment.

Ironically, the king had put his skeptical officer **in charge of the gate.** When the news of the abandoned Syrian camp with its abundance of food hit the city, there had been an instant rush through the gates, and **the people trampled him in the gateway.** The story is repeated to impress upon us the precision with which the Lord fulfills even his most unlikely promises. It was God who gave victory, not the king or his army, and it came through the agency of his prophets. God's true prophets speak the truth and must not be mocked, opposed, or ignored.

The Shunammite Woman (8:1–6)

> **SUPPORTING IDEA:** *When God's people act on the basis of the word of God's prophet, God meets their needs.*

8:1–6. This brief paragraph takes us out of the realm of the national back into the realm of the personal. The story of the Shunammite, the woman whose son Elisha **had restored to life**, was given in 4:8–37. Now she reappeared, as the symbol of the believing remnant in Israel that acted on the basis of the prophet's word. At some unspecified time, **Elisha** had warned the woman of a coming seven-year **famine**. It was probably another act of God's judgment on his rebellious people. Elisha advised her to leave Israel and **stay for a while wherever you can.** There is no mention of her husband, and it seems reasonable to believe that she was now a widow. She acted on the word of the prophet and **stayed in the land of the Philistines seven years**.

When the woman returned to her homeland, she found a major problem. Her house and land had been seized. The land may have been confiscated by the king or perhaps misappropriated by someone else. Her only hope was a favorable hearing from the king, so she **went to the king to beg for her house and land.** But a single woman approaching the king had little hope for a fair hearing. Furthermore, her problem in large measure had come because she had followed the direction of the prophet. Would the Lord help her in her time of need?

At the very moment she entered the royal court, the king was asking **Gehazi**, Elisha's servant, to tell him about **all the great things Elisha** had done. We are surprised to read about the presence of Gehazi. This may mean that this episode took place before the Naaman miracle or that he had a low-grade leprosy, allowing him to continue public service. We are also surprised by the king having a positive interest in the deeds of Elisha. But the major point of the story is that it was just as Gehazi was telling the king how Elisha had restored the dead to life that the woman and her son appeared. Gehazi interrupted his story to declare: **This is the woman, my lord the king, and this is her son whom Elisha restored to life.**

The king turned his attention to the woman to get her account of events. Then he issued orders that her land should be returned, along with **all the income from her land from the day she left the country until now.** This was not an example of "good timing." It was God's providential care for those who are rightly related to his word through his prophet. Elisha had helped her even though he had not been present. The Lord had been faithful to her in her need.

D The "Appointing" of Hazael (8:7–15)

> **SUPPORTING IDEA:** *When God speaks through his prophet even about pagan nations, his word is sure.*

8:7–15. This is the only occasion on which Elisha traveled outside the land of Israel. We are not told the reason, but it seems likely that it was related to God's unfulfilled commissioning of Elijah to "anoint Hazael king over Aram" (1 Kgs. 19:15). His presence in **Damascus** did not go unnoticed.

King Ben-Hadad of Syria was sick. He did not send for a personal interview with Elisha. Rather, he sent a trusted officer, **Hazael**, to **consult the LORD through him**. The king wanted to know if he would recover from this illness. As a pagan, Ben-Hadad was willing to seek help wherever he could, and he had seen the Lord's healing power in the case of his general Naaman. Ben-Hadad obviously trusted Hazael, and he had no way of knowing that his choice was providential. The Lord had a special message for Hazael as well.

Hazael made his way to Elisha with an extravagant gift: **forty camel-loads of all the finest wares of Damascus**. He asked the question he had been commissioned to ask. But Elisha's reply was not what he expected: **Go and say to him, "You will certainly recover"; but the LORD has revealed to me that he will in fact die**.

Although this sounds as if Elisha was telling Hazael to deceive his king, the larger context makes his meaning clear. Ben-Hadad's illness was not fatal; he would recover from it. But Ben-Hadad would be murdered by Hazael. Elisha then stared at Hazael, his eyes piercing into his soul and making it clear that he was reading Hazael's intentions. Hazael turned away **ashamed**, and at that point Elisha **began to weep**. The prophet revealed that he not only read Hazael's intentions; he also knew his future: He would make trouble for the nation of Israel.

Hazael was the king of Syria from about 843 to 806 B.C. For much of his reign, he would be involved in bloody warfare against Israel. From this point on, he would be the scourge of Israel, unleashing the horrors of war. This was the sovereign judgment of God upon his people, punishing them for their rebellion and purging baalism from their midst. The Lord would use Hazael as his rod of judgment. He did not cause the evil Hazael inflicted, but he used it to accomplish his judicial purpose.

Hazael's response was striking: **How could your servant . . . accomplish such a feat?** Hazael's description of himself as **a mere dog**, that is, a nobody, was mock humility. He was a commoner, and the Assyrian annals describe him as "a son of a nobody." He heard Elisha's description of his activities as a feat, literally, "a great thing." He was a man drawn to violence and power. Elisha left no doubt about the future: **the LORD has shown me that you will become king of Aram**.

Events unfolded quickly. Hazael returned to give the king Elisha's message of recovery from his illness. But the following day, he took a thick cloth, soaked it in water, and spread it over the king's face. The Lord was sovereign in Syria, just as he was in Israel. He knew the evil of Hazael's heart. He was in control of human evil, turning it to his own ends. Once again God's prophet was at work behind the scenes.

E The Kings of Judah (8:16–29)

SUPPORTING IDEA: *When God speaks through his prophet, he is faithful to his promises, even to an unfaithful people.*

Once again the writer of 2 Kings freezes the frame of Israel's history and moves the history of Judah forward, so that the two histories run parallel. Elisha was not active in Judah, but something else was: the promise the Lord had made to David. The ultimate difference between the nations of Judah and Israel was not the character of the kings, but the Lord's gracious promise to David.

8:16–24. Jehoram, son of Jehoshaphat, ruled Judah from 848 to 841 B.C., preceded by a five-year co-regency with his father (1 Kgs. 22:50). He was married to Ahab's daughter, who is unnamed here but identified in 2 Kings 8:26 as "Athaliah, a granddaughter of Omri king of Israel." His name was the same as the king of Israel (NIV uses *Joram* for the king of Israel to minimize confusion). The identity of names was only the least significant way in which the two nations had converged. Jehoram **did evil in the eyes of the LORD.** Baal worship had come in full force to the land of Judah, and matters were only going to get worse. The writer of 2 Chronicles indicates that to secure his hold on the throne, Jehoram "put all his brothers to the sword along with some of the princes of Israel" (2 Chr. 21:4). Full-fledged paganism now occupied David's throne. The compromise of Jehoshaphat was bearing bitter fruit!

Judah's kingdom began to unravel under its ungodly king. **Edom**, which had long been subservient, **rebelled against Judah**, and Jehoram was not able to suppress the rebellion. The border town of **Libnah**, which was part of Judah, revolted at the same time. Even Judean towns were breaking away! Spiritual rebellion had a high price. Jehoram died from a severe bowel disease (2 Chr. 21:18–19).

8:25–29. In 841 B.C. Jehoram's son **Ahaziah** (who also bore the name of an earlier Israelite king; 1 Kgs. 22:51–2 Kgs. 1:18) succeeded his father on the throne. He was the youngest of Jehoram's sons, since raiders had killed Jehoram's other sons (2 Chr. 21:16–17; 22:1). He also was a practitioner of Baal worship, since he **walked in the ways of the house of Ahab and did evil in the eyes of the LORD . . . for he was related by marriage to Ahab's family.** Not only was his mother a follower of Ahabite, so was his wife!

Ahaziah's reign was brief, less than **one year.** He joined in a coalition with **Joram son of Ahab king of Israel** to try once again to retake **Ramoth Gilead.** In an earlier attempt Ahab had been killed (1 Kgs. 22). On this occasion Israel's king was **wounded** and **returned to Jezreel to recover from his wounds.** Ahaziah went to keep him company. The writer of 2 Kings leaves the two kings together at Jezreel, ready for the decisive change that was about to occur in the histories of the two nations.

MAIN IDEA REVIEW: *Because God's prophet was his spokesman, people's response to his prophet determines blessing or judgment.*

III. CONCLUSION

Person of the Year

At the end of every calendar year, the media loves to honor the person of the year. Invariably they are people who have made headlines—politicians, entertainers, business people, military leaders, or even sports figures. But there is a great difference between celebrity and significance. Almost no one can name the "person of the year" of the previous decade. Research shows that the accomplishments that once seemed so significant tend to vanish without a trace.

The "people of the year" in Syria were kings and military leaders such as Ben-Hadad, Joram, Jehoram, Hazael, and the general who led Syria's army against Dothan. But the man of real power was the man who knew the living God and shaped his life around sharing and obeying his word. He was the one who shaped history; he also brought God's blessing and God's judgment to others. He was God's secret agent through whom God was accomplishing his purposes. He seemed to be in a terrible minority, but he lived by a great truth: "Those who are with us are more than those who are with them" (2 Kgs. 6:16). Elisha is a profound reminder that it is not those people who live for today who have the most influence—but those who live for eternity.

PRINCIPLES

- When God's people follow God's word through his spokesman, they experience divine protection.
- God is present with his people at all times. His invisible army is more powerful than any earthly force.
- God's grace persists in his faithfulness to his covenant promises, in spite of his people's unfaithfulness.
- God is sovereign over all the nations and works his purposes with amazing creativity.
- Spiritual rebellion has a high price.

APPLICATIONS

- Live in obedient trust, so that you can live with confidence in God's presence and protection.

- You can choose to blame God or to trust God when you find yourself in trouble. Trust is the appropriate response.

- Take the warnings of God seriously. He means what he says.

- You don't need to know how God will accomplish his purposes. You can trust in his sovereignty and faithfulness.

IV. LIFE APPLICATION

No Place to Hide

One of the great truths of the Bible is that God is infinite in relation to space, time, knowledge, and power. He is the unlimited God. But our delight in that truth will be directly related to our relationship with him.

The Syrian king encountered a God unlike any he could imagine—one who knew his state secrets, could hear his most intimate conversations, and would reveal them to his enemies. It was frustrating, and his instinctive response was to try to kill the prophet of such a God. The secretive military attaché of the Syrian king was convinced that his plan to seize power by killing his king was known only to him. But when Hazael stood before the prophet of the Lord and heard his most secret plans unveiled, he could only blush with shame. He had been found out. When the king sent an official to kill the prophet, he arrived on the scene to discover that Elisha already knew what he intended. "Everything is uncovered and laid bare before the eyes of him to whom we must give account" (Heb. 4:13).

On the other hand, for those loyal to God, the truth of the Lord's total knowledge is a precious truth. Before the enemy attacks, God is able to warn his people. Before the enemy arrives in force, he is able to put his angelic army in place. Before the famine has ended or the enemy has fled, he is able to give promises of encouragement. Before the widow arrives to plead her case, he is able to engineer the perfect scenario for her to present her need. God is always looking out for the welfare of his people. This means that we can live confidently in his presence.

V. PRAYER

Father, help us to trust your word and your ways, even when we cannot see how current events or circumstances will turn out for our good and your glory. Help us to see the hidden chariots of God that surround us at every step and to walk faithfully before you. Amen.

VI. DEEPER DISCOVERIES

A. Blaming Elisha (6:31)

Jehoram's attack on Elisha for causing the famine is a reminder that being a prophet has always been dangerous business. Sinners do not like to be told about their sin; they hate to be told that they are reaping the consequences of their sin. Jesus warned his disciples that as they faithfully followed him, they could expect to be treated like the prophets: "Blessed are you when people insult you, persecute you and falsely say all kinds of evil against you because of me. Rejoice and be glad, because great is your reward in heaven, for in the same way they persecuted the prophets who were before you" (Matt. 5:11–12).

B. "O LORD, Open His Eyes" (6:17)

Elisha knew what his servant did not know, and it made all the difference in the way he saw events in Dothan. The army of God was already present to protect his prophet. Because Elisha was convinced about God's promises, he was able to be more concerned about his servant than about the enemy. God fights for his people and does not abandon those who trust in him.

VII. TEACHING OUTLINE

A. INTRODUCTION

1. Lead Story: Conspiracy Theory
2. Context: Elisha now finds himself in the middle of international events, where it seems that kings and armies determine events. But the main shaper of events was a man who spoke for God and brought his truth to bear on the present situation.
3. Transition: War between Israel and Syria was to be a continual fact of life in the time of Elisha. But as the prophet of God, he was a secret weapon for his nation.

B. COMMENTARY

1. Syria's Attack on Dothan (6:8–23)
2. Syria's Siege of Samaria (6:24–7:20)
3. The Shunammite Woman (8:1–6)
4. The "Appointing" of Hazael (8:7–15)
5. The Kings of Judah (8:16–29)

C. CONCLUSION: PERSON OF THE YEAR

VIII. ISSUES FOR DISCUSSION

1. Are there times in your life when the Lord has "opened your eyes" and you have been aware of his special presence? What difference does it make that the protection was already in place for Elisha and his servant before they were even aware of it?

2. God is sovereign. But his relation to events is very different in each situation. Is God sovereign or are people ultimately in charge? How are we to understand that our God is sovereign?

2 Kings 9:1–10:36

The Sword of the Lord

I. INTRODUCTION
A Severe Mercy

II. COMMENTARY
A verse-by-verse explanation of these chapters.

III. CONCLUSION
Spiritual Surgery

An overview of the principles and application from these chapters.

IV. LIFE APPLICATION
The Right Thing in the Wrong Way

Melding these chapters to life.

V. PRAYER
Tying these chapters to life with God.

VI. DEEPER DISCOVERIES
Historical, geographical, and grammatical enrichment of the commentary.

VII. TEACHING OUTLINE
Suggested step-by-step group study of these chapters.

VIII. ISSUES FOR DISCUSSION
Zeroing these chapters in on daily life.

"*To* have a right to do a thing is not at all the same as to

be right in doing it."

G .   K .   C h e s t e r t o n

BIOGRAPHICAL PROFILE: JEHU

- Served as a military officer under Ahab and Joram
- Designated by God and anointed as the instrument of judgment on the house of Ahab
- Carried out a bloody purge that removed the house of Ahab and official Baal worship from Israel
- Responsible for the killing of much of the royal family of Judah
- Ruled in Israel from 841 to 814 B.C.
- Was a syncretistic worshiper of the Lord and tolerated the corrupt worship of the Jeroboam cult
- Submitted to Shalmaneser III of Assyria, paying a large tribute
- Unable to prevent Hazael from taking possession of his territory east of the Jordan River
- Founded the longest-lived royal dynasty in Israel

IN A NUTSHELL

The time came for the Lord to remove Baal worship and the influence of Ahab from Israel. Only radical surgery would do. So the Lord raised up a man of zeal who purged Israel of baalism and the family of Ahab, including Jezebel. But in his zeal Jehu went beyond the Lord's directions on many occasions and stopped short of full reform of Israel's worship.

The Sword of the Lord

I. INTRODUCTION

A Severe Mercy

*W*hen I was a young high school student, a good friend suffered a severe hand injury on a construction job. When I got to the hospital, I was horrified to discover that the surgeon was seriously considering amputating several of his fingers. What made it seem even worse was that this surgeon was a close family friend. How could a good man like Ted even consider cutting off my friend's fingers? I had been seriously thinking of a career in medicine, but if that was what it took, no thanks!

My response was, of course, evidence of my ignorance and immaturity. In fact, my doctor friend was able to save my friend's fingers. But amputation, although always unpleasant, is sometimes necessary. My surgeon friend could not be swayed by emotion or sentiment, if that would endanger my friend's health or lead to even greater impairment. Surgeons can be ruthless with infected organs or tumors or crushed limbs, because they are concerned about the whole patient. They will not spare the unhealthy because they care about the healthy. And sometimes extreme measures are called for.

As a pastor, I have had occasions when people have confessed to inappropriate or sinful relationships. Almost always they want to know how they can manage this relationship differently. They rarely appreciate it when I tell them that management is not the option; amputation is. Inevitably they argue for more limited solutions and often seek other opinions. But I have learned, from hard experience with too many people, that such temptations cannot be managed; they must be removed.

Conditions in Israel had reached the point where God found it necessary to appoint a surgeon to remove the cancer of baalism from the nation of Israel. The family of Ahab had brought terrible evil to the nation, and Elijah had announced the Lord's intention to perform radical surgery to cut out the evil (1 Kgs. 21:20–29). Because the cancer had spread so far and embedded itself so deeply, it would require drastic measures.

The surgeons God uses to operate on his people often surprise us. At a later stage he would use the pagan kings of Assyria and Babylon. On this occasion he used a very flawed instrument, a military man named Jehu. He was a man who would boast of his "zeal for the LORD" (2 Kgs. 10:16), but his zeal was incomplete and misguided. He did not pursue God's will consistently (10:29,31), and at times he resembled a butcher more than a surgeon. As a result, he would come under the condemnation of Hosea (Hos.

1:4). Nevertheless, he was God's man for the task, and he was used by the Lord to excise a spiritual cancer from the nation.

II. COMMENTARY

The Sword of the Lord

MAIN IDEA: *Zeal for the Lord is no substitute for obedience of the Lord.*

A The Anointing of Jehu (9:1–13)

SUPPORTING IDEA: *A sovereign and righteous God may call human beings to serve as his agents of judgment.*

9:1–3. Years before, God had commissioned Elijah to "anoint Jehu son of Nimshi king over Israel" (1 Kgs. 19:16). His failure to do that is never explained, and so it fell to **the prophet Elisha** to carry out the mission, just as he had done with Hazael (2 Kgs. 8:7–15). The anointing of a royal successor while the ruling king was still alive was a volatile act. So Elisha chose to work through a surrogate, **a man from the company of the prophets**. Anointing by a prophet gave divine legitimacy. The man was to take a **flask of oil** given to him by Elisha and hurry to the Israelite military camp at **Ramoth Gilead**, where the army remained while King Jehoram recovered from his wounds at Jezreel (8:28–29). There he was to arrange a private audience with **Jehu**. He was then to pour the oil on his head and declare, **This is what the LORD says: I anoint you king over Israel**.

This phrase occurs three times in the immediate context (vv. 3,6,12). It emphasizes that the coup of Jehu was instigated by God himself. One of the major themes of this section is the fulfillment of God's word in the purge of Ahab's family. But the young man also needed to realize that he was engaged in a dangerous mission. The army's reaction to Jehu's anointing was uncertain. After performing his duty, Elisha's agent should **open the door and run**.

9:4–10. The man went to Ramoth Gilead, found Jehu, and anointed him in private as Elisha had directed. Following the anointing, he gave Jehu his commission, following the directions of Elisha. Jehu had two responsibilities: **to destroy the house of Ahab** and to deal with Jezebel. Jehu was to act as the agent of the Lord, carrying out the word of God. The purging was to be complete: **the whole house of Ahab . . . every last male**. This must be remembered if Jehu is to be evaluated fairly. He was God's surgeon, carving out the cancer of Ahab. Jehu would be the instrument of God's justice to **avenge the blood . . . of all the LORD's servants shed by Jezebel**. This recalls the butchery of God's prophets, mentioned in 1 Kings 18:4,13.

God's retaliation had not been swift, but it was certain. Jehu's purge would also be the fulfillment of God's prophecy through Elijah. The statement **as for Jezebel, dogs will devour her on the plot of ground at Jezreel** recalls Elijah's prophecy in 1 Kings 21:23. There were thus two reasons God's judgment was falling on the house of Ahab. Elijah had pronounced judgment for the murder of Naboth. The reference to **Jezreel** makes evident that this sentence was being carried out. The greater reason was the murder of God's messengers and the rejection of God's message. God's word does not fail. After completing his assignment, the prophet **opened the door and ran**.

9:11–13. The sight of the man who had acted with such secrecy and then bolted with such haste aroused questions in the minds of the officers in the outer room. **Is everything all right? Why did this madman come to you?** Jehu was apparently suspicious that all this had been a practical joke by his fellow officers. When assured that they knew nothing of what had happened, he repeated to them the prophetic declaration: **This is what the LORD says: I anoint you king over Israel.**

The response of the officers was remarkable. They accepted the truth of Jehu's statement and backed his claim. Making an impromptu throne by spreading **their cloaks . . . under him on the bare steps**, they blew a trumpet and shouted, **Jehu is king!**

This instant acceptance of Jehu as king suggests that great disenchantment with Jehoram and the house of Ahab already existed. Conditions were ripe for revolution. But there is no indication of a plan by Jehu to seize the throne, as had been true in the case of Hazael. Jehu's emergence was the product of God's initiative through his prophet. The elimination of the followers of Ahab was the act of God through his chosen instruments.

Ⓑ The Zeal of Jehu (9:14–10:29)

SUPPORTING IDEA: *When God uses us as his instruments, we must be careful to be guided by his will.*

9:14–26. A coup is successful only if power is seized quickly and completely. Jehu was aware of this, and he took immediate steps to consolidate his power. The first task was to deal with the king, who was in **Jezreel**, about forty-five miles away, recuperating from wounds he had suffered in a battle with **Hazael king of Aram**. Dealing with the ruling king was not a task that could be delegated to another. So Jehu ordered his fellow-conspirators to seal the military camp at Ramoth lest **anyone slip out of the city to go and tell the news in Jezreel.** He then set out with a small team for Jezreel to engage **Joram** and **Ahaziah** of Judah.

The narrator recounts Jehu's approach to the city in great detail. King Joram of Israel was anxious for any news of military affairs at the front. When the guard announced that troops were approaching, the king sent a messenger with the question, **Do you come in peace?** While this is a possible translation, Joram had no reason to be suspicious. The phrase is literally, "Is it peace (*shalom*)?"—an expression that means, "Is everything all right? Did we win?" Jehu refused to answer the question and told the king's messenger to fall in with his men. The process was repeated a second time. By now the entourage was close enough for the watchman to recognize Jehu by his style of chariot riding: **he drives like a madman.** The king was increasingly anxious for information, but his suspicions had not been aroused by Jehu's arrival. These were, after all, his soldiers. His only concern was for the status of the conflict against Syria.

Joram and Ahaziah mounted their chariots and rode out to meet Jehu, not accompanied by a military guard. It was providence and not mere accident that caused them to meet Jehu at **the plot of ground that belonged to Naboth the Jezreelite**, a fact of which Jehu was fully aware (9:25). God's retribution was about to fall. Joram asked the same question he had sent his messengers to ask: **Have you come in peace, Jehu?**

Joram learned quickly that he had a more immediate problem than Syria. Jehu's angry response announced his intent: **How can there be peace . . . as long as all the idolatry and witchcraft of your mother Jezebel abound?** Jehu had thrown down the gauntlet. There could be no *shalom* in Israel while the house of Ahab and its Baal worship was in place. Joram recognized Jehu's intent, shouted **Treachery** in warning to Ahaziah, and turned to flee. He did not get far. Jehu **shot Joram between the shoulders**, then ordered his officer **Bidkar** to dump his body **on the field that belonged to Naboth.**

Jehu then reminded Bidkar of an unrecorded prophecy from an unnamed source (presumably Elijah) they had heard when they had accompanied Ahab: **I will surely make you pay for it on this plot of ground.** This was a prophecy that had been pronounced more than twenty years earlier, but now it was being fulfilled. The repetition of the text drives home the truth that these events were the outcome of the word of the Lord.

9:27–29. Ahaziah was not only the king of Judah; he was also a relative of Ahab (his grandson). Jehu had not been commissioned to deal with the kings of Judah, but perhaps fearing retribution from Ahaziah if he were allowed to escape or seeing him as a supporter of Ahab, he ordered his officers to pursue and **kill him too.** They managed to wound him, but Ahaziah escaped to **Megiddo**, a major fortress city in Israel, only to die there. He was returned to Jerusalem and buried. Now the kings of both nations had been killed. The vacant throne in Judah would prove to be disastrous, as we shall see in chapter 11. There is no mention of the fulfillment of prophecy in this killing. Jehu was acting on his own.

9:30–37. Word of the killing of two kings spread quickly. By the time **Jehu** reached **Jezreel**, Jezebel knew what had happened and what was likely to happen to her. She was a proud, haughty woman who knew that confrontation with the usurper was inevitable. She was determined to meet him looking like a queen. So **she painted her eyes, arranged her hair and looked out of a window.** Seeing Jehu, she challenged him in words of sarcasm and defiance: **Have you come in peace, Zimri, you murderer of your master?** By calling Jehu "Zimri," she was calling him a traitor and reminding him that Zimri had reigned as king only seven days before he was killed by Ahab's father, Omri (1 Kgs. 16:8–20).

These were hardly words intended to placate Jehu! When he called out for those on his side to declare themselves, **two or three eunuchs** or royal servants displayed their willingness to help. At Jehu's command to **throw her down**, they complied, and Jehu's horses trampled Jezebel. As a sign of his contempt for the dead queen, he went in to Jezebel's residence **and ate and drank.** After a considerable period he thought better of leaving her unburied. But when his servants went out to bury her, **they found nothing except her skull, her feet and her hands.** They were on the very plot of ground where Ahab had once desired to put a vegetable garden. The wild dogs that ran in packs in the cities had devoured her.

When Jehu heard the news, he saw it as another fulfillment of prophecy. There was a crude humor in the fact that the only remains of Jezebel would be dog droppings (**refuse on the ground**) on the piece of ground for which she had arranged Naboth's murder.

10:1–11. Jehu's mandate had been to eliminate "every last male" of Ahab's family (9:8). **Seventy sons** ("sons" probably has a more general sense of "male heirs") were located in the royal capital of **Samaria**, under the care of palace officials and the city leaders. They posed a continuing threat to Jehu's new regime, but the way he chose to deal with that threat showed his shrewdness and his brutality.

Jehu made no attempt to attack the capital directly. He tested the strength of the opposition by issuing a challenge to the royal household intended to intimidate them: **Choose the best and most worthy of your master's sons and set him on his father's throne. Then fight for your master's house.** Samaria's leaders had already taken the measure of Jehu. They knew that he was a determined, ruthless man, and that all resistance melted before his threat. They surrendered and submitted to Jehu's rule.

The next part of Jehu's plan was to have the leaders of Samaria carry out the extermination of Ahab's family. He sent a letter with a brutal demand, especially for those who had been charged with the care and protection of the royal family: **take the heads of your master's sons and come to me in Jezreel by this time tomorrow.** The order was shrewdly stated. Although he clearly meant it the way they interpreted it, he could always claim that all he meant was for them to bring the leaders ("heads") of Ahab's sons to him. But the cowardly officials understood that this was a test of loyalty to the new regime—the bloody elimination of the former regime.

Jehu was motivated by some sense of obedience to the divine command, but these men were concerned only with self-protection. They executed and decapitated the royal descendants and sent the heads to Jehu. He, in turn, piled them at the entrance of the city of **Jezreel**. This was a form of intimidation common in Eastern warfare—an act of terrorism that served as a warning against rebellion.

The execution of Ahab's family had been commanded by the Lord, but one cannot help but be repelled by this public atrocity. But Jehu's methods meant that he was not personally guilty of the direct killing of the royal family. He admitted to killing his master, but he made clear that guilt was not on his head alone (**who killed all these?**). He absolved them (**you are innocent**), but he also declared that this was the fulfillment of prophecy: **The LORD has done what he promised through his servant Elijah.**

Jehu had turned a divine prediction into a buttress for his regime, implying that opposition to him was opposition to God. But the surgeon was becoming a butcher, as he extended his bloodshed far beyond the divine mandate: **Jehu killed everyone in Jezreel who remained of the house of Ahab, as well as all his chief men, his close friends and his priests.**

10:12–14. As Jehu set out to take control of Samaria, he met **some relatives of Ahaziah** at a place called **Beth Eked**, north of Samaria. When asked why they were in the region, they claimed they had come down to visit **the families of the king and of the queen mother.** Their explanation was suspicious at best. It would have been almost impossible at this point not to have known of the death of Ahaziah and Jezebel. A journey from Jerusalem to Jezreel would not normally have taken them north of Samaria. They may have had a more devious purpose, or they may simply have been in the wrong place at the wrong time. Jehu clearly viewed them as suspicious and ordered them seized and killed: **forty-two men. He left no survivor.** This again exceeded his mandate. Jehu had become a man of blood.

10:15–17. As Jehu made his way from Beth Eked, he met a man who was coming to meet him, **Jehonadab son of Recab.** The founder of a strict religious group (see "Deeper Discoveries"), he apparently saw in Jehu a kindred spirit. His support would give credibility to Jehu among more conservative elements of Israel. The two declared their mutual commitment. Jehu then invited Jehonadab to go with him **and see my zeal for the LORD.**

"Zeal for the Lord" was a quality of those such as Phineas (Num. 25:10–13) and Elijah (1 Kgs. 19:10,14) who refused all compromise with paganism. Jehu's claim was not well-founded, as we will see in 10:31. But he was obedient to his divine mission with respect to Ahab's house: **when Jehu came to Samaria, he killed all who were left there of Ahab's family.**

10:18–29. Jehu had not specifically been commissioned to eliminate Baal worshipers, but that mandate had already been established in the law. The Baal worshipers in Samaria did not know of his religious convictions. They knew only that he had eliminated Ahab's family. So they were willing to believe him when he boasted of his devotion to Baal: **Ahab served Baal a little; Jehu will serve him much.** This was, of course, an act of deception. When their new king declared his intention **to hold a great sacrifice for Baal,** they assumed that the coup had only been military and political, not religious. However, Jehu's true intention was not sacrifice but slaughter.

Jehu's cunning was revealed by his methods. After gathering the Baal worshipers from throughout the nation in **the temple of Baal** in Samaria, he provided **robes for all the ministers of Baal.** He further insisted that they police themselves and remove all **servants of the LORD** from their midst. In the meantime, he had the temple surrounded with **eighty men,** sworn on their lives to not let anyone escape. Jehu went so far as to make **the burnt offering.** At that precise moment he issued the order that the Baal worshipers were to be killed.

As a result, there was a wholesale slaughter of the Baal worshipers, **the sacred stone of Baal** (a cult object of some kind) was demolished and burned, and **the temple of Baal** was demolished. In a supreme act of insult, the Baal temple was turned into a public latrine. Baalism had gone from temple to toilet!

Jehu's greatest achievement was the destruction of Baal worship. It marked the end of state-sponsored Canaanite religion in Israel. The royal family would no longer patronize or protect baalism. Jehu had completed what Elijah had begun. But that was only part of the story. Jehu's zeal for God had a major defect: **He did not turn away from the sins of Jeroboam son of Nebat.** His zeal was not under the authority of God's law. In some brutal acts that he committed, he went too far. In the matter of genuine worship, he did not go far enough. He did the right thing when he stamped out baalism, but **the worship of the golden calves at Bethel and Dan remained.**

The Evaluation of Jehu (10:30–36)

SUPPORTING IDEA: *Partial reform will produce an ambiguous legacy.*

10:30–31. Jehu's zeal left a curiously mixed legacy, reflected in the way his life was summarized by the writer of 2 Kings. On the one hand, he was God's instrument to remove the cancer of baalism and the supporters of Ahab from the nation of Israel. That was a great achievement. For that reason he received divine approval unique for the kings of Israel: **you have done well in accomplishing . . . all I had in mind to do.** This accomplishment was so significant that the Lord was willing to look beyond Jehu's excesses and shortcomings.

As a result, the Lord blessed Jehu with a promise: **your descendants will sit on the throne of Israel to the fourth generation.** This would be the longest-ruling royal dynasty in Israel's history, occupying the throne from 841 to 752 B.C. But the promise, though generous, was limited. This was not the everlasting dynasty of David or even the conditional perpetual dynasty offered to Jeroboam.

But we are not allowed to overlook Jehu's failure. His reform was partial. He was not a man consistently under the word of God. Spiritually, he may have been the best of the Israelite kings, but he fell far short of the standard of David. To underline this, we are told once again: **he did not turn away from the sins of Jeroboam, which he had caused Israel to commit.** The Lord's grace gave Jehu full credit for all that he accomplished in doing the will of God. But the Lord's truth would not allow him to ignore the sins of Jehu's life. His partial reform caused him to receive an ambiguous approval from the Lord.

10:32–33. Jehu's ambiguous reform also caused him to leave an ambiguous legacy. When Jehu seized power in 841 B.C., Hazael of Syria was under siege by Shalmaneser III of Assyria. He blockaded Hazael in his capital of Damascus and captured the city. The military expedition was memorialized in the Black Obelisk, which portrays King Jehu of Israel paying tribute to Shalmaneser. This was not recorded in Scripture, but it is obvious that Jehu's bloody purge of leadership in his nation would have left it in no condition to resist Assyria. He chose payment over opposition.

After 838 B.C. Assyria withdrew from the region, and Hazael turned his attention southward in battle against Israel, as Elisha had foreseen (8:12). He **overpowered the Israelites throughout their territory east of the Jordan** (the entire Transjordan area). This meant loss of its buffer zone against Syria and loss of control of the major trade routes through the region. But Israel's problem wasn't just with Hazael. These military defeats were the judicial hand of God: **The LORD began to reduce the size of Israel.** This is an ominous note which once again suggests the shortcomings of Jehu's reform. The nation had retreated from Baal worship; it had not returned to the true worship of the Lord. Therefore, God's hand was against his people.

10:34–36. Jehu ruled over Israel for **twenty-eight years.** Yet the writer tells us almost nothing of his accomplishments. He speaks of **all his achievements** (literally, "mighty deeds"), but we are left to guess at what they might have been. The focus has been on the great moments of his purge of the followers of Ahab and baalism. But we are left with the sad impression that, although Jehu came a long way, he stopped far short of where he should have. It is also obvious that he never involved the people as a whole in the process of reform. It happened "top down" and therefore never took deep root in the soil of the nation.

In the final analysis Jehu was memorable for the people he killed and the things he destroyed but not for the positive things he built or established. As a result, his tenure on the throne must receive, at best, the grade, "Incomplete."

> **MAIN IDEA REVIEW:** *Zeal for the Lord is no substitute for obedience of the Lord.*

III. CONCLUSION

Spiritual Surgery

Jehu was a man called by God to perform a critical task for the well-being of his people. At a time when the nation was desperately sick, God appointed him to be his surgeon, to excise the tumors of the supporters of Ahab and of baalism. It was major surgery. No minor treatments would do. The cancer must be completely removed, and no traces must be allowed to remain. It was not a pleasant task, since it would require violence and bloodshed.

Jehu went about his task with a zeal that was often commendable. He was aware that he was doing the will of God, and he would not allow a false sentimentality to stay his hand. By the end of the operation, his was a very different nation. The house of Ahab had been destroyed, and state sponsorship of baalism was a thing of the past. Jehu had rooted out the sins he had been sent to deal with.

But a surgeon who removes two tumors while allowing a major one to remain has done his patient no favors, especially if the remaining one is malignant. Jehu failed his duty in two critical ways: he did not excise the tumor of Jeroboam's cult, and he used a butcher's ax rather than a scalpel on part of his mission. In the final analysis he was a spiritual failure. Zeal for the Lord is no substitute for obedience of the Lord.

PRINCIPLES

- God may graciously delay judgment, but he will certainly carry it out in his time.
- Sin cannot be dealt with partially. It must be removed at its roots.
- Zeal is no substitute for obedience. It must be guided by the word of God, not by emotions.
- In the final analysis partial obedience is disobedience.

APPLICATIONS

- The Lord wants you to be a person of zeal for his glory, but your zeal must be regulated by his word. Your zeal must be tempered with knowledge.
- Don't deal with sin in your life in partial measures; attack it at its roots.
- Beware of a zeal for the Lord in one area of your life but a blindness to your disobedience in another.

IV. LIFE APPLICATION

The Right Thing in the Wrong Way

Purging a nation of the cancerous effects of an evil dynasty and a false religion is not a task that could be accomplished without bloodshed and violence. It is impossible to be fair to Jehu if we do not admit that much that he did was at God's direction. But his killing of Ahaziah, his heaping of the heads and the terrorizing of the citizens of Jezreel, and the slaughter of Ahaziah's relatives went beyond the boundaries. He seemed to cross the line from godly zeal to ungodly zeal and fanaticism.

It is possible to do the right thing in the wrong way. The means we use contaminate the ends we seek. A zeal to protect the lives of the unborn has led some fanatical pro-lifers to take the lives of the born, murdering abortion doctors. A zeal for biblical morality has led some people to a fanaticism that oppresses homosexuals. Zeal to share the gospel has led some people to fanatical acts that disregard the dignity of those whom they are trying to reach.

Jehu is an example of zeal without godly controls. The Lord Jesus was a person of zeal. When he cleared the temple, "his disciples remembered that it is written, 'Zeal for your house will consume me'" (John 2:17). We are exhorted in Romans 12:11: "Never be lacking in zeal." But we need to be sure that ours is the zeal of Jesus, not the zeal of Jehu.

V. PRAYER

Father, help us to have a passion and a zeal for you. May the flame of our love for you not flicker and die. But, Father, give us a sensitivity to you and to others, so that our flame does not consume the wrong things and damage your name. Amen.

VI. DEEPER DISCOVERIES

A. The Death of Ahaziah (9:27–29)

The account of Ahaziah's death in 2 Chronicles 22:9 seems to be somewhat different. There he is said to be found hiding in Samaria and is brought to Jehu, who put him to death. The two accounts are both apparently incomplete and supplementary to each other. Ahaziah was wounded, made it to Samaria, was found there, and taken to Jehu, who by this time was in Megiddo. There he died. But it is difficult to reconstruct the events based on our present knowledge.

B. Jezebel's Makeup (9:30)

Jezebel's motivation in "painting" her eyes and doing her hair has aroused considerable speculation. Some have suggested that she was trying to seduce Jehu. But given her age (Ahab had come to the throne thirty-three years earlier) and her defiant words to Jehu, that is extremely unlikely. It is much more likely that this was the response of a proud woman, who was haughty and unrepentant to the end.

C. Jehonadab Son of Recab (10:15)

The Recabites are mentioned elsewhere only in Jeremiah 35:1–19. That account, occurring more than two hundred years later, makes clear that Jehonodab was their founder. They were an ascetic, traditionalist group who lived in tents, not in cities. They did not drink wine, nor did they plant crops. They had apparently come to believe that the nomadic lifestyle Israel had experienced in its desert wanderings was the ideal, divinely approved lifestyle. They would certainly have joined with Jehu in his rejection of baalism and the royal pretensions of the supporters of Ahab.

VII. TEACHING OUTLINE

A. INTRODUCTION

1. Lead Story: A Severe Mercy
2. Context: The Lord had told Elijah that others would finish what he had begun in his work against Baal and Ahab. Jehu is the last of the three whom God had named to appear on the scene. He does so with a passion and zeal as he sets out to wipe out baalism and the supporters of Ahab.
3. Transition: Jehu came on the scene by the direct intrusion of the Lord into the affairs of the nation through his prophet Elisha.

B. COMMENTARY
1. The Anointing of Jehu (9:1–13)
2. The Zeal of Jehu (9:14–10:29)
3. The Evaluation of Jehu (10:30–36)

C. CONCLUSION: SPIRITUAL JOURNEY

VIII. ISSUES FOR DISCUSSION

1. There is sometimes a fine line between zeal and fanaticism. What is the difference between the two? How do we know when we are crossing that line?
2. The problem for many of us is not excess zeal but an apathy and lukewarmness that accepts the status quo of Jeroboam's idols. What would true zeal for the Lord look like in those areas of your life?
3. When Jehu was at his best, he dealt ruthlessly with Ahab's family and the Baals, a zeal the Lord approved. Our cultural setting is very different, but do we try to apply halfway measures to the Jezebels we encounter? What applications can you see in this aspect of Jehu's purge?

2 Kings 11:1–12:21

Back from the Brink

Quote

"*G*od can achieve his purpose either through the absence of human power and resources, or the abandonment of reliance on them. All through history God has shown and used nobodies, because their unusual dependence on him made possible the unique display of his power and grace. He chose and used somebodies only when they renounced dependence on their natural abilities and resources."

Oswald Chambers

BIOGRAPHICAL PROFILE: JOASH

- The only surviving male of the Davidic line, after the murder of his siblings by his grandmother Athaliah
- Placed on the throne at the age of seven under the direction of the priest Jehoiada
- Reigned from 835 to 796 B.C. Because of his youth, his early reign was under the direction of Jehoiada
- Restored the temple and reorganized the temple finances
- Turned away from the Lord and ordered the execution of Jehoiada's son, the prophet Zechariah (not the author of the biblical book)
- Wounded at the hands of the Aramean army (2 Chr. 24:23-25)
- Assassinated by officials in his administration for his part in the death of Zechariah
- Buried in Jerusalem but not in the royal tombs (2 Chr. 24:25)

2 Kings 11:1–12:21

IN A NUTSHELL

Although Baal worship has been uprooted from Israel by Jehu, it has found a home in Judah under the reign of Ahab's daughter, Athaliah. In spite of the great weakness of the Davidic line, God uses a faithful priest and a child king to restore the Davidic line and to begin to restore proper temple worship.

Back from the Brink

I. INTRODUCTION

A Brand Plucked from the Burning

About midnight on the evening of February 9, 1709, fire swept through the parsonage in Epworth, England, in which the family of Samuel Wesley lay sleeping. Awakened by smoke and flames, the family struggled out of the house. When they reached safety, they realized that one child was not with them but had been left behind in his upstairs bedroom. When he appeared at a second-story window, his father tried several times to reach him, but the heat forced him back. But a persistent neighbor, standing on the shoulders of others, was able to reach him and pull him out through the window, just as the walls collapsed.

His mother Susannah never forgot that moment. It gave her the conviction that her son John Wesley was a child with a special mission, a person of divine destiny. She told him that he was "a brand plucked from the burning," a term he used on the epitaph he composed for himself when he thought he was dying decades later. God's hand indeed was on John Wesley. Years later, after he came to saving faith in Christ, he saw his life in terms of pulling people from the flames of divine judgment by proclaiming the gospel. He became one of the primary figures in the spiritual awakening that swept through the British Isles and spread to the thirteen colonies in the eighteenth century, reshaping both nations.

The rescue of a child from certain death is always dramatic and moving. The chapters before us recount the story of a baby rescued from certain death who became a child of special destiny. The nation was at the brink of destruction. All that made Judah distinct—the worship of God and the Davidic line—was in danger of total destruction. He was the only surviving link to the great messianic promises God had made to David, and he was the means through which his nation was prevented from sliding into the baalism that had engulfed its neighbor to the north, Israel. He is also a vivid reminder of the importance of godly influences in our lives—in this case an elderly priest named Jehoiada.

II. COMMENTARY

Back from the Brink

MAIN IDEA: *Spiritual recovery demands the recognition of God's true king and the restoration of God's proper worship.*

A On the Brink of Destruction (11:1–3)

SUPPORTING IDEA: *There are times when it appears that the darkness is about to overcome the light.*

11:1–3. Jehu's purge had removed baalism from the Northern Kingdom. But his execution of Judah's king Ahaziah (9:27–29) had opened a door for baalism to lodge in the south. **Athaliah,** Ahab's daughter and Ahaziah's mother, was already in a position of power as the queen mother. There was no obvious candidate for the throne among Ahaziah's sons (2 Chr. 22:9 indicates that "there was no one in the house of Ahaziah powerful enough to retain the kingdom"). It must be noted that Joram, Ahaziah's father and Athaliah's husband, had murdered all his brothers on his ascent to the throne (2 Chr. 21:4), and that his older sons had been killed by Philistine and Arab raiders (2 Chr. 21:16–17). The Davidic line was under great attack.

Athaliah determined to fill the vacuum personally. As the daughter of Ahab (see 8:18,26), her marriage to the royal family had been arranged by Jehoshaphat. That good king's compromise was now bearing bitter fruit for his descendants! **When Athaliah . . . saw that her son was dead, she proceeded to destroy the whole royal family.** A grandmother determined to murder her own grandchildren to seize power is a brutal picture of the depths of human depravity.

This would be the only time in Judah's history when its throne was under the control of a usurper. Judah now had its own Jezebel! The text does not indicate whether Athaliah was Jezebel's physical daughter; she certainly was her spiritual daughter. Her motive is not indicated, but at least part of it was religious. Her pernicious influence on her husband (8:18) and on her son (8:26) had already been suggested. Second Kings 11:18 makes clear that a Baal temple was constructed in Jerusalem, with a functioning Baal priest. Second Chronicles 24:7 indicates that her followers (called "sons of that wicked woman Athaliah") had vandalized the temple of the Lord and used its objects for the worship of the Baals.

Perhaps Jehu's purge of baalism in the North had made Athaliah determined to turn Judah into a safe refuge for Baalists in the South. Whatever her motive, a false queen now ruled in Judah. She was determined to stamp out the legacy of the Mosaic covenant, which insisted on the exclusive worship of God, and the Davidic covenant, which promised a Davidic king.

It is impossible to exaggerate the depth of this crisis. The future of God's program through his people was in dire jeopardy. The courageous action of another woman, **Jehosheba, the daughter of King Jehoram and sister of Aha-ziah**, saved the day. Although we are not told so in 2 Kings, she was also the wife of the priest Jehoiada (2 Chr. 22:11). At a critical moment she **took Joash son of Ahaziah**, who at this point was about a year old (cp. vv. 3,21), **and stole him away from among the royal princes, who were about to be murdered**. She then arranged for his nurse to keep him in **a bedroom** (or the term may refer to a storeroom, "a room for beds") in the temple. For six years Joash remained hidden. The public believed that the Davidic dynasty had been terminated and that the wicked queen now controlled the destiny of the nation.

It is important to put this in the larger context of the Davidic covenant. The writer of 1 and 2 Kings has reminded us that God had promised "a lamp for David and his descendants forever" (1 Kgs. 11:36; 15:4; 2 Kgs. 8:19). But now that lamp was barely flickering, reduced to a one-year-old baby. If the light should go out, God's messianic promise would fail. While theologically we know that the sovereign God would not fail to keep his promise, we must be impressed by how fragile he allowed it to become. Two women stood in direct contrast. A wicked queen was determined to destroy the dynasty; a courageous woman who followed the Lord was committed to protect and preserve it.

Ⓑ Risky Obedience (11:4–21)

SUPPORTING IDEA: *The Lord uses faithful people who commit themselves to risky obedience to fan the flame.*

11:4–8. The Book of 2 Kings suddenly introduces a mysterious figure named **Jehoiada**. Only later does it become clear that he is a priest (v. 9), and 2 Kings never tells us that he was Jehosheba's husband. As a priest, he had been responsible for the care and protection of the boy king in the temple. In the dark years of Athaliah's oppression, he had been planning the restoration of the Davidic dynasty as well as pure worship of the Lord. The situation was obviously dangerous, and he had to proceed with caution. He was the prime mover who organized the events, plotted the action, and instigated the revolt. This was a new movement in the nation—a priest rather than a prophet following God's law to bring about reformation.

Jehoiada's plan took shape **in the seventh year** of Athaliah's usurpation, when he gathered together in the temple **the commanders . . . the Carites and the guards**. The Carites were apparently mercenaries, linked to the Kerethites, who had served as royal bodyguards (2 Sam. 20:23). Jehoiada entered into **a covenant** with these men. This covenant obviously involved an **oath** of secrecy and a commitment to restore the Davidic dynasty. After putting them under sacred oath in the sacred precincts of the temple, **he showed them the king's son.** This must have been a very emotional moment. The royal son had been hidden even from the temple guard! For a people who believed that the Davidic dynasty had come to a violent end, and with it the divine promises, this must have been a profound and stunning occasion.

Athaliah as the ruling queen was powerful enough that the seizure of power had to be swift, unexpected, and sure. Jehoida's instructions detailing the precise movements of the guard are not entirely clear, but the main point was that Jehoiada chose **the Sabbath** day, and the time when the changing of the guard normally occurred. The presence of so many troops in the temple at that point would arouse the least possible suspicion on the part of Athaliah's supporters. The three guard companies were to muster at different places in the temple complex. At the appropriate signal they were to guard the temple for the king and to station themselves around him, prepared to kill anyone who interfered.

11:9–12. The commanders carried out their orders **just as Jehoiada the priest ordered.** He added to the solemnity of the occasion by giving **the commanders the spears and shields that had belonged to King David.** These weapons were now more than two hundred years old! Their use was symbolic rather than military. Jehoiada was investing this occasion with reminders of David so that everyone involved would recognize the significance of the enterprise in which they were engaged. This was not just a battle for power; it was a struggle for the identity of the nation as God's covenant people.

With the guards in place, Jehoiada brought out the **king's son,** by now a seven-year-old boy. Within the temple precincts, surrounded by the large crowds that would likely be present on a Sabbath, he **put the crown on him . . . and proclaimed him king.** The act of public coronation was followed by public acclamation: **the people . . . shouted, "Long live the king!"** With a reigning monarch on the throne, this was a revolutionary act! Joash's restoration thus had the support of the priests, the temple guards, a significant segment of the military, and the general public.

11:13–16. Strong rulers are sensitive to danger. Athaliah was drawn by **the noise made by the guards and the people** and was perceptive enough to realize that something momentous was afoot. She did not send officials to investigate; unattended, **she went to the people at the temple of the LORD,** adjacent to the royal complex. A single glance was enough to reveal what was happening. **There was the king, standing by the pillar.** It seems unlikely that Athaliah recognized the seven-year-old boy as her grandson, but there was no mistaking the intent of the occasion, especially since he had a crown on his head!

The pillar was presumably Jakin or Boaz (1 Kgs. 7:21), which had become the traditional place for a coronation. As a usurper, Athaliah would have been sensitive to any attempts at a countercoup. The actions of the people made clear that her worst fears had been realized: **all the people of the land were rejoicing and blowing trumpets**. It was obvious that the restoration of the Davidic monarchy had received instant and widespread popular support.

Athaliah **tore her robes and called out, "Treason! Treason!"** This had been the call of Joram, when confronted by Jehu (9:23), but there is more than a little irony in such words being found in the mouth of the arch-traitor, who had murdered her own grandchildren!

Jehoiada reacted decisively. He ordered Athaliah seized and executed. Then he ordered his men to escort her from the temple premises. She was taken out of the temple complex to the entrance to the neighboring palace complex, **the place where the horses enter the palace grounds** (referred to simply as "the palace" in 11:20). **There she was put to death** with a sword. She died alone, with no one rallying to her support. Judah's Jezebel had been removed with surgical precision.

11:17–18. Joash was obviously too young to provide leadership for his nation. So Jehoiada served as his regent. His first act was of crucial importance: to have the nation recommit itself to the Lord. The central issue was not Judah's relation to the Davidic king but to the divine King. Spiritual reform was an even higher priority than political reform. **Jehoiada then made a covenant between the LORD and the king and people that they would be the LORD's people**. This national covenant involved a formal renewal of the national covenant with God, reaffirming Judah's status as the people of Yahweh (Deut. 4:20; 7:6; 14:1–2; 26:18; 27:9).

Jehoiada **also made a covenant between the king and the people**. The exact content of this royal covenant is not indicated. Perhaps it involved the people's commitment to the Davidic dynasty (2 Sam. 7) and the king's commitment to rule according to the law (Deut. 17:14–20). All pagan ideas of royalty derived from Athaliah needed to be purged.

Baalism also needed to be purged. It had been allowed to flourish under the influence of the supporters of Ahab, from the time of King Jehoram. So **all the people . . . went to the temple of Baal and tore it down**. This purging involved not only the destruction of the temple and of Baalite **idols** and **altars**, but also the execution of **Mattan the priest of Baal**. This reform had obvious parallels to the work of Jehu in Israel six years earlier, but it was done with less bloodshed and more popular support.

11:19–21. The remarkable day engineered by Jehoiada came to an end with a procession from the temple of the Lord into the palace. **The king then took his place on the royal throne, and all the people of the land rejoiced.** Judah's long national nightmare was over. A Davidic king once again ruled, even though he was only seven years old. In spite of the drama of the revolution, **the city was quiet**, because the usurper had been removed and with her the entire system of evil she represented. The people were at peace.

C Restoring the House of the Lord (12:1–16)

SUPPORTING IDEA: *True renewal requires the recovery of right leadership as well as the restoration of proper worship.*

12:1–3. It is typical of the method of the writer of 1 and 2 Kings to give us a summary of a king's reign. He had not done so with Athaliah because she was a usurper. Joash ruled as king in Jerusalem from 835 to 796 B.C., one of the longest Judean reigns. He received an evaluation of restrained approval. As was true of most of the Judean kings, the high places were not removed. That would remain true until the time of Hezekiah. But even the positive evaluation of Joash had an important limitation: **Joash did what was right in the eyes of the LORD all the years Jehoiada the priest instructed him.** This suggests that he did right initially. But what happened after the removal of Jehoiada's influence? We are never told explicitly in 2 Kings (the writer of 2 Chronicles is very explicit about Joash's final days of failure; 2 Chr. 24:17–22), but the writer does leave some clues which suggest that Joash did not finish as well as he began.

12:4–16. The major accomplishment of Joash's reign was the repair of the temple and the reorganization of the temple finances that made it possible. The author goes into considerable detail about the process of reorganization. His discussion of the details sometimes is obscure and hard to follow. What is obvious is that he approved of Joash's commitment to put the care of the temple on a different basis than it had been. By this time the structure was about 150 years old. It had suffered not only from aging but also from the abuse of the Ahab-influenced rulers who had preceded Joash.

The repair of the temple came at the initiative of Joash, not Jehoiada, as we might have expected. The king issued orders to **the priests** that money given to the temple from **the census . . . from personal vows** and from the funds **brought voluntarily** should be devoted **to repair whatever damage is found in the temple.** Priests lived on the basis of offerings of food and funds made to the temple by worshipers. Those funds had been used to this point exclusively by the priests for their own needs. Now a major portion was to be dedicated to temple repairs.

We are not told when Joash gave this order. But by **the twenty-third year of King Joash**, when he would have been thirty years old, no progress had been made on repairs. Joash summoned the priestly leaders, including Jehoiada, and rebuked them for their lack of action: **Why aren't you repairing the damage done to the temple? Take no more money from your treasurers, but hand it over for repairing the temple.** It is surprising to find Jehoiada guilty of such neglect. But the writer of 2 Chronicles notes that he died at the age of 130 (2 Chr. 24:15), and he would have been a very old man at this stage, perhaps unable to exercise much leadership.

Perhaps at the specific direction of the king, the priests agreed to distance themselves from the collection and the expenditure of the temple funds. The temptation for them to use funds for their own needs was too strong. They needed a system that would divide responsibility, provide accountability, and remove the temptation to divert funds for personal use.

The new system developed by Jehoiada and Joash centered on a new money collection and distribution system. Money given to the priests would be placed in a single **chest** and placed **beside the altar** near **the entrance** to the temple court. Only they would handle such contributions. When **they saw that there was a large amount of money in the chest**, they would summon **the royal secretary and the high priest**. They in turn would count or weigh the money and then distribute it to **the men appointed to supervise the work on the temple**. The supervisors would then distribute the money to the skilled workers who were responsible for the actual work.

This involved a major change in the way the temple was viewed. It was not a private royal chapel under the financial and personal control of the king. Nor was it a religious institution run by the priests for their own benefit. It was the house of God. It would be financed by public giving. The money brought into the temple was not to be spent at the discretion of the priests alone, even for sacred objects such as **silver basins** and **wick trimmers**. The men chosen for repairs were men of such integrity that they could be trusted; they acted with complete honesty.

On the other hand, the priests were to be supported for the ministry they provided. Their source of revenue was not to be used for temple repairs. In accordance with the Mosaic Law (Num. 5:5–10), **the money from the guilt offerings and sin offerings was not brought into the temple of the LORD; it belonged to the priests.**

It is not clear why the writer of 2 Kings is fascinated with such detail and why this reorganization of temple finances was so important to him. It is clear that he wants us to see that Joash made care of the temple a central concern of his reign, and for this he deserved full credit. It was not enough that a Davidic king should occupy the throne. It was also crucial that the proper worship of the Lord should be at the center of the nation's life.

D Reversing Course (12:17–21)

[handwritten: Joash mother Zibiah]

[handwritten marginal notes: parents / uncle's / aunt / cousin / Pg 749]

SUPPORTING IDEA: *A good beginning does not guarantee a good ending.*

12:17–18. Both Israel and Judah had been preoccupied with internal affairs, with the purge of the influence of the supporters of Ahab from both nations. But their enemies from other nations had not vanished. **Hazael** of Syria's main adversary was Israel, not Judah. But he also had designs on Judah. At some point he moved along the coastal plain into Philistine territory, **attacked Gath and captured it.** This gave him control of the valuable coastal trade routes and also made Judah vulnerable militarily and economically. In a panic Joash determined to pay him tribute and buy him off. Although restoring the temple had been the major accomplishment of his reign, he stripped the temple of its special treasures. He then sent these to Hazael, who **withdrew from Jerusalem.**

12:19–21. The writer of 2 Kings gives us his usual summary of a king's life, but this one contains a major surprise: His officials conspired against Joash and **assassinated him at Beth Millo.** He thus became the first king of Judah to suffer such a fate. We have come a long way from the joyful celebration that ends chapter 11. We are not told what motivated their action. The names of his assassins are given: **Jozabad son of Shimeath and Jehozabad son of Shomer.** These men were not outsiders but Joash's own **officials.**

The writer of 2 Chronicles gives us crucial information, which takes us back to the cryptic statement of 12:2 that Joash pleased the Lord "all the years Jehoiada the priest instructed him." When Jehoiada died, Judah's officials led him to abandon the Lord and his temple and to worship pagan gods. Much of his behavior had been motivated more by a desire to please his mentor than to please God. When the Lord sent his prophet Zechariah, the son of his protector Jehoiada, to rebuke Joash for his sin, "by order of the king they stoned him to death in the courtyard of the L ORD's temple" (2 Chr. 24:21).

The writer of 2 Chronicles then goes on to say, after describing Joash's wounds at the hands of the Arameans, "his officials conspired against him for murdering the son of Jehoiada the priest, and they killed him in his bed" (2 Chr. 24:25). It was an act of ingratitude and coldheartedness on a scale that is hard to describe. It is not clear why the writer of 2 Kings did not record the specifics of his sad ending, but one cannot help but reflect on the difference between Joash's beginning and his end. The boy who had come to the throne in a coup intended to put God in his rightful place in his nation had to be forcefully removed because he had become a stumbling block to that purpose. At the end of his life, he had reversed course and was leading his nation back toward the very cliff from which he had been rescued!

Joash was buried in the city of David (v. 21), but his body was not placed in the royal tombs (2 Chr. 24:25). He ended his life in disgrace and shame.

MAIN IDEA REVIEW: *Spiritual recovery demands the recognition of God's true king and the restoration of God's proper worship.*

III. CONCLUSION

After Darkness, Light

The tragedy of Joash's ending must not be allowed to obscure what a significant place he had in the history of his nation. The nation of Judah was one small infant away from the extinction of its hope. Even after his life had been spared, the powerful presence of Athaliah must have made even the most determined believer feel that God's kingdom program was a hopeless cause. But a few faithful people chose to do what was right. They were used by a sovereign God to bring a nation back from the brink of disaster. The first requirement of recovery was the recognition of God's true king, the replacement of Athaliah by Joash. The second requirement was carried out by Joash: the recovery of the worship of the Lord from neglect and abuse. He stopped short, but his repair of the temple was an act of major significance.

The sovereign God cannot and will not be defeated. But at the same time he has entrusted his affairs into the hands of feeble, failing human beings, Even as good a man as Jehoiada can delay doing what was right in the temple because it had personal financial consequences. A man like Joash can be the recipient of amazing grace and still turn away from those who have loved him and imitate those who sought to destroy him. But weak as he may allow it to become, the Lord will not allow the flame to die. The lamp of David could not be extinguished. Even the failure of Joash did not extinguish God's light.

The history of the church is full of similar moments, when God's promise seemed about to be swallowed up by a combination of the enemy's power and its own weakness and failure. But in times of great darkness, the Lord has used those people who have chosen to do the right thing. Then the Spirit has fanned the flame into a blaze. One of the great slogans of the Protestant Reformation was *post tenebras lux,* "after darkness, light." It is never too late for God! That is our hope and our call to faithful action.

PRINCIPLES

- God will sometimes allow his kingdom program to come to times of great weakness.
- The Lord uses faithful people who are committed to risky obedience for the sake of his kingdom.

- Wise kingdom agents not only pray; they plan carefully.
- God must be honored by treating the place where he places his name with great respect.
- Kingdom work should be carried out with practical wisdom that manages the weaknesses and biases of people.
- A good beginning does not guarantee a good ending.

APPLICATIONS

- Don't allow times of great weakness to cause you to despair that God has abandoned his work.
- Think carefully, plan wisely, and administrate realistically your work for God's kingdom.
- Let your faith be a matter of deep personal conviction that will survive the loss of your mentors.
- You can't run the race well if you don't finish well.

IV. LIFE APPLICATION

The Gift of Administration

Administration can often seem tedious. People with a concern for proper management are often considered to be roadblocks on the highway of progress. But it is apparent from Joash's experience that restoration of the temple could not happen without the reorganization of temple financial management. As long as the priests were getting personal support from the same funds from which temple repairs were to be financed, there was temptation to defer repairs for the sake of personal needs.

The reorganization recognized several fundamental principals. One was the need for a division of responsibilities between those being paid and those paying. If even Jehoiada was guilty of failing to make temple repairs a priority, what about those of lesser character and conviction? Second, they needed to avoid the comingling of funds. Third, they needed a carefully monitored and centralized collection system that kept people from the temptation to make personal use of contributions.

In the work of God's kingdom, money must be handled with great care. There needs to be a realism about the danger of temptation with attendant safeguards. Value should be placed on the gift of administration that advances God's work. And there must be a recognition that the supreme concern in all we do must be the glory of God. As long as the temple was in disrepair because money was being mishandled, God was being dishonored. And when our financial practices leave us open to abuses, he is also dishonored.

[handwritten margin notes: Joash credit with / who managed the temple finances before reform? / who was Jehoiada? a priest]

V. PRAYER

Father, help us to finish well. Thank you for those who have invested in our lives as children and as younger persons to set our feet on the right path. But, as you call them home, help us to stay the course, to finish well for you. Amen.

VI. DEEPER DISCOVERIES

A. Saving the Baby (11:2–3)

The Lord's promise to David was "I will establish your line forever" (Ps. 89:4,29). The survival of that son was essential to the fulfillment of the Davidic covenant, which had as its ultimate fulfillment the coming of the Lord Jesus Christ as the son of David (Matt. 1:1). Humanly speaking, that line never came as close to extinction as it did at this moment in history. Because of Jehoram's purge of his brothers (2 Chr. 21:4), the killing of the royal family by Philistine and Arab raiders (2 Chr. 21:16–17), and the slaughter of her grandsons by Athaliah (2 Kgs. 11:1), only one male child of the Davidic royal line survived. The preservation of Joash was an event of great significance.

Satan was trying to blow out David's "lamp," and he almost succeeded. He attacked the "lamp" again when he tried to kill the Lord Jesus with the others boys in Bethlehem (Matt. 2:16–18). The slaughter of the infants was another attempt by Satan to prevent the fulfillment of God's program of salvation. The Lord's sovereign plan is certain, but he may allow it to appear that the Evil One has triumphed, as his program reaches points of precarious weakness. There is no greater illustration of this than the cross. But the living God is always victorious.

B. The Anointed One (11:12)

Kings were anointed in Old Testament times as a way of consecrating them to office. Saul and David were anointed by the prophet Samuel (1 Sam. 10:1; 16:3), while Solomon was anointed by the priest Zadok (1 Kgs. 1:39). Priestly anointing was the normal pattern, as we see in the case of Joash. So a king was an "anointed one" (Hb., *Meshiach*). Thus David speaks with respect of Saul as "the LORD's anointed" (1 Sam. 24:6,10; 26:11). The progressive revelation of the Old Testament that a king descended from David would establish God's perfect kingdom on earth led to anticipation of the coming of this "Anointed One," or Messiah.

The hope of the promised Davidic king occurs many times in the prophetic Scriptures, but the title itself occurs directly for this coming King only in Daniel 9:24–27. The Greek equivalent is *Christos*. So the New Testament proclaims the fulfillment of God's promise in the coming of Jesus the Christ, the Anointed One of the Father and the Spirit (Luke 4:18).

C. Joash's Sad Ending (12:19–21)

The facts of Joash's sad ending have already been recounted in the commentary. It is hard to imagine Joash could reach such depths of ingratitude that he would order the murder of the son of the couple who had spared his life and the man who had mentored and guided him. The killing of the prophet-priest Zechariah is referred to by the Lord in Luke 11:49–51. Because of the order of the books in the Hebrew Old Testament (Chronicles is the last book in the Hebrew canon), his murder was the last one mentioned in the Old Testament, while Abel's was the first.

VII. TEACHING OUTLINE

A. INTRODUCTION
1. Lead Story: A Brand Plucked from the Burning
2. Context: The story shifts to the Southern Kingdom, where the cause of the Lord has fallen into deep crisis. An ardent Baal worshiper has seized power. Only one little baby remains of the Davidic line. God's program of salvation has been reduced to one infant!
3. Transition: God's solution came not in the form of dramatic divine intervention but by the faithfulness of ordinary people.

B. COMMENTARY
1. On the Brink of Destruction (11:1–3)
2. Risky Obedience (11:4–21)
3. Restoring the House of the Lord (12:1–16)
4. Reversing Course (12:17–21)

C. CONCLUSION: AFTER DARKNESS, LIGHT

VIII. ISSUES FOR DISCUSSION

1. The recovery under Joash is notable for its careful planning on the part of Jehoiada and then on the part of Joash in the repair of the temple. What place do good plans and solid business practices play in the work of the Lord? What are the dangers of such things?
2. God's cause in Judah reached a place of great weakness in this section. Why do you think the Lord permitted that? Can you think of any similar contemporary situations?

2 Kings 13:1–15:31

Squandered Opportunities

| Q u o t e |

"*F*our things come not back—the spoken word, the sped arrow, the past life, and the neglected opportunity."

A r a b   P r o v e r b

HISTORICAL PROFILE: THE KINGS OF ISRAEL AND JUDAH (EIGHTH CENTURY B.C.)

ISRAEL	JUDAH
	Joash (835–796 B.C.)
Jehoahaz (814–798 B.C.)	
Jehoash (798–782 B.C.)	
	Amaziah (796–767 B.C.)
Jeroboam II (793–753 B.C.)	
	Azariah (Uzziah) (792–740 B.C.)
Zechariah (753–752 B.C.)	
Shallum (752 B.C.)	
Menahem (752–742 B.C.)	
	Jotham (750–732 B.C.)
Pekaiah (742–740 B.C.)	
Pekah (753)740–732 B.C.)	
	Ahaz (735–715 B.C.)
Hoshea (732–725 B.C.)	
	Hezekiah (715–686 B.C.)

2 Kings 13:1–15:31

The nation of Israel had chosen a course of covenant disloyalty and rebellion that put it on a collision course with the righteous wrath of a holy God. When a strong enemy appeared in the guise of Assyria, Israel's lack of strong and godly leadership, its internal instability and moral weakness, and its abandonment of God made its fate inevitable. In this section Israel's downhill slide accelerates toward the day of reckoning.

Squandered Opportunities

I. INTRODUCTION

"My Life Is Going in the Right Direction"

At one time he had been one of the brightest stars on the baseball horizon, but now he stood before a judge, dressed in an orange-colored jail uniform. He had been Rookie of the Year, an eight-time All-Star, the owner of four World Series rings. But he had also violated parole six times, and now he awaited sentence. The prosecutor told the judge, "He doesn't like someone telling him what to do. At some point, he should be punished for that." The judge agreed, sentencing him to eighteen months in prison. "You've been given several opportunities to avoid incarceration," the judge said. "You've squandered those opportunities, and now it's time for you to face the consequences." Just before the prisoner shuffled off to jail, he insisted, "My life is going in the right direction."

If so, it was apparent only to him. Sadly, his life had become a trail of squandered opportunities, wasted potential, and missed chances. He had engaged in self-defeating, self-destructive behavior, and now he would reap the consequences. Fans could only hope that this time he would learn his lessons and make a permanent change.

The history of the nation of Israel was also one of squandered opportunities and wasted chances. The Lord had given its first king the promise of a lasting dynasty (1 Kgs. 11:34–39). But in classic self-destructive behavior, this king had turned his back on the promise-making God and constructed a false religion. Like the baseball player, he didn't like anyone telling him what to do. So judgment had come upon him and his nation (1 Kgs. 14:14–16). Sadly, none of his successors ever reversed Jeroboam's religious innovation. There seemed to be a kind of national death wish as the nation insisted, "We're going in the right direction," marching ever closer to the edge of the cliff.

When we reach 2 Kings 13, the narrator's pace increases notably. In three chapters we meet eight kings of Israel within about eighty years, as the day of final reckoning draws closer and closer. The nation moved to the brink of anarchy and military disaster, all the while refusing to engage God in true repentance. Affairs in the Southern Kingdom were only marginally better. They lagged behind Israel in the rate of defection, but they were also engaged in self-defeating, self-destructive behavior that made divine retribution inevitable. The crisis to come in chapter 17 was already becoming visible. It is a sad story of squandered opportunities.

II. COMMENTARY

Squandered Opportunties

MAIN IDEA: *We pay a terrible price when we squander the opportunities given by God's grace.*

A Jehoahaz and Jehoash of Israel (13:1–25)

SUPPORTING IDEA: *Sin and lukewarmness cause us to squander our God-given opportunities.*

13:1–9. Jehu had died as Hazael and the Syrians were putting great military pressure on Israel (10:32–36). Jehu's son **Jehoahaz** became king in 814 B.C., when Syrian power was at its pinnacle and Assyria was occupied in another part of the region. Jehu had removed baalism from Israel, but he had not dealt with **the sins of Jeroboam son of Nebat.** Jehoahaz's son Jehoash did not revert to baalism, but he continued his father's flawed policy: **he did evil in the eyes of the LORD because he did not turn away from the sins of Jeroboam.** In response, **the LORD's anger burned against Israel, and . . . he kept them under the power of Hazael king of Aram and Ben-Hadad his son** (serving as military commander). God was using a pagan king as his agent of judgment against his rebellious people.

For the only time in the history of the northern kings, we read that **Jehoahaz sought the LORD's favor.** The description of the writer of 2 Kings is patterned after the Book of Judges. Sin aroused God's anger, leading to military defeat or bondage. But Israel's cry of pain stirred God's compassion, causing him to send a deliverer. Jehoahaz sought the Lord but not in deep-seated repentance. It was a cry of pain and need, as the oppression of Hazael followed the terrible course of Elisha's vision (2 Kgs. 8:12), driving the Israelites from their homes.

In condescending grace the Lord listened to him, **for he saw how severely the king of Aram was oppressing Israel.** As a result, **the LORD provided a deliverer for Israel, and they escaped from the power of Aram.** The identity of this deliverer is a matter of conjecture, since no figure comparable to the judges emerged during this time. The reference may be to Elisha, but no public activity is attributed to him at this time. The "deliverer" was probably Adad-Nirari III, king of Assyria. In 805 B.C., he reappeared in the region, lured Syria's armies away from Israel to protect their own homeland, and then defeated the Syrians, ending their oppression of Israel.

Life quickly returned to normal: **The Israelites lived in their own homes as they had before.** But they also worshiped as they had before—at the golden calves of Jeroboam and even at pagan shrines, with **the Asherah pole.**

They wasted God's delivering grace by failing to turn from their sins. As a result, they were reduced to military weakness. The nation's deliverance could only be attributed to the Lord, and it could only be maintained by him. By wasting grace and indulging in sin, they had sentenced themselves to weakness.

13:10-19. Jehoahaz was succeeded by his son **Jehoash** (798–792 B.C.). For a brief period (Joash of Judah died in 796   B.C.), both Israel and Judah were ruled by a king of the same name! The writer of 2 Kings records nothing of consequence from the reign of Jehoash. Spiritually, he was just like his father. The standard description of his death is given both here and in 14:15-16.

Jehoash would have vanished virtually without a trace, were it not for a significant encounter with the prophet **Elisha**. By this time he was old and ill. He had come on the scene as Elijah's protégé before the death of Ahab in 853 B.C. Since Jehoash came to the throne in 798   B.C., Elisha had served as a prophet for at least fifty-five years. Jehoash was not a man of authentic faith in the Lord, but he regarded Elisha as a national treasure. His absence would leave a gaping hole. Jehoash went to see Elisha   **and wept over him**, using the same words to describe Elisha that Elisha had used to describe Elijah at his dramatic departure (2:12): **My father! My father! . . . The chariots and horsemen of Israel!**

Elisha was an army in himself, the source of the nation's victories with Syria, such as those recorded in 2 Kings 6–7. He was a far more certain source of protection than Israel's paltry army (13:7). Jehoash's respect for Elisha was appropriate: he represented his link to God. But Israel was not dependent on its prophets, even ones as great as Elijah and Elisha. The king's trust needed to be in his never-changing God.

Elisha's last message took the form of two acted-out prophecies. The first involved the king taking **a bow and some arrows**, opening **the east window** and, with **his hands on the king's hands**, shooting an arrow in the general direction of Syria. So there would be no doubt about the meaning of the action, Elisha spelled it out: **You will completely destroy the Arameans at Aphek.** Aphek was a strategic border town between Syria and Israel. Considering the massive military weakness of Israel, this was a stunning promise.

We have no way of knowing whether Jehoash believed this promise. It was quickly followed by another command from the prophet: **Take the arrows . . . Strike the ground.** Since these were the same arrows, there was every reason to believe they had the same significance. Jehoash took them and struck the ground **three times and stopped.** It was a perfunctory response, humoring the strange request of the aged prophet. Elisha exploded in anger: **You should have struck the ground five or six times; then you**

would have defeated Aram and completely destroyed it. But now you will defeat it only three times.

But Jehoash did not trust the Lord or the prophetic word. He just went through the motions. Like king; like nation. They were going through the motions of worship of the Lord, without any passionate commitment to him. Israel would know victories because God was faithful to his promise. But they would not know victory as they could have because their king had stopped short. He had squandered a God-given opportunity.

13:20–25. The chapter ends with an unusual story, but a careful look shows that it contains a powerful message. **Elisha died and was buried**, probably in a cave or a hewn-out sepulcher. Such gravesites would be reused, over and over. That led to a bizarre incident, linked to Israel's military weakness. At harvest time in the late spring, **Moabite raiders** would enter the country to seize as much food as they could. On one occasion a band of raiders surprised a burial party. Fearing for their lives, they quickly discarded the body, throwing it **into Elisha's tomb**. When the body touched Elisha's bones, **the man came to life and stood up on his feet**.

There is no comparable event in the Bible. And it never occurred again. Otherwise any death in the region would have been reversed by casting the corpse into Elisha's tomb! It was a unique event, but there is no reason to dismiss it as nonsensical superstition. What follows shows that the writer of 2 Kings considered it to have symbolic importance. He does that by using the Hebrew word *threw* once again in verse 23: **To this day he has been unwilling to destroy them or banish (*throw*) them from his presence.** In verses 22–23 the writer reverts back to the time of Jehoahaz and the oppression of Hazael, which he had covered in 13:1–9.

The Lord's deliverance of the nation at that time was grounded in his prophetic covenant: **The LORD . . . showed concern for them because of his covenant with Abraham, Isaac and Jacob.** Israel's hope did not ultimately rest in its own merit but in the covenant promises of God. The writer knew that his readers were in exile in Babylon and also was keenly aware of the destruction of the nation of Israel in 722 B.C. (described in ch. 17). The nation, on more than one occasion, appeared to be dead. But when the corpse hit the bones of God's prophetic promises, the nation would spring back to life. This remarkable rebirth of the nation would take place after the Babylonian exile, and in some measure, in our own day, with the rebirth of the nation in 1948. But it will be at the return of the Lord Jesus that the dead bones of the nation will fully return to life (Ezek. 37).

To confirm that the promises of the prophets outlive the prophets, the chapter ends with the fulfillment of Elisha's promise: **Three times Jehoash defeated him** (Ben-Hadad son of Hazael), **and so he recovered the Israelite**

towns. But it could have been so much more, if only the king had trusted God. The victories were a vivid reminder of lost opportunities.

B Amaziah of Judah (14:1–29)

SUPPORTING IDEA: *Pride and arrogance cause us to squander the victories God has given.*

14:1–7. While the writer of 2 Kings momentarily freezes events in Israel, he catches up with events in Judah. Joash's life had ended at the hands of assassins (12:20), but in distinction from Israel, the assassins did not take the throne. Instead his son **Amaziah** succeeded him. His rule would be an unprecedented one, in that while he is credited with twenty-nine years on the throne (796–767 B.C.), his actual sole rule was much shorter, since he shared the throne with his father **Joash** and with his son Azariah. He received qualified approval: **In everything he followed the example of his father Joash. The high places, however, were not removed.** Thus, he received a grade of "relatively good."

To his credit Amaziah acted justly in his punishment of his father's assassins. Contrary to common Near Eastern patterns, he moderated his revenge in response to the law. The citation of Deuteronomy 24:16 contains the command that restrained Amaziah. In this matter he modeled an appropriate response to God's Word.

Another event proved to be far more determinative to Amaziah's reign, since it contained the seeds of his downfall. The opening words suggest that this episode brought him fame: **He . . . defeated ten thousand Edomites in the Valley of Salt and captured Sela.** Victories had been rare in Judah at this time. His father had only escaped from Hazael by paying him off (12:17–18). Although Edom was hardly a major power, the defeat of an army of ten thousand was a major achievement. Even more impressive was the capture of Sela. Traditionally identified with the site of Petra, it was an almost impenetrable fortress. Its capture was an achievement to be proud of.

14:8–14. Flushed with success, Amaziah returned to Jerusalem full of confidence. Second Chronicles indicates that the behavior of some Israelite mercenary troops had heated tensions between Judah and Israel. Amaziah had contracted the help of Israelite troops, but at prophetic direction he had dismissed them. Furious, they had attacked Judean cities, killed three thousand, and spoiled the area (2 Chr. 25:6–10,13). Amaziah was emboldened to issue a **challenge** to Israel's king, Jehoash: **Come, meet me face to face.** This represented a major shift in the relations between the two countries. Since the time of Omri and Ahab, the two nations had formed an alliance. Amaziah's challenge represented a renewal of tensions as well as open conflict between the two states.

Jehoash's response combined congratulations, contempt, and warning, in the form of a fable: **A thistle in Lebanon sent a message to a cedar in Lebanon, "Give your daughter to my son in marriage." Then a wild beast in Lebanon . . . trampled the thistle underfoot.** The wild thistle, ugly and unwanted, obviously represented Amaziah, while Jehoash "humbly" compared himself to a majestic cedar of Lebanon. The wild beast trampling the thistle also referred to Israel. Jehoash was clearly contemptuous of Amaziah and fully confident of his ability to defeat him. But he was seeking to avoid a fight. So he made his warning as clear as possible: **You have indeed defeated Edom and now you are arrogant. Glory in your victory, but stay at home! Why ask for trouble and cause your own downfall and that of Judah also?** In other words, "Enjoy your Little League victory, but you're not ready for the Big Leagues!" There is no way to know whether Israel had obvious military superiority or whether this was just royal bluster. Whatever the facts, it was a challenge that Amaziah could not ignore.

Recognizing war was inevitable, Jehoash chose to strike first. Meeting Amaziah's forces at **Beth Shemesh**, deep within Judean territory, about fifteen miles southwest of Jerusalem, he routed Judah's army and **captured Amaziah king of Judah.** We are not told where or for how long Amaziah was held captive. But there are significant reasons for believing that it was for a considerable time. **Then Jehoash . . . broke down the wall of Jerusalem.** A breach of **about six hundred feet** was made in the northern defense wall, **the temple** and **royal palace** were looted, and **hostages** were taken to Jerusalem. These were traumatic and unprecedented events: the defeat of the army, the capture of the king, the breaching of the walls, the looting of the temple, and the taking of hostages. Judah and its king had been completely humiliated.

This would not be the last time the walls of Jerusalem were breached and hostages were taken. The event signified the destiny of both nations. The hostages, apparently including the king, represented a kind of human collateral against Judah's attempt to retaliate.

14:15-22. Having paused once again to summarize Jehoash's reign, repeating 13:12-13 almost exactly, the writer of 2 Kings recounts the story of Amaziah's sad ending. There is a subtle shift from the normal formula: Amaziah **lived** (rather than reigned) **for fifteen years after the death of Jehoash.** The chronology of his son Azariah's life suggests that Azariah was recognized as the king as early as 792 B.C. If this coincided with Amaziah's capture, it would make sense. The text does not indicate when Amaziah was set free. But it is evident that his disastrous military adventurism had long-term consequences. He would be especially resented in Jerusalem. At some point after Amaziah's release, **they conspired against him in Jerusalem.**

Amaziah fled for his life to the fortress city of **Lachish**, but the conspirators **sent men after him to Lachish and killed him there.** This was not intended as an attack on the Davidic dynasty, but on Amaziah himself, since **all the people of Judah took Azariah . . . and made him king in place of his father**. This may refer to an act carried out years earlier—Azariah's enthronement with the broad support of the people at the time of Amaziah's capture. This is consistent with Azariah's age and his fifty-two-year reign. For the first twenty-five of those, he was co-regent with his father, who was a prisoner of war for an unknown part of that time.

For the second time in a row, Judah's king had been assassinated. Israel's instability was beginning to appear in the Southern Kingdom. The only bright spot in Amaziah's legacy was that Azariah was able to follow up his father's victory in Edom by rebuilding the port city of **Elath** and restoring it to Judah—a fleeting glimpse of Solomonic glory (1 Kgs. 9:26). But Amaziah's pride had brought the nation very low.

Ⓒ Jeroboam II of Israel and Azariah of Judah (14:23–15:7)

SUPPORTING IDEA: *The complacency of success can lead us to squander the opportunity for godly change.*

14:23–29. Jeroboam II's reign of forty-one years (793–753 B.C.) was the longest in the nation's history as well as its most illustrious and prosperous. He was the fourth king in the Jehu dynasty (10:30), but he was a true follower of his namesake, Israel's first king: **He did evil in the eyes of the LORD and did not turn away from any of the sins of Jeroboam**. His was a reign of military success, political expansion, and financial prosperity. Under his leadership Israel recovered from its appalling weakness under Jehoahaz (13:7) to become the major power in the region. Its boundaries rivaled those of the time of Solomon (see 1 Kgs. 5:1; 8:65): **from Lebo Hamath** (on the north, the Bekaa Valley of Lebanon) **to the Sea of the Arabah** (the Dead Sea, indicating control of much of modern Jordan). In a few years Jeroboam II built a nation on the brink of extinction into a great regional power.

The writer of 2 Kings wants us to know two things about Jeroboam II's success. The first is that it occurred in accordance with God's prophetic word through **his servant Jonah**. It was God's Word, not Jeroboam's skill, which determined events in Israel. The second was that Israel's respite from oppression and defeat was the product of God's grace on his people. Israel's constant rebellion and covenant unfaithfulness warranted divine judgment, but God's amazing grace continued to grant time to repent. Even when judgment finally came, Israel would not be blotted out. God would preserve a remnant.

The writer of 2 Kings cites Jeroboam's **military achievements, including how he recovered for Israel both Damascus and Hamath** (see "Deeper Discoveries"). These were remarkable achievements by secular standards, but the writer is unimpressed. In the long run, did they really matter if the greater issues of spiritual faithfulness and covenant obedience were not attended to?

15:1–7. The reign of Azariah in the South was not as illustrious as that of his contemporary Jeroboam II, but it was very impressive. Judah's longest reigning king (792–740 B.C.), he began his sole reign in 767 B.C. with the assassination of his father. He is known by two names: Azariah ("Yahweh has helped") and Uzziah ("Yahweh is my strength"). He is categorized as a moderately good king: **He did what was right in the eyes of the LORD. . . . The high places, however, were not removed.** In spite of the length of his reign, Azariah is passed over quickly by the writer of 2 Kings. He ignores his military victories and building achievements. We are told that **the LORD afflicted the king with leprosy.** The reason for this affliction is not given here, but 2 Chronicles tells us that it was because of his intrusion into a role reserved for the priests (2 Chr. 26:16–21).

As a result, Azariah **lived in a separate house,** literally, "a house of freedom." This indicates that he was relieved of his royal duties, while **Jotham the king's son . . . governed the people of the land.** His father had been a prisoner of Israel; Uzziah became a prisoner of the Lord because of his sinful arrogance. The year of his death is best known as the occasion of God's great self-revelation to his prophet Isaiah (Isa. 6:1). As a royal leper, he was **buried near** (but not with) his fathers **in the City of David.**

🄳 Israel's Last Kings (15:8–31)

SUPPORTING IDEA: *Squandered opportunities produce dire consequences.*

15:8–12. Zechariah, the final king of the promised four-generation dynasty of Jehu, reigned for only six months in 753–752 B.C. Only Zimri reigned for a shorter time. He was publicly assassinated by **Shallum,** the first man in the ninety years since Jehu to lead a coup. This act not only marked the completion of the promise of the Lord to Jehu but the beginning of a period of great internal instability.

15:13–16. Shallum seized power, but he also unleashed the animals of prey. After only one month of rule, he found himself the victim of a ruthless conspirator named **Menahem.** Menahem's base was the old royal capital of **Tirzah.** As if to establish his credentials as a ruthless terrorist, he prepared to do whatever it took to gain or hold power. Menahem **attacked Tiphsah and everyone in the city and its vicinity. . . . He sacked Tiphsah and ripped open all the pregnant women.**

What is not clear is where this appalling atrocity was carried out. Tiphsah was located on the Euphrates River. If that was the site, it was in territory

brought under control by Jeroboam II and far from home. But the distances
make it unlikely. Many interpreters suggest that the Greek translation retains
the original reading of *Tappuah*, an Israelite town. Whatever the location, this
was an atrocity unprecedented for its brutality, perhaps committed against
fellow citizens. The Israelites had become as brutal as the Syrians (8:12) or
the Assyrians.

15:17–22. Menahem remained in power for a decade (752–742 B.C.). His
reign was not motivated by a desire for religious reform: **He did evil in the
eyes of the LORD.** It was the only relatively stable reign in the period, but it
was achieved at the cost of capitulation to Assyria. For the first time in the
period the Assyrians, who have loomed in the background, are mentioned. As
king of Assyria, **Pul** (Tiglath-Pileser) . . . **invaded the land.** This did not drive
Menahem to trust in the Lord but to his own strategies. He made himself a
vassal, paying **a thousand talents of silver** to gain Pul's support and
strengthen his hold on the kingdom. A thousand talents amounted to about
thirty-five tons, an amount Menahem raised by taxing the people of wealth in
his nation fifty talents of silver, about one and one-fourth pounds.

As a result, the king of Assyria withdrew, but not for long. In his annals
Tiglath-Pileser wrote, "As for Menahem, I overwhelmed him like a snow-
storm and he fled like a bird, alone and bowed at my feet."

15:23–26. Menahem was the only king of this period to die a natural
death. His son **Pekahiah** ruled from 742 to 740 B.C., when he became the victim of one of his political officers, **Pekah.** Pekah was accompanied by **fifty
men of Gilead.** This may indicate that his coup had a regional base. He executed Pekahiah, along with two otherwise unknown Israelite officials **Argob
and Arieh**, apparently in a surprise attack on the palace.

15:27–31. Pekah is given credit for a reign of **twenty years.** Since that figure is ten years too long to fit into the chronology, it seems best to presume
that Pekah had royal power regionally in Gilead as a rival of Menahem and
Pekahiah for a period of ten years and then ruled the entire nation from 740
to 732 B.C. During his reign **Tiglath-Pileser** reappeared, destroying Damascus
in 732 B.C. Pekah was a close ally of Rezin the king of Syria (see 15:37;
16:5–6). So he experienced the dire effects of Assyria's presence, losing
Gilead and Galilee as well as other strategic towns. Most ominously, Pul
deported the people to Assyria.

This was the first wave of deportation, a punishment that had hung over
the nation since 1 Kings 8:46–51, with roots in the warnings of the Deutero-
nomic covenant (Deut. 28:63–68). Deportation served the purposes of punishment, intimidation, and weakening, as well as providing a population for
Assyria's projects elsewhere in the world.

Assyria's ravaging of Pekah's nation because of his disastrous alliance with
Syria left Pekah without any support for his leadership. As a result, his life

came to a violent end at the hands of **Hoshea, who attacked and assassinated him, and then succeeded him as king**. It was an unenviable position. Hoshea had become king just in time to preside over the total destruction of his nation. The trail of squandered opportunities and wasted grace had reached its bitter end.

> **MAIN IDEA REVIEW:** *We pay a terrible price when we continually squander the opportunities given by God's grace.*

III. CONCLUSION

A Long, Downhill Road

"There is a way that seems right to a man, but in the end it leads to death" (Prov. 14:12). Few statements capture the lessons of Israel's history as clearly as this. As we near the end of 2 Kings 15, we have almost reached the end of a long, downhill road. Since Jeroboam I took his first fateful step away from God, the outcome had been inevitable, especially since none of the eighteen kings who followed him took any steps to reverse his spiritual rebellion. The unraveling of the nation was not instantaneous, since God, in his grace, slowed the process of self-destruction and often intervened with special kindness. But Israel's history was a long, downhill road of chosen sin and squandered opportunities. Now, as the end drew near, the nation's self-defeating and self-destructive behavior grew more and more extreme. It seemed almost as if a national death wish had fallen upon the people.

Judah was only a short way behind on its own path of destruction. Its sin had not been the patronizing of a false cult based on golden calves, but the toleration of high places and false gods. They would soon plunge into sins as degrading as those in which Israel had indulged. They could see the unfolding disaster in Israel, but they learned nothing from it. But the promises God had made to David and the pattern set by their great ancestor was at least slowing their downhill journey.

The story of both nations at this point is a reminder that, while God is patient and gracious, he is also holy. We may choose to squander the opportunities he gives and to try to convince ourselves that our life is going in the right direction. But at the end of the road, death awaits.

PRINCIPLES

- God's grace responds to the cry of his people, in spite of their unfaithfulness.
- We "waste grace" when we revert to former sinful patterns.

- When we stop short of passionate obedience, we lose the opportunity for blessings that God desires for us.
- Pride makes us foolish before people as well as God.
- Secular standards of greatness are very different from spiritual standards.
- Success can blind us to our true condition.

APPLICATIONS

- Assess the depth of your realization of God's grace in your life.
- What portion of your communication with God consists of gratitude?
- Is there a connection in your life between realizing God's grace toward you and your obedience to him?
- Listen carefully to the Word of God so that it reveals your true condition.

IV. LIFE APPLICATION

Blinded by Success

The middle period of the eighth century in Israel and Judah was a time of success. Both nations boasted secure borders, prosperous economies, and strong military forces. From the vantage point of 755 B.C., it seemed impossible that within thirty years one of the nations would cease to exist, and the other would be a petty vassal of a great empire. Jeroboam and Uzziah could boast of their victories, their achievements, and their reputation among the nations. So when prophets such as Hosea and Amos railed against their sins and shortcomings, it was easy to dismiss them. When things were going well, why would anyone want to change? Why go back to the old ways when the new ways were working so well?

Success can breed complacency. In one form complacency becomes delusion. Israel's prosperity was a product of temporary political circumstances and God's grace. It was easier to believe that it was due to Israel's greatness and that it would always be this way. Complacency also produces arrogance, the feeling that we are invincible because we know how to do it and no one can take it away from us.

Israel and Judah's prosperity was a window of opportunity, a period of blessing and success that could have been the occasion for a self-evaluation that looked beneath surface conditions. But the leaders of the two nations chose to be blinded by success. Wise people *find the truth, face the truth, and follow the truth*. They reject the superficial counsel that says, "If it ain't broke, don't fix it." Whether we are talking about our business, our church, our marriage and family, or our personal life, it is important that we refuse to be blinded by "success" and choose to be illumined by the Lord and his will.

V. PRAYER

Father, you know our tendency to deceive ourselves—to excuse our sins and exaggerate our merits. Our hearts are deceitful. Undeceive us, Father. In your grace, show us our condition as you see us. Help us to live authentically before you and others. Amen.

VI. DEEPER DISCOVERIES

A. A Tale of Two Prophets

Elijah and Elisha were alike in many ways. Both stood for the exclusive and authentic worship of the Lord. But they were also different. Elijah spent much of his ministry on his own, engaged in acts of God-directed confrontation with the king. Elisha was regularly seen in the company of the prophets and lived in the capital city of Israel. Elijah's ministry was relatively brief; Elisha's was remarkably long. Elijah did not die; Elisha, the miracle worker, died of a lingering illness as an old man. Yet each of them was God's man for his times. God is not stuck on a single pattern for his servants.

B. Striking the Ground (13:18)

The word Elisha used when he told Jehoash to "strike" the ground was the same one he used when he commanded him to "shoot" the arrow. He may have been commanding the king to shoot the arrows into the ground rather than to strike it. Either way the significance of the action is the same.

C. Reviving the Corpse (13:20–25)

The biblical prediction that the corpse of the nation of Israel would be resuscitated took on new significance with the miraculous reappearance of the nation of Israel in 1948 after more than eighteen hundred years of nonexistence. The famous prophecy of the dead bones in Ezekiel 37 depicts first the gathering of dead bones and their formation into a skeleton without life. That is modern Israel's present state, which exists—but in a state of unbelief. Israel is restored to the land but not spiritually reborn. National rebirth will occur at the time of Messiah's return, with the moving of the Spirit and the repentance of the nation. We may marvel at the restoration of the nation, but the current nation is not yet the restored people of God, in a full biblical sense. It stands in need of repentance and rebirth.

D. Yaudi (14:28)

The statement of this verse has puzzled commentators. The Hebrew text speaks of "Damascus and Hamath, which had belonged to Judah." The text is identical to the statement in verse 22: "restored it to Judah." The problem is that Damascus and Hamath never belonged to Judah, except perhaps in the times of David and Solomon. The reading of the NIV "Yaudi" is a conjecture, based on Assyrian inscriptions, but has little support. Others believe an early scribe wrongly inserted "Judah" rather than the original "Israel". Certainty is impossible, but I am inclined to see a reference to Judah, in terms of David and Solomon.

VII. TEACHING OUTLINE

A. INTRODUCTION

1. Lead Story: "My Life Is Going in the Right Direction"
2. Context: As Israel's history moves toward its closure, the country grows weaker and weaker, with a brief interlude of glory. But every experience of God's grace is squandered or abused. It seems as if a kind of death wish has beset the nation.
3. Transition: God's prophet Elisha makes one last appearance. But even at the end of his life, Israel's king squanders the opportunity that Elisha represents.

B. COMMENTARY

1. Jehoahaz and Jehoash of Israel (13:1–25)
2. Amaziah of Judah (14:1–29)
3. Jeroboam II of Israel and Azariah of Judah (14:23–15:7)
4. Israel's Last Kings (15:8–31)

C. CONCLUSION: A LONG, DOWNHILL ROAD

VIII. ISSUES FOR DISCUSSION

1. Jehoash lost his opportunity because he stopped short of what God intended. Are there ways in which we "stop short" and deny ourselves the blessings that God desires for us?
2. Amaziah's pride led him into a disastrous defeat at the hands of Jehoash. What is the difference between confidence, appropriate pride in one's accomplishments, sinful pride, and arrogance?

2 Kings 15:32–17:41

Dealing with the Devil

Quote

"*P*eople do not drift toward holiness. Apart from

grace-driven effort, people do not gravitate toward godliness,

prayer, obedience to Scripture, faith and delight in the Lord.

We drift toward compromise and call it tolerance; we drift

toward disobedience and call it freedom; we drift toward

superstition and call it faith."

D . A . C a r s o n

HISTORICAL PROFILE: THE KINGS OF ASSYRIA

Tiglath-Pileser III
- Reigned 745–727 B.C.
- Personal name was Pul (2 Kgs. 15:19); throne name was Tiglath-Pileser (2 Kgs. 15:29)
- Leaders preceding him were weak; he reawakened the power of Assyria, making it the dominant power in the Fertile Crescent
- Made thirty-eight drives to the west, with two major campaigns, the first in 743 B.C. when Menahem paid him tribute (2 Kgs. 15:19–20) and the second in 734 B.C.
- Conquered Damascus and dismembered Aram (Syria) in 732 B.C.; also despoiled Israel at this time (2 Kgs. 15:29–30)
- Returned east, and in 729 B.C. conquered Babylon, where he died in 727 B.C.

Shalmaneser V
- Reigned 727–722 B.C.
- Moved west in 725 B.C., and besieged Samaria until he captured it in 722 B.C., dying just at the moment of victory

---

Sargon

- Reigned 722–705 B.C.

- Claimed the capture of Samaria. It is highly probable that he was taking credit for the work of Shalmaneser

- Hurried back to Assyria to claim the throne

- Annals record numerous campaigns in the west during his reign. The only one referred to in the Old Testament is found in Isaiah 20:1, where Judah is not involved

- Died in 705 B.C. Hezekiah's rebellion against the king of Assyria (2 Kgs. 18:7) may have been at this time or earlier

2 Kings 15:32–17:41

IN A NUTSHELL

Throughout its history Israel had chosen the path of rebellion and spiritual compromise. But now it had reached the end of the road where it encountered the harsh judgment of God in destruction and deportation. At the very time this was occurring, Ahaz pursued the same course in Judah. It is a prescription for disaster.

Dealing with the Devil

I. INTRODUCTION

Feeding the Crocodile

*N*eville Chamberlain was convinced that Adolf Hitler was a reasonable and trustworthy man. As the prime minister of Great Britain in the late 1930s, Chamberlain was committed to keeping his nation out of a disastrous war. He was sure that if he met some of the Nazi leader's demands, he would be satisfied and live peaceably with the rest of Europe. Unfortunately, appeasing Hitler meant breaking treaty commitments to friendly nations. He felt it was a price he had to pay. So on September 29, 1938, Britain, France, Germany, and Italy signed the Munich Pact. Chamberlain returned home in triumph, waving the pact and proclaiming that it meant "peace in our time, peace with honor." His claim was received with great popular relief and acclaim.

One man was not convinced. Winston Churchill observed that "an appeaser is one who feeds a crocodile, hoping it will eat him last." He arose in the House of Commons to voice a lonely but prophetic opinion: "Britain and France had to choose between war and dishonor. They chose dishonor. They will have war. . . . The people should know that we have sustained a defeat without war. They should know that we have passed a terrible milestone. . . . And do not suppose that this is the end. This is only the first sip, the first foretaste of a bitter cup."

As events proved, Churchill was right. Hitler was an insatiable crocodile. Compromise with such a man was defeat, and the course that follows such compromise goes steadily downhill. When you deal with the devil, disaster results.

In these chapters Israel reaches the end of the line. After 2 Kings 17, the nation never again appeared on the stage of history, represented only by scattered refugees, some who fled to Judah. They had dealt with the devil and despised their covenant with God. Now they would pay the price. As Israel was destroying itself, the king of Judah was imitating Israel's policies in his own nation, bringing it to the lowest point in its history. He would try to feed the crocodile of a pagan king and pagan gods, and his nation would only barely escape being devoured. So even as Israel vanished into the mists of history, Judah's king was rushing along the same trail.

II. COMMENTARY

Dealing with the Devil

MAIN IDEA: *Corrupt worship first corrupts us and then condemns us.*

Ⓐ Jotham and Ahaz (15:32–16:20)

SUPPORTING IDEA: *Short-term solutions that involve spiritual compromise have long-term consequences.*

15:32–38. The writer of 2 Kings once again freezes the account of Israel to update the history of Judah. He does this for the last time, since Israel was about to disappear. We have already been introduced to **Jotham** in 15:5, as he governed the nation during the incapacity of his leprous father Uzziah. Jotham reigned from 750 to 732 B.C., sharing the first ten years with his father and the final three years with his son Ahaz. Jotham received a conditioned approval: **he did what was right in the eyes of the LORD. . . . The high places, however, were not removed**.

This is a pattern we have become all too familiar with in the Book of 2 Kings. Many of Judah's kings were relatively good, but they could only be compared with one another, not with David. We are told little else of Jotham's reign. The author of 2 Chronicles evaluated him more positively (2 Chr. 27:1–9).

The writer of 2 Kings observes that **the LORD began to send Rezin king of Aram and Pekah son of Remaliah against Judah**. This was not just a military attack but an act of God—a judgment upon the nation of Judah. For the first time the Lord had sent, not just allowed, attacks on his holy city. The alliance of **Rezin** and **Pekah** was inspired by their mutual fear of Assyria. They wanted Judah to join in their mutual opposition, as the superpower moved in their direction. But Jotham refused to join such an alliance. So Israel and Syria attacked, with double purpose: to remove Jotham from the throne so they could install a king sympathetic to their plans and to eliminate Judah's military threat as a potential ally of Assyria on their exposed southern flank.

16:1–20. The reign of Ahaz turned out to be a disaster. He plunged Judah into a period of royally sanctioned idolatry and paganism, far more extensive even than that of Athaliah. He apparently shared three years as co-regent with his father, and then ruled from 732 B.C., the year in which Damascus fell to the Assyrians, until 715 B.C. (see "Deeper Discoveries"). The evaluation of his reign is more severe than that of any previous king.

Ahaz was **unlike David**, since he was a man with no heart for God, but he was like **the kings of Israel** (said elsewhere only of Ahab's son-in-law Jehoram;

8:18) who were leading their own nation over a cliff! But Ahaz resembled Ahab most of all, enshrining pagan worship as the officially sanctioned worship, even in the temple of the Lord in Jerusalem.

The extent of Ahaz's paganism is detailed. He engaged in child sacrifice, not only permitting it—but he **even sacrificed his own son in the fire**. Not even the kings of Israel had wallowed in such spiritual and moral filth! Other Judean kings have been sanctioned for not removing the high places and allowing the people to patronize them. Ahaz not only did not remove them; he constantly participated in them. He turned out to be the most evil of the descendants of David to ascend to the throne to this point in the nation's history.

Once again the Syrian-Israelite alliance attacked Judah (15:37). The account in 2 Chronicles 28:5–8 indicates a massive invasion in which Judah lost hundreds of thousands by way of death or capture. But they were not able to take Jerusalem: they **besieged Ahaz, but they could not overpower him**. Syria did, however, break Judah's hold on **Elath**, and the Edomites reoccupied the valuable port. What went on inside Jerusalem at this time is vividly portrayed by Isaiah in Isaiah 7, a chapter that contains the famous "refused sign" of the virgin birth (see "Deeper Discoveries"). The invasion of Rezin and Pekah had a powerful effect on the king. Isaiah tells us that "the hearts of Ahaz and his people were shaken, as the trees of the forest are shaken by the wind" (Isa. 7:2).

Facing an enemy he could not resist, Ahaz had several choices. He could surrender to the Syrian-Israelite alliance, a course he refused to take, probably realizing the futility of resisting Assyria. He could appeal to the Lord in trust and reliance, an option Isaiah begged him to take (Isa. 7:3–12). Or he could play the diplomatic card and appeal to the king of Assyria as his lord and protector. This was the course he chose. He sent **messengers** to grovel before the pagan king **Tiglath-Pileser** in humble submission. The man who refused to trust in the Lord was more than willing to trust the crocodile of Assyria! He then stripped the temple and its palace as **a gift to the king of Assyria**. The NIV translation obscures the fact that "gift" is more precisely translated "bribe." Bribes were forbidden in God's law, but Ahaz had placed his trust in man, not God.

In 733 B.C. the Assyrians marched against Damascus, laid siege for eighteen months, and captured the city in 732 B.C. Syria, as it had existed up until this time, ceased to exist. It was only a matter of time until Israel suffered the same fate. Second Kings 15:29 indicates that Tiglath-Pileser also seized a good part of Israel's territory and deported many of its people. Hoshea, Pekah's assassin and successor, became Assyria's vassal (17:3).

Ahaz had escaped Rezin and Pekah, but he could not afford to stop feeding the crocodile of Assyria. The Assyrians had set up regional headquarters in **Damascus**, and Ahaz made a pilgrimage there to swear allegiance to his deliverer, **Tiglath-Pileser**. During his visit **he saw an altar** that impressed him. While it is possible that this was a Syrian altar, it was more probably a "superior" Assyrian altar to a "superior" Assyrian god. Ahaz was not prepared to let the "newest thing in worship" pass him by. Jeroboam-like, he determined to introduce his own innovations into the temple worship of the Lord. He sent **a sketch of the altar** to the high priest **Uriah**, who had one built **in accordance with all the plans** of Ahaz.

When Ahaz returned to Jerusalem, he approached the pagan altar **and presented offerings on it**, in total defiance of the commands of God's law. He also had the now antiquated and redundant (but God-designed) **bronze altar that stood before the LORD** moved to a secondary position **on the north side of the new altar**, where he used it **for seeking guidance**, apparently a pagan practice of divination.

This was a great religious occasion, but it was also a paganizing of God's holy place of worship. We are not told that Ahaz did this at the direction of the Assyrians. He was doing his own thing. But when the Assyrians spoke, he was glad to comply. We read that he made other changes to the temple furnishings, **in deference to the king of Assyria**. It is not clear why the Assyrians would have any concern about such things. All that matters is that Ahaz would do whatever they desired, even in matters related to worship in the temple of the Lord. The crocodile was in full control! The glory of Solomon's temple was a far-distant memory.

Ahaz left a legacy of political and spiritual appeasement. His was a policy that would sap his nation of any capacity to withstand the onslaught of a powerful adversarial culture. His policy of appeasement would have led to the complete assimilation of his people. They might have maintained their existence but only at the cost of their unique identity. He was a man on whom the Assyrians could count. But his was a policy that could only lead to the disappearance of his nation. While the Northern Kingdom was in terminal decline, he was pushing his people down the same path.

B Hoshea of Israel (17:1–6)

SUPPORTING IDEA: *Change can come too late to avoid the consequences of past failure.*

17:1–6. The end of the nation of Israel is told with remarkable brevity and restraint. We are not invited to watch the pain of its last moments, to see the terrors that must have fallen as a nation was dismembered and its people scattered among the nations. The depth of human suffering can only be imagined as families were torn apart and an entire culture and way of life were dismantled. The writer of 2 Kings spares us all that. He reports simply that the assassin (15:30) **Hoshea** ascended to the throne in 732 B.C. Remarkably, he received the least negative evaluation of any Israelite king. In the light of all the other evaluations, this can only mean that he did not support or patronize the false cult of Jeroboam. But it was too little, too late. There was no way to escape the consequence of more than two hundred years of rebellion against God.

Shalmaneser succeeded his father as king of Assyria in 727 B.C. Hoshea, who had recognized Tiglath-Pileser's suzerainty, became **Shalmaneser's vassal and had paid him tribute**. But Shalmaneser was preoccupied with events in the east. Hoshea seized the opportunity to declare his independence by sending **envoys to So king of Egypt** and withholding **tribute** from Assyria. But the weakness of Egypt made reliance upon her foolish, and Hoshea soon paid the price. Shalmaneser branded Hoshea **a traitor**, attacked in force, and took him as his prisoner. We learn nothing more about his fate.

The Assyrians then turned on **Samaria**. Shalmaneser **laid siege to it for three years**, captured it, and then dismantled the nation. He **deported** large segments of the population, stripping the region of the capacity for rebellion and providing a work force for projects elsewhere. There had already been one such deportation (15:29). Assyrian records indicate 27,900 deportees, which probably included only males of a certain status. Their destination was the upper regions of the Tigris-Euphrates valley, where they soon vanished among other captive peoples. They did not have a spiritual identity strong enough to keep them from assimilation.

In the course of just over two hundred years (931–722 B.C.), nineteen kings had presided over the nation of Israel, all of whom "did evil in the eyes of the Lord." Ahijah's prophecy, made almost two centuries before, had reached its sad fulfillment: "He will uproot Israel from this good land that he gave to their forefathers and scatter them beyond the River, because they provoked the LORD to anger" (1 Kgs. 14:15)

Israel's Removal from the Land (17:7–23)

SUPPORTING IDEA: *When we rebel against the Lord, persist in sin, and reject God's repeated warnings, we will face his anger.*

17:7–12. The central issue throughout 1 and 2 Kings has always been the same: God's claim to exclusive loyalty. There is a long list of Israel's specific sins, but the Lord's basic indictment is couched in words deliberately reminiscent of the first commandment: "I am the LORD your God, who brought you out of Egypt, out of the land of slavery. You shall have no other gods before me" (Exod. 20:2–3). The relevance of this to the writer of 2 Kings is clear: **All this took place because the Israelites had sinned against the LORD their**

God. God had a covenant claim on Israel, but they worshiped other gods and followed the practices of the pagan nations.

Although 2 Kings focuses on the behavior of the nation's kings, the people also stood under divine indictment. It is what **the Israelites** had done, not just their kings, that brought divine retribution. God will be satisfied with nothing less than exclusive loyalty. Anything less demeans his glory and debases his uniqueness. This is an important message in our pluralistic times!

The specific sins of which Israel was guilty are now listed. The piling up of offenses makes clear how extensive the violations had been. The claim that **the Israelites secretly did things against the LORD their God that were not right** is surprising, especially since the things that follow hardly seem secret. The verb "do secretly" is used only here in the Old Testament and probably has more of the sense of doing something hypocritically. They did all these things while claiming to be the Lord's people. **They built themselves high places . . . burned incense . . . did wicked things . . . worshiped idols**. Their model had not been God's faithful people, but the pagan nations. They **provoked the LORD to anger** and violated his clear commands.

In the background of the indictment stands the command of Deuteronomy 12:1–4 that conditioned possession of the land on destruction of pagan worship: "You must not worship the LORD your God in their way" (Deut. 12:4).

17:13–15. God had not only given Israel his covenant law; he had also given her **all his prophets and seers**, who had called them to repentance and obedience. Throughout 1 and 2 Kings continued attention is paid to the place of the prophets in God's program. It was the prophet Ahijah who had been used to declare the emergence of the nation in 1 Kings 11 and the inevitable failure of the nation in 1 Kings 14. Major attention is given to Elijah and Elisha. But the response was consistent: **they would not listen and were as stiff-necked as their fathers**.

17:16–17. The final stage of the indictment adds more specifics, all of which stand in violation of God's law. The making of **two idols cast in the shape of calves** was forbidden in the Ten Commandments (Exod. 20:4–6). The worship of **the starry hosts** was forbidden in Deuteronomy 4:19; 17:3. The worship of Baal shattered the first commandment, while sacrificing **their sons and daughters in the fire** was not only detestable; it was forbidden (Lev. 18:21). **Divination and sorcery** also had no place among the covenant people, but their prevalence showed that the Israelites had become spiritual prostitutes, who **sold themselves to do evil in the eyes of the LORD**. Their sins were not sins of ignorance and excess; they were the products of aggressive, active, continual rebellion against their covenant Lord.

17:18–23. God had only one response to such contemptuous behavior: he **removed them from his presence**, literally, "from before his face." The expression is repeated three times (vv. 18,20,23) to drive it home. We are not to take this in physical terms, since God is omnipresent. The terms are relational, describing punishment, specifically deportation and dispersion. The Lord is slow to anger, but he is also sure to anger when he is persistently defamed. The writer of 2 Kings will not let us forget the fundamental sin of the nation. He describes once again the great sin of **Jeroboam**, which the people **persisted in**. God only did what he had said he would do: **the people of Israel were taken from their homeland into exile in Assyria**.

But what about Judah? It alone was left, but even Judah did not keep the commands of the Lord. They followed the practices Israel had introduced. This stands as an editorial comment on the history of Judah that we are about to consider. If judgment had fallen on Israel, it would also fall on Judah, unless the nation reversed direction. But the prospect for this was not good.

Ⓓ The Resettlement of the Land (17:24–41)

SUPPORTING IDEA: *Corrupt worship is confusing and corrupting.*

17:24–26. Having described why Israel no longer possessed the land, the writer of 2 Kings also explained how the situation in the land at the time he was writing had come about. The key word in the section, occurring eleven times, is **worship**. Because the worship of the region was corrupt and syncretistic, the result was corruption and confusion. Assyrian policy was to remove the native population to quench rebellion. But control of an empty region had little attraction and no capacity to enrich the conquering nation. So they repopulated the area with people from other conquered areas: **Babylon, Cuthah, Avva, Hamath and Sepharvaim**. They were not temporary residents: **They took over Samaria and lived in its towns**.

The movement of these people groups probably occurred over a prolonged period, but the result was a mixed population that **did not worship the LORD**. God was not a local deity, as the pagan gods were, but he had a special commitment to the promised land. **So he sent lions among them and they killed some of the people**. This was the third time in 1 and 2 Kings that lions served as instruments of divine judgment (see 1 Kgs. 13:24; 20:36). The new residents of the lands had a distorted, polytheistic understanding of theology, but they recognized that the God of Israel was making a claim on the land. So they sent a message to the king of Assyria, asking for instruction in the worship of the one true God: **The people you deported and resettled in the towns of Samaria do not know what the god of that country requires**.

17:27–33. The king of Assyria responded by sending one of the deported priests to **teach the people what the god of the land requires**. He was almost certainly a devotee of the corrupt Jeroboam worship, indicated by his taking up residence at **Bethel**. So when he taught them **how to worship the LORD**, it was distorted instruction. Their response was to add the Lord to the list of gods being worshiped in the land. Each group had its own gods and local shrines. The names of the various gods are largely unknown outside this passage, but the purpose of the list is not to identify the gods so much as to display the spiritual confusion that filled the land. The land had moved even further away from the exclusive worship of God. Polytheism characterized the land.

The writer of 2 Kings was not just describing past history to his first readers. They would have been appalled as they read about the false worship that now filled the land. But their greatest danger in Babylon was that they would adopt the gods of the land, mix Babylonian customs with their own, and develop a form of worship that blasphemed God.

17:34–41. Such "worship" was not true worship. God would not accept or tolerate syncretism. The only acceptable worship was the exclusive worship of the Lord in accordance with God's law. Three times the writer of 2 Kings repeats the divine command: **Do not worship any other gods or bow down to them** (vv. 35,37–38). This was a message the exiles in the hand of their enemies in Babylon needed to hear, and one that we, in a pluralistic and syncretistic age, need as well. The only acceptable worship is the worship of God alone, in his chosen way.

But were things in Samaria really so different than they had been in Israel before the Assyrian invasion? Or than what they had become in Judah? Or what they had the potential to become in exile in Babylon? The description that ends the account of the northern territory after the Israelites had been removed differed only in degree from what had prevailed before. It was a picture of spiritual confusion from which any worshiper of the Lord would recoil. The warning with which the apostle John ends his first letters rings down to us today: "Dear children, keep yourselves from idols" (1 John 5:21).

MAIN IDEA REVIEW: *Corrupt worship first corrupts us and then condemns us.*

III. CONCLUSION

The Cost of Compromise

A nationally televised memorial service held in a large church featured representatives of various faiths memorializing a girl who had been murdered and attempting to provide comfort. Over and over we were told how her death was bringing us together. But at what cost? There was no comfort of the Scriptures or of Christian hope. In fact, the concept of an "infinite something" presented by at least one participant bore no resemblance to the God of Scripture. Were we celebrating unity or obscuring truth and misleading people?

Once spiritual compromise begins, it continues to grow until we lose our identity by assimilation or we lose our freedom by divine judgment. This is especially true when we are tempted to compromise our exclusive loyalty to God. Whatever King Jeroboam of Israel intended by his golden calves, they corrupted the nation's worship. A corrupt view of God and a corrupted practice of worship led to corrupt and corrupting practices that finally called down the judgment of God.

PRINCIPLES

- Compromise with evil leads to further acts of compromise and corruption.
- When God's judgment comes, resistance is futile.
- The Lord is slow to anger, but he is also sure to anger if we persist in sin.
- God will not accept or tolerate anything less than exclusive loyalty to him.
- We become like what we worship.

APPLICATIONS

- Guard your heart against anything that compromises authentic biblical convictions.
- Let the certainty of divine judgment be a central part of your worldview.
- Be aware of temptation to syncretism. Do you observe this among your friends?

IV. LIFE APPLICATION

Syncretism Then and Now

A bishop in a major denomination recently presided over a Eucharist in which female priests in a procession invoked African and ancient Egyptian deities. Christians in interfaith meetings are told that they can pray using the name of God, but they must not invoke the name of Jesus. A pastor in a mainline denomination compares those who believe that Jesus is the only way of salvation to terrorists: "This is the same kind of absolutism that the September 11 terrorists expressed, claiming that their way is the one, the true, and the only way. This kind of absolutism leads to disrespect, and disrespect leads to intolerance, and intolerance leads to discrimination, and in extreme cases, as we've seen with terrorists, it can lead to violence."

Apparently the extremism of his own words and their incitement to hatred of biblical Christians is morally acceptable! Another liberal church-man boasts of reaching out to people of other faiths without trying to convert them: "We're all children of Abraham and worship the same God."

Our culture has embraced a pervasive tolerance and pluralism that rules all final truth claims as arrogant, inappropriate, and even oppressive. But the demand of the living God for exclusive loyalty and the claims of our Lord Jesus Christ to be the only way to the Father have not evaporated. Certainly, there is a place in our society for interfaith respect and the recognition of diversity. Followers of Christ have a responsibility to honor their Lord not only by the integrity of the message they proclaim but also by the integrity of their obedience to the lifestyle he commanded and displayed. But we also need to be clear in our mind that the spiritual confusion in our society bears a resemblance to conditions in Samaria in the seventh century B.C. Syncre-tism has taken a third-millennium form. Its message not only imperils people by holding out a false promise of "salvation," but it also demeans the glory and majesty of God.

V. PRAYER

Father, voices are attacking all claims to absolute truth and exclusive views of God. Help us to respect those with different understandings. But help us to hold passionately to the truth about yourself revealed supremely in the Lord Jesus, the one Mediator between God and man. Amen.

VI. DEEPER DISCOVERIES

A. The Chronology of Ahaz (16:1–2)

The chronology of 2 Kings is difficult to unravel in the times of Ahaz and his son Hezekiah. If Ahaz came to the throne at twenty and ruled for sixteen years, and if Hezekiah was twenty-five when he came to the throne (18:2), Ahaz would have been only eleven when Hezekiah was born. This is not impossible but highly unlikely. The "seventeenth year of Pekah" (16:1) would have been 735 B.C. But Ahaz's reign extended to 715 B.C., and Jotham died in 732 B.C. There is thus a three-year period of co-reign not included in Ahaz's sixteen years. Ahaz thus shared the throne with his father in 735 B.C., at the age of twenty. From 732 to 715 B.C., he was king in his own right. Chronological issues are too complex for our space constraints. Helpful discussions can be found in the works of Edwin Thiele and Eugene Merrill, and in the commentary by Robert Hubbard.

B. Ahaz and Isaiah (16:5–6)

Isaiah provides an inside view of the attack by Rezin and Pekah in Isaiah 7. Isaiah exhorted the faithless king to trust in the Lord: "Be careful, keep calm and don't be afraid. Do not lose heart because of these two smoldering stubs of firewood" (Isa. 7:4). He then gave Ahaz God's solemn promise that the invasion would not succeed, and within sixty-five years Samaria would be shattered. To confirm this promise, Isaiah encouraged Ahaz to ask of God any sign he desired. Ahaz had already decided to trust Assyria, not God, and he refused to ask for a sign, claiming it would be "testing the LORD." His words were pious, but his heart was rebellious.

Isaiah condemned his unbelief and gave God's sign to Ahaz, the sign of the virgin birth (Isa. 7:14). The essence of the sign was that, in the time it would take for a virgin to conceive, give birth to a child, and grow into early childhood, God would bring Ahaz's "ally," Assyria, against Judah. If Syria was bad, Assyria would be far worse! Events unfolded exactly in this way. But the prophecy of the virgin birth gave more than a time frame for the coming invasion of Assyria; it provided a preview of the miraculous conception of the Messiah. He was the true hope of the nation—a hope fulfilled in the coming of the Savior, our Lord Jesus Christ (Matt. 1:18–25; Luke 1:26–45).

VII. TEACHING OUTLINE

A. INTRODUCTION

1. Lead Story: Feeding the Crocodile
2. Context: The history of Israel had led downhill from the very moment of King Jeroboam's rebellion against God when he set up the golden calves. None of the following kings had reversed that rebellion, and now the debt was due. Judgment day had arrived.
3. Transition: As judgment day arrived in Israel, Judah was anything but a righteous spectator. Its king was pursuing a policy that would land the nation in the same predicament.

B. COMMENTARY

1. Jotham and Ahaz (15:32–16:20)
2. Hoshea of Israel (17:1–6)
3. Israel's Removal from the Land (17:7–23)
4. The Resettlement of the Land (17:24–41)

C. CONCLUSION: THE COST OF COMPROMISE

VIII. ISSUES FOR DISCUSSION

1. The description of life in Samaria in the resettlement depicts a group of religions coexisting and interacting. Many people in the modern world promote such a "parliament of religions." What should be our attitude toward such things in a pluralistic society? What boundaries must be set by those who are loyal to the Lord?

2. How are you tempted to compromise exclusive loyalty to the Lord? How have you dealt with such temptations?

2 Kings 18:1–19:37

Under Attack

"*An* average view of the Christian life is that it means deliverance *from* trouble; it is deliverance *in* trouble, which is a very different thing."

O s w a l d   C h a m b e r s

2 Kings 18:1–19:37

 I N   A   N U T S H E L L

*W*hen a godly king of Judah finally appears in the person of Hezekiah, he and his people find themselves facing the greatest threat the nation had ever known, the attack of Assyria. Without adequate resources to defend Jerusalem, Hezekiah casts himself in faith upon the Lord and receives not only the promise of victory through God's prophet Isaiah, but also the experience of victory through the Lord's special intervention.

Under Attack

I. INTRODUCTION

Living in a War Zone

I had just gotten out of bed to head to a meeting when my phone rang just after 6:00 A.M. It was my son, calling from North Carolina. "Dad, are you up? Turn on the TV quick. Some planes have just flown into the World Trade Center." And so began a day of watching a series of unbelievable events that not even the most creative Hollywood mind had imagined.

When the first fully loaded passenger plane hit one of those massive towers, it was possible to regard it as a terrible accident. But when the second plane hit, it became evident that this was something more. By the time another one hit the Pentagon, and a fourth plane was reported down in Pennsylvania, it was clear that someone had declared war on the United States and was carrying out a series of carefully developed, skillfully executed, and ruthlessly cruel attacks. We had become the target of people who had made themselves our enemy.

The first rule of warfare is "know your enemy." American officials knew that Osama bin Laden was a declared enemy of the United States. But September 11, 2001, made clear that we had underestimated the ability and determination of al-Qaeda, and that had made us very vulnerable.

The Bible makes clear that Christians live in a spiritual war zone. We face three relentless enemies—the world, the flesh, and the devil. They all oppose us but not in the same way. The world attacks our hearts, seducing us to conformity. Satan attacks our minds, driving us to doubt. The flesh attacks our wills, luring us to indulgence. As long as we are on earth, we will face their opposition to a God-honoring life.

There is much to be learned about living under attack by those occasions in the Bible when good people found themselves under great opposition. In this section of 2 Kings, it is a relief to meet a good and godly king. One evidence of the significance of Hezekiah is that his story is told three times in the Old Testament (2 Kgs. 18–20; 2 Chr. 29–32; Isa. 36–39). Each account has its own emphasis, although Isaiah and 2 Kings are very similar. The focus in 2 Kings is on the time when Hezekiah found himself under the onslaught of Assyria, the superpower of his time. It is a story that highlights his faith and the faithfulness of God to those who trust him.

II. COMMENTARY

Under Attack

> **MAIN IDEA:** *When we trust in the living God and his promises, even in the most desperate circumstances, we experience his deliverance.*

Hezekiah's Character (18:1–12)

> **SUPPORTING IDEA:** *Whatever our background, we can make wise choices that please God and build godly character.*

18:1–4. Hezekiah had every reason to view himself as the victim of circumstances. Following his father's death in 715 B.C., he assumed the throne and **reigned in Jerusalem twenty-nine years** until 686 B.C. (the chronology of Hezekiah is difficult; see "Deeper Discoveries"). He had shared royal responsibility with his father since **the third year of Hoshea**, around 728 B.C. Young as he would have been (twelve, if he was twenty-five in 715 B.C.), he had gained firsthand exposure to his father's spiritual rebellion, his pro-Assyrian policies, and the offering of one of his brothers as a sacrifice to a pagan god (16:2–4).

Ahaz had been a disaster as a king and even more so as a father and spiritual influence. In addition, he had seen the brutal power of Assyria as it obliterated the nation of Israel. Hezekiah also would have been aware of his own nation's sin as it followed the destructive path of Israel (17:18–19). It would be easy to excuse Hezekiah if he had simply perpetuated the past, taking the path of least resistance.

Instead, we read the strongest affirmation of a king in 2 Kings, rivaled only by that of his great-grandson Josiah: **He did what was right in the eyes of the LORD, just as his father David**. There are no qualifications. Indeed, we read, for the first time, that **he removed the high places, smashed the sacred stones and cut down the Asherah poles**. Hezekiah was the polar opposite of his father; he was also a king like David who led his nation in external reform and spiritual renewal. His crusade to rebuild his nation is described in considerable detail in 2 Chronicles 29–31.

Moreover, King Hezekiah dealt with a previously unmentioned abuse. The bronze serpent Moses had made under God's direction (Num. 21) had somehow survived, had been given a special name (**Nehushtan**), and had become an object of superstitious worship. Compared to the abuses introduced by his father, it was a relatively minor matter. But not in Hezekiah's mind. He broke the bronze serpent **into pieces**, turning it from an object of worship into scrap metal (see "Deeper Discoveries").

18:5–8. Hezekiah's God-pleasing life was not an accident. He had made godly choices. He had three major characteristics. First, he **trusted in the LORD**. It was the quality of faith that would be most directly tested by the Assyrian onslaught, but it set him apart. The second quality was exclusive loyalty: **He held fast to the LORD** (in contrast to Solomon, who held fast to his wives; 1 Kgs. 11:2). The third quality was Hezekiah's consistent obedience: **he kept the command the LORD had given Moses.** As a result, **the LORD was with him; he was successful in whatever he undertook.**

Hezekiah's father had been a cringing supporter of the pagan superpower. Hezekiah rebelled, probably around 705 B.C., when Sargon died, and he got away with it, although by a narrow margin. The defeat of the Philistines made him a worthy successor to David. He also regained areas lost by his father (2 Chr. 28:18–19).

18:9–12. The writer of 2 Kings takes us back to 724 B.C., when the Assyrian king **Shalmaneser** attacked **Samaria**, and to 722 B.C., when it fell. By reviewing the events of chapter 17, he reminds us of the power of Assyria, against which Hezekiah had rebelled, and of the penalty for sin. He also contrasts Hezekiah with the weakness that characterized the Northern Kingdom. He does not say it in so many words, but he wants us to see the great difference a godly king makes. Israel had **neither listened to the commands** of the Lord **nor carried them out.** Now we will see what could happen when a king listened and obeyed.

Ⓑ Hezekiah's Crisis (18:13–37)

SUPPORTING IDEA: *The ungodly forces always try to strip us of our reliance on the Lord.*

18:13–16. Sennacherib of Assyria, who succeeded Sargon in 705 B.C., had no intention of allowing Hezekiah's rebellion to go unpunished. That would encourage other vassals to attempt the same. At the same time he intended to attack Egypt, and he could not afford to have a hostile state at his rear. So in 701 B.C. he **attacked all the fortified cities of Judah and captured them.** He made his headquarters at **Lachish**, twenty-five miles southwest of Jerusalem, and wrote in his annals that he had Hezekiah "shut up in Jerusalem, his royal capital, like a bird in a cage."

Hezekiah suffered an uncharacteristic but understandable lapse of faith. He sent a message to the Assyrian king, confessing the "sin" of rebellion: **I have done wrong** (literally, "I have sinned"). He then asked the king to **withdraw**, offering to pay whatever price he demanded. The demand was for **three hundred talents of silver and thirty talents of gold.** Hezekiah could pay this amount only by emptying the temple and royal treasuries of their **silver** and stripping off the **gold** he had used to cover the temple doors and doorposts.

Notably absent is any reference to seeking divine guidance or aid. At this moment Hezekiah was like his father, giving in to the pagan power.

18:17-27. The Assyrians didn't play by the rules. Rather than withdrawing, the king sent his military officers with **a large army** to negotiate with Hezekiah. Actually, he had no intention of settling for anything less than Judah's surrender. Hezekiah was an unreliable vassal; Sennacherib could not allow him to survive, and his people would share his fate. The royal representatives met just outside the city walls, near **the aqueduct of the Upper Pool**, a place of strategic importance if the city were to come under siege. It was a place where people gathered for meetings. Sennacherib's team, with his large military force and his high-ranking officials, was meant to intimidate the Judeans. When they demanded a meeting with the king, Hezekiah sent his most trusted officials.

The Assyrian **field commander** was a skilled propagandist. He used a combination of truths, half-truths, threats, promises, and mockery to deride Judean confidence. He not only spoke the Hebrew language; he was well-versed in Judean affairs. His major goal in this opening salvo was to undermine confidence in the Lord and Hezekiah. He wanted to show that trusting anything other than **the great king, the king of Assyria** was foolishness. His question, **On what are you basing this confidence of yours?** was a dagger aimed at the heart of Judean resistance.

The Assyrian commander first mocked Judah's feeble defenses. Their **strategy and military strength** were **only empty words**. Assyria was overwhelmingly superior. He also mocked the idea that Judah was **depending on Egypt** to sustain its rebellion. Egypt was a **splintered reed of a staff, which pierces a man's hand and wounds him if he leans on it**. Egypt was good to look at but not to lean on.

The Assyrian commander also claimed that reliance on the Lord was senseless, since Hezekiah had offended him by removing his **high places and altars**. He was speaking as a pagan, but he was probably tapping in to underlying concern on the part of many Judeans that Hezekiah's reforms had offended some powerful deities and maybe even the Lord.

The field commander's final barb was to point out that Judah's resistance was only bluster. They lacked the power to resist. He offered to supply Jerusalem with **two thousand horses**, knowing they could not find enough soldiers to **put riders on them**. He once again derided Egypt and depending on this nation for horses and chariots. Finally, he claimed that Sennacherib was the agent of the Lord: **The LORD himself told me to march against this country and destroy it.** Since God had used pagan agents to accomplish his purpose against his own people in the past, this claim had some plausibility. In fact, in Isaiah God refers to "the Assyrian, the rod of my anger, in whose hand is the club of my wrath" (Isa. 10:5). It was also a common Assyrian claim that they were an agent of the gods.

At this point Hezekiah's representatives interrupted, claiming that the Assyrians were not playing by the common decencies of diplomacy. They were not negotiating in good faith because they were speaking in a language (**Hebrew**) and at a volume that allowed the general public, **the people on the wall**, to hear. They asked him to **speak to your servants in Aramaic**, the official language of the western Assyrian empire, as well as the usual language of diplomacy.

The Assyrian rejected the request, claiming that the consequences of their discussion would affect the people. The men on the wall would have to pay the harsh price of famine under siege, if they did not submit to the Assyrians. It was a masterful propaganda ploy. The people's confidence in the Lord and Hezekiah must have been shaken as they listened to this exchange. It was an act of verbal terrorism, bolstered by a powerful military presence.

18:28–37. The commander shifted his target, now speaking directly to the assembled crowd in the name of **the king of Assyria**. The main word now became **deliver**, and his specific target was Hezekiah, whom he slandered. He accused Hezekiah of deception by holding out the false hope of deliverance and of intervention from the Lord. He also attacked Hezekiah by claiming that the Assyrians had a better offer. If they would surrender, **every one of you will eat from his own vine and fig tree and drink water from his own cistern.**

Until now the Assyrian commander's attack had been directed at the people's false confidence and at Hezekiah's leadership. But now he crossed into the realm of blasphemy by demeaning God: Judah's God was only one god among many. His statements were consistent with the worldview of polytheism. If the gods of stronger nations had been powerless before him, **How then can the LORD deliver Jerusalem from my hand?** Judah's God was just another god. But ridiculing the Lord would prove to be a fatal mistake.

With that assertion, the public negotiations came to an abrupt end. **The people remained silent**, following the directions of Hezekiah. It was an indication of the respect they had for him. Hezekiah's negotiators returned to the king to make their report, **their clothes torn** as a symbol of their grief and concern. Judah was in real trouble!

C Hezekiah's Response (19:1–34)

> **SUPPORTING IDEA:** *When we are under enemy attack, our refuge is prayerful trust in the Lord.*

19:1–7. If the true test of leadership is performance under pressure, Hezekiah was in the middle of a profound test. His first responses were indicative of the man. After hearing the report, he went downward in humility before the Lord (**he tore his clothes and put on sackcloth**) and outward into his presence (he **went into the temple of the LORD**). He was now aware that Assyria could not be bought off by tribute money; only God could deal with the problem. He went one step further in seeking a word from **the prophet Isaiah**. Many previous kings had been confronted by prophets; rarely did a king seek a prophet out for God's message.

Two of Hezekiah's negotiators, **Eliakim** and **Shebna**, and **the leading priests, all wearing sackcloth**, were sent to the prophet with a message from Hezekiah. The king was realistic about the situation. It was **a day of distress and rebuke and disgrace**. Hezekiah's hope was based on the blasphemy of the Assyrians. This was now an issue of God's honor and glory: **It may be that the LORD your God will hear all the words of the field commander**. The key issue in Hezekiah's mind was that God alone was **the living God**. It was true that Assyria had conquered the "no-gods" of the nations. But the Lord was totally unlike them. The Assyrian king had claimed for himself the title "the great king;" but God was the Great King. Hezekiah asked Isaiah to **pray for the remnant that still survives**.

Isaiah's response came quickly and with divine authority: **Do not be afraid of what you have heard**. The issue was not between Hezekiah and Sennacherib but between Assyria and the Lord: they **have blasphemed me**.

God would do two things. First, he would cause Assyria's king to withdraw. Jerusalem would be spared as a result. This would be entirely the work of God; Hezekiah would contribute nothing. The second promise was that the Lord would bring about Sennacherib's death in Nineveh: **there I will have him cut down with the sword**. The Assyrian king had reduced God to the status of a local god. He would discover that God was the universal Lord whom Sennacherib could not escape even in his homeland.

19:8–13. The Assyrians escalated the attack on God. The commander had earlier called Hezekiah a deceiver (18:29); now he accused the Lord of deception: **Do not let the god you depend on deceive you when he says, "Jerusalem will not be handed over to the king of Assyria."** The Assyrians had left a trail of defeated gods and defeated kings. How could Judah imagine that its fate and the fate of its God would be any different? The Lord's character had become the main issue.

19:14–19. Hezekiah's view of the Lord was different from that of the pagan king, as he revealed by his response to the Assyrian letter. Having read it, **he went up to the temple . . . and spread it out before the LORD**. The temple was where God dwelt in a special way among his people. By spreading the letter before the Lord, Hezekiah was not displaying a crude belief in God's physicality but a profound sense of trust and dependence. Earlier he had asked the prophet Isaiah to pray (v. 4); now he himself prayed.

Hezekiah's prayer is a striking illustration of the principles of effective prayer. He began with adoration of God. In spite of the claims of the Assyrians, he was the **God of Israel**, but he was also the exalted, universal, unrivaled, all-powerful Lord. He was the Creator of all things, having **made heaven and earth**.

Having begun with praise, Hezekiah expressed his sense of urgency. The heaping up of appeals to hear and see reflect the intensity of need. Before God, he was realistic about his situation. He was, on the one hand, aware of Assyrian power. He did not minimize their reign of terror or the history of their conquests. The major feature of Hezekiah's prayer was his passion for God's glory and honor. The Assyrian had dared to **insult the living God**. Hezekiah obviously desired deliverance from his enemy. But more was at stake than the peace and security of Jerusalem: **O LORD . . . deliver us from his hand, so that all kingdoms on earth may know that you alone . . . are God**. Prayer that is more concerned with God's glory than with our peace, prosperity, or pleasure is prayer that the Lord delights to answer.

19:20–34. We are not specifically told how much time elapsed before Isaiah responded to Hezekiah. But the king's prayer led directly to a prophetic declaration. The translation of the NIV in 2 Kings 19:20–21 does not show this connection as clearly as the way the exact same Hebrew phrase is translated in Isaiah 37:21: "Because you have prayed to me concerning Sennacherib king of Assyria, this is the word the LORD has spoken against him." That word is recorded in verses 20–28, which contain a taunt song against the foolish pretensions of the Assyrian king. It is followed by a sign of assurance to Hezekiah in verses 29–31 and a promise of protection for Jerusalem in verses 32–34.

Isaiah also had a word of hope for Hezekiah. Jerusalem would not be destroyed. Good times were ahead, because **the zeal of the LORD Almighty will accomplish this**. Lest there be any doubt, Isaiah spelled out God's promise in the most specific terms. With a threefold **he will not**, Isaiah declared that not only would Sennacherib not enter the city; he would not besiege it or even attack it. God himself was the city's salvation. Judah's hope was never its merit. It was always God's commitment to his own glory and his faithfulness to his covenant purposes. Assyria's arrogance could not stand in the face of the Lord's character and his covenant with his people.

D God's Intervention (19:35–37)

SUPPORTING IDEA: *The Lord's faithfulness to his promises is his people's source of confidence against the enemy.*

19:35–37. The account of the attack of Sennacherib has been told with a level of detail rare in 2 Kings. But the outcome is told with great brevity. The

Lord fulfilled his promise of 19:7 precisely. The "spirit" that caused Sennacherib to break camp and retreat came because of an angelic visit reminiscent of the visit of the angel of death on the first Passover night (Exod. 12:29–30). Details are sparse. We are told only that **the angel of the LORD . . . put to death a hundred and eighty-five thousand men in the Assyrian camp**. Those not directly affected slept through the night, but they awoke to find dead bodies everywhere! No wonder Sennacherib **broke camp and withdrew**. There is no mention of such a massive death toll in the Assyrian annals. This is hardly surprising since no ancient king would record a disaster of such magnitude.

One final piece needed to fall into place. Sennacherib had returned to Nineveh. Twenty years later, in 681 B.C., **while he was worshiping in the temple of his god Nisroch**, his sons assassinated him. The Assyrian chronicles record that he was killed by his sons in a rebellion and succeeded by another son, Esarhaddon. The irony must not be missed. Hezekiah, in complete distress, had gone into the temple of his God—and he found help and deliverance. Sennacherib, the "great king," had gone into the temple of his god—but he found death from his own family in the presence of a god of whom he had foolishly boasted.

MAIN IDEA REVIEW: *When we trust in the living God and his promises, even in the most desperate circumstances, we experience his deliverance.*

III. CONCLUSION

The Posture of Victory

When the crisis comes, our understanding and experience of God will make all the difference. Hezekiah began to prepare for the day of crisis the very first time he made a choice that moved him away from the path of his father to the path of a God-pleasing life. He met the supreme challenge of his life fortified with years of walking in obedience to his Lord. By the time the Assyrians arrived, he was a man who knew God.

When the enemy attacks a follower of Christ, his prime target will always be our trust and confidence in the Lord. He will seek to shake our confidence in God's goodness and power. The antidote for this attack is a knowledge of God grounded in his promises and forged in the school of experience. But no matter how experienced we may be in the faith, the posture of counterattack is always on our knees. Hezekiah received victory over Sennacherib not on the battlefield but in the temple, as he spread his letter before God and poured out his heart to him. He found deliverance for his nation as a man of prayer.

PRINCIPLES

- A person who trusts and obeys the Lord will make God-honoring choices.
- The enemy will use every method to undermine trust in the Lord.
- The enemy will attack God by slandering his people.
- The major issue in times of attack is always the character of God.
- In our weakness, humble dependence on the Lord is a sure place of refuge and strength.
- Our confidence is based on God's commitment to his own glory and his faithfulness to his promises.

APPLICATIONS

- The antidote for the enemy's attack is a worthy view of God; make it a priority to know him.
- Develop a passion for God that is greater than your commitment to your personal safety.
- Bring your problems into the presence of the Lord and place them before him.

IV. LIFE APPLICATION

"Pray-ers" and "Do-ers"

Although prayer is the most important thing we can do, it is rarely the *only* thing we can do. If we read this account as suggesting that all Hezekiah did was pray, we misread it. Aware that Assyria would attack, he prepared his city and his people, as 2 Chronicles 32:2–8 indicates. He had a long tunnel dug through the rock from the Gihon Spring to the Pool of Siloam to protect the water supply (2 Kgs. 20:20). He also rebuilt the existing city walls, added exterior walls, reorganized his military, and rearmed the people. But in the midst of these preparations, his message to his people was "do not be afraid or discouraged because of the king of Assyria and the vast army with him, for there is a greater power with us than with him. With him is only the arm of flesh, but with us is the LORD our God to help us and to fight our battles" (2 Chr. 32:7–8). Hezekiah knew the need for preparation, but he also knew that plans have limits. Deliverance would have to come from the Lord.

We need to pray first, and we need to pray last. Sometimes all we can do is pray. But more often, we can also plan *and* prepare. Christians tend to fall into two opposing camps—the "do-ers" and the "pray-ers." Hezekiah shows us we need to be both.

V. PRAYER

Lord, when the enemy comes or when problems threaten to overwhelm us, our first instinct is to yield to despair or to rush into frantic activity. Teach us the ways of Hezekiah: to humble ourselves before you and to cast our cares and needs upon you. Amen.

VI. DEEPER DISCOVERIES

A. The Chronology of Hezekiah (18:1–2)

Hezekiah's chronology is difficult to reconstruct. He became king in the third year of Hoshea (around 728 B.C.). But 18:13 indicates that Sennacherib invaded in Hezekiah's fourteenth year, an event that happened in 701 B.C. This would make the first year of Hezekiah's reign 715 B.C. Some interpreters have suggested that verse 13 has suffered from a corruption and should read "twenty-fourth." That solution has some attraction, but it lacks any manuscript evidence. Others have postulated that the 728 B.C. date refers to a co-regency with his father, and his sole reign is to be dated from 715 B.C. This seems the far more likely solution. But it also raises another question: Are Hezekiah's twenty-nine years to be dated from about 728 B.C., putting his death around 698 B.C. or from 715 B.C., putting his death around 687 B.C.? I have opted for the latter solution. For details, see the works of Thiele, Merrill, and Hubbard.

B. Nehushtan (18:4)

During Israel's wilderness years, the people complained constantly, blaming God and Moses. On one occasion the Lord sent poisonous serpents that bit the people. When the people confessed their sin and asked Moses to intercede for them, God instructed him to "make a snake and put it up on a pole; anyone who is bitten can look at it and live" (Num. 21:8). Moses made a bronze (*nehoshet*) snake (*nahash*), which came to be called "Nehushtan." At some unknown time, this bronze object became a relic or a fetish, endowed superstitiously by the people with magical properties. The people turned it into an object of veneration. Hezekiah's destruction of this idol is a powerful reminder of the danger of religious relics.

VII. TEACHING OUTLINE

A. INTRODUCTION

1. Lead Story: Living in a War Zone

2. Context: Hezekiah came to the throne at a difficult time. His father had debased the nation internally. Externally it faced the power of Assyria, which had just destroyed Israel. Hezekiah shows the difference a godly leader can make.
3. Transition: The change from Ahaz, Judah's worst king so far, to Hezekiah, its best king, is stunning and encouraging. We are first given an overview of Hezekiah's life, then a detailed look at his defining moment.

B. COMMENTARY

1. Hezekiah's Character (18:1–12)
2. Hezekiah's Crisis (18:13–37)
3. Hezekiah's Response (19:1–34)
4. God's Intervention (19:35–37)

C. CONCLUSION: THE POSTURE OF VICTORY

VIII. ISSUES FOR DISCUSSION

1. How do you account for a Hezekiah, a faithful follower of the Lord, in a very hostile setting? What makes a person stand out spiritually and refuse to conform to what he sees around him?
2. Describe a time when you felt most like Hezekiah with the enemy at your gate and no apparent solution. What did you learn about yourself and the Lord in this situation? What could you have learned from the example of Hezekiah?

2 Kings 20:1–21:26

A Study in Contrasts

Quote

"*When* a man is getting better, he understands more and more clearly the evil that is still left in him. When a man is getting worse, he understands his own badness less and less. A moderately bad man knows he is not very good; a thoroughly bad man thinks he is all right. . . . Good people know about both good and evil; bad people do not know about either."

C .   S .   L e w i s

HISTORICAL PROFILE: THE KINGS OF ASSYRIA

Sennacherib
- Reigned 705–681 B.C.
- Attacked Hezekiah and Jerusalem 701 B.C.
- Moved his capital to Nineveh and assimilated Babylonia into the Assyrian orb
- Assassinated by two of his sons in 681 B.C. (2 Kgs. 19:37–38)

Esarhaddon
- Reigned 681–669 B.C.
- Seized power after his father's assassination
- Listed Manasseh among his vassals in his annals
- Appointed Ashurbanipal prince over Assyria, and another son, Samas-sum-ukin ruler of the province of Babylon

Ashurbanipal
- Reigned 669–627 B.C.
- Defeated the Egyptians in 664 B.C., when Manasseh is listed as one of his allies
- Took Manasseh captive to Babylon and later released him (2 Chr. 33:10–13)

- Had increasing trouble with the Mesopotamian states, led by Babylon
- Made his son his co-regent in 630 B.C. After his death Assyria weakened, and the empire began to collapse under internal pressures and the rise of Egypt and Babylon

2 Kings 20:1–21:26

IN A NUTSHELL

At last we have seen the impact a good king can have for good upon his nation. Perhaps we have reached a turning point in Judah's life. But after learning ways the Lord prepared Hezekiah for his great crisis, we are plunged back into the depths of corruption by the actions of Hezekiah's son.

A Study in Contrasts

I. INTRODUCTION

Family Mysteries

*H*annah Whitall Smith was the author of one of the most popular Christian devotional books of all time, *The Christian's Secret of a Happy Life,* first published in 1875. By 1894 it had already sold ten million copies. In her time she was a sought-after speaker at "Higher Life" conferences. The title of her book could lead a casual reader to believe that she had lived a trouble-free life. In fact, she had more than her share of heartaches. Her husband, a famous preacher, was involved in several moral scandals, suffered from bouts of depression and mental illness, and finally abandoned the faith.

Hannah had three children who survived until adulthood. Her oldest daughter Mary abandoned her Roman Catholic husband and her two children for an extramarital affair. Her daughter Alys married the outspokenly atheistic and hedonistic philosopher Bertrand Russell and abandoned the faith. Her son Logan became a well-known writer who moved in circles hostile to the Christian faith and had no place in his life for the Lord Jesus.

Hannah was not without her faults, but one cannot help but wonder how someone who was of so much help to others could fail to see even one of her children follow her in faith. Certainly her husband's negative influence played an important role, as did some elements of Hannah's own defective theology.

The contrast presented to us in the chapters before us is far more dramatic. Ahaz was the worst king to his time in Judah's history, a man who "promoted wickedness in Judah" (2 Chr. 28:19). Yet his son Hezekiah was the most godly king since the time of David. Hezekiah brought revival and reform to his nation. But Hezekiah's son Manasseh was even worse than Ahaz, setting out to undo every one of his father's reforms. Manasseh's son Amon would be "a chip off the old block," doing evil like his father. But Amon's son Josiah rivaled Hezekiah for personal godliness and spiritual leadership.

If ever a passage reminded us that parents may influence their children but they do not determine their character or faith, it is this one. The passage does not pretend to explore the intriguing family dynamics that must have been involved. It does call us to accept responsibility for our own choices and to avoid falling into an unbiblical deterministic or victimization mind-set. At the same time it depicts a nation bent on self-destruction, quick to follow those who have led it into sin, in spite of the legacy of godly leaders.

II. COMMENTARY

A Study in Contrasts

> **MAIN IDEA:** *Our relation to God determines whether we live constructive lives or destructive lives.*

 ## Hezekiah's Healing (20:1–11)

> **SUPPORTING IDEA:** *When we turn to the Lord in our weakness, he hears our prayer.*

In 701 B.C. Assyria arrived at the gates of Jerusalem, determined to wipe out the reign and the realm of King Hezekiah. The most godly and gifted king since David, Hezekiah found himself "shut up like a caged bird" facing extinction, with no assets to rely on except God's promises. Chapters 18–19 of 2 Kings told the story of God's miraculous deliverance of his embattled people.

We would expect chapter 20 to pick up the story from there, describing the final fourteen years of Hezekiah's role. But they don't. The writer does here what he does nowhere else in 2 Kings. The key to understanding these episodes is to recognize that they are flashbacks, events that occurred before Sennacherib arrived on the scene. They tell us how the Lord had prepared Hezekiah for his great crisis, building within him the character and spiritual confidence that became his resource under the attack of Sennacherib.

20:1–3. The phrase **in those days** indicates the time of the following episode in only the most general terms. But verse 6 provides two important clues: the episode occurred fifteen years before Hezekiah's death, and it preceded the attack of Assyria in 701 B.C. Since Hezekiah died around 687 B.C., this puts Hezekiah's illness in 702, when he was about forty years old. The writer gives no details of Hezekiah's illness, simply indicating that he **became ill and was at the point of death**. The only medical symptom indicated was some kind of skin eruption ("boil," v. 7).

The prophet Isaiah **went to him**, apparently sent by God, with the warning that the disease was terminal: **Put your house in order, because you are going to die.** This was a call to Hezekiah to attend to his personal and royal affairs. Time was short, since death was imminent. But his death at a relatively young age was not said to be caused by some sin in his life. There was no call for repentance and no instinctive response of confession.

The news stunned Hezekiah. He **turned his face to the wall**, apparently seeking privacy and wishing to hide his emotions. More important, he **prayed to the LORD.** The prayer was not a prayer of confession, and it did not contain a spoken request. It was an appeal to the Lord based on his covenant faithfulness to his Lord. We should not see in this prayer a claim of self-righteousness but a recognition that the law sometimes promised longevity to the obedient (Deut. 4:40; 5:16; 30:15–20). It was also a response to the Lord's requirement that a Davidic king must "walk before me in integrity of heart and uprightness, as David your father did" (1 Kgs. 9:4). Hezekiah had done what God had commanded. This was not a rote prayer: he **wept bitterly.**

20:4–7. God's response came quickly: **Before Isaiah had left the middle court** (the intermediate area of the palace-temple complex), **the word of the LORD came to him.** The message came as an oracle from the Lord himself, and it was grounded in the covenant promise made to David. God not only hears our words; he sees our tears. The answer went far beyond the request. On the most direct level, God promised healing and a quick recovery. The Lord went one step beyond to promise the extension of Hezekiah's life. For a person facing imminent death, this was a marvelous promise.

The deliverance of Hezekiah from imminent death became the basis of God's promise for the nation: **I will deliver you . . . from the hand of . . . Assyria.** Assyria was not yet present, but Hezekiah was being prepared for their arrival. They would arrive soon enough, and with them the apparent "terminal illness" of the nation. But the Lord had placed his name in Jerusalem and had made covenant promises to David. It was thus for his own sake and for David's sake that he would act. This was the promise with which the Lord armed Hezekiah for the encounter described in chapters 18–19.

God's miraculous healing does not always occur in the absence of medical means. Thus, Isaiah ordered the king's attendants to **prepare a poultice of figs.** Dried figs were used medicinally in the Ancient Near East. The healing did not come from the figs, but it was somehow linked to the application of the poultice. It was placed on the boil or skin eruption.

20:8–11. Even before the poultice was applied, Hezekiah asked for a **sign** to confirm the divine word. The reason is not indicated, but the Lord granted his request and even offered a choice. The sign would be more impressive than the healing! Isaiah offered the alternatives: **Shall the shadow** (of the sun) **go forward ten steps, or shall it go back ten steps?** The reference to the ten steps, later said to be **on the stairway of Ahaz,** is enigmatic, but it apparently referred to a structure that served as a kind of sundial. The shadow moved as the sun moved across the sky. Hezekiah chose what he thought to be the harder and the more relevant (the promise was about turning back time): **Have it go back ten steps.** If God could turn back time, he could surely turn back disease.

In response to Hezekiah's request, **the LORD made the shadow go back the ten steps it had gone down on the stairway of Ahaz.** We are to think of this as a miracle of refraction, not of the rotation of the earth, since it was a local phenomenon (2 Chr. 32:24). But it must have been a powerful faith-building experience for Hezekiah. It fortified him for his coming encounter with Sennacherib. In his weakness he had experienced the power and received the promise of God.

B Hezekiah's Failure (20:12–21)

SUPPORTING IDEA: *When we respond to God's rebuke in our failure, he sustains us.*

20:12–13. One of the strange habits of the human heart is to feel proud about what we receive by grace. When the Lord does something special for us, we are tempted to believe it is about us, rather than about him. The writer of 2 Chronicles tells us that "Hezekiah's heart was proud" (2 Chr. 32:25). The writer of 2 Kings describes one form it took. A delegation arrived from **Merodach-Baladan son of Baladan king of Babylon**, bearing **letters and a gift**. Merodach had been deposed by Sargon of Assyria in 709 B.C., after having reigned from 721 to 710 B.C. He regained power after Sargon's death for nine months in 704–703 B.C. and then was deposed by Sennacherib. This was the first appearance of Babylon as a player in the politics of the region, and Hezekiah would have had no idea of the ominous role Babylon was to play in the future life of his nation.

Merodach sent a delegation **because he had heard of Hezekiah's illness**. The parallel passages in Isaiah 39:1 and 2 Chronicles 32:31 make clear that he had heard of the illness, the healing, and the miraculous sign. The news of Hezekiah's healing had spread far and wide. But there was probably a more basic reason for Babylon's interest in Hezekiah. The king of Judah had rebelled against Assyria, and Merodach was canvassing for potential allies. He was hoping to enlist Hezekiah in an anti-Assyrian movement.

Hezekiah's welcome was wholehearted. It is not clear whether he was naïve about Merodach's intentions or whether he was seriously interested in an alliance. What is clear is that he was flattered by the attention of a more powerful king, and he sought to impress him by showing them **everything found among his treasures**. No wise king at any time reveals all his state secrets, even to his most trusted ally. At their first meeting Hezekiah revealed all his possessions to pagan visitors in a pathetic attempt to make an impression and perhaps in a faithless attempt to enter an alliance.

20:14–19. Isaiah was not present during this visit, but he came to Hezekiah demanding to know the identity of his visitors, their message, and what they had seen. Because Hezekiah recognized Isaiah as an authentic prophet, he answered his questions. The prophet's answer made the foolishness of Hezekiah's actions clear. He had treated Babylon as a trusted ally; they would, in fact, prove to be a deadly enemy who would destroy the nation:

The time will surely come when everything . . . will be carried off to Babylon. Isaiah did not suggest that this would happen because of Hezekiah's actions. It was a rebuke of Hezekiah for putting trust in a pagan nation without seeking divine direction, and for his personal foolishness in seeking to impress them in such a nonsensical way. Showing them state treasures was an invitation to attack, even more than it was an incentive to alliance. The coming disaster would be total, but it would fall on his descendants, not on Hezekiah.

It would be a full century before this judgment would fall on Judah. Hezekiah was not given any specific information on how long it would be. He would have known, however, that Babylon did not have the military power in his time to present this kind of danger. It must have been startling to learn that Assyria did not pose the greatest danger. He had already been told that the Lord would deliver him from Assyria, but this did not mean that Judah would escape divine judgment. Implicit in Isaiah's words was the warning that whatever we turn to as a substitute for the Lord will turn on us. What we pursue as an immediate solution, apart from the Lord's guidance, may prove to be a long-term catastrophe.

Hezekiah's response to Isaiah's message can be read in two different ways: **"The word of the LORD you have spoken is good," Hezekiah replied. For he thought, "Will there not be peace and security in my lifetime?"** Some find Hezekiah guilty of self-centered concern only for his own well-being. At least he wouldn't have to deal with Babylon's attack. Others believe Hezekiah was responding in humble submission to God's righteous judgment on his nation. It seems more in keeping with the tenor of his life to see this as a mixture of pious resignation and genuine gratitude. He submitted to God's rebuke rather than fighting it so that when the Assyrians came, he could call upon the Lord's help.

Whatever Hezekiah's emotions, he was confident that the Lord would deliver him from the Assyrians and that Babylon would not be a threat in his lifetime. This confidence was also preparation for his ensuing encounter with Sennacherib. Hezekiah may also have hoped that the Lord's delay of judgment would provide time for a national repentance that would forestall divine judgment.

20:20–21. The formula that concludes the account of Hezekiah's life follows the usual format of the writer of 2 Kings. The reference to **the pool and the tunnel by which he brought water into the city** is a reference to the remarkable 1,770-foot tunnel that took water from the Gihon Spring to the Pool of Siloam in the lower part of Jerusalem. Built to enable the city to withstand the Assyrian siege (2 Chr. 32:30), it still can be seen today. However, the achievements of Hezekiah that mattered most were not physical but spiritual and political. He instituted spiritual reforms in a nation that had long wallowed in spiritual rebellion.

Manasseh's Sin and Rebellion (21:1–18)

SUPPORTING IDEA: *When we turn from the Lord in deliberate rebellion, we unleash great corruption.*

21:1–2. Spiritual integrity is not inherited. Hezekiah was succeeded on the throne by a man who has the notoriety of being the worst king ever to rule in Judah. Manasseh came to the throne in 697 B.C. at the age of twelve, in a co-regency with his father. It seems that Hezekiah, knowing that he had limited years, appointed his son co-regent at an early age. Ironically, Manasseh was the longest reigning Judean king. During his tenure Assyria remained the dominant power, and Manasseh adopted a pro-Assyrian policy. He is mentioned in the Assyrian chronicles twice.

The first time Manasseh is included in a list of vassals who supplied building materials for Esarhaddon (681–669 B.C.), and the second he is depicted as aiding Ashurbanipal (669–627 B.C.) in a campaign into Egypt. Toward the end of his life, Manasseh incurred the wrath of the Assyrians, who took him in shackles to Babylon (2 Chr. 33:11). He was eventually released back to Jerusalem.

The evil done by Manasseh is something the writer of 2 Kings does not want us to miss. His evil was not just equated with that of Ahab and Israel, as had been true of Ahaz (2 Kgs. 16:2–3). Rather, we are told that Manasseh **did evil in the eyes of the LORD, following the detestable practices of the nations the LORD had driven out before the Israelites.** These Canaanite detestable practices ("abominations") were the antithesis of all that his father had pursued, and he seemed to have set out deliberately to undo every reform his father had instituted. The extent of Manasseh's evil rings like a bell through the passage: "He did much evil in the eyes of the LORD" (v. 6) . . . "Manasseh led them astray" (v. 9) . . . "He has done more evil than the Amorites" (v. 11) . . . "they have done evil in my eyes" (v. 15) . . . "Manasseh also shed so much innocent blood" (v. 16).

When the Babylonian onslaught finally came, we are told that "these things happened to Judah according to the LORD's command, in order to remove them from his presence because of the sins of Manasseh and all he had done" (24:4).

21:3–9. Lest we have any doubt about the extent of Manasseh's spiritual rebellion, we are given a catalogue of his sins. In his rebellion against his father and his father's God, he became a thorough pagan. The first sin overturned the very thing that made his father distinctive: **He rebuilt the high places his father Hezekiah had destroyed.** He also imitated Ahab by erecting

altars to Baal . . . as Ahab . . . had done. Baalism now had received state sanction in Judah. The days of Athaliah had returned. Manasseh also introduced pagan astral worship that was popular with the Assyrians but abhorrent to God.

Manasseh's major attack was on the sanctity of the temple. His intention was to pollute the temple with polytheism. **He built altars in the temple of the LORD** to gods other than the Lord and **altars to all the starry hosts.** Both Jeremiah (Jer. 7:18) and Ezekiel (Ezek. 8:1–18) would describe the penetration of idol worship into the very heart of the temple, an outcome for which Manasseh was primarily responsible. Manasseh also followed Ahaz in the outrage of child sacrifice, putting **his own son in the fire.** Added to this were other pagan practices, such as **sorcery and divination**, and consulting **mediums and spiritists.**

Manasseh may have led the way, but the people followed him eagerly. Their sin was intended and determined, not accidental. To reinforce the defiant nature of their sin, the writer of 2 Kings takes us back to the great promise God had made when he established Jerusalem and the temple as the place of his name: **I will not again make the feet of the Israelites wander from the land I gave their forefathers.** The temple was a fulfillment of the Abrahamic promise as well as the Davidic covenant. But there was a condition: they had to keep God's law. The deliberate nature of their covenant violation meant that the promise could not be kept and that exile was now inevitable. If Manasseh had seduced the people, they had followed willingly and wholeheartedly.

21:10–15. Just as the Lord had raised up Elijah and Elisha to oppose and pronounce judgment on Ahab and Israel, he now raised up unnamed individuals, **his servants the prophets,** to pronounce the divine verdict on Manasseh and Judah. The summary of the prophetic indictment begins and ends with a statement of the extent of the sin involved. At the start we are told again of the extent of Manasseh's sin. It concludes by declaring the participation of the general public: **they have done evil in my eyes and have provoked me to anger.** We are reaching the end of a long trail of rebellion.

In between the indictment comes the divine sentence. The repeated **I will** emphasized that the judgment was coming from the hand of God. He would use the same standards he had used against Samaria and Ahab, **the measuring line** and **the plumb line**, and the disaster would be as complete because he would give **their enemies** and **all their foes** free reign. The Lord did not indicate when this judgment would come, but he left no doubt that it would happen. The destruction of Judah and Jerusalem was now inevitable.

21:16. We are given one more insight into the depth of Manasseh's depravity. He not only engaged in idolatry; he engaged in violence. His victims were probably those who opposed his descent into paganism. It was a purge of those loyal to the Lord who had enthusiastically followed the reforms put in place by his father. State-sponsored terror and the elimination of all who opposed his pagan ways is indicated. With the reign of Manasseh, Judah had turned a corner. It was now headed for certain judgment.

21:17–18. The end of Manasseh's long reign is given in a formulaic pattern, typical of the book, with a final reminder of **the sin he committed.** The identity of **the garden of Uzza** is unknown. But there is an ominous association with the man whom God had struck down in sudden judgment (2 Sam. 6:1–7). What is missing from 2 Kings is any reference to Manasseh's personal deportation to Babylon, his repentance and recognition of the Lord, and his subsequent return to Jerusalem, where he carried out many reforms. These are described in 2 Chronicles 33:10–17 (see "Deeper Discoveries"), but it is likely that the writer of 2 Kings viewed them as late, short-lived, and limited. The conversion had great personal significance, but little national importance. The die had been cast.

Amon's Sin and Rebellion (21:19–26)

SUPPORTING IDEA: *If we imitate our parents' ungodliness, we are held accountable.*

21:19–26. Amon was only **twenty-two** when he came to the throne. Since his father had ruled for fifty-five years, he was presumably one of Manasseh's younger sons. Morally, politically, and especially spiritually, he was every bit his father's son: **He did evil in the eyes of the LORD, as his father Manasseh had done.** Paganism and polytheism had now become engrained in the fabric of Judean life. Whenever the repentance of Manasseh occurred, it was the rebellious Manasseh, not the repentant Manasseh, that his son imitated.

Manasseh held power for fifty-five years; Amon for only two. Then a palace coup took place: **Amon's officials conspired against him and assassinated the king in his palace.** There is no way to be sure of the motives of the assassins. They did not act for spiritual reasons. It was either a vicious grab for power or, more likely, an anti-Assyrian, pro-Egyptian conspiracy. But the people did not allow the coup leaders to have their way. They **killed all who had plotted against King Amon, and they made Josiah his son king in his place.** The people of the land consistently supported the Davidic dynasty (see 11:12–20; 14:19–21). Amon thus passed off the scene unlamented.

MAIN IDEA REVIEW: *Our relation to God determines whether we live constructive lives or destructive lives.*

III. CONCLUSION

The Greatest Difference

It is hard to imagine a greater contrast than that between Hezekiah and Manasseh, father and son. The central issue was not their relation to each other but their relation to God. Hezekiah had a God he could trust, even against the most formidable military power of the day. His confidence in God drove him to order his life by God's word, even if it meant going against the tide of his culture, the example of his father, and the realities of politics. His commitment to the Lord made Hezekiah a courageous leader who changed the course of his nation for the better.

Hezekiah's son was a stranger to God. He was only one god among many to Manasseh. His standards were too rigid, his requirements too restrictive, his worship too nonsensual. Manasseh sampled what all the other gods had to offer, but he did not find any god powerful enough to give him courage against the Assyrians. They were the real powers in his world, and he submitted to the rules they set. Besides, much of what Manasseh represented appealed to the appetites of many people in his culture, and if they wanted it, he would supply it. As a result, he changed the course of his nation. But it was a course change that put the people on a collision course with disaster.

Hezekiah and Manasseh shared much in common—genetically, culturally, and ethnically. But what they did not share was a common understanding and relation to God. And that made all the difference.

PRINCIPLES

- Personal crises are often ways in which the Lord prepares us for future challenges.
- When we turn to the Lord in our weakness, he hears our prayers.
- Pride remains the great enemy of all of us, even the godly.
- When we respond humbly to the Lord's rebuke in our failure, he sustains us.
- When we turn from the Lord in deliberate rebellion, it leads to deep corruption.

APPLICATIONS

- Think of your trials not only as immediate problems but also as times of training for what the Lord has in store for your future.
- Turn to the Lord in your times of need.
- Respond humbly to the Lord's rebuke.

- Guard your heart, knowing that you are capable of great evil if you turn away from the Lord.

IV. LIFE APPLICATION

The Marks of a Leader

Leadership is all about influence. Both Hezekiah and Manasseh were significant leaders, but one was a disaster, the other a blessing. Not everyone in a position of leadership is a good leader. Some are maintainers who just hold a position and fill a role. Others are manipulators. They use their position for their own selfish goals, concerned with the benefit of an exclusive few. They are willing to see harm done to the many for the benefit of their circle. The collapse of Enron in 2001 revealed that a corrupt view of leadership responsibility had infected many people in high levels of leadership in some corporations. Authentic leaders are people who do the right thing. They commit themselves to godly priorities. And they lead with integrity, by example.

Hezekiah is a model of a godly leader. He had the courage of his convictions, and he was willing to take great risks to destroy the evil things in his nation. He had a vision of his people becoming what God intended them to be. His character was in tune with his message. He was committed to God's promises, seeking the guidance of God's prophet and submitting to the rebuke of Isaiah when it was appropriate. Most of all, he was humble before God, relying upon him. He was a man of strength and vision who knew how to be weak as well as strong. We will make a difference as leaders if we follow the pattern of Hezekiah.

V. PRAYER

Father, thank you for your willingness to hear and answer when we call on you in our need. But when you answer our prayers, help us to respond in gratitude, not pride. Help us to remember that it is about you and your grace, not us and our merit. Amen.

VI. DEEPER DISCOVERIES

A. Death in the Old Testament (20:3)

One of the great truths of the Christian faith is "the appearing of our Savior, Christ Jesus, who has destroyed death and has brought life and immortality to light through the gospel" (2 Tim. 1:10). The resurrection of the Lord Jesus made everything different. We now know that, for a genuine believer in the Lord Jesus, "to die is gain" since it is "to depart and be with Christ" (Phil.

1:21,23). Old Testament saints had no such certainty. Death was, at best, mysterious—like sleep. It brought fear and terror (Ps. 55:4–5); nowhere in the Old Testament is it embraced with a sense of hope. There are glimmers of hope in passages such as Psalms 16:10–11; 49:15; 73:24; and Daniel 12:2, the experiences of Enoch and Elijah, and the confession of Job in Job 19:25–27. But there is nothing like the bright light of resurrection hope. Hezekiah's tears are understandable in such a context.

B. Hezekiah's Tunnel (20:20)

Hezekiah's tunnel (the Siloam Tunnel) contains an official inscription at its entrance to commemorate its completion. It is the only inscription in biblical Hebrew that exists from the first temple period. The inscription describes the workmen, working from opposite ends of the tunnel, hearing the voices of one another because of a natural fissure in the rock. "And on the day when the tunnel was cut through, the stone cutters struck toward one another, ax against ax. Then the water flowed from the source to the pool for 1200 cubits." It is possible to walk through the tunnel today and to observe water running through it. The spring gushes (Hb., *gihon*) at different times in the day, so the water level varies.

C. Manasseh's Repentance (21:17–18)

The lack of any mention in 2 Kings of Manasseh's repentance has led many interpreters to dismiss it as an invention of the writer of 2 Chronicles (see 2 Chr. 33:10–17). But it is a mistake to believe that the writer of each book had the same purpose and therefore needed to choose the same materials. Biographers and historians select from a vast amount of material the facts that support their major argument. The purpose of 2 Chronicles was to show the centrality of the temple and the way in which a right relation to God, demonstrated by a proper response to the temple, determined the nation's blessing. In such a context Manasseh's changed relation to the temple, belated and limited as it was, had great significance.

The writer of 2 Kings was more concerned to show why the exile had taken place. The depth of Manasseh's descent into sin—and the fact that his belated repentance had no effect on his son who followed him—made the exile certain. He had a long-range, national view. Manasseh's repentance was "too little, too late."

VII. TEACHING OUTLINE

A. INTRODUCTION

1. Lead Story: Family Mysteries

2. Context: We have had the story of Hezekiah's great deliverance, but now the writer of 2 Kings surprises us in two ways: by giving us two episodes that precede the great crisis with Assyria and with the kind of son who followed Hezekiah.
3. Transition: We sometimes see a person performing at a high level of competence but forget the training that brought him to that point. We are given an insight into the way the Lord refined Hezekiah through discipline.

B. COMMENTARY
1. Hezekiah's Healing (20:1–11)
2. Hezekiah's Failure (20:12–21)
3. Manasseh's Sin and Rebellion (21:1–18)
4. Amon's Sin and Rebellion (21:19–26)

C. CONCLUSION: THE GREATEST DIFFERENCE

VIII. ISSUES FOR DISCUSSION

1. How do you account for the differences between parent and child, as illustrated by Ahaz, Hezekiah, and Manasseh? What is the extent of parental influence, and what are its limits? What message is there for parents in this contrast? For children?
2. The nation embraced the corruption of Manasseh enthusiastically, even though they had seen the godly life of Hezekiah. What about the human heart causes us to gravitate so quickly to the sinful and the corrupt? For example, why are pornographic sites the most profitable ones on the Internet?

2 Kings 22:1–23:30

Spiritual Renewal

I. INTRODUCTION
A Great Awakening

II. COMMENTARY
A verse-by-verse explanation of these verses.

III. CONCLUSION
Making a Difference

An overview of the principles and application from these verses.

IV. LIFE APPLICATION
Losing God's Word

Melding these verses to life.

V. PRAYER
Tying these verses to life with God.

VI. DEEPER DISCOVERIES
Historical, geographical, and grammatical enrichment of the commentary.

VII. TEACHING OUTLINE
Suggested step-by-step group study of these verses.

VIII. ISSUES FOR DISCUSSION
Zeroing these verses in on daily life.

"*T*he Sword of the Spirit, which is the Word of God,

is the only weapon which has always been mightily used in a

revival."

J o n a t h a n   G o f o r t h

HISTORICAL PROFILE: THE TIMES OF JOSIAH

Assyria

- Overextended its empire and had to expend its energy trying to put down rebellious states
- Following the death of Asshurbanipal in 627 B.C., the empire was beset with civil strife
- Its major cities—Asshur (614 B.C.) and Nineveh—(612 B.C.) fell to the Medes and Haran to the Babylonians and Medes in 610 B.C.
- Pursued by the Babylonians westward to northern Syria

Egypt

- Moved into Palestine's coastal plain and Syria, in dispute of Assyria's claims in the 630s
- Following the fall of Nineveh in 612 B.C., allied with Assyria to try to resist Babylon
- In 609 B.C. moved troops to northern Syria when appealed to by the Assyrians

Babylon

- Nablopolassar proclaimed himself king in 626 B.C. and led Babylon to independence
- Became the dominant power in the region, allying with the Medes and putting increasing pressure on Assyria
- Moved to engage the Egyptian-Assyrian coalition in northern Syria under the military leadership of Naplopolassar's son, Nebuchadnezzar

HISTORICAL PROFILE: THE WRITING PROPHETS OF JOSIAH'S TIME

- Zephaniah (about 640–609 B.C.)
- Nahum (663–612 B.C.)
- Jeremiah (627–562 B.C.)

2 Kings 22:1–23:30

IN A NUTSHELL

Josiah came to the throne as a boy, inheriting a nation in terrible spiritual condition. But he made a deep personal commitment to the Lord that shaped his life. When the Word of God was providentially discovered, he heard it as God's Word and led the nation in spiritual renewal and reformation. But far-reaching as Josiah's reforms were, they could not change the sinful predisposition of his nation or God's intention to judge them for their sustained sin.

Spiritual Renewal

I. INTRODUCTION

A Great Awakening

*T*he new nation was in trouble. Seven years of war for independence had taken their toll morally and spiritually. Drunkenness was widespread—an estimated three hundred thousand of a population of five million. Dueling had become a national fad; fear of assault made women reluctant to go out at night; bank robberies were a common experience; and the number of illegitimate births was soaring. As a massive number of people rushed to settle the West, life on the frontier was rough, crude, and turbulent.

The spiritual state of the United States was at a low ebb. Whereas 40 to 50 percent of the population had attended church in the 1770s, estimates in the 1790s were in the 5 to 10 percent range. The deist Tom Paine gloated, "Christianity will be forgotten in thirty years." Chief Justice John Marshall wrote to Bishop Madison of Virginia, "The church was too far gone ever to be redeemed." A poll taken at Harvard uncovered no students willing to declare themselves as believers; Princeton discovered two and Yale five. Churches in the settled areas of the East battled with internal divisions and low morale, while on the frontier they were few and far between. As one preacher lamented, "How many thousands . . . never saw, much less read, or ever heard a chapter of the Bible!"

In New England a Baptist pastor named Isaac Backus called Christians to pray, and they began to set aside the first Monday of each month for that purpose. A committed follower of Christ named Timothy Dwight was named president of Yale. The students challenged him to a debate on the Scriptures. Dwight's presentation of the gospel on that occasion and in the years that followed resulted in a third of the student body professing faith in Christ by 1802 and launching a movement of the gospel across university campuses. On the frontier, preachers such as James McGready began to pray and preach. Soon tens of thousands were being swept into the kingdom in a powerful moving of God's Spirit.

The Second Great Awakening reshaped America in the early years of the nineteenth century. In the first four decades of the century, America's population increased fourfold; church membership increased tenfold! God's Word was the spark of revival, the prayer of God's people the fan, and practical obedience the fuel. These have always been the essentials of spiritual renewal and awakening. No one embodies commitment to those essentials more than Josiah, one of Judah's last kings. His example has been encouraging and relevant to believers who long to see renewal in their time. Josiah did not rescue his nation from judgment, but he did make an indelible difference for good and for God. His example resonates into the twenty-first century.

II. COMMENTARY

Spiritual Renewal

MAIN IDEA: *When God's people respond properly to God's Word, God's Spirit moves in renewing power.*

A Josiah Cleanses the Temple (22:1–7)

SUPPORTING IDEA: *The first step of renewal is to see where we are and to desire change.*

22:1–2. Like Hezekiah, **Josiah** was not a man whose life could be explained by the life of his ancestors. His father had a short but evil rule; his grandfather a long but even more evil rule. Still, only Hezekiah rivaled Josiah for personal righteousness and godly leadership. Josiah **did what was right in the eyes of the LORD . . . not turning aside to the right or to the left.** Hezekiah may have swerved somewhat in his attempt to buy off Sennacherib and in his encounter with the Babylonian envoys. Josiah had no such deviations. So the writer of 2 Kings repeated his accolades as he looked back on his life in 23:25: "Neither before nor after Josiah was there a king like him who turned to the LORD as his did—with all his heart and with all his soul and with all his strength, in accordance with all the Law of Moses." Here is a life worth studying!

Josiah came to the throne at the age of **eight**. He was placed there by the people who rejected and executed those who had killed his father. He **reigned in Jerusalem thirty-one years**, from 640 to 609 B.C. Obviously, as a boy of eight, he was king in title only, with someone else acting as regent. We are not told who may have influenced him for the cause of the Lord. The writer of 2 Chronicles indicates that "in the eighth year of his reign, while he was still young, he began to seek the God of his father David" (2 Chr. 34:3). That choice, at the age of sixteen, shaped Josiah's life. At the age of twenty (his twelfth year), he began to undo the paganism of his father and grandfather by purging idolatry (2 Chr. 34:3–7).

22:3–7. The eighteenth year of his reign, when Josiah was twenty-six years old, was his defining moment. He had become unsettled by the state of the temple. His immediate forbears had showed no respect for it as the place of God's name and had neglected and abused it. Josiah's conviction that the current state of the temple and worship of God was not right drove all that followed. There is no indication that the cleansing of the temple was the first stage in a master plan of reform; he was simply acting on what he could see was wrong in care for the temple. He commissioned his secretary **Shaphan** to direct **Hilkiah the high priest** to initiate a program of repair and refurbishing.

It had been almost two hundred years since Joash had repaired the temple, and it had suffered both aging and abuse. Josiah's plan for repairing the temple was patterned on that of Joash (see 12:4–16). It involved a public collection system, with money given to the care of supervisors who would oversee and pay the workmen. The repairs were extensive, requiring **carpenters, the builders and the masons**, and using **timber and dressed stone**.

🅱 Josiah Hears God's Law (22:8–23:3)

> **SUPPORTING IDEA:** *The central step of renewal is to see ourselves in the light of God's Word and to respond appropriately.*

22:8–10. In the course of cleaning the temple, a remarkable event occurred. **Hilkiah the high priest said to Shaphan the secretary, "I have found the Book of the Law in the temple of the LORD."** This book of the law contained at least the Book of Deuteronomy and perhaps the entire first five books of the Old Testament (see "Deeper Discoveries"). The expression "Book of the Law" is found regularly in Deuteronomy (28:61; 29:21; 30:10; 31:26), and what follows reflects the blessings and curses sections of Deuteronomy.

It is hard to imagine such an important scroll being lost, until it is remembered that the pagan worship of Manasseh and Amon would have had no use for such a book, since it condemned all they were doing. It had first been ignored, then neglected and finally lost (or perhaps even hidden by someone wanting to preserve it). The book would have been in the form of a scroll, and Shaphan, having received it, **read it**. He then reported to the king, first informing him of the progress made on the temple repairs and then reporting the providential discovery to Josiah.

It is intriguing that he introduced it without any indication of what it was or where it had been found: **Hilkiah the priest has given me a book**. Josiah had never seen or heard a copy of the Word of God. **And Shaphan read from it in the presence of the king**. If this was the Book of Deuteronomy, this would have taken two or three hours; if the entire book of the law, it would have taken the entire day.

22:11–14. The Word of God has innate power and is self-authenticating. This is especially true when one's heart is sensitive to the Lord. The message of God's Word penetrated immediately and deeply into the heart of Josiah: **When the king heard the words of the Book of the Law, he tore his robes**. His first response was one of conviction. Tearing one's garments was a sign of grief, and this was due to Josiah's recognition of the way his nation had violated the requirements of God's covenant and come under his judgment. The Lord's standards stood in judgment on the condition of his people.

Since Josiah had never before encountered the Word of God, he had a desire to have it confirmed by a godly person whom he trusted and also to have a prophetic perspective on the interpretation he had given it. He was aware of the need to test his understanding of God's Word in the light of the understanding of spiritual people whom he respected. So he commissioned a team of highly regarded officials: **Hilkiah the priest, Ahikam son of Shaphan, Acbor son of Micaiah, Shaphan the secretary and Asaiah the king's attendant**. The careful listing of their names suggests that this was an official, formal delegation.

Their orders were to **go and inquire of the LORD for me . . . about what is written in this book**. "Inquiring of the Lord" is often used elsewhere of using the Urim and Thummim in the hands of the high priest, but here it meant seeking the insight of God's prophet.

Josiah was convinced that what he had heard was bad news for his nation. His evaluation was devoid of any rationalization or excuse making. He was overwhelmed with the realization of the guilt of his people. His reference to the sins of his fathers was not putting the blame elsewhere. It was recognizing the corporate responsibility of the nation for their sins.

The delegation **went to speak to the prophetess Huldah, who . . . lived in Jerusalem**. Huldah is one of five prophetesses named in the Old Testament (Miriam, Exod. 15:20; Deborah, Judg. 4:4; Isaiah's wife, Isa. 8:3; and Noadiah, Neh. 6:14), but we know nothing more about her other than what we read in this passage. Since both Jeremiah and Zephaniah were active as prophets at this time, it shows the great respect in which she was held. As "keeper of the wardrobe," her husband Shallum apparently had responsibility for either the royal or priestly garments (cp. 2 Kgs. 10:22).

22:15–20. Huldah had a double message for Josiah. The first message confirmed Josiah's worst fears. God would **bring disaster on this place and its people**. The catalogue of offenses resembled the acts of Manasseh recorded in the previous chapter—offenses which violated the first and second commandments. The nation had been guilty of spiritual abandonment and sin. Huldah's words at this point are strongly reminiscent of Deuteronomy 29:20–28. The awful truth is stated: **my anger will burn against this place and will not be quenched**. Not even the godliness of Josiah could hold back the outpouring of divine judgment.

That, however, was not all the prophet had to say. One of the great principles of the Bible is that "God opposes the proud but gives grace to the humble" (Prov. 3:34; Jas. 4:4; 1 Pet. 5:5). Josiah's heart was David-like. The Lord had declared through Isaiah: "This is the one I esteem: he who is humble and contrite in spirit, and trembles at my word" (Isa. 66:2). Josiah's response to

God's Word was what the Lord had always desired of his people. Therefore, although judgment could not be avoided, it would be delayed. Josiah was told that disaster would not happen in his time, but it would surely happen.

23:1–3. Josiah could have received the prophetess's words with selfish gratitude and fatalistic resignation. That was not the kind of man he was. He now understood what the Lord required, and he would honor God by doing all he could to bring the nation into conformity with his will. So he **called together all the elders of Judah and Jerusalem** in a solemn covenant ceremony. He was determined to lead his nation in renewal and reformation. Having gathered **the men of Judah, the people of Jerusalem, the priests and the prophets** in the temple courts, **he read in their hearing all the words of the Book of the Covenant.** For the first time in at least sixty-five years, the people heard the Word of God read publicly.

But Josiah was not content simply to read the law. **The king stood by the pillar** (see 1 Kgs. 7:21), as Joash had done at his coronation (2 Kgs. 11:14). This suggests it was a place of special ceremonial significance. He then led the people in a commitment similar to that led by Moses (Deut. 29:1–32:52) and Joshua (Josh. 24:1–27). He began with a personal covenant renewal as the king. The people followed. No other Judean king had led such a movement!

🅒 Josiah Reforms Judah's Worship (23:4–23)

> **SUPPORTING IDEA:** *Spiritual renewal always leads to practical steps of reformation.*

23:4–14. Josiah's reforms touched every part of the nation, but **the temple** received special attention. The indication of what Josiah purged shows how thoroughly polluted by paganism it had become. He enlisted **Hilkiah the high priest, the priests next in rank and the doorkeepers** to remove the offensive materials and to shame and degrade these pagan symbols. The temple contained **all the articles made for Baal and Asherah and all the starry hosts** (v. 4; the latter reveals particularly Assyrian influence). These were **burned** outside the city and the **ashes** were taken **to Bethel** and the Jeroboam cult center. He also **took the Asherah pole** (v. 6) from the temple, **burned it** and **ground it to powder.**

It is amazing to read that living **quarters of the male shrine prostitutes** had been constructed in the temple itself. These were torn down, as well as areas where women did **weaving for Asherah.** The entrance to the temple had been polluted by objects of **sun** worship (v. 11), ornamental **horses,** and **chariots** dedicated to the sun. Such objects were well-known in Assyrian religion. Usually they were devoted to the gods Asshur and Sin. Manasseh himself had been responsible for placing dedicated figurines or statues in a section of the temple courtyard. Josiah had these removed and burned.

Manasseh and Amon had also built pagan altars on the roof near the **upper room of Ahaz** (a location that cannot be determined today) and in **the two courts of the temple of the LORD** (v. 12). Josiah had them removed, smashed, and discarded.

Josiah also dealt with other abuses. **Pagan priests appointed by the kings of Judah** served in various high places **to burn incense** to Baal and various Assyrian idols (v. 5). They were stopped. There were also other **priests** (vv. 8–9) who served at various towns throughout the country. These were not pagans, but their practices violated the requirement that worship was to be conducted at one central place. These compromised priests were returned to Jerusalem, where they were not allowed to serve in the temple **at the altar of the LORD**, but were allowed to share in the priestly food. The **high places** and **shrines** at which they had served, some at the **city gate** of Jerusalem, were desecrated and broken down.

Josiah also attacked **Topheth** (v. 10), the grotesque shrine where children had been sacrificed. He also terminated the false worship established by **Solomon** on **the Hill of Corruption** southeast of Jerusalem. It is amazing that this had endured for more than three hundred years, but it was not until Josiah that these pagan places of worship were dealt with.

23:15–20. Josiah's zeal for the Lord's glory and law was not contained within the boundaries of his nation. His listening to the law had given him a concern for the entire twelve tribes. So for the first time since the disruption of Jeroboam, a Davidic king extended his authority to the north. The weakness of Assyria at this time and the lack of strong government in Samaria probably gave him opportunity to move into the area of the former Northern Kingdom. He first removed the center of Jeroboam's deviant religion, **the altar at Bethel, the high place made by Jeroboam son of Nebat, who had caused Israel to sin.** Nineteen Israelite kings had done nothing to remove this syncretistic cult center, but Josiah attacked it with vigor.

Alert to his surroundings, Josiah saw **the tombs that were on the hillside.** Burning bones on an altar desecrated it and made it unusable. So Josiah ordered the tombs to be exhumed and bones **burned on the altar.** Josiah's only intention may have been to defile the Jeroboam altar, but in doing so he was acting **in accordance with the word of the LORD.** This prophecy had been made in 1 Kings, when the anonymous man of God from Judah had told Jeroboam three hundred years earlier that a Davidic king named Josiah would burn human bones on Jeroboam's false idol (1 Kgs. 13:2).

Josiah also recognized a special tombstone. Told that it marked the tomb of the man of God who **pronounced against the altar of Bethel the very things you have done to it,** Josiah commanded that the tomb be left undisturbed. The old prophet had declared that the man of God's prophecy would come true (1 Kgs. 13:32), and indeed it had. Josiah's entire life was directed by the word of God, whether written or given through a prophet.

Bethel had been the center of Jeroboam's cult, **Samaria** of the royal family and the Baal cult. So Josiah continued north to Samaria, where he removed **all the shrines at the high places that the kings of Israel had built**. He also fulfilled 1 Kings 13:2 by slaughtering **all the priests of those high places on the altars and burned human bones on them**. Then he went back to Jerusalem, having reclaimed the entire land for the Lord. He had removed the objects that defied God's claim on his people.

23:21–23. Removal of idols was only the negative side of spiritual renewal. There was also the need to celebrate the nation's covenant with the Lord by positive obedience. So Josiah called the people to **celebrate the Passover to the LORD your God, as it is written in this Book of the Covenant**. The Passover was to be celebrated each year, as a reminder of the deliverance of Israel from Egypt, which led to the covenant at Sinai (Exod. 12:1–11; Deut. 16:1–8). The Passover had been celebrated down through the centuries to some degree. We read of a special national celebration in the reign of Hezekiah (2 Chr. 30:1–27). But it had apparently not been held in strict accordance with the requirements of the law, most notably the call to a celebration centralized in the temple. That careful following of the law is apparently the reason we read that **not since the days of the judges . . . had any such Passover been observed. But in the eighteenth year of King Josiah, this Passover was celebrated to the LORD in Jerusalem**. This was the crowning act of the reformation of Judah in submission to the Word of God.

D Josiah Finishes Well (23:24–30)

SUPPORTING IDEA: *Great times of spiritual renewal do not guarantee the reversal of God's declared judgments.*

23:24–25. The year 622 B.C. had been a glorious year of spiritual renewal in Judah. But Josiah did not allow it to become just a passing event. He continued his faithful walk before the Lord. He also dealt with other abuses: **Josiah got rid of the mediums and spiritists, the household gods, the idols and all the other detestable things**. These were more private spiritual abuses, carried on out of the public gaze. But Josiah was not content to deal with public sins only.

Once again the writer of 2 Kings celebrates the special character of Josiah: **Neither before nor after Josiah was there a king like him who turned to the LORD as he did—with all his heart and with all his soul and with all his strength**. The last part of this statement is intentionally written in such a way as to resonate with what the Lord Jesus called the Great Commandment: "Love the LORD your God with all your heart and with all your soul and with all your strength" (Deut. 6:5). Josiah is thus the epitome of love for the Lord and passionate obedience to his law.

23:26–27. Although Josiah was a great reformer, his righteousness could not hold back the wrath of God on his sinful people. Reform had come too late, through no fault of Josiah. The sins of the nations, having reached their pinnacle in Manasseh, demanded a divine response. In fact, it would be in the furnace of Babylon that idolatry would be burned out of Judah's soul. Only major surgery would prevent relapse. Josiah's reforms would not long survive him. Jeremiah and Ezekiel portray the extent to which the people plunged into idolatry after his death. So we hear the divine verdict: **the LORD did not turn away from the heat of his fierce anger, which burned against Judah because of all that Manasseh had done to provoke him to anger.**

We have traveled a long, sad journey from the glorious days of the dedication of the temple in 1 Kings 8! But the inevitability of judgment is exactly what Huldah had indicated in 2 Kings 22:16–18.

23:28–30. External events have not so far played any part in the account of Josiah's rule. But in 609 B.C. they conspired to bring Josiah to an early death, at the age of only thirty-nine. The Assyrian Empire had come unraveled. In the west, Egypt had become a major power, while in the east, Babylon had emerged as a budding superpower under the leadership of Nablopolasser. Egypt had forged an alliance with what remained of Assyria to resist Babylon, which obviously represented the greatest threat. The Assyrian king appealed to **Pharaoh Neco** (ruled 609–595 B.C.), the influential ruler of Egypt. Neco responded and **went up to the Euphrates River** in northern Syria **to help the king of Assyria** against Babylon. As he passed through Palestine, **Josiah marched out to meet him in battle.**

Josiah's motives are unclear. He was badly outmanned, but perhaps his determination to oppose Assyria drove him. His cause was hopeless. **Neco faced him and killed him at Megiddo.** A harmonization with 2 Chronicles suggests that Josiah was fatally wounded at Megiddo but was transported back to Jerusalem where he died (2 Chr. 35:24). For reasons that are not stated, **the people** took his youngest son **Jehoahaz** and **anointed him . . . king.**

With the death of Josiah, the disintegration of Judah under the judicial wrath of God and the military might of the Babylonians would come with bewildering speed. But the contribution of Josiah would continue to shine, like a bright light in the midst of darkness.

MAIN IDEA REVIEW: *When God's people respond properly to God's Word, God's Spirit moves in renewing power.*

III. CONCLUSION

Making a Difference

Josiah was a man who made a profound difference in his nation because he took God and his Word seriously. The fact that his spiritual renewal did not hold back the judicial hand of God in no way minimizes his spiritual greatness or the lessons he teaches about spiritual renewal.

The central message of his life is that we must not accept the spiritual status quo, no matter how hopeless things seem. A person with a passion for God who is concerned about God's place of honor will not be content to sit back. Josiah's reform began with a simple desire that the place where God was to be worshiped should be treated with respect. Then, when providentially confronted with the Word of God, he recognized it for what it was and humbled himself before God and his truth. But he was not content with an emotional response to God's Word. He was committed to bring every area of his life and kingdom into conformity to God's will. That is the passion of all who yearn for spiritual renewal.

We do not read of any encounters between Jeremiah and Josiah in 2 Kings, but the Lord's words quoted in the Book of Jeremiah about Josiah provide a fitting epitaph: "'He did what was right and just, so all went well with him. He defended the cause of the poor and needy, and so all went well. Is that not what it means to know me?' declares the L ORD" (Jer. 22:15–16).

PRINCIPLES

- Spiritual renewal begins with a dissatisfaction with the status quo.
- God's Word is self-authenticating.
- Spiritual renewal involves hearing God's Word and responding to it properly.
- God gives grace to the humble.
- Personal renewal must be linked to public commitment.
- Spiritual renewal must be linked with practical reformation and active obedience.
- Great times of spiritual renewal do not guarantee the reversal of God's declared judgment.

APPLICATIONS

- Don't criticize or lose heart at the current state of things, but actively pursue what honors God.
- Place yourself under the Word of God as your judge.

- God's Word, not good intentions or good feelings, must be our guide in all we do.

IV. LIFE APPLICATION

Losing God's Word

In a day in which Bibles can be purchased at low prices and when modern translations abound, it is impossible to imagine how we could physically lose the Word of God. However, we should not forget the incredible sacrifices made by people who were determined to make the Word of God available to the average Christian by heroes of the faith such as John Wycliffe and William Tyndale. We should also pray for those parts of the world where access to the Scriptures is denied by the government and where ownership of God's Word is a criminal offense. Because we know the treasure of the Word, we need to support the work of organizations such as Wycliffe Bible Translators that labor to give each people group the Bible in its own language.

But it is possible to lose the Word of God—and to lose it "in the temple." One way is by an unbelief that denies that the Bible is God-breathed Scripture. We lose it when it becomes a record of human strivings after God rather than a divine revelation. Sadly, the liberal churches have almost entirely "lost" the Bible. But even those with a high view of Scripture can "lose" it. When we make our experiences or the claims of powerful teachers more authoritative than the Bible, we have "lost" it. When we substitute even the best of human insight for God's authoritative Word, we have "lost" it. When we pay it lip service but make little effort to understand it and apply it, we have "lost" it. When we apply sophisticated arguments to explain why it doesn't really say what it clearly does say, or to explain why modern culture has antiquated it, we have "lost" it. When we are more familiar with the celebrities of our culture than with the heroes of Scripture, we have "lost" it. Until we "find" God's Word in the modern church, we will not have the spiritual renewal we so desperately need.

V. PRAYER

Father, help us never to allow your Word to be lost, either in your church or in our lives. Keep us from just knowing it. Give us a passionate desire to do it, for your glory. Amen.

VI. DEEPER DISCOVERIES

A. The Book of the Law (22:8)

It is clear from the following context that this "Book of the Law" contained the Book of Deuteronomy and perhaps all or most of the first five books of the Old Testament. Before the age of the mass production of manuscripts by printing, biblical scrolls would have been very expensive and therefore rare. It is tragic but not surprising that under the reign of an evil king such as Manasseh, copies of God's law would be neglected and even suppressed. We are not told how long it had been lost. But tracing the loss to the time of Manasseh seems feasible.

Biblical critics have contended that the book was not lost at all but that it was the product of prophetic circles, which was surfaced at this point by Yahweh loyalists, and attributed to Moses in a "pious fraud" to give it credibility. This is a view required to support critical theories of the evolution of the Old Testament documents. However, such a conspiracy theory is not only improbable on its face; it goes against the clear witness of the text and the unanimous witness of Hebrew tradition.

B. Passover (23:21–23)

The writer of 2 Chronicles devotes considerably more space to this great Passover than the author of 2 Kings (2 Chr. 35:1–19). His account helps us understand the special quality of this occasion. Its major feature was Josiah's concern that it conform precisely to the requirements of the law, by focusing on the temple and the one place of sacrifice. A second feature was the huge quantity of sacrifices involved (35:7–10; cp. 30:24). A third was the presence of "all Judah and Israel" (35:18). The presence of those from Israel, perhaps drawn by the destruction of the northern centers of worship, was something that had not taken place since the Jeroboam disruption. This was a great national celebration of a unity that had long been broken.

C. The Death of Josiah (23:29–30)

Judah was no match at this time for Egypt's military might, so Josiah's actions seem reckless. It is hard to understand why he would have wanted to support Babylon. It would have meant ignoring the clear statement of Isaiah to Hezekiah that Babylon represented Judah's greatest danger (20:16–18). His action was more probably inspired by deep-seated opposition to Assyria and any nations allied with her, as well as fear of the results of an Assyrian-Egyptian victory. Better to engage Egypt when she was alone. The author of 2 Chronicles indicates that Neco tried to dissuade Josiah from a foolish attack

(2 Chr. 35:21), and suggests that Josiah was ignoring a divine message from a pagan king (35:22).

There was something tragic about Josiah's death, and the people immediately recognized their loss. "Jeremiah composed laments for Josiah, and to this day all the men and women singers commemorate Josiah in the laments. These became a tradition in Israel and are written in the Laments" (2 Chr. 35:25).

VII. TEACHING OUTLINE

A. INTRODUCTION

1. Lead Story: A Great Awakening

2. Context: The hour was getting late for Judah. But in one of its darkest hours, the Lord raised up a king who was committed to follow him. The Word of God sparked a movement of great renewal, even though judgment could not be avoided.

3. Transition: Once again, one godly leader makes a difference in the life of the nation.

B. COMMENTARY

1. Josiah Cleanses the Temple (22:1–7)

2. Josiah Hears God's Law (22:8–23:3)

3. Josiah Reforms Judah's Worship (23:4–23)

4. Josiah Finishes Well (23:24–30)

C. CONCLUSION: MAKING A DIFFERENCE

VIII. ISSUES FOR DISCUSSION

1. In what ways can the Word of God be "lost" in the church or in our lives? Do you think that is a concern in the modern evangelical community? Do you think we could be characterized as "trembling at his Word" in reverence and awe?

2. In your opinion, what about the present status quo is dishonoring to God? What are some preliminary steps of change?

2 Kings 23:31–25:30

The Day of Reckoning

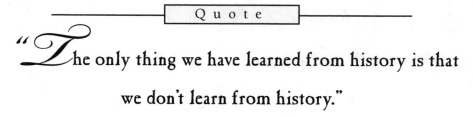

"*The only thing we have learned from history is that we don't learn from history.*"

W i n s t o n   C h u r c h i l l

HISTORICAL PROFILE: GOD'S PROPHETS IN JUDAH'S LAST DAYS

Habakkuk
- Prophesied before the Babylonian invasion, perhaps shortly after Josiah's death
- His theme was that God would use pagan Babylon to judge his sinful people, but he would judge Babylon as well

Daniel
- Taken captive to Babylon in 605 B.C., in the reign of Jehoiakim
- Lived his adult life in Babylon, serving first the Babylonians and then the Persians
- His great theme was God's outworking of kingdom history, while Israel is under Gentile power

Ezekiel
- Taken captive to Babylon with Jehoiachin (Ezek. 1:1–3)
- His prophecy was directed primarily to the exiled community, although his prophecy contains a vivid picture of the religious corruption of the temple in Jerusalem's last days

Jeremiah
- Lived in Jerusalem through its destruction and then was taken with the final refugees to Egypt
- His public ministry stretched from the reign of Josiah past the destruction of Jerusalem in 587 B.C.
- A major prophetic antagonist of the sins of the final four kings of Judah and the people. He especially attacked their magical trust in the temple

2 Kings 23:31–25:30

*J*udah has reached the end of its road. Its final four kings turned away from the exclusive worship of the Lord practiced by Josiah. In the presence of the power of first Egypt and then Babylon, Judah proved to be weak and foolish. In a series of attacks, Jerusalem is captured and totally destroyed, and its people are deported to Babylon. It looks like the nation is finished, but in the end, a tiny flicker of hope remains, in the person of a Davidic king.

The Day of Reckoning

I. INTRODUCTION

A Swift and Sudden End

ooking back, it's still hard to believe how quickly it all happened. The Soviet Union was one of the world's superpowers, a military colossus with its tentacles reaching all over the world—an "evil empire," according to President Reagan's famous expression.

When Mikhail Gorbachev came to power in 1985, he wanted to revitalize what he felt had become a stagnant and closed society. He declared his commitment to "perestroika" (restructuring) and "glasnost" (openness), throwing open the windows to let in light and fresh air. But when light and fresh air are let into a sealed room, they often hasten the rate of disintegration. The Soviet Union was riddled with problems, such as economic stagnation, political corruption, nationalistic dissatisfactions, yearnings for freedom, and military overspending. His new policies only served to feed the cause of dissidents, while a series of military and technological disasters such as Afghanistan and Chernobyl further undermined government credibility. The increasing military superiority of the United States played its part, as did the new information technologies that made it increasingly difficult for the Soviet leadership to hide the truth from its people. Gorbachev had raised expectations, but the failure of his reforms only increased disillusionment.

In 1989, the "evil empire" began to unravel. The Warsaw Bloc countries declared their independence of Moscow, and in December Berliners tore down the infamous Berlin Wall. By 1990 the Baltic Republics asserted their independence, and ethnic conflicts broke out in many places. The Ukrainian president later observed, "The whole country was falling apart before our very eyes and not because we planned it." In August 1991, as the economy plummeted, the Gang of Eight, a group of hard-liners, attempted a coup, which failed as democratic forces rallied behind Boris Yeltsin. Within days the republics declared their independence, and in December the Union of Socialist Soviet Republics disbanded. One empire had become fifteen countries, and a power only decades before on the brink of world domination was consigned to history's ash heap.

As we come to the final chapters of 2 Kings, we are struck by how fast the end comes. Events rush downhill with increasing speed. The day of reckoning had arrived. In one sense the nation destroyed itself. The Babylonians were the external agents of destruction, but what happened was the inevitable result of Judah's long history of rebellion against the Lord and his law. The great reforms of Hezekiah and Josiah had only been brief interruptions in the process of self-destruction. Judah's terminal events revealed the judicial hand of God, doing what he had warned he would from the beginning of the nation's history. Judah's day of reckoning was a day of encountering the wrath of their offended covenant Lord.

II. COMMENTARY

The Day of Reckoning

MAIN IDEA: *God will not be mocked. Persistent violation of his covenant results in judgment.*

A The Capture of Jerusalem (23:31–24:17)

SUPPORTING IDEA: *God's judgment on Judah's sin results in the nation's loss of its freedom.*

23:31–35. When Josiah was killed unexpectedly at the hands of Pharaoh Neco in 609 B.C., the people made **Jehoahaz** king. Jehoahaz was a throne name; his personal name was Shallum (1 Chr. 3:15; Jer. 22:10–12). He was not Josiah's oldest surviving son, since his brother Jehoiakim was two years older (2 Kgs. 23:36). It is not clear why he was chosen. It may have been because of his mother (**Hamutal** was also the mother of Zedekiah; 24:18), because of his political viewpoints, or because of his perceived leadership abilities. If it was the latter, his brief reign of **three months** provided no opportunity to display them. But in that short time Jehoahaz revealed that he was no Josiah: **He did evil in the eyes of the LORD, just as his fathers had done**. This can only mean that he reintroduced idolatry, undoing the reforms of his father.

Josiah had encountered **Pharaoh Neco** of Egypt on his march to the north. Neco continued to northern Syria, where he made his headquarters at **Riblah**, a city north of Damascus on the Orontes River, **in the land of Hamath**. He apparently summoned Jehoahaz and **put him in chains . . . so that he might not reign in Jerusalem**. Judah was now under the direct control of a foreign power that determined its kings. Pharaoh imposed a levy, reducing Judah to vassal status, and placed his choice on the throne, **Eliakim son of Josiah**. To further make Judah's vassal status clear, Neco **changed Eliakim's name to Jehoiakim**. The names mean essentially the same thing ("God [El] has established"; "Yahweh has established"), so this was simply a display of Pharaoh's power.

The new king was responsible for raising the tribute (**a hundred talents** [about four tons] **of silver and a talent** [seventy-five pounds] **of gold**), which he did by imposing a tax to meet the burden. In the meantime, his brother was carried off **to Egypt, and there he died.**

23:36–24:7. The reign of Jehoiakam (Eliakim) lasted for **eleven years,** from 609 to 598 B.C. Spiritually, he was a clone of his brother Jehoahaz (he had a different mother) rather than his righteous father: **he did evil in the eyes of the LORD, just as his fathers had done.** During the first period of his reign, he was under the suzerainty of Egypt. But that ended abruptly when King Nebuchadnezzar of Babylon invaded the land. In 605 B.C., at the battle of Carchemish on the Euphrates River, Nebuchadnezzar defeated an alliance of Assyria and Egypt (Jer. 46:2). He moved down into the region, pushing Egypt back. During this invasion **Jehoiakim became his vassal.**

The writer of 2 Chronicles indicates that Jehoiakim was "bound . . . with bronze shackles" and taken to Babylon, along with the temple treasures (2 Chr. 36:6–7). At this same time Daniel and his companions were trans-ported to Babylon (Dan. 1:1–4). Apparently Jehoiakim was allowed to return to Jerusalem, where he remained loyal **for three years.** In 601 B.C. Nebuchad-nezzar attempted to invade Egypt. He was repulsed and forced to return to Babylon to rebuild his army. The defeat and withdrawal apparently embold-ened Jehoiakim: **he changed his mind and rebelled,** probably by withholding tribute. Nebuchadnezzar did not return immediately in force, but he used forces in the region to harass Judah until he could return.

But these events cannot be understood only on the geopolitical level. **The LORD sent Babylonian, Aramean, Moabite and Ammonite raiders against him.** These raiders may have been doing the bidding of their respective kings, but they were, in fact, God's agents. The Lord was the prime mover of Judah's downfall. Throughout 1 and 2 Kings, we have seen God's prophets declaring history in advance. Most recently that word had been proclaimed by Isaiah (2 Kgs. 20:16–18), an anonymous group of "his servants the prophets" (21:10–15), and Huldah (22:16–17). What God says surely comes to pass! We must have no illusions: this was Judah's day of reckoning, the time when it would begin to receive in full the wages of its sin. Time and God's patience had run out.

Jehoiakim **rested with his fathers,** but we are given no details about the form of his death. Jeremiah had predicted that he would have the burial of a donkey (Jer. 22:18–19), which suggests an ignominious ending. He died just in time to avoid the Babylonian onslaught, leaving his son **Jehoiachin** to deal with the consequences of his rebellion.

24:8–17. Jehoiachin (also called Jeconiah and Coniah) was **eighteen years old** when he came to the throne for **three months** in 598 B.C. Spiritu-ally, he was a clone of the two preceding kings. The armies of Babylon laid siege to Jerusalem, and **Nebuchadnezzar himself came up to the city while his officers were besieging it.** On March 15 or 16, 597 B.C., the city fell.

Everything had changed, as the writer of 2 Kings shows by dating this event in **the eighth year of the reign of the king of Babylon**. This is the first event to be dated by pagan kings. The royal chronology of Judah had come to an end; the times of Gentile dominance had begun. Nebuchadnezzar not only took the king prisoner; he also unwittingly fulfilled God's word (see 20:17). As the Lord had declared, **Nebuchadnezzar removed all the treasures from the temple of the LORD . . . and took away all the gold articles that Solomon . . . had made for the temple**.

The reference to Solomon is clearly meant to reveal how far the nation had fallen because of its sin. These objects were not only sacred objects devoted to the worship of the Lord; they were also historical symbols and national treasures. The city itself was spared because it had surrendered rather than resisted. But the things set apart for the worship of the Lord were now under the control of a pagan king.

The end of Judah was now in view as Nebuchadnezzar began to strip the kingdom of its most valued people. He took King Jehoiachin captive to Babylon, as well as **the king's mother, his wives, his officials and the leading men of the land**. He also deported **the entire force of seven thousand fighting men . . . and a thousand craftsmen and artisans**. The prophet Ezekiel was apparently among this group of exiles (Ezek. 1:1–3). Thus, the nation lost its leaders. Nebuchadnezzar's plan was to enrich his own kingdom by finding talented people among the enemy, and to strip the occupied nation of its ability to resist by removing its qualified leaders. He put his own puppet on the throne, **Mattaniah, Jehoiachin's uncle . . . and changed his name to Zedekiah**.

𝔹 The Fall of Jerusalem (24:18–25:21)

SUPPORTING IDEA: *God's judgment on Judah's sin results in the nation's loss of its homeland.*

24:18–20a. Zedekiah was Josiah's son by **Hamutal**. She was also the mother of Jehoahaz (23:31). Zedekiah's reign lasted for **eleven years**, from 597 to 587 B.C. In spite of the obvious failure of his brother, he modeled himself after him: **He did evil in the eyes of the LORD, just as Jehoiakim had done**. It was his destiny to reign over the nation when it suffered its tragic end, and his stupidity and spiritual rebellion hastened the day. But beyond royal stupidity and pagan power stood a sovereign God, pouring out his judgment.

24:20b–25:7. The end began with an ill-fated attempt of Zedekiah to break free of the Babylonian yoke. Jeremiah had warned Zedekiah against such behavior, telling him that it was God's will for him to submit to the yoke of Babylon (Jer. 22). But Zedekiah chose to believe false prophets, who claimed the nation could expect aid from Egypt. The author of 2 Kings was not concerned about the futile and foolish rebellion but about the Babylonian reaction. **Nebuchadnezzar** attacked in force. In December 589 B.C. he **marched against Jerusalem with his whole army**. He used siege towers rather than siege ramps, with the goal of starving the population and forcing surrender. The siege lasted for a terrible eighteen months, until **the famine in the city had become so severe that there was no food for the people to eat**.

In July of 587 B.C., the city wall was broken, and the city was entered by the Babylonians. Judah's army, accompanied by the king, attempted to escape. The Babylonian blockade apparently was weak enough in certain areas to allow men familiar with the terrain to escape. But the effort was in vain. As Zedekiah fled toward the east, **the Babylonian army pursued the king and overtook him in the plains of Jericho**. There is a divine irony in the fact that Israel's sovereignty ended near the place where its occupation of the land had begun with the conquest of Jericho under Joshua.

Zedekiah was now a helpless prisoner. Nebuchadnezzar had established his regional headquarters at **Riblah**, the same place where Pharaoh Neco had established his twenty years earlier (23:33). Zedekiah was marched north to face his royal master, and **sentence was pronounced on him**. The judgment involved typical Babylonian brutality: **They killed the sons of Zedekiah before his eyes**. This removed potential claimants to the throne and terrorized any would-be rebels. Zedekiah's last sight was to be of his dead sons: **they put out his eyes, bound him with bronze shackles and took him to Babylon**. He was treated like a rebellious slave, which is how the Babylonians perceived him.

25:8–17. Meanwhile, back in Jerusalem, the city was being dismantled. In August, Nebuchadnezzar sent **Nebuzaradan . . . an official of the king of Babylon** to reduce the city. The offense of repeated rebellion meant that looting, pillage, and partial destruction was insufficient punishment. **He set fire to the temple of the LORD, the royal palace and all the houses of Jerusalem**. Since much of the city was made of limestone, the flammable materials in the buildings would reduce the limestone to lime. Thus, **every important building he burned down**. In addition, **the whole Babylonian army . . . broke down the walls around Jerusalem**. Without a wall a city was not really a city. The walls were extensive, so this would have required a great deal of effort. Jerusalem the glorious was reduced to a smoldering ruin.

Nebuzaradan then began to deal with the people. The population had been greatly reduced in the deportation ten years earlier, but now he **carried into exile the people who remained in the city, along with the rest of the populace and those who had gone over to the king of Babylon**. There was no longer urban life. The Babylonians left only **some of the poorest people of the land to work the vineyards and fields**. In contrast to Assyrian practice, there was no corresponding importation of other captured peoples. The land was to be left underpopulated. The prophet Jeremiah was among those left in the land (Jer. 39:11–40:6).

All of this destruction is described in the briefest and most unemotional way. A reading of Lamentations is helpful to get a sense of the anguish felt by the citizens as they saw all that was valuable being destroyed, dismantled, or deported. The writer of 2 Kings returns once again to the temple. He began there with a depiction of the glories of Solomon's temple (1 Kgs. 5–8); he ends his account with a vivid picture of the glory being reduced to shame. He describes in some detail the elements of the temple that were removed to Babylon. The larger elements made of bronze were broken up so they could be more readily transported. The remaining pieces of service equipment were carried to Babylon for pagan uses. To remind us of the glory days of old, the writer of 2 Kings reminds us of the immensity of **the two pillars, the Sea and the movable stands, which Solomon had made for the temple of the LORD.** The glory of Solomon was now part of the irretrievable past.

25:18–21. The final act of Nebuzaradan was to purge the nation of its leaders. A group of leading citizens was taken prisoner. This included leading temple officials as well as officers, royal advisers, the official in charge of conscription, and sixty military figures. These were taken **to the king of Babylon at Riblah.** There, **the king had them executed.** By this time any possibility of finding gifted leaders for resistance had been virtually eliminated.

The death sentence of the nation is stated in stark terms: **So Judah went into captivity, away from her land.** This national obituary echoes the statement of Israel's demise in 17:23: "So the people of Israel were taken from their homeland into exile in Assyria, and they are still there." However, unlike chapter 17, there is no further theological reflection on the fate of the nation. That has been given throughout the entire history.

C The Flight into Egypt (25:22–26)

SUPPORTING IDEA: *God's judgment on Judah's sin results in the nation's virtual destruction.*

25:22–26. Although the population had been greatly reduced, it had not been eliminated entirely. Nebuchadnezzar apparently did not think the remaining population was worth leaving a Babylonian official to govern the people. Instead, he **appointed Gedaliah . . . to be over the people he had left behind in Judah.** Gedaliah was a member of an influential family. His grandfather **Shaphan** had been a scribe under Josiah (22:3) and his father **Ahikam** had served both Josiah (22:14) and Jehoiakim (Jer. 26:24), saving Jeremiah from the latter. His pedigree made him a natural choice as a local administrator for the Babylonians. With the destruction of Jerusalem, **Mizpah**, about eight miles north of Jerusalem, became the center of the new government.

There were Judean army veterans still in the land. On hearing of the appointment of Gedaliah, **all the army officers and their men** went to meet him. They were concerned about their status and whether they were viewed as enemies of the state because they had fought for Judah. **Gedaliah took an oath to reassure them and their men.** He promised them that Babylon's purge was finished. They should **settle down in the land and serve the king of Babylon.** It was a call for submission and nonresistance.

That was too much to expect. One of their members, **Ishmael . . . who was of royal blood**, apparently had aspirations of reestablishing the Davidic kingship. Whatever his motive, he **came with ten men and assassinated Gedaliah.** Jeremiah indicates that the king of Ammon had inspired this action (Jer. 40:13–14) and that it led to further atrocities on the part of Ishmael (Jer. 41:1–10). The people recognized that this atrocity would bring the wrath of Babylon down upon its perpetrators. As a result, **all the people . . . fled to Egypt for fear of the Babylonians.** This flight took place against the advice of Jeremiah, but he finally joined them (Jer. 42–44). This was a reversal of the exodus, an anti-exodus! Jeremiah depicts the settling of these refugees in Tahpanhes, in the northeastern Nile delta region of Egypt (Jer. 43:7).

Jerusalem was now a ghost town. Its walls were broken down; its people had been exiled; its leaders had been executed; its remnant had fled. "How deserted lies the city, once so full of people! . . . After affliction and harsh labor, Judah has gone into exile. . . . Our end was near, our days were numbered, for our end had come" (Lam. 1:1,3; 4:18).

Ⓓ A Faint Glimmer of Hope (25:27–30)

SUPPORTING IDEA: *God's judgment on Judah's sin does not terminate the hope represented by his covenant promises.*

25:27–30. But the end of Jerusalem is not the end of the story. Suddenly we are transported twenty-seven years into the future, to **the thirty-seventh year of the exile of Jehoiachin king of Judah.** Since **Jehoiachin** had been taken captive in 597 B.C. (24:15), we have reached the year 561 B.C. Just when we thought the story of the Judean kings had come to a tragic end with the deportation of the blind Zedekiah (25:7), we discover that the long-forgotten Jehoiachin is still alive. Not only was he alive, but also **in the year Evil-Merodach became king of Babylon, he released Jehoiachin from prison.** It was customary to declare an amnesty for political prisoners on the occasion of a new ruler's accession. So when the son of Nebuchadnezzar came to the throne, Jehoiachin was released. He had outlived his captor! He was not only released; he was treated with respect, was honored as the first among the captive kings, and was given a royal pension.

Jehoiachin was a king in name only, without a people or a state. The Solomonic days of glory were far behind. But hope for a better future remained. God had not died; his covenant with the patriarchs had not died; and a link to the Davidic covenant had not died. But Davidic kings have never ruled in Jerusalem since that day. The great Son of David gave his life for his people in that city. One day he will return in power and glory. Then the Davidic king will sit on his eternal throne in the city where he will once again put his name in a glory that will transcend anything that Solomon ever knew. "Now one greater than Solomon is here!" (Matt. 12:42).

MAIN IDEA REVIEW: *God will not be mocked. Persistent violation of his covenant results in judgment.*

III. CONCLUSION

Grace in the End

We have apparently reached the end of the line. The Book of Numbers had warned: "You will be sinning against the L ORD; and you may be sure that your sin will find you out" (Num. 32:23). First Israel's and then Judah's sin had found them out. The day of reckoning had come in the form of judgment. Destruction had come because both nations had violated the requirements of their covenant with the Lord, especially the call to exclusive loyalty found in the first commandment and the prohibition of idolatry found in the second commandment. One of the major reasons for the history was to explain to the exiles why they were in captivity. Understanding this, they should recommit themselves to obedience to the great covenant commandments.

But even when the people's continued sin had reduced their once-glorious capital to a smoldering pile of rubble, the grace of God remained. God has acted throughout the history of the nation for his own sake and for the sake of his covenant with David. The hope is not in Jehoiachin personally, but in what he represents—the Davidic promise and the promised Davidic king. As we end the Book of 2 Kings, this "lamp of David" has been reduced to a flicker. But the Lord will bring it to full flame. In the exilic and postexilic years, the light of the messianic hope grew brighter and brighter until the Lord Jesus came "when the time had fully come" (Gal. 4:4). He was the Son of David, fully qualified to take his place as the Lord of all things. We wait with eager anticipation for "the Lion of the tribe of Judah, the Root of David" (Rev. 5:5) to return in glory as " KING OF KINGS AND LORD OF LORDS" (Rev. 19:16).

PRINCIPLES

- When we turn back to sin after a spiritual breakthrough, our corruption will be swift and complete.
- Sin carries a heavy price because God will not be mocked.
- Leaders weakened by their indulgence in sin will have neither the character nor the wisdom to lead in a time of crisis.
- The hope of God's people is his enduring grace and his faithfulness to his promises.

APPLICATIONS

- There is always a danger that in our depravity we will turn back to sin; we must make no allowance for compromise.
- Take God's warnings of judgment and discipline as seriously as you take his promises of grace and love.
- Insist on loyalty to the Lord and mature, godly character as the prime qualities in our leaders.
- Rely on the faithfulness of God, even when you cannot see how he will fulfill his promises.

IV. LIFE APPLICATION

No Shortcuts

As we come to the end of our study of the history of the kings of Israel and Judah, it is worth asking what it has shown us. The writer did not have us in his gaze as he wrote. His audience was made up of fellow Jews in exile in Babylon who longed for a homeland and a way of life that was now in shambles. They worried about what the future held, wondered why things had turned out the way they had, and were enticed to join in with the lifestyle and belief system of Babylon. They heard all kinds of suggestions about how to resolve their current situation. Second Kings was written for all of those reasons, but most of all it was written to help people avoid shallow and superficial solutions to deep spiritual issues. There were hundreds of voices offering advice. Where could truth be found?

It was only as they looked at their past in the light of God-given insights that they would choose wisely for the future. Every answer that did not confront the need for exclusive, consistent, uncompromised, obedient loyalty to the Lord was either an invitation to disaster or a dead end. The answer was not to be found in pluralism, syncretism, legalism, ritualism, nationalism, or any one of a dozen other possibilities. It was to be found only in repentance, faith, and obedience.

Many of the suggestions about how God's people should live in the modern world offer either substitutes, shortcuts, or compromises. We are prone to follow the latest fad, adopt the latest program, or submit to the most convincing spokesman. But if Israel's history tells us anything, it is that every deviation from the command of God is an invitation to disaster. If we look back wisely, we can walk ahead confidently, never forgetting the most basis call of all: "You shall have no other gods before me" (Exod. 20:3). "For there is one God and one mediator between God and men, the man Christ Jesus" (1 Tim. 2:5).

V. PRAYER

Father, cause us to see sin as you do, not as something desirable and attractive to be played with, but as something ugly and detestable, to be avoided and rejected. Help us to see that its promises are lies and its wages are death. Give us even more of a passion to please you. Thank you that you always keep the lamp of your promises lit in the Lord Jesus. Amen.

VI. DEEPER DISCOVERIES

A. Jehoiakim and Jeremiah (23:37)

The prophet Jeremiah agreed with the assessment of 2 Kings that Jehoiakim "did evil in the eyes of the L ORD" (23:37). He had disdain for him as a king who promoted evil and persecuted righteousness. Jeremiah accused him of dishonesty, self-aggrandizement, violence, and exploitation of the poor (Jer. 22:13–23). Jehoiakim killed the prophet Uriah (Jer. 26:10–23), tried to have Jeremiah imprisoned (Jer. 36:19,26), and burned the prophetic scroll that contained God's Word (Jer. 36:20–26).

B. Zedekiah and Jeremiah (25:19)

Jeremiah helps us to understand the character of Zedekiah more clearly. He was an indecisive and weak leader who found himself caught between the "hawks" who wanted to resist Babylon and Jeremiah. Jeremiah had no use for Babylon, but the Lord had clearly revealed to him that it was God's agent of judgment, and Judah was to submit to Babylon and not resist (Jer. 29; 34:1–22; 38:19–26). False prophets claimed that the exile would be over within two years (Jer. 28:1–4). At times Zedekiah refused to listen to Jeremiah (Jer. 37:1–2) and allowed him to be imprisoned (Jer. 37:11–16; 38:4–6). At other times he spoke to Jeremiah secretly (Jer. 37:17; 38:14–16). In the final analysis, Zedekiah listened to the hawks, rebelled, and reaped the disaster Jeremiah had warned him about.

C. Jehoiachin in Babylon (25:27–30)

The final picture of Jehoiachin's release in Babylon has been understood in very different ways. Some interpreters have seen it as a final picture of Israel's tragedy. The only king Israel has is a captive, in a foreign land, with no chance of return. That seems to be a very unlikely reason for reintroducing Jehoiachin to the story. He was dead and gone, but now he suddenly appears once again. He has survived, even outliving his powerful conqueror, Nebuchadnezzar. It is hard not to see here a picture of hope. The Davidic covenant is not dead and gone; a Davidic line remains.

This note of hope is very strong in Jeremiah. No one insisted more strongly than he that the Babylonian invasion was the judicial will of God to which the Judeans must submit. But he also insisted that the Lord had "a hope and a future" for his people that would come to pass within seventy years (Jer. 29:10–14). The Davidic hope was not finished. After judgment would come blessing: "They will serve the LORD their God and David their king, whom I will raise up for them" (Jer. 30:9). Judah's hope for the future could not rest in its obedience or the godliness of its kings. But it could rest in the promises and character of their covenant God.

VII. TEACHING OUTLINE

A. INTRODUCTION

1. Lead Story: A Swift and Sudden End
2. Context: We have now reached the "final four," the last four kings to sit on the throne of David. In many ways they represent why Judah has reached the day of reckoning. All of them turn to evil, and none of them trusts in the Lord. As a result, their resistance to Babylon is futile and foolish. God's judgment falls on his wayward people, but even in the depth of judgment, the lamp of hope shines.
3. Transition: The last days of Judah involve a deadly formula: weak and foolish leaders and a powerful and determined enemy. It did not take Josiah's sons long to give up all the ground he had gained.

B. COMMENTARY

1. The Capture of Jerusalem (23:31–24:17)
2. The Fall of Jerusalem (24:18–25:21)
3. The Flight into Egypt (25:22–26)
4. A Faint Glimmer of Hope (25:27–30)

C. CONCLUSION: GRACE IN THE END

VIII. ISSUES FOR DISCUSSION

1. The continuing existence of the people of Israel, in spite of their sins and the actions of their enemies, is one of the great wonders of history. But the present nation is not related to the triune God in faith. In the light of God's unconditional commitment to his covenants with Israel—but its present unbelieving state—how should we evaluate events in the Middle East? Should Christians support Israel, whatever they do?

2. Imagine you are a Jew in Babylon, hearing 2 Kings for the first time. What would be the primary message of the book to you? As you reflect on it as a Christian, what have been the major lessons of the book to you?

Glossary

angel—A messenger from God, either heavenly or human, who delivers God's message of instruction, warning, or hope

confession—Admission of personal sin and seeking forgiveness from others

consecration—Setting apart for God's use

covenant—A contract or agreement expressing God's gracious promises to his people and their consequent relationship to him

discipline—Instruction or training used by God to train his children in righteous living

evil—Anyone or anything that opposes the plan of God

exile—Israel's life in the Assyrian kingdom after 722 B.C. and Judah's life in Babylon after 587 B.C.

exodus, the—The most important act of national deliverance in the Old Testament when God enabled the Israelites to escape Egypt

Gentiles—People who are not part of God's chosen family at birth and thus can be considered "pagans"

grace—Undeserved acceptance and love received from another, especially the characteristic attitude of God in providing salvation for sinners

high priest—The chief religious official for Israel and Judaism appointed as the only person allowed to enter the holy of holies and offer sacrifice on the Day of Atonement

holy—God's distinguishing characteristic that separates him from all creation; the moral ideal for Christians as they seek to reflect the character of God as known in Christ Jesus

holy of holies—The innermost and most sacred area of the tabernacle and temple, where God was present and where sacrifices were made by the high priest on the Day of Atonement

idolatry—The worship of that which is not God

Jerusalem—Capital city of Israel in the Old Testament

law—God's instruction to his people about how to love him and others; when used with the definite article "the," *law* may refer to the Old Testament as a whole but usually to the Pentateuch (Genesis through Deuteronomy)

Messiah—the coming king promised by the prophets; Jesus Christ who fulfilled the prophetic promises

miracle—An act of God beyond human understanding that inspires wonder, displays God's greatness, and leads people to recognize God at work in the world

monotheism—Belief in only one God

pagans—Those who worship a god or gods other than the living God to whom the Bible witnesses

Passover—The Jewish feast celebrating the exodus from Egypt (Exod. 12); celebrated by Jesus and his disciples at the Last Supper

Pentateuch—First five books of the Hebrew Bible: Genesis, Exodus, Leviticus, Numbers, Deuteronomy

polytheism—Belief in more than one god; a heresy prevalent in biblical times

prophet—One who speaks for God

repentance—A change of heart and mind resulting in a turning from sin to God that allows conversion and is expressed through faith

righteousness—The quality or condition of being in right relationship with God; living out the relationship with God in right relationships with other persons

Sabbath—The seventh day of the week corresponding to the seventh day of creation when people in the Old Testament were called on to rest from work and reflect on God

sacrifice—According to Mosaic Law, an offering to God in repentance for sin or as an expression of thanksgiving

Septuagint—Translation of the Hebrew Old Testament into Greek produced in the third century B.C.

shalom—Hebrew word for peace and wholeness meaning fullness of life through God-given harmony with God, the world, others, and oneself

sin—Actions by which humans rebel against God, miss his purpose for their life, and surrender to the power of evil rather than to God

sovereignty—God's freedom from outward restraint; his unlimited rule of and control over his creation

Yahweh—The Hebrew personal name of God revealed to Moses; this name came to be thought of as too holy to pronounce by Jews; often translated LORD or Jehovah

Bibliography

Auld, A. Graeme. *I & II Kings.* The Daily Study Bible. Philadelphia: Westminster, 1986.

Bright, John. *A History of Israel.* 3rd edition. Philadephia: Westminster, 1981.

Bronner, Leah. *The Stories of Elijah and Elisha as Polemics against Baal Worship.* Leiden: Brill, 1968.

Brueggemann, Walter. *1 Kings.* Knox Preaching Guides. Atlanta: John Knox, 1982.

_____. *2 Kings.* Knox Preaching Guides. Atlanta: John Knox, 1982.

_____. *1 and 2 Kings.* Smith and Helwys Bible Commentary. Macon, Ga.: Smith and Helwys, 2000.

Cogan, Mordechai. *I Kings.* Anchor Bible. Garden City: Doubleday, 2000.

Cogan, Mordechai, and Hayim Tadmor. *II Kings.* Anchor Bible. Garden City: Doubleday, 1988.

Cohn, Robert. *2 Kings.* Collegeville, Minn: Liturgical Press, 2000.

Crockett, William Day. *A Harmony of the Books of Samuel, Kings and Chronicles.* Grand Rapids: Baker, 1951.

Davis, Dale Ralph. *The Wisdom and the Folly: An Exposition of the Book of First Kings.* Fearn, Ross-Shire: Christian Focus, 2002.

De Vries, Simon. *1 Kings.* Word Biblical Commentary. Waco: Word, 1985.

Dillard, Raymond. *Faith in a Time of Apostasy: The Gospel According to Elijah and Elisha.* Phillipsburg, N.J.: Reformed and Presbyterian, 1999.

Ellul, Jacques. *The Politics of Man and the Politics of God.* Grand Rapids: Eerdmans, 1972.

Gray, John. *I and II Kings: A Commentary.* Old Testament Library. Philadelphia: Westminster, 1963.

Hamilton, Victor. *Handbook on the Historical Books.* Grand Rapids: Baker, 2001.

Handy, Lowell K. (ed.) *The Age of Solomon: Scholarship at the Turn of the Millennium.* Leiden: Brill, 1997.

Harrison, R. K. *Old Testament Times.* Grand Rapids: Eerdmans, 1970.

Hauser, Alan J., and Russel Gregory. "From Carmel to Horeb: Elijah in Crisis." *Journal for the Study of the Old Testament Supplement Series 85.* Sheffield, England: Almond Press, 1990.

Hendricks, Howard. *Standing Together.* Gresham, Oreg.: Vision House, 1995.

Hobbs, T. R. *2 Kings.* Word Bible Commentary. Waco: Word, 1985.

Honor, Leo L. *Book of Kings 1*. The Jewish Commentary for Bible Readers. New York: Union of American Hebrew Congregations, 1955.

House, Paul. *1, 2 Kings*. The New American Commentary. Nashville: Broadman & Holman, 1995.

_____. *Old Testament Theology*. Downers Grove: InterVarsity Press, 1998.

Howard, David. *An Introduction to the Old Testament Historical Books*. Chicago: Moody Press, 1993.

Hubbard, Robert L., Jr. *First and Second Kings*. Everyman's Bible Commentary. Chicago: Moody Press, 1991.

Jones, Gwilym H. *1 and 2 Kings, Volume I and II*. The New Century Bible Commentary. Grand Rapids: Eerdmans, 1984.

_____. "The Nathan Narratives." *Journal for the Study of the Old Testament Supplement Series 80*. Sheffield, England: JSOT Press, 1990.

Kaiser, Walter C. *A History of Israel*. Nashville: Broadman & Holman, 1998.

_____. *Revive Us Again*. Scotland: Christian Focus, 2001.

Keil, C. F. *The Books of Kings*. Biblical Commentary on the Old Testament. Grand Rapids: Eerdmans, 1954.

LaSor, William. *Great Personalities of the Old Testament: Their Lives and Times*. Westwood, N.J.: Fleming H. Revell, 1959.

Long, Burke O. *1 Kings: With an Introduction to Historical Literature*. Forms of Old Testament Literature. Grand Rapids: Eerdmans, 1984.

_____. *2 Kings: With an Introduction to Historical Literature*. Forms of Old Testament Literature. Grand Rapids: Eerdmans, 1991.

Merrill, Eugene. *Kingdom of Priests: A History of Old Testament Israel*. Grand Rapids: Baker, 1987.

Montgomery, James A., and Henry Snyder Gehman. *A Critical and Exegetical Commentary on the Books of Kings*. The International Critical Commentary. Edinburgh: T & T Clark, 1951.

Moore, Rick Dale. *God Saves: Lessons from the Elisha Stories*. Sheffield: Sheffield Academic Press, 1990.

Nelson, Richard. *First and Second Kings*. Interpretation. Louisville: John Knox, 1987.

Patterson, R. D., and Hermann Austell. *First and Second Kings*. Expositor's Bible Commentary. Volume 4. Grand Rapids: Zondervan, 1988.

Payne, David F. *Kingdoms of the Lord*. Grand Rapids: Eerdmans, 1981.

Phillips, Richard D. *Turning Back the Darkness*. Wheaton: Crossway, 2002.

Provan, Iain. *1 and 2 Kings*. New International Biblical Commentary. Peabody, Mass.: Hendrickson, 1995.

_____. *1 & 2 Kings.* Old Testament Guides. Sheffield: Sheffield Academic Press, 2001.

Rice, G. *Nations under God: A Commentary on the Book of 1 Kings.* International Theological Commentary. Grand Rapids: Eerdmans, 1991.

Roper, David. *Seeing Through.* Sisters, Oreg.: Multnomah, 1995.

Swindoll, Charles. *Elijah.* Nashville: Word, 2000.

Thiele, Edwin R. *The Mysterious Numbers of the Hebrew Kings.* 3rd edition. Grand Rapids: Eerdmans, 1983.

Wallace, Ronald S. *Elijah and Elisha.* Grand Rapids: Eerdmans, 1957.

_____. *Reading in 2 Kings.* Eugene: Wipf and Stock, 1997.

Walsh, Jerome T. *1 Kings.* Collegeville, Minn.: Liturgical Press, 1996.

Whitcomb, John. *Solomon to the Exile.* Grand Rapids: Baker, 1971.

Wiersbe, Warren W. *Be Distinct.* Colorado Springs: Cook, 2002.

_____. *Be Responsible.* Colorado Springs: Cook, 2002.

Wiseman, Donald J. *1 and 2 Kings.* Tyndale Old Testament Commentaries. Downers Grove: InterVarsity, 1993.

Wood, Leon. *A Survey of Israel's History.* Grand Rapids: Zondervan, 1970.

_____. *Israel's United Monarchy.* Grand Rapids: Baker, 1979.

Zuck, Roy B. (ed.). *A Biblical Theology of the Old Testament.* Chicago: Moody Press, 1991.

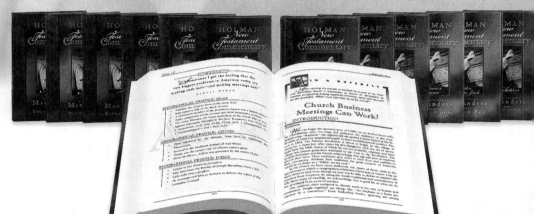